Baedeker

GW00320475

Andalusia

www.baedeker.com

Verlag Karl Baedeker

SIGHTSEEING HIGHLIGHTS ★ ★

The list of things to see is long, but where are the real highlights in Andalusia? Beaches and coast, the mountains and plains of the interior, nature parks and lively cities, formidable castles and Moorish palaces – we have summarized everything that you should not miss!

1 ★ ★ Úbeda
Pearl of Renaissance architecture with a picturesque old town like no other, and an ideal base for an excursions into the Sierra de Cazorla. ▶ **page 188**

2 ★ ★ Baeza
This picture-postcard Renaissance town with many charming plazas and streets lies high above the Guadalquivir valley. ▶ **page 184**

3 ★ ★ Sierra de Cazorla
Rugged mountains, rocky gorges, thickly wooded valleys and peregrine falcons – hikers will fall in love with these wild and romantic mountains. ▶ **page 412**

4 ★ ★ Seville
At night party in the bars, during the day marvel at the magnificent buildings and, if you go for Semana Santa, do penance and then dance wildly – when you have done that, you have experienced Seville.
▶ **page 382**

5 ★ ★ Carmona
Country town with several thousand years of history and an outstanding Roman necropolis with tombs dating from the 2nd century BC to the 4th century AD.
▶ **page 207**

6 ★ ★ Medina Azahara
The ruins of the caliph's palace city from the 10th century are testimony to one of the most magnificent seats of power in the world, which Abd ar-Rah-man III named after his favourite wife, Al-Zahra »the flower«. ▶ **page 332**

© Baedeker

1 Úbeda
3 Sierra de Cazorla
2 Baeza
7 Córdoba
6 Medina Azahara
5 Carmona
4 Sevilla
11 Granada
12 Sierra Nevada
10 El Torcal
8 Coto de Doñana
Cueva
13 de Nerja
16 Costa de la Luz
9 Ronda
15 Jerez de la Frontera
14 Gibraltar

Velez Blanco

According to Gautier, southern Spanish light is like a »battle between the blue of the sky and the glistening silver of the sea«.

Vejer de la Frontera
White village in a marvellous setting

BAEDEKER'S BEST TIPS

To make the most of your trip it is important to know the highlights of Andalusia. But to have a really enjoyable time, it's good to know a little more than the others: the best Andalusia tips from Baedeker.

■ Bathe like a caliph
Treat body and soul in the Moorish hammam of Cördoba. ▶ page 67

■ Be a cave man
in a dwelling where the greatest convenience is an open fireplace. ▶ page 82

■ Oil, oil, everywhere
There is a lot to be said about olive oil — as you will realize when you learn that there are 712 types of olives.
▶ page 184

Alhambra
The pinnacle of Moorish-Arab architecture in Europe

■ Alhambra in moonlight
A stroll at night through the Nasrid palace is unforgetable. ▶ page 262

■ Fresh trout
can be enjoyed on the idyllic terrace of the Venta Riofrio country inn in the village of Riofrio. ▶ page 282

Tapas
The Rinconcillo has been an institution in Seville since 1670.

Hammam
It is in Córdoba but looks just like a bath in the Middle East.

🚩 Classical guitar
Spanish guitar music of the highest quality is presented in Andrés Segovia's hometown ▶ **page 315**

🚩 Temptation
will get the better of you in Medina Sidonia, the bastion of the confectionery trade ▶ **page 335**

🚩 Beach racehorses
Don't miss the horse races on the beach at Sanlúcar. ▶ **page 380**

🚩 Tapas in Seville
Go into a tapas bar, order a small drink and tapas to go with it and a chat a bit – sometimes it doesn't take much to be happy. ▶ **page 403**

🚩 Off to the tablao
What is there in a tablao? Flamenco, what else! ▶ **page 410**

🚩 Safe in the wilds
of the sierras with Quercus, on foot, horseback or in a Land Rover
▶ **page 415**

🚩 Whale-watching
in the straits between Tarifa and Africa with a Swiss marine research organization ▶ **page 423**

Flamenco
An absolutely rousing dance with fire, fury, pride and passion

Most important Spanish painter of the 17th century – Diego Velázquez
▶ **page 79**

BACKGROUND

Moorish: calligraphic frieze in the Alhambra
▶ **page 65**

PRACTICALITIES

Price categories

► **Hotels (double room)**
Luxury: over €180 / £125
Mid-range: €120–180 / £85–125
Budget: €60–120 / £40–85

► **Restaurants (main course)**
Expensive: over €20 / £15
Moderate: €10–20 / £8–15
Inexpensive: less than €10 / £8

The major parades
of Semana Santa
take place in Seville.
► page 382

*The seemingly endless forest of columns
in the Mezquita of Córdoba reveals
a different perspective with each step.* →

Background

BRIEF AND CONCISE, CLEARLY WRITTEN, AND QUICK AND EASY TO CONSULT: FACTS WORTH KNOWING ABOUT ANDALUSIA AND ITS MOORISH LEGACY, ABOUT THE COUNTRY AND ITS PEOPLE, ITS ECONOMY AND POLITICS, ITS SOCIETY AND EVERYDAY LIFE.

»SO COME ... AND SEE«

The words which the Moor Ibn Zamrak used in the 14th century as an invitation to come to his native city of Granada, the queen of Andalusian cities, are best understood as an invitation to visit the whole of Andalusia.

There is so much to see in Al-Andaluz: the bright, life-embracing lustre of the Moorish palaces and the gloomy, melancholic austerity of Christian cathedrals focusing on the afterlife; the ochre and brown tones of barren landscapes and the gay play of colours of the gardens and orange groves; the fields of sunflowers and corn shimmering in the heat and a hilly landscape speckled with olive trees stretching to

The legacy of the caliphs

A stroll through the Generalife gardens behind the Alhambra is refreshing and relaxing.

the horizon; the blue sea and snow-covered peaks; peaceful, whitewashed villages, craggy castles and proud cities like Granada, Córdoba, and Seville. Granada, with its extraordinarily charming location at the foot of the Sierra Nevada, a history that merges Moorish culture and Christianity in a unique manner and magnificent monumental buildings like the Alhambra, is one of Andalusia's major attractions. Córdoba also experienced its golden age under the rule of the Moorish Umayyad dynasty. At that time, Córdoba was a densely populated city with countless mosques, palaces, public baths, schools and colleges. It was the centre of the Islamic culture of the West. Under Caliph Abd Ar-Rahman III (891–961), the Mezquita, the Alcázar and the caliph city of Medina Azahara were built. As for Seville, the city can only really be experienced by visiting during Semana Santa.

Moorish Legacy

It is Arab and Moorish legacies which make Andalusia so fascinatingly different from all the other southern regions. The Moors not only gave the region its name, but also brought a culture to fruition during their 700-year presence that lived from a spirit of tolerance between Muslims, Jews and Christians. Science, the arts and poetry blossomed in al-Andaluz in a way unknown in Europe until then,

Andalusia far from the coast
Snow-covered mountains, picturesque villages and a far horizon like here on the Guadix plateau are characteristic of the hinterland.

Semana Santa
Holy Week is celebrated flamboyantly in all of Andalusia, but especially in Seville.

Costa de la Luz
It is called »The Coast of Light« because the sun makes the Atlantic glisten.

Corrida
Whether one considers bullfighting to be brutal or actually »arte de lidiar«, the »art of captivating the bull«, Andalusia is unimaginable without it.

Giralda
»A smile on the face of life« is what Stefan Zweig called Seville – the Giralda is the symbol of the city.

Flamenco
Deeply emotional singing, explosive dancing and brilliant guitar playing tell of love, pride and pain.

and which spread out to the rest of the continent – not everyone is aware that it was the Moors who brought the seasoning of food with herbs and spices and pleasant table manners to Europe.

The culture of the Orient did not only manifest itself in southern Europe in the form of magnificent historical architecture, such as in the Alhambra in Granada and the Mezquita of Córdoba; the Moorish legacy can also be felt in the lifestyle and everyday life of the Andalusians.

Vivacity and Passion

But Andalusia doesn't live from this legacy alone. It is also everything seen as »authentically Spanish«: corrida, flamenco, caballeros, señoritas and sherry. With a little luck though, those venturing into one of the less hectic corners of the country might just discover what lies hidden behind the stereotype: in a small bodega for example, where everybody brings their own food. After two or three copas of dry fino, visitors will experience how the proud, almost cold Andalusians thaw out, buy a drink for the stranger and even offer him some of their bread and ham. As the evening progresses, it may be that one or the other of them stands up and starts to dance while the rest clap in time and actually call out »olé« every so often. That's the way it is in a country where life only really gets going when elsewhere in Europe the lights are being switched off.

Tapas bars
Ham, sherry and olives – there is not only food and drink in the bars, but life itself.

Composure and a Zest for Life

On Sundays, the Andalusians can also be seen serenely enjoying life with their families on the beach promenades. Dressed in their Sunday best, they treat themselves to a break out-of-doors: a little relaxation, fresh air and some sunshine before a new week begins. The strollers do not give the impression that they would ever give a second thought to the meaning and purpose of the Sunday promenade that has been passed on from generation to generation. They simply walk on by – with a spring in their step.

Facts

The roots of an ancient farming culture can still be felt in Andalusia. There was no sustained industrialization here. Agriculture and tourism have remained the pillars of the economy right up to the present day. Expanses of olive plantations, fields of sunflowers and seemingly endless seas of plastic sheeting beneath which vegetables are cultivated dominate the landscape.

Nature

Geographic Divisions

Andalusia is divided into two natural environmental zones: **Upper Andalusia** with a small strip of the Costa del Sol, and **Lower Andalusia** in the north. Andalusia also shares a part of the Castilian plateau bordering Sierra Morena.

Upper Andalusia is made up of two mountain ranges that run parallel forming a west-east axis, the inner Penibetica range (Cordillera Penibética) and the outer sub-Betica range (Cordillera Subbética). These are separated by the Betic intermountain basin running in the same direction. They are the result of over-thrusting and basal folding processes during the Lower Triassic **approximately 37–38 million years ago**, a geological event which also created the Pyrenees. Steppes, pastureland, and maquis scrubland cover the detritus-strewn mountain regions; cork-oak and chestnut-tree woods thrive in lower areas.

Upper Andalusia

The mountains of the inner range stretch from Río Guadiaro that flows into the Mediterranean about 20km/12mi north of Gibraltar to Cabo de Palos on the coast of Alicante. The limestone and clay slate mountains of the Málaga Mountains dominate in the west, reaching their highest point with the Sierra de Tolox at 1,919m/6,296ft above sea level and possessing **one of Spain's most impressive mountain landscapes**, the Jurassic limestone landscape of Torcal de Antequera. The Valle de Lecrín marks the cleft behind which there is a rise northeastwards to the Sierra Nevada all the way to Pico de Veleta and to Mulhacén (3,481m/11,421ft above sea level), **Spain's highest peak on the mainland**. They continue in the Sierra de Baza and Sierra de los Filabres, which rise no higher than 2,300m/7,500ft above sea level. To the south, a strip of lower coastal mountains walls off the Mediterranean coast. It stretches from Sierra Bermeja in the west across the Sierra de Gádor to the Sierra de Alhamilla (highest point 2,242m/7,356ft), Europe's only natural desert region. The valley of the Río Guadalfeo cuts between the coastal mountains and the Sierra de Gádor and forms the **terraced landscape of Las Alpujarras**.

◄ Cordillera Penibética

The Andalusian Mediterranean coastline is characterized by relatively short, sandy beaches, occasionally with shingle, which are repeatedly interrupted by cliffs, as well as by the towering mountains only a few miles behind the coastal strip – the **snow-covered peaks of the Sierra Nevada**, for example, can be clearly seen from the beach. It is divided into the universally known Costa del Sol that reaches from the tip of Gibraltar to the eastern parts of the province of Málaga

◄ Mediterranean coast

← *Not an unusual view – fields of sunflowers along with olive tree plantations are typical of the countryside in the province*

The peaks of the Sierra Nevada can be seen from Andalusia's Mediterranean coast, here near Nerja.

and the eastern Costa de Almería that passes around Cabo de Gata in the west; the Costa Tropical has become the accepted name for the short section that lies in between in the province of Granada.

Cordillera Subbética ▶ Starting with the distinctive Jurassic limestone rock of Gibraltar (425m/1,394ft), the ridge of mountains of the outer sub-Betica range runs north of the inner chain of Campo de Gibraltar, rising sharply from the north toward the south around the Málaga Mountains, and reaching its first point of culmination in the **rugged Sierra de Grazalema**. It continues on with the peaks of the Sierra de Cazorla y Segura, which are almost as sharp and rise to above 2,000m/6,500ft, **where the Río Guadalquivir has its source**.

Betic intermountain basin ▶ The Betic intermountain basin lies nestled between these two main mountain ranges and rises from west to east from approx. 400m/1,300ft to a final 1,300m/4,250ft. It consists of the basin landscape of the Serranía de Ronda – where the Río Guadelevín **breathtakingly breaks through** to join the Río Guadiaro – the high-altitude basin of Antequera, the fertile central countryside of Granada's Vega and finally the Guadix and Baza basins.

Lower Andalusia ▶ The second natural environmental zone, Lower Andalusia, is essentially comprised of the Guadalquivir river basin that extends in a stretched-out triangular form between the Sierra de Morena in the north and the Upper Andalusian mountains to the south.

Atlantic coast ▶ The Atlantic coast in the west, the **Costa de la Luz**, dominates the landscape. The up to 100m/328ft-wide strips of sand dunes with seemingly endless beaches are characteristic of the region, as are the »marismas«, the wetland region north of the Río Guadalquivir which reaches the Atlantic here near Sanlúcar de Barrameda. Another marsh area is to be found near Huelva around the mouths of the Río Tinto and Río Odiel rivers flowing out of the mining region of Aracena, as well as at the Bay of Cádiz in the south into which the Río Guadalete flows.

Adjacent to the coastal strip is Campiña, undulating hill country on either side of the Guadalquivir, in summer **one of the hottest zones in Europe** with temperatures often exceeding 40°C/104°F. The still extensive pastures grazed by fighting bulls and Andalusian horses are being increasingly squeezed out by artificially irrigated fields of wheat and vegetables, vineyards and citrus tree plantations.

◄ Campiña

Lower Andalusia is bordered to the northeast by the nearly 250km/150mi-long Loma de Úbeda plateau that rises from 900m/2,950ft to 1,300m/4,265ft. This landscape in the eastern part of the Jaén province is marked by **gently rolling hills** with fields of grain and olive plantations, bounded in the distance by **sheer mountain peaks**.

◄ Loma de Úbeda

The Sierra Morena mountains rise up to the north of the Guadalquivir Plateau as a natural border to the Castilian Meseta or central plateau. The thinly populated mountain range, **bedecked with woods of cork and holly oak**, stretches across the provinces of Huelva, Córdoba and Jaén, reaching a top altitude of 1,323m/4,341ft. From time immemorial, the most important route between Castile and Andalusia was the 1,009m/3,310ft-high Desfiladero de Despeñaperros pass (»Pass of the Overthrow of the Dogs« – so called because in a battle between Christians and Moors many were thrown from the cliffs to their deaths). The journey through this remote landscape was once feared because of its **bands of robbers**.

Sierra Morena

Andalusia is not blessed with water. The water level in the major rivers is below average for six months of the year while many smaller rivers dry up completely in the hot summers. The main watershed between the Atlantic and the Mediterranean runs along the inner Betic mountain range. The Río Guadalquivir (from the Arabic »great river«), Andalusia's major river, flows into the Atlantic. It has its source at an altitude of 1,369m/4,492ft in the Sierra de Segura; after Seville it spreads out into a

Water

delta that forms the »Las Marismas« of the **Coto de Doñana** and then empties into the Gulf of Cádiz near Sanlúcar de Barrameda in a 3km/2mi-wide estuary. The estuary up to Seville – where the tides are still noticeable – is navigable even for ocean-going ships. In the province of Huelva, the Río Tinto and Río Odiel rivers flow into the Atlantic, while the Guadalete ends near Cádiz. The major Mediterra-

The green gold of Andalusia – the province of Jaén is the largest olive-growing region on earth.

nean rivers are the Río Guadiaro and the Río Guadalhorce, whose mouth is situated near Málaga.

Reservoirs, primarily those of the Guadalquivir, play an important role in irrigation and as a source of energy. The reservoir system on the river's upper course and the tributaries flowing out of the Sierra Morena (including Laguna de las Yeguas near Andújar and Embalse Puente Nuevo north of Córdoba) and the Sierra Nevada (Embalse de Iznájar / Río Genil) hold several thousand million cubic feet of water. Large reservoirs have also been created with dams along the Río Guadalete and the Río Guadalhorce.

Water shortage The lack of rain from 1991 to 1995 showed how fragile Andalusia's hydrologic balance is. But precipitation during the following three winters also assumed catastrophic dimensions in some regions, ruining crops. Although water rationing was lifted in 1996, the problem has not been solved as **water consumption** continues to rise – though less through showering tourists and the watering of golf course greens than through the proliferation of often inefficiently managed crops grown on irrigated land: the cultivation of cotton, maize and sugar beet requires much more water than traditional fruit growing. Agriculture accounts for 80% of water consumption! The National Water Plan passed in 2001 provides for the construction of a gigantic canal and reservoir system from the Ebro Delta to Andalusia. Critics suggest it would be better to invest the estimated cost of 40 thousand million euros in refurbishing the water mains systems, improving the methods of irrigation, closing down illegally irrigated areas, and raising the extremely low price of water.

Climate

Andalusia, like all of Spain, has a characteristically Mediterranean climate that is generally marked by hot, dry summers and damp, mild winters, as well as – once away from the coasts – by temperatures that vary greatly according to the time of day and the season. The

Land of the sun

Climate Andalusia

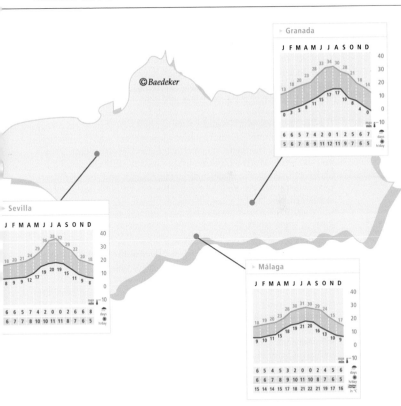

─── Maximum day-time temperature   ─── Minimum night-time temperature
🌧 Days with rain   ☀ Hours of sun   ≈ Water temperature in °C

good news for tourists is the **high number of hours of sunshine**, reaching a Spanish peak on the Costa del Sol and the Costa de la Luz with 3,000 hours annually. Thanks to the powerful wedge of **Azores highs** that keep the Atlantic low pressure areas at bay, the sun shines almost without interruption from May to the middle of October. From mid-October until the end of April, when the highs shift to the south in the autumn, areas of rain are more often able to reach Andalusia. But even in the dampest months, November and December, the duration of sunshine still reaches up to 60% of the amount of time astronomically possible, greater than in northern European summers.

Temperatures in summer

Andalusia isn't called »the frying pan of Europe« for nothing. The temperature during the day in the interior exceeds the 30°C/86°F mark on over 100 days in the year. On average, between June and September, the mercury reaches 32 to 36°C/90 to 97°F; such temperatures are even typical in July and August for 700m/2,300ft-high Granada. On individual days it can even get decidedly higher, especially in Lower Andalusia, where the Guadalquivir river basin, the **hottest region in Europe**, averages ten days of temperatures of 40°C/104°F or higher between mid-July and mid-August. Only along the coast is it somewhat cooler because there the sea breeze blows during the day, bringing relief from the summer heat.

Autumn, winter and spring ▸

Spring and autumn are much more pleasant, but winter is particularly mild too, thanks to the sheltering effect of the Sierra Nevada and the Sierra Morena blocking off the cold northern winds. This is above all true for the coasts, where the Atlantic and the Mediterranean, whose temperatures do not fall below 14°C/57°F, act like a **hot water radiator**. For this reason daytime temperatures there, even in the coldest month of January, usually still reach 16 to 18°C/61 to 64°F; at night it hardly ever cools down below 9°C/48°F. It is different inland: with daytime temperatures similar to those of the coast, the thermometer in the lowlands of the interior drops down on average to 5°C/41°F; in the central hill country it approaches 0°C/32°F. Authentic **winter weather** can be found above 2,000m/6,560ft. In the higher regions of the Sierra Nevada up to 50 days of snowfall are recorded annually, and from the end of October to the beginning of June the highest peaks are crowned by a solid blanket of snow or at least snow patches.

Particular feature of the extreme south ▸

An **unexpected climatic characteristic** of the extreme south of the European mainland between Tarifa and Gibraltar, of all places, is that the summers are the coolest there, averaging 22 to 24°C/72 to 75°F, and the winters the mildest, with an average of 12°C/54°F. The reason is that the moderating influence of the very evenly tempered Atlantic waters (max. 20°C/68°F; min. 15°C/59°F) is particularly strong in this section of coastline which protrudes far out into the ocean. At the same time, strong winds blow from the east (»**Levante**«) or the west (»**Poniente**«) that are additionally fanned by the jet-like effect

Desert-like – the Cabo de Gata is the driest region in Europe.

of the strait, building down-draughts in the Bay of Gibraltar that can become dangerous for smaller boats.

Water temperatures

The water temperature is influenced by the Atlantic, whose cool currents have an effect through the Strait of Gibraltar all the way to the eastern Costa del Sol. As a rule of thumb, **the sea gets warmer moving eastwards.** The water is warmest in mid-August when temperatures average 21°C/70°F on the Gulf of Cádiz, 22°C/72°F on the Costa del Sol near Málaga and 23°C/73°F on the beaches of Almería. The sea is coolest at the beginning of March with temperatures between 14 and 15°C/57 and 59°F.

Precipitation

The Cordillera Bética is a prominent **rain trap** for the moisture-bearing west winds. As a result, many of the regions lying on the leeward side of the mountain range are particularly dry and feature **steppe-like landscapes.** Precipitation is extremely low on the eastern Costa del Sol, where downright desert-like conditions reign, as well as on Cabo de Gata, where **Europe's driest climate station** is located. Moving southwest, precipitation rises. July and August, the **drought months,** are practically precipitation-free, while the **most rain** falls from November to January and in April. Even then, the **risk of rain** is still very low with 10–20% on the coasts and a maximum of 30% inland and along the Strait of Gibraltar. Periods of pronounced bad weather are rare; however, individual storms with strong rainfall, especially in autumn and winter, are more frequent.

Effects of climate change

Spain is suffering more and more from the consequences of global climate changes. Since the 1980s, little or the complete lack of winter precipitation has led to a worsening **drought**.

But the real **danger** comes from the mountains. The failing winter precipitation is causing the snow cover on the peaks of the Sierra Nevada to shrink, which has severe consequences for the water supply in the dry areas of East Andalusia. Until now, the melting snow has supplied enough drinking and industrial water to meet the needs of the major cities, tourist centres and irrigated agriculture, which are partially in totally arid climate zones. Modern horticulture and irrigation techniques involving cultivation under plastic sheeting and the growing of fruit trees with avocados and chirimoyas revolutionized agriculture in the 1980s (▶ill. p.30). With the continuing **trend toward aridity** which the climate experts predict for the whole Mediterranean area, all of this is at risk.

Flora and Fauna

Flora

High Andalusia ▶

The immense forests that once covered Iberia fell victim to merciless **campaigns of deforestation** in ancient times. The flora characteristic of the lower terrains consists of woods of holly oak and cork oak and the »dehesas«, areas of pasture grasslands grazed by goats, cattle and pigs and scattered with holly oak and cork oak. **Exotic plants** such as agaves, which develop metre-high inflorescences, also thrive in these zones. Higher up, stands of red and black pine are to be found with an undergrowth of aromatic shrubs and herbs such as rosemary, juniper, hawthorn and gorse. A **rarity** is the Spanish fir, an endemic fir found only in the Sierra de Grazalema. The upper regions of the Sierra Nevada are dominated by robust types of shrubs with the occasional sprinkling of alpine grasses and foliage, forming the so-called »hedgehog heath«.

Alpha and esparto grasses dominate in the province of Almería in eastern Upper Andalusia and are used in **traditional wickerwork**. Maquis shrubland consisting of typical Mediterranean foliage and shrubs also thrive on the mountainsides, as do Indian fig cacti, often planted to mark off parcels of land. Another **endemic variety** often seen is the European fan palm.

Mediterranean varieties of palms can be seen growing along the **Costa del Sol**. Crops requiring intensive irrigation such as citrus fruits and vegetables such as bell peppers, tomatoes, aubergines and so on are cultivated over wide areas. The

The dwarf fan palm only grows here.

sugar cane and banana plantations to be found primarily on the Costa Tropical are smaller. Although located at a high elevation, the climatic conditions in Alpujarras are very favourable and citrus fruits, vegetables and grapes thrive in large terraced gardens.

◀ Lower Andalusia

The flora found in Lower Andalusia includes forest communities of holly oak, cork oak and Lusitanian oak. These formations were once typical for the hill country lying beyond the coastline, but have visibly degenerated to Maquis shrubland of rockrose, pistachio, myrtle, arbutus and a variety of herbage. Grape vines for **sherry** thrive behind the sand dunes along the Atlantic coastline, along with pine and eucalyptus trees, which, however, are the product of afforestation measures. Plants that survive in salty soil like the sea holly are characteristic of the »marismas«. Extensive areas of Lower Andalusia are covered with endless rows of olive trees that reach into the regions of Upper Andalusia and make up the **largest olive-growing area in the world**.

Fauna

Wolves and lynx find a habitat in Andalusia in the foothills of the Sierra Morena. It is only in the fertile river marshlands of Coto de Doñana that the extraordinarily rare **Iberian or pardel lynx** and the ichneumon, a variety of civet cat, have managed to survive. Also among the endangered animals are genets (a viverrine), otters and the Iberian ibex. An animal that is not rare but whose absence from this landscape is impossible to imagine is the ancient breed of half-wild **fighting bulls** (»toros bravos«), mainly bred in the southwest of the province of Cádiz in the ancient countryside of the big landowners.

◀ Mammals

Original and copy – »toros bravos« and the popular Osborne bull

Birds ▶ The imperial eagle, golden eagle and the booted eagle have withdrawn to the lonely mountain regions. The monk vulture and the griffon vulture are also frequently observed there. **Innumerable seabirds and water fowl** live in the wetlands of the »marismas«, among them the only European breeding colony of purple swamp hens; there are also herons, and rare varieties of duck such as the white-eyed pochard and the white-headed duck, as well as the ruddy shelduck. In addition there are flamingos, and, in the Coto de Doñana, imperial eagles and short-toed eagles, and occasionally also ospreys and azure-winged magpies. A lot of white storks are to be seen, as well as cranes; much rarer, though, are the black storks.

Reptiles and amphibians ▶ The world of the reptiles and amphibians is represented by varieties of snakes (snub-nosed vipers, the Montpellier snakes), geckos, aquatic turtles and swamp turtles, as well as fire salamanders.

Nature conservation areas 19 ecologically valuable areas are under protection in Andalusia – close to 17% of its total area, the **highest in Spain**. Two regions – ▶ Coto de Doñana and the ▶ Sierra Nevada – can claim to be national parks; the rest are designated as »parques natural« (nature parks), in which restricted agricultural exploitation is still possible.

Population • Politics • Economy

Population structure The majority of the Andalusian population is concentrated around the provincial capitals, in the tourist centres and in the areas intensively used for agriculture. Accordingly, the **areas of high population**

Semana Santa lives from religious worship and the joy of celebrating.

Facts and Figures Andalusia

Location
▶ Southern Spain

Area
▶ 87,268 sq km/33,694 sq mi
(a little more than 17% of the total
area of Spain; similar in size to
Portugal)

Length of coastline
▶ 800km/497mi

Population
▶ Major cities:
Seville (701,100),
Málaga (528,000),
Córdoba (310,000),
Granada (288,000)
▶ Population:
with around 7.2 million inhabitants
(18% of the Spanish population),
including 600,000 Gitanos (Roma;
1.5 % of the Spanish population) and
about 200,000 Africans, Andalusia is
the most densely populated of Spain's
17 autonomous regions.
▶ Population density:
84 persons per sq km/135 persons per
sq mile (United Kingdom: 245 per sq
km/638 per sq mi)

Language
▶ Spanish

Religion
▶ 95 % Roman Catholic
▶ 5 % Muslims, Jews and Protestants

Government
▶ Capital: Seville
▶ Administration (»Junta de Andalucía«):
The government of the region is
responsible for cultural, education,
health and infrastructure policies; the
social-democratic orientated PSOE
(Partido Socialista Obrero Espanol) has
been in power since 2000. The elections of 14 March 2004 again gave the
PSOE a comfortable absolute majority.

Andalusia

© *Baedeker*

▶ Andalusia is the southernmost and
second-largest (after Castilia-León) of
the 17 autonomous communities of the
Kingdom of Spain.
▶ 8 provinces (Huelva, Sevilla, Córdoba,
Jaón, Cádiz, Málaga, Granada, Almeria), plus the North African enclaves
surrounded by Moroccan sovereign
territory, Ceuta and Melilla; Gibraltar,
as a crown colony, belongs to Great
Britain.

Economy
▶ Andalusia and the region of Extre-
madura bring up the economic rear in
Spain (25% of all EU aid for Spain
flows into Andalusia).
▶ Per capita income (20% below the
national average): 14,400 euros
(US$19,700, £9,800).
▶ Above average number of unemployed:
around 19%
▶ Economic structure:
Services: 67%
Industry and construction: 26.2%
Agriculture: 6.8%
▶ Tourism: about 20 million visitors
annually

density are Greater Seville (approx. 1 million), the Mediterranean coast around Málaga (approx. 650,000) and the industrial area around Cádiz (approx. 600,000). Most sparsely populated are the Sierra Morena, the Betic Cordillera mountain ranges and the desert regions of East Andalusia. The age pyramid in the villages has gradually been turned on its head as the youth have left their homes and headed in the direction of Málaga, Seville or Madrid to secure employment in the big cities.

Religion The majority of Andalusians are Catholics. There are a small number of Muslims, Jews and Protestants. Islam plays a bigger role in the North African enclaves of Ceuta and Melilla; the Islamic community is also growing in Granada.

Gitanos The Gitanos (**Roma**) originally came from **northwest India**, migrating from there as early as the Middle Ages. They came by way of North Africa with the Moors to Spain, where today approx. 600,000 individuals live. Despite popular preconceptions, only a few actually still move about the country. Many have settled in the province of Granada. High unemployment, no vocational training, widespread illiteracy, low life expectancy and high infant mortality characterize the situation of this people, to whom Andalusia in particular owes a debt of thanks for flamenco, a **significant contribution to its culture**

Andalusia *Provinces*

and folklore. Integration into society is hampered by the persistent antipathy of the population on the one hand, and the resistance of the Gitanos on the other, who – through a lack of social recognition – cling to their traditions and their pronounced common identity and sense of solidarity.

Illegal immigrants

In recent years, the number of illegal immigrants being brought across the Strait of Gibraltar for huge amounts of money by people traffickers has risen sharply. In 2004, the Guardia Civil apprehended a total of more than 17,000 immigrants, 44 being found dead. Most of them are Moroccans, who since 1991 have needed a visa to enter Spain, which is difficult to obtain. The rest are from Black Africa with a scattering coming from India, Pakistan, Iraq and Palestine. Without valid residency papers, they have no chance of finding regular employment in Spain, so in order to earn a living the best they can do is find jobs as **day labourers** on vegetable and fruit plantations. In the province of Almería, for example – as even tourists can see – they are forced to exist under the **most wretched of working and living conditions**. Added to that is their almost complete **isolation** from the locals that can even escalate into acts of racial violence – as happened in the year 2000 in El Ejido.

Government

Since October 1981 Andalusia has been an autonomous community which traditionally bears the colours green-white-green. It is governed by the »Junta de Andalucía« with its seat in Seville. Although the powers of the Spanish central government in Madrid are more comprehensive than those of the German Federal government, it is still possible to compare the autonomous communities with the German states.

Economy

A poor region

Andalusia is among the less developed regions of Spain. There are still large numbers of landless seasonal workers, who find work only as day labourers (»jornaleros«) during harvest time and thereby also find themselves facing the strong competition of African immigrants – a cause for xenophobic antagonism. There is no government support for the times without work; no wonder that **illegal employment** is flourishing.

Although Andalusia is indeed profiting from the positive development of the Spanish economy, and there is also no lack of aid – 25% of all EU aid funds for Spain flows into Andalusia – **structural problems** stand in the way of a real upswing. Among them remains the ownership situation in agriculture in particular, where 270,000 operations with half of the developed land are in the hands of about 9,000 big landowners. Naturally, they profit from the blessings of EU funds: 6% of the monies from Brussels are divided among the 200 largest agrarian enterprises.

As if Christo had wrapped it – the »sea of plastic« in the province of Almeria

Agriculture The **main products** of Andalusian agriculture are wheat, olives, vegetables, fruit, and wine. Predominantly wheat, oats, barley, beans and chick-peas, as well as maize, are found where only dry farming can be conducted. Olive tree cultivation covers about a third of the arable land of Lower Andalusia. The regions around Jerez de la Frontera, Málaga, Montilla-Moriles and Huelva are the focus of wine growing. Cork is produced primarily in Sierra Morena.

The fact that extensive areas of Andalusia is farmland at all is thanks solely to large-scale irrigation, the areas under cultivation in the Guadalquivir basin and in the provinces of Huelva and Almería being of major importance. Citrus fruits, sunflowers, potatoes, sugar beet, cotton and even rice are grown there. Thanks to irrigation under transparent plastic sheeting, the provinces of Almería (tomatoes, cucumbers, beans, peppers, melons) and Huelva (strawberries) are able to reap **multiple harvests per year**, which has made them the major centre of Spanish horticulture that supplies large parts of Europe with its products –making up **80% of Spanish vegetable exports**. With an average annual production of three hundred thousand tons on 7,500ha/18,500ac, Spain is **Europe's largest producer of strawberries** and indeed, after the USA, the second largest producer in the world. 5% of the Spanish production comes from Huelva. The production methods, however, are **ecologically questionable** because of the wide use of pesticides. They are also **socially dubious** because the major part of the workforce are Africans who have immigrated – either legally or illegally – and who live in third-world conditions. Finally, the landscape is ruined. The farmland around Almería is not called »mar plástico« for nothing: the plastic hothouses stretch for mile upon mile.

Animal husbandry now only has relatively little significance in the **Animal** total economy. Large herds of sheep graze the Sierra Morena in sum- **husbandry** mer. Dairy farming and the breeding of horses and fighting bulls are carried out on the pastures of Marismas. Traditional goat keeping still occurs in Upper Andalusia; pig breeding, especially fattening pigs with acorns, is traditionally at home in the Sierra Morena and Sierras Béticas. Up until the 1950s, **fishing** was practised in every settlement on the coast, but today the spread of tourism, over-fishing of the traditional fishing grounds and restrictive quotas have led to a sharp decline. The most important fishing locations are Huelva, Cádiz, Algeciras, Málaga, Almuñecar and Motril. The catch includes sar-

Seemingly antediluvian farming in the province of Jaén

dines, anchovies, tuna and octopus. Fish and shellfish farming in aqua-farms have now taken the place of traditional fishing, above all in Cádiz province.

Although Andalusia is rich in mineral resources, the situation on the **Mining** world markets has plunged Andalusian mining into a **crisis**. The cupriferous pyrite deposits in the provinces of Seville and Huelva are still of particular importance, above all in the regions of Río Tinto.

Economic prospects for Andalusia are being created from the use of **Solar and wind** renewable energy, for which there are favourable climatic conditions **power** such as those enjoyed by the Tabernas solar power station near Almería. The generation of wind energy in the mountains between Tarifa and Algeciras has gained **special significance**. Andalusia supplies 20% of the total amount of energy produced by wind power in Spain.

Industry remains relatively weak in Andalusia. Seville is developing **Industry** into an **important economic centre**. Not only are the food, beverage and tobacco industries concentrated here, but Seville is also home to iron and steel works and the metalworking industry. The chemical and petrochemical industries have established themselves in Algeciras and Huelvat, and shipbuilding takes place in Cádiz. Added to that are the traditional industrial sectors such as sea salt production – above all in Almería province – and the reprocessing of ores. Until now, the high-tech era has as good as passed Andalusia by; the hopes of creating a Spanish Silicon Valley in Seville as a result of the World Exposition of 1992 were not fulfilled.

Building trade ▸ The building trade employs over 20% of the workforce. The times when the coastline was mercilessly cemented over are gone, but the construction of more discriminating holiday facilities at least guarantees seasonal jobs.

Tourism Tourism is by far the most important economic factor in Andalusia. The figures speak for themselves. Tourists annually spend about 14 thousand million euros; directly or indirectly, tourism provides close to 258,000 jobs.

The rise to becoming a **holiday paradise** was tentatively initiated in the 1950s with the first charter flights, and in the 1960s tourism began developing into the most important source of revenue. The core area is, as it always was, the Costa del Sol on either side of Málaga, where holiday centres like Torremolinos, Fuengirola, Marbella, Estepona, San Roque, Almuñecar, Motril, Castell de Ferro, Roquetas de Mar and Aguadulce are lined up one after the other – every one of them once a sleepy fishing village that was transformed within a short time into a conglomeration of hotels for tens of thousands of holidaymakers. This development triggered, on the one hand, a great migration of job hunters to the coasts and, on the other, eventually resulted in **80% of all Andalusia's beaches becoming built-up and spoiled**. An attempt was made in 1988 to counter this with the

Twenty million tourists visit Andalusia annually.

coastal law (»Ley de Costa«), according to which it was no longer allowed to build within 100m/328ft behind the beach and 1km/0.6mi distance from a river estuary. Andalusia experienced its first **tourism crisis** in the 1990s as a result of unimpeded expansionism that placed more emphasis on quantity than quality and, for example, hardly provided for sewage treatment plants. That has been made up for in the meantime: in 1990, 33 beaches had to be closed because of poor water quality, but since 1997 there has not been one closure.

The future of tourism in Andalusia will very much depend on whether environmentally sustainable development can be brought about and whether the efforts of the government aiming at a **qualitatively better, individual holiday experience** are successful, which also include the hinterland. It can only be hoped that what has been achieved by the coastal law will not be ruined by the reform of the land law, which allows the municipalities extensive freedom in the allocation of building land.

History

Ever since the campaigns of conquest of the Phoenicians, Celts, Romans, Visigoths and the Moors, Andalusia has been used to waves of immigrants. The Moors preached tolerance and brought Andalusia to a cultural flowering – during the period of their reign, al-Andalus was economically, artistically and academically vastly superior to the rest of Christian Spain.

From Prehistory to the Arab Invasion

8th–6th century BC	Tartessos Culture
237 BC	The Carthaginians advance into Spain.
219–206 BC	Second Punic War; 201 BC, Carthage relinquishes all claims to Spain in the peace settlement.
27 BC	The province of Baetica is established under Augustus with about the same boundaries as today's Andalusia.
AD 100	Christianization of the Iberian Peninsula begins.
507–711	The Visigoths rule from Toledo.
711	Landing of the Arabs

The **first pieces of cultural evidence** of human settlement are cave paintings dating to the Palaeolithic (2000–10,000 BC), found, among other places, in the Cueva de la Pileta near Ronda and the Cueva de Nerja on the Costa del Sol. The first town-like settlement was built by the Los Millares culture, considered to be part of megalith culture (3000–2000 BC). The large **burial complex near Antequera**, dating from a thousand years later, is also considered to be their work. The beginnings of the Bell-Beaker culture also occurred in this time period (approx. 2000–1500 BC); one of its largest settlement centres was in today's Almería province.

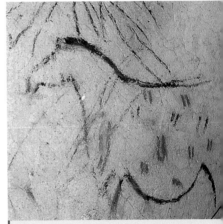

Prehistoric cave paintings in Cueva de la Pileta

The ancients viewed the world as ending at the Strait of Gibraltar with the »**Pillars of Hercules**« – Jebel Musa on the African side and the Rock of Gibraltar on the European. The **Phoenicians** were the first to dare to venture beyond this point and in around 1100 BC founded the trading settlement of Gadir (Cádiz), **Europe's oldest city**. Malaka (Málaga), Sexi (Almuñecar) and Abdera (Adra) followed.

← *Moorish arch forms in the Mezquita of Córdoba*

Tartessos
Burial mounds provide evidence of the legendary Tartessos culture that has been located by most historians in the area of the Guadalquivir estuary and whose flowering is dated from about the 8th to the 6th century BC. The most important reports of this culture, which has been equated by some with Atlantis, are from later Greek (Herodotus) and Roman sources, which agree that the Tartessos supplied the Phoenicians and Greeks with ore. The later, mainly Asia Minor Ionians from the Phocaian colony of Massalia (Marseille) established a few ports on the Mediterranean coasts as early as 700 BC, including Mainake near today's Torre del Mar.

Greeks ▶

Carthaginians
The Greeks lasted for only a century. They were ousted by the Carthaginians around 600 BC, whose conflict with Rome spread out to include Iberia. After the loss of Sicily in the First Punic War (237 BC), Hamilcar Barcas, Hasdrubal and Hannibal concentrated on Iberia and pushed up from the south to Ebro. This border was recognized by Rome.

219–206 BC Second Punic War ▶
At the beginning of the Second Punic War, Hannibal destroyed Sagunt, which was allied with Rome. The Romans then advanced ever deeper into Carthaginian territory and in 208 BC reached the Guadalquivir River near Baecula (Bailén). Carthage's defeat was ensured two years later with Publius Cornelius Scipio's victory near Ilipa (Alcalá del Río). Scipio settled his veterans not far from the battlefield in what became **Itálica**. In the peace settlement with Rome in 201 BC, Carthage relinquished all its Iberian possessions.

Romans
The Romans divided Iberia into two providences, »Hispania citerior« in the northeast and »Hispania ulterior« in the southwest. In 45 BC during the Roman Civil War, Julius Caesar defeated the sons and supporters of Pompey near Munda (southwest of Córdoba) and became the dictator of the Roman Empire. When the Iberian Peninsula was reorganized under Augustus in 27 BC, **Baetica province** (named after the Guadalquivir, called by the Romans »Baetis«) was created, which had approximately the same boundaries as today's Andalusia. Major centres were Hispalis (Seville), Corduba (Córdoba) and Itálica. The Christianization of the Iberian Peninsula began around AD 100.

Vandals
Over a period of a little more than 20 years during the great migration at the beginning of the 5th century, the Vandals moved out of eastern Germany and settled in southern Spain. In 429, led by Geiseric, they moved over to North Africa and founded a kingdom there. They left practically nothing behind in Andalusia except the name – it comes from the Arabic »al-Andalus«, a derivation of the Gothic **»landahlauts« (= landless)** used to denote the Vandals.

Visigoths
King Euric (466–484), ruler of the Visigothic Kingdom in Toulouse founded by Theodoris, spread Visigoth rule to Spain. After their de-

feat at the hands of Clovis I in 507 at Poitiers, the Visigoths withdrew completely back into Spain and ruled there in Toledo until 711. From 551 on, they had to fend off the Byzantines, who had taken the southern coast of Spain, until they were able to force them out again in 624. Under Reccared I, the Third Council of Toledo dissolved the Visigoths from Arianism (that recognized only a God-like Christ) and professed Catholicism (that postulated a Christ equal to God).

The Arab general **Tariq Ibn Ziyad** crossed over the Strait of Gibraltar with his 7,000-strong army in the year 711 and landed in the vicinity of today's Tarifa.

Landing of the Arabs in 711

Al-Andalus

July 711	Tariq defeats Roderic in the Battle of Jerez de la Frontera.
732	Charles Martel defeats the Muslims as they advance into France near Tours and Poitiers.
756–929	Emirate of Córdoba
929–1031	Caliphate of Córdoba
1086–1147	Rule of the Almoravids, a Muslim sect from Morocco
1147–1212	Reign of the Moroccan Almohad dynasty

Tariq's troops met an opponent weakened by internal disputes. In July, they decisively defeated the Visigoth army led by King Roderic in the seven-day battle of Jerez de la Frontera. In thefollowing three years, the Muslim army conquered almost the whole of the Iberian Peninsula up to the mountains of Asturia, Galicia and the Basque Country. Named »al-Andalus«, the region was made a **province of the Umayyad Caliphate** in Damascus. Increasing numbers of Muslims poured in, among them many North African Berbers from the former Roman province of Mauretania, which is why one generally speaks only of the »Moors«. The triumphant progress of the Muslims was finally halted by Charles Martel's victory at the Battle of Tours.

Conquest of Iberia
◄ July 711
Battle of Jerez de la Frontera

The Umayyad Abd ar-Rahman I, the sole survivor of his family in the fight against the Abbasids of Baghdad, fled to al-Andalus and in 756 founded the **Emirate of Córdoba**, which encompassed the whole Pyrenean Peninsula. New crops (including rice and sugar cane), artificial irrigation and the increasing production of silk and weapons facilitated a great economic and cultural flowering. In general, the Moors practiced religious tolerance towards the Christians (Mozarabs) and Jews living among them. Many Christians converted to Is-

756–929 Emirate of Córdoba

Important Battles between Moors and Christians

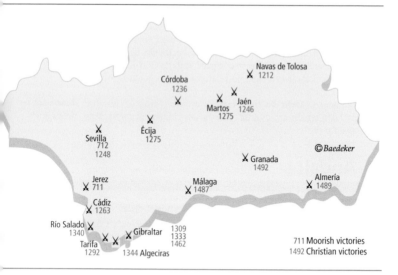

Córdoba 1236

Navas de Tolosa 1212

Martos 1275 Jaén 1246

Écija 1275

Sevilla 712 1248

©Baedeker

Granada 1492

Jerez 711

Málaga 1487

Almería 1489

Cádiz 1263

Río Salado 1340

Gibraltar 1309 1333 1462

Tarifa 1292 1344 Algeciras

711 Moorish victories
1492 Christian victories

lam and adopted the Arab language and customs. In 785, Abd-ar-Rahman I began the construction of the **Mosque in Córdoba** as a visual symbol of his rule. He died in 788.

From the beginning, however, there was a stirring of Christian resistance to the Moors that originated in the non-occupied regions in the mountains of Asturia in the north of the Iberian Peninsula, and the emirate found itself constantly on the defensive.

929–1031 Caliphate of Córdoba

Abd-ar-Rahman III declared himself caliph in 929. This was **a tremendous event**, because in the Islamic world the only recognized caliph – and as such the legitimate successor to the Prophet – was the caliph of Baghdad. Despite that, Moorish culture reached its zenith in Andalusia, most clearly expressed in the **palace complex of Medina Azahara** that was begun in 936. The caliph was also successful in his fight against the advancing Christians. In 930 he conquered Toledo; a year later he even reached out into Northwest Africa (to Tahert), which was lost again in 979. Under Almansur (»Victorious by Grace of God«), the grand vizier of Caliph Hisham II, Spain experienced the **peak of the development of the Moors' military might**. One after another, Almansur conquered Barcelona (985), León (987) and Santiago de Compostela (997). With his death in 1002, the end was in sight, which was sealed with the overthrow of the last Umayyad caliph, Hisham III, in 1031. The caliphate broke up into more than 20 **independent emirates** (»Taifas«), which mostly warred against each other.

The Christians took advantage of the disunity of the Muslims. Alfonso VI of Castile retook Toledo in 1085 and threatened Seville. In 1086, the local emir sent for help from Yusuf ibn Tashfin, the leader of the fundamentalist Berber sect, the Almoravids, based in North Africa. Within a short time, they had forced back the Christians and united the Islamic southern part of Spain with their North African kingdom.

1086–1147
Almoravids

The Almohads, led by Abd al-Mum, were also Berbers, and conquered the Almoravid kingdom. They were incessantly forced to fight against the Christian kingdoms and in 1195 gained the last great Muslim victory over the Christians in the Battle of Alarcos. Nevertheless, they displayed lively building activity – the Alcázar and the mosques, of which the Giralda still stands today, were built in their capital Seville.

1147–1212
Almohads

The Reconquista

1212	Battle of Las Navas de Tolosa; the beginning of the Reconquista with the victory of the Christian armies over the Almohads
1236	Conquest of Córdoba by Ferdinand III
1248	The Christians conquer Seville.
1238–1492	The Nasrid Emirate of Granada
2 January 1492	Catholic monarchs enter Granada.

The Almohad caliph, Mohammed ibn Nasr, suffered a crushing defeat in 1212 against the allied armies of Castile, Aragón and Navarre at the Battle of Las Navas de Tolosa. That signalled the downfall of Islamic rule and the final re-conquest by the Christians (»**Reconquista**«). Again, smaller states emerged that were, however, unable to stop the disintegration. The losses of the Moors against Ferdinand III, called the Saint, and Alfonso X the Wise included Córdoba (1236), Seville (1248) and Cádiz (1263).

The advance of the Christians

The last Moorish state able to survive over a longer period of time was the Emirate of **Granada** founded in 1238 by Mohammed ibn al-Ahmar of the Beni Nasr dynasty. It stretched from Gibraltar to Almería. Its capital was the richest city of the peninsula and, at the same time, its cultural centre. The Nasids left behind a unique legacy of their reign, the **Alhambra**, built in the 14th century. A fragile peace was bought with the Christians in 1246 by submitting to Castile, to whom the Nasrids were required to pay tribute. Granada even went into battle on the side of the Christians in the conquest of Sev-

1238–1492
Nasrid Emirate of Granada

ille in 1248. The Christians continued a policy of pin pricks. Although King Mohammed II defeated the Castilians with the help of the Marinid sultan of Morocco, Abu Yûsuf, in 1275 at Écija and Martos, Granada lost Tarifa in 1292 and Gibraltar in 1309 (which was regained in 1333 and remained Moorish until 1462). In 1340, Yûsuf I, in alliance with the Moroccan sultan, suffered a severe defeat at Río Salado north of today's Vejer de la Frontera. The Castilians entered Algeciras in 1344.

The two great Christian kingdoms of Spain were united with the marriage of Isabella of Castile and Ferdinand of Aragón (the **»Catholic monarchs«**) in 1479. The couple was determined to drive out the Muslims, and they became overpowering adversaries of the Moors. In 1481, open war between Castile-León and Granada began, with Granada weakened internally by disputes over the throne between Muley Hassan (ruled 1464–1482) and Abu abd-Allah (Boabdil, ruled 1482–1492). In 1487, the Spaniards stood in Málaga, cutting Granada off from the sea. In 1491 the city was besieged.

2 January 1492: the Moors surrender Granada to the Catholic Monarchs.

On 2 January 1492, the Catholic monarchs entered into Granada.   **2 January 1492**
The **last Moorish ruler, Boabdil**, withdrew to Africa, ending almost
eight hundred years of Islamic culture in southern Spain. The subsequent expulsion of several hundred thousand Moors and Jews meant
a grave setback for Spain's cultural life and further economic development.

The Era of the Habsburgs and Bourbons

1492	Founding of Spain's colonial empire
1496	Spain falls to the Habsburgs.
1700–1873	Reign of the Bourbons
1713	British awarded Gibraltar.
1808	Napoleon's troops occupy Spain, except Cádiz.
1812	Cádiz Constitution
1814	French driven out, return to absolutist order
1820	National uprising, return to the Cádiz constitution
1823	French troops crush the revolt.
1834–1876	Carlist Wars

Even before entering Granada, Isabella of Castile concluded a con-   **Columbus**
tract with Christopher Columbus enabling him to seek a western   **discovers the**
route to India. Andalusian ports were used as the starting points for   **New World**
his four **voyages of discovery**. In 1492, he set sail from Palos de la
Frontera, in 1493 from Cádiz, in 1498 from Sanlúcar de Barrameda
and in 1502 again from Cádiz.

The marriage of Isabella's daughter, Joanna the Mad, to Philip the   **Habsburg King**
Handsome in 1496 gave Spain to the **Habsburgs**.

The **discovery of the New World** founded the Spanish colonial em-   **Golden**
pire. Communication with the colonies was maintained from Anda-   **Age**
lusia, where their immense wealth would first arrive, resulting in a
great blossoming of trade, industry and, in their wake, also art – for
this reason the 16th century is referred to as Andalusia's golden age.
Seville, where the galleons laden with gold and silver landed after
crossing the Atlantic, profited the most. In 1503, the city became the
seat of the Casa de la Contratación, the chamber exclusively responsible for trade with the new colonies. It was from there that in 1519
the Portuguese mariner Magellán set sail on the **first circumnavigation of the globe**. The **Habsburg Empire** reached its greatest extent

Columbus – the discoverer of the New World

under Charles V (ruled 1516–1556), who was at the same time Holy Roman Emperor. He immortalized his reign with the construction of his palace on the Alhambra in Granada and the erection of a **cathedral** in the middle of the Great Mosque of Córdoba.

For the Moors who stayed in Granada after its conquest, the so-called **Moriscos**, the age was anything but golden. Many retreated to the Alpujarras. Constantly under pressure from the Church, even threatened with forced baptism in 1502, they tried to improve their conditions through revolts, as in 1568 to 1570 in the Alpujarras, which Philip II had brutally crushed. Beginning in 1609, the last Moriscos, and Jews as well, were **driven out** once and for all.

Charles II, the last Habsburg, died in 1700 without designating a successor. With Philip V, the Bourbons ascended to the throne of Spain. This ignited the War of the Spanish Succession – Philip V and France on the one side, Charles of Habsburg and Great Britain on the other – during the course of which in 1704 the British **conquered Gibraltar**, which was awarded to them in the Treaty of Utrecht in

1700–1873 Bourbons

1713. In return, they accepted the Bourbons on the throne. Andalusia became appreciably poorer under their reign. The gap between the big landowners and the landless peasants became ever greater. The wealth from the colonies was scarcely still flowing; the Guadalquivir was silting up and the ships could no longer reach Seville. In 1717, the Casa de la Contratación was transferred from there to Cádiz. An attempt, begun in 1767 by Charles III who was influenced by the Enlightenment, to revive agriculture by settling German farmers in the Sierra Morena failed.

Napoleon and the consequences

On 21 October 1805, the English fleet under the command of **Admiral Nelson** destroyed the combined French and Spanish fleets in the

Battle of Trafalgar. The French-controlled politics of the monarchy elicited a revolt in 1808; Napoleonic troops occupied Spain and suddenly found themselves facing a guerrilla war. Only Cádiz in Andalusia remained unconquered. The French were defeated for the first time in Europe in July 1808 at the Battle of Bailén.

The parliamentarians who had fled from Napoleon to Cádiz passed a **liberal constitution** in 1812, which among other things guaranteed free speech and freedom of the press, and established a separation of powers. However, after the French had been ousted in 1814 and the Spanish throne reinstated, Ferdinand III threw it out and restored **the old absolutist order**.

The Liberals, however, did not accept defeat. In 1820, Rafael de Riego Nuñez instigated a popular uprising in Cádiz, which at first forced the king to accept the constitution again. French troops sent by the »Holy Alliance« crushed the revolt in 1823. **Mariana de Piñeda** from Granada, who was executed for her avowal of liberty, became a folk heroine.

On the path to the First Republic

While the **Carlist Wars** flared up over the throne (1834–1839, 1847–1849, 1872–1876) **Spain failed to become involved in the industrial revolution**. Economically, Andalusia fell further and further behind. In particular, the position of the farm workers worsened dramatically.

For this reason, socialist and anarchist ideas won increasingly more followers among the farm workers in the last quarter of the 19th century, who became vocal about their dire situation in revolts and strikes.

From the First Republic to the Death of Franco

1873–1874	First Spanish Republic; the period after its demise; the restoration of the monarchy
1923–1930	Dictatorship under General Primo de Rivera
1936–1939	Spanish Civil War
1939–1975	Franco's reign

The First Spanish Republic lasted only from 1873 to 1874. After it was crushed by General Pavía, the monarchy was restored. The situation in Andalusia did not improve. In 1910, Andalusia's first ancho-syndicalist trade union was founded. At the same time, intensified emigration to North America began. With King Alfonso XIII's approval, **General Primo de Rivera** governed dictatorially between 1923 and 1930.

Republic and restoration

The Málaga front in the Spanish Civil War

Under Franco

1936–1939
The Spanish Civil War ▶

The Second Republic was formed following Alfonso XIII's abdication. In 1936, on the eve of the civil war, the People's Front won the parliamentary elections in Andalusia. During the Spanish Civil War, Andalusia was the **deployment area** for the insurgent army under General Franco that advanced from Morocco. Franco set foot on Spanish soil again near Barbate. Morón near Seville was one of the most important bases of the German Condor Legion (air force) that supported Franco. The west of Andalusia was on the side of the Nationalists, while the east defended the Republic.

His victory in the civil war brought »Caudillo« Francisco Franco **unrestricted power to rule** over Spain. Efforts to move toward democracy and autonomy were suppressed. Politically, Franco turned to the West. Through agreements signed in 1953, Spain was able to gain millions in **economic aid** in return for hosting American military bases. The Americans were given Morón air base and the harbour of Rota, which they developed into a huge marine base. In 1954, »Marbella Club« was opened in Marbella and with it began **Costa del Sol's rise to become a holiday region**. Its immense popularity in the 1960s only increased in the 1970s.

New Democracy

1975	Franco's death and Spain's return to democracy
1992	EXPO World's Fair in Seville
2000	Racial riots

The path to autonomy

Spain's return to democracy began after Franco's death in 1975. **Juan Carlos**, a Bourbon, became King of Spain and persistently supported the process of democratization. On 15 June 1977, **democratic elec-**

tions were held for the first time since 1936. As early as 1978, Andalusia experienced its first demonstration for autonomy. In 1981, the majority of the Andalusians voted in a referendum for a statute of autonomy. The Socialists won the first election for an Andalusian regional parliament in 1982, and the same party emerged as winners in the overall Spanish elections as well, with Felipe González, an Andalusian from Seville, becoming prime minister.

World's Fair

Seville hosted the World's Fair, EXPO '92, on the occasion of the 5th centennial of Columbus's first voyage. A portion of the funds were used to improve Andalusia's infrastructure. Among other things, the east-west motorway from Seville to Almería and a stretch of track for the high-speed train AVE from Madrid to Seville were built. However the hoped-for lasting economic boom, and in particular the establishment of hi-tech industry, failed to materialize.

Economy

At the beginning of the 1990s, tourism suffered a setback – there had been too much reliance on unbridled growth. Since the turn of the century tourist numbers have started rising again thanks to the construction of well-tended beach promenades and sewage treatment plants, as well as a **reorientation** toward high quality, environmentally friendly tourism.

Domestic policies

Andalusia has increasingly had to deal with the problem of illegal immigrants. Xenophobia is the result. In February 2000, a woman was murdered by a mentally deranged Moroccan fieldworker in El Ejido (Almería province), leading to three days of race riots in which the police did not intervene.

The illegal immigrants, also called »boat people«, come over the Straits of Gibraltar.

Art and Culture

What are the distinguishing features of Moorish-Islamic art? What are the typical characteristics of Mudéjar style? Who was the most important Spanish painter of the 17th century? Remarkable artistic and architectural monuments from the Phoenician, Roman, Moorish, Jewish and Christian past have survived and provide an insight into an authentic aspect of Andalusia.

Art History

Glossary p.432

Early History and Antiquity

The oldest forms of artistic expression of the former inhabitants of today's Andalusia have been found near Málaga and near Huelva, as well as in the interior near Ronda. For the most part, these people left behind drawings and petroglyths that have survived for **20 to 25 centuries** on the underside of overhanging cliffs and in caves. The favourite subject of these hunters was animals, but there are also hand prints and symbols whose meanings still remain uncertain today. As the pictures were found in rather remote parts of the caves, it is assumed that they did not have a decorative but rather a ritual function. The caves of Pileta and Nerja, both in the province of Málaga, have most of these drawings.

Cave paintings of the Stone Age

The remains of Los Millares in Sierra de Gádor are, if not in their state of preservation then in their extent, the most important evidence of the megalith culture of the 3rd millennium BC, at least a millennium before the burial mounds or dolmens of Antequera were built.

Megalith culture

At the end of the 3rd and the beginning of the 2nd millennium BC, a culture which was to extend throughout the whole of Europe began on the Andalusian coast. The early inhabitants of the Iberian Peninsula laid decorated bell-shaped ceramic beakers in the graves of their dead and, additionally, often a bone or stone vambrace that served as protection against the snapping back of the bow string. These people, or at least their cultural technology, quickly conquered the **whole of the central European area** – such beakers have been found in England, across France and Germany and into Hungary.

Bell Beaker culture

Large deposits of copper, along with tin the basic raw material for bronze, were present in Andalusia. At the beginning of the 2nd millennium BC, trade relations based on these commodities were established between southern Spain, Egypt and the Aegean. At that time, the »**El Argar culture**« (2200–1500 BC), evidence of which was discovered in the province of Almería, were a people engaged in mining, metalworking and agriculture, who developed their own language of forms with their sparsely decorated tools, weapons and pottery.

Copper ore and Mediterranean trade

Cádiz, Spain's oldest city, was founded in the 11th century BC by the Phoenicians in their westernmost colony of the time and named

Phoenicians, Greeks, Carthaginians

← *Pleasantly warm water splashed in the time of the Moors in the today restored baths in Jaén.*

»Gadir«. Málaga and Córdoba also date back to this time. The local museums, especially in Cádiz, and in particular the archaeological museum in Madrid, show the historical cultural evidence of this period. In the 7th century BC the Greeks and Carthaginians began to establish further cities on the Mediterranean coast. Southern Spain became an important source of metal and ore and also a **trading base** for the world powers of the time. Their influence is strongly displayed in the Iberians' pottery and sculptures; their most significant legacy is the head of the Lady of Baza.

Romans In the peace settlement with the Romans after the Second Punic War, the Carthaginians were forced to relinquish to Rome all of their

territory on the Iberian Peninsula – this was an event of the greatest significance for the Andalusians, as well as Spanish culture as a whole. From then on, Roman culture shaped the country. The most obvious legacy of the Romans is, naturally, the **Spanish language** itself. Moreover, at least for today's autonomous community of Andalusia, the borders have remained similar; its territory corresponds approximately with the Roman province of Baetica. The introduction of Roman culture above all meant the **advancement of the technologies of civilization**. Roads, bridges, aqueducts, temples, theatres and baths were built and irrigation systems laid out. An important archaeological excavation site close to Seville is **Itálica**, founded in 207 BC. There, the Roman occupiers formed the political and social upper class and orientated

The Museo de Cádiz possesses a collection of Roman sculptures.

their tastes strongly along »Roman Empire« lines, so that the so-called provincial Roman »mixed style« did not develop in Baetica as in other Roman provinces. Further important excavations have been carried out in Bolonia near Tarifa and in the necropolis of **Carmona**.

Early Christianity

Migration In the year 325, the year of the Council of Nicaea, Christianity was already widely spread in Baetica. The famous sarcophagus of Écija, which serves as an altar in the church there in Santa Cruz, dates from that time. Later, tribes moving through Baetica primarily influenced arts and crafts. The Vandals, however, who plundered Baetica on their way to North Africa, left next to nothing of artistic or cultural value.

The Visigoths (Spanish: »visigodos«), at first allied with the Romans, dominated the region of southern Spain for close to 300 years (418–711), but stimulated no new artistic achievements. It was mainly churches that were built under their early feudalistic rule. Along with the Roman elements already found there, they primarily used Byzantine, Coptic and Syrian construction details such as horseshoe arches and stone vaults. The **Visigothic calendar pillar** in Santa María church in Carmona is of some importance.

Visigoths

Moorish Art and Culture

From the conquest of southern Spain in 711 by Tarik to the handing over of the keys to the city of the last Moorish bastion in Granada to the Catholic monarchs in 1492, the **Moorish-Islamic Culture** had determined the production of art in Andalusia for 780 years. Its influence lasted much longer, however: the later art of the region also clearly referred to and cited the Moorish era, and this applies to some extent even up to the present day.

Centuries-long influence

? DID YOU KNOW …?

■ that due to the centuries-long influence of the Arabic tongue, 4,000 words entered the Spanish language? Even the word that to our ears sounds the most Spanish of all – »olé« – goes back to »Allah«.

Although Islam was hardly 100 years old at the time of the Moorish invasion of Andalusia, it had already developed its own, in part synthetized, artistic features. There are no devotional images in Islam, for example, so therefore no contrast was drawn between art that served ritual purposes and profane art. Primarily, art had a **decorative role**, and space-filling ornamental decorations were therefore predominant. Ornamentation created as sculpture or as plaster relief dominated the architecture of the façades. Plaster work was either carved or, where the pattern is repeated, formed with moulds. A third decorative technique consisted of rhombic patterns laid with bricks, the »**ajaracas**«. In the interior, ornaments were used on the ceilings and above all in the colourful wall tiles typical of the country, the »**azulejos**«. Depictions of humans and animals are very rare; the ornamentation principally takes its themes from plants and geometric designs. Often Arabic characters expressing praise to Allah or individual rulers were also integrated into the ornaments.

An essential feature of Moorish construction, however, is the **multiplicity of arch forms**. Above all the horseshoe arch, which was already known in Iberia in Visigoth times, was used with many variations in every building project. The typical twin windows (»ajimez«), for example, were developed from the basic form of two horseshoe

Characteristics of Moorish-Islamic art

Types of arch

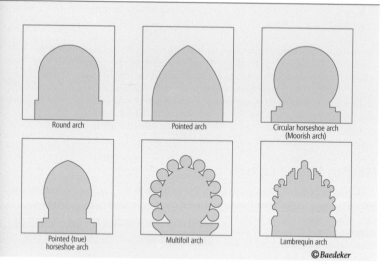

Round arch

Pointed arch

Circular horseshoe arch (Moorish arch)

Pointed (true) horseshoe arch

Multifoil arch

Lambrequin arch

© Baedeker

arches. Columns, often re-used Roman **spolia**, divide the interiors of mosques, private homes and palaces or separate covered promenades from the inner courtyard. The artistic design of the ceilings likewise led to a specific type of ceiling, the richly carved coffered ceiling (**»artesonado«**). The art of the stonemason, plasterer and gilder reached their peak in the stalactite vaulted ceilings that still can be marvelled at, primarily in the **Alhambra** in Granada, but also in the Capilla Villaviciosa in the **Mezquita** of Córdoba.

Umayyad Emirate Córdoba was made the **seat of the Moorish emirs** as early as 712. The outstanding flowering of Moorish-Andalusian culture began with the arrival from Damascus of Abd ar-Rahmans I, the last survivor of the Arab Umayyad dynasty, in the year 756. He had work begun in 785 on the first section of the **Mezquita**, which after the Grand Mosque of Mecca is the largest (former) Islamic place of worship still in existence today. The building followed the **Umayyad tradition** with a square ground plan and forecourt. In contrast to the popular image of pencil-shaped minarets, the towers for the Muezzin in Andalusia had a basic square form and were adorned with brick patterns, following the manner of construction in the North African Maghreb. The most important spot in the mosque was the **Mihrâb**, the prayer niche orientated toward Mecca. The Friday prayers were held from the pulpit-like Mimbar.

Delicate plaster work with a love for detail adorn →
the Alhambra in Granada.

Al-Andalus Caliphate In the year 929, Emir Abd ar-Rahman III, who had by then both in political and economic terms optimally consolidated his Spanish emirate, declared himself caliph in Córdoba. Under his government, Moorish Spain with Córdoba as its centre achieved its **cultural zenith**. Medicine, poetry, astronomy, mathematics, as well as luxuries, conveniences and lifestyle experienced a blossoming unknown to the rest of the world of that time. The **Medina Azahara**, the palace-city close to Córdoba, was founded in this period and today its remains provide an extremely impressive picture of the caliph's need to demonstrate his power and wealth.

Almohads The last Umayyad caliph was overthrown in 1031 and the caliphate disintegrated into more than 20 **independent minor kingdoms**, some of which, however, were united again in 1039 by the North African Berber dynasty of the Almoravids, who took their seat in Seville. Their successors, the **Almohads**, erected a magnificent mosque there in 1172 under Emir Abu Jacûb Yûsuf, probably comparable to the one in Córdoba. A cathedral stands on its former site today. Only a minaret, the »Giralda«, today the city's landmark, has survived with slight changes and is an outstanding example of the form of western Islam's minarets.

Granada A ruling dynasty also declared itself independent in Granada, namely the Zirids in 1031. Though they resided on Alhambra hill, it was not in today's palace but in an earlier building. The palace that stands today was first constructed by the Nasrids. Mohammed I, who came to power in 1232, began with the first section in the eastern part. By that time, the Reconquista had already made great advances. Mohammed saw the writing on the wall and allied himself with Ferdinand III. Though this alliance contributed to Seville also being taken by the Christians in 1248, it also ensured that the Islamic kingdom of Granada was able to coexist with the Christian kingdoms for almost 250 years, and a separate artistic development – represented today above all by the Alhambra – was able to take place there. The **Patio de los Leones**, created under Mohammed V in the second half of the 14th century, shows this development toward a more filigree language of form in architecture and decoration and, through the Fountain of Lions, toward more figurative representation, which also demonstrated an opening toward Christian art.

Western Christian Art before 1492

Romanesque and Mozarabic Styles Evidence of Romanesque art and architecture that dominated Christian Europe of the 11th and 12th centuries can hardly be found in al-Andalus, though some buildings and stonemasonry in areas that were re-conquered early do exist. In Cantillana, in a little town in the vicinity of Carmona, the small Romanesque Ermita San Bartolomé still stands. A few monasteries also continued to exist in Muslim al-Andalus and along with the Carolingian script and the greatly influential Beatus Commentaries (commentary on the apocalypse by the monk Beatus of Liébana from the 8th century), they also adopted Arabic graphic elements in their illumination workshops. This individual language of form of Christian-influenced art mixed with Arab elements was named after the so-called **Mozarabs**, the Christians under Muslim rule.

The Andalusia of today, with the exception of the kingdom of Granada, was **conquered by the Christian kings** in the first half of the 13th century. The building of churches, frequently on the sites of destroyed mosques, took priority in the construction plans of the new regents.

But monasteries were also specifically established to make the dominance of the »new« religion visible in their urban development. From the 14th to 16th centuries, Gothic cathedrals were built in all the major cities, including the **largest Gothic church in the world**, the Cathedral of Seville with its nave and double aisles, begun in 1402 on the site of the mosque which was just 200 years old and essentially completed around 1500. As a monument to the victory of the cross over the crescent, it was provided with a gigantic sculpted doorway on the west side. The former minaret of the Almohad mosque (»Giralda«) remained standing with little change. A characteristic feature of the interiors of all Spanish cathedrals is the **freestanding choir** in the nave in front of the chancel.

Gothic

Stellar and reticulated vaulting decorate the cathedral of Seville.

»Estilo mudéjar« is taken from the Arab word »mudejalat« (»conquered«), the **style of the conquered Moors**. The Catholic conquerors, after centuries of battle, were primarily proficient in the art of warfare. They did not have a sufficient number of their own craftsmen, artisans and master builders and so in large part the subjugated Moorish master craftsmen were entrusted with the new building projects. The result, a successful merging of Gothic and Arab elements of form, later also incorporating those of the Renaissance, can be admired in Andalusia and particularly in Seville. This style is tan-

Mudéjar style

Honeycomb-shaped plaster in the Alhambra's Patio de los Leones

gible most notably in architecture and arts and crafts and seen at its most beautiful in **Alcázar**, begun around 1360 for Pedro the Cruel. The craftsmen from Granada given the job brought with them their experience from the building of the Alhambra and within a few decades built the palace for the Christian ruler using spolia from Córdoba and Medina Azahara. **Casa de Pilatos** is an example of the use of this style in the private residence of a rich Sevillian.

The Catholic monarchs, Isabella and Ferdinand, entered Granada in 1492. The New World had just been discovered, the rejection and racism against the Moors and Jews had escalated and as a consequence more and more **French and Flemish masters** were being brought into the country. An influence from the North became noticeable, particularly in sculpture. This development is discernable even before 1492 in the terracotta sculptures of the west façade of the Cathedral of Seville created by the Breton sculptor Lorenzo Mercadante and by Pedro Millán. Lavish filigree embellishments are characteristic for this »Isabelline Gothic style«.

From the Renaissance to Classicism

Architecture Pedro Machuca, a student of Bramante and Michelangelo, built a palace in pure Italian Renaissance style (Spanish: »renacimiento«) in 1526 for **Charles V** on the grounds of the Alhambra. The wealth of the New World had also helped the Spanish royal house to gain great political clout. Accordingly, a new thrust came in the production of art that was mostly reflected in secular construction. Examples of this are the Renaissance palaces in Úbeda and Baeza, particularly the Palacio de Jabalquinto there.

The structuring elements of the Renaissance together with the dense and highly complex ornamentation of the Mudéjar style are denoted as **»Plateresque = in the manner of a silversmith«** (Spanish: platero). The town hall of Seville (1527–1564) and the chapter house and sacristy of the local cathedral are examples of this language of form used in architecture and wall decoration; the architect of the

Capilla Real in Granada, Enrique de Egas, and Diego de Siloé, who constructed the cathedrals in Granada and Málaga, are its most famous representatives. However, there were still some resemblances to Gothic style in the construction of churches.

It was not only the last Christianized Moors (**»moriscos«**) and Jews that were driven out by Philip II and the Holy Inquisition, inflicting great injury to the cultural diversity; changes had also occurred in the politics of art and the zeitgeist. The consciousness of being a world power paired with asceticism and religious fanaticism banished the lavish ornaments for some decades in favour of a plain **deornamentation** of the façades (»desornamentado«). In the painting of the time, the mythological themes otherwise so popular in the Renaissance were no longer to be found. Luis de Morales (approx. 1505–1585), for example, strictly preferred **Christian subjects** stressing suffering, such as *Pietà*, *Mater Dolorosa* or *Ecce Homo*. His works are represented in the art collection of every provincial town in Andalusia.

Painting in the 16th and 17th centuries

The spirit of this era was expressed above all in the dark, serious faces of the portrait paintings. The Greek **El Greco**, who painted the test-piece *The Dream of Philip II* in 1579, failed to gain favour with the king with his subsequent work for El Escorial near Madrid because of its garish colours and received no more commissions. This did not prevent him, however, from giving form to his deeply mystical images and visions of light in the service of the Church thus enabling **Spanish Mannerism** to flourish. El Greco, however, worked for the most part in Toledo. In Seville, the only place in Andalusia where a politically significant middle class had formed, other foreign Mannerists were also working, including the Dutchman Pedro de Campaña (Pieter de Kempeneer).

The demand for art from the court and the aristocracy shifted more and more, however, to the young capital of Madrid, at the latest after the construction of El Escorial. The history of art in Andalusia from this point on can hardly be separated from Spain as a whole.

The 17th century is known as the **»Golden Age«** of Spanish art, even though the country was experiencing a political and an economic decline. The gold supply from America inflated the domestic market and famine among the needier in the population was the result. On the other hand, the royal family, the aristocracy, the Church and in turn the arts profited from colonialism. The painting of the time was predominately orientated toward **Caravaggio** and Correggio. The artists' order books were full.

Francisco de Zurbarán (1598–1664), the »painter of monks«, and **Bartolomé Esteban Murillo** (1618–1682) are the important representatives of the styles that made up the **Seville School**. Zurbarán had led Spanish painting, after José de Ribera (worked in Naples) and Francisco de Herrera the Elder, up to the point when **Velázquez** gained international standing. What was new, beginning in the

Bartolomé Murillo,
»The Little Fruit Seller«

1630s, was his abandonment of chiaroscuro, the bold contrast between dark and light. The Carthusian Order, his main source of commissions, was not alone in recognizing his qualities. In 1632, he was named **court painter to the king**, given state commissions and remained successful until around 1645 or 1650 when Murillo outshone him as court painter. The **Museo de Cádiz** owns the most important collection of Zurbarán paintings in Andalusia. Murillo, who in his delightful Genre paintings and scenes of everyday life painted commoners' children just as charmingly and warm-heartedly as he did saints and is therefore considered to be Spain's most demotic painter, came from Seville, as did the somewhat older Diego Velázquez de Silva (1599–1660).

Madrid School **Diego Velázquez** landed in Madrid soon after his training with **Francisco Pacheco**, among others, which he completed while still in Seville. Working at the Spanish court from 1623, he became the **most important Spanish painter of the 17th century**. His talent and his independent position at court made it possible for him to revolutionize whole genres, to introduce new subject matter and to pursue new paths with his more strongly realistic perception of images. He worked primarily in Madrid and in Italy. Some of his paintings hang in the archiepiscopal palace and, naturally, in the **Museo de Bellas Artes in Seville**, Spain's second largest art gallery; but the most important ones such as *Las Meniñas*, the famous picture of the Spanish royal family, which includes his own portrait, are to be seen in the Prado of Madrid (►p.79).

Sculpture Andalusian Sculpture produced notable artists who restricted themselves solely to **religious themes**. Alonso Cano (1601–1667) stands out among them. He produced the façade of the Cathedral of Granada and left behind numerous portrayals of Mary. The choir stalls in the cathedral in Málaga are by Pedro de Mena (1628–1688); Martínez Montañés (1568 to 1646) specialized to a certain extent in processional figures.

Baroque architecture Baroque architecture, which replaced desornamentado style, is named **Churriguerism** after its most important proponent, **José de Churriguera** (1665 to 1725). The figured decoration became more and more opulent, reaching its peak in altar retables usually inun-

A Churriguesque altar of the Virgin in El Rocio

dated with putti. Luis de Arévalos' design for the sacristy of Cartuja in Granada is regarded as an outstanding example of Churriguerism. With the spreading of the Order of the Jesuits, the effort to provide the masses with an impressive **spectacle** became popular; magnificent altars, retables adorned with gold and silver and luxuriously clad »virgen«, who today still retain their importance in processions in Semana Santa and other places.

In the second half of the 18th century, the absolutist monarchs made much use of foreign artists. Along with **Tiepolo** and his son, both of whom worked for only a few years in Madrid, it was principally **Anton Raphael Mengs** who embodied academic Classicism in the newly-founded Academy of San Fernando.

Rococo and Classicism

Against this backdrop, Francisco de Goyay Lucientes (1746–1828) occupies a unique position. In a period when the academic and court art of Spain was no longer in any way setting the tone Europe-wide, he began working on a »modern« version of art. At first, Goya also pursued a career at the Academia San Fernando, but was soon able to win over the heir to the throne, Charles IV, and became **court painter**. His contact with Andalusia was of a significant nature: he travelled to Cádiz in 1792, was seized by a severe illness and from then on was **deaf**. This fateful event is generally judged as the impetus for his individual, new conception of art. A second trip soon followed in 1796, which took him to Sanlúcar de Barrameda, where he

Goya

Goya's »St Justa and St Rufina«
in the cathedral of Seville

stayed in the country residence of the Duchess of Alba, with whom he is said to have had an affair – although this is disputed among art historians. Sketchbooks exist from the time and are preserved in the Prado in Madrid. Goya's significance primarily lies in his **new, realistic point of view**, a view of the world that – after the French Revolution – became pivotal, questioning the distribution of power as a God-given absolute, and which he was the first to express in his work. His most important works in Andalusia are the paintings of the patron saints of Seville, **Justa and Rufina**, in the Cathedral of Seville.

From the 19th Century to the Present

Although an enormous amount of building took place in Andalusia in the 19th century, classic and historical architecture barely achieved any greater significance in this period. Things were the same in the field of sculpture. Even painting hardly reflected the politically troubled times – but perhaps the **sugar-coated folklorism** was precisely a reaction to the uncertain times, projecting a romanticized image of Andalusia, an Andalusia of »majas«, of »bandoleros« and of »toros«. The real situation – not represented in the arts – was that through the ever-increasing **loss of colonies** in the 19th century, the country was economically bankrupt. The Spanish philosopher Ortega y Gasset formulated it thus: »Art is not capable of bearing the gravity of our lives«. It wasn't until the turn of the century that a painter, Rodríguez Acosta (1878–1941), appeared in Granada who represented a new realism.

? DID YOU KNOW ...?

■ Probably one of the most beautiful Andalusian clichés, namely that of Carmen, the vivacious gypsy from the Sevillian tobacco factory, was created by two Frenchmen: Prosper Mérimée, who wrote the literary work in 1845; and George Bizet, who immortalized it in his world-famous opera in 1875.

Julio Romero de Torres (1885–1930) was highly famous in Córdoba. As a painter, he was a unique figure at the beginning of the 20th century and his **idealized, sensuous images of Andalusian women** are still being used today on bullfight posters and in advertising. Even during his lifetime, he was so popular with his contemporaries and particularly the female ones that, according to legend, hundreds of women lined the streets crying at his funeral.

Naturally, this account would not be complete without mentioning the most famous painter and Andalusian of all: Pablo Picasso (▶Famous People). Picasso was born in Málaga and lived mostly in France, making world art history there.

Picasso

In 1929, 31 years after the loss of all Spain's colonies, the Ibero-American Exhibition was held in Seville. The Parque de María Luisa was laid out for it and huge buildings were erected, in front of which even today almost every wedding party has its picture taken. Aníbal González (1876–1929) was the architect of the **Plaza de España**, a semi-circular enclosure surrounding the eclectic Palacio Central. Every historical style from Spanish history is supposed to have been used in this building; regional historicism with an Arab touch and a clear debt to the Renaissance was intended to convey the nation's continuing great importance. The architecture of some of the buildings for the EXPO '92 in Seville were very innovative; for example, the Santa Justa train station by the architects **Cruz and Ortiz** or the extravagant Puente de la Barqueta by **Santiago Calatrava** – in Spain, bridge architecture is associated with modernity. During the Second World War, as also under the Franco regime, Spanish artistic work was concentrated in the industrial regions of the north and in the capital Madrid. Only since the 1970s have Andalusian sculptors and painters tried to regain access to the international scene. Various groups of artists have formed, mostly in Seville. The political transition to democracy that took place in the 1970s and 80s brought forth a wide variety of directions in art, which are now – without political or ideological functions – relating to social development. Because contemporary art was seen as a synonym for progress and modernity, it was not only tolerated, it was supported. New exhibition centres were created all over Spain, such as the **Centro Andaluz de Arte Contemporáneo in Seville**. In the 1980s and 90s, it was almost exclusively painters and sculptors that set the scene. They worked in the most diverse directions, from Expressionism to Conceptual Art.

Ibero-American Exhibition Seville 1929

◀ EXPO-architecture

◀ Recent history

Calatrava's Puente de la Barquerta in Seville was constructed as an unsupported suspension bridge.

Better known names today are Guillermo Paneque (born 1963), Guillermo Pérez Villalta (born 1948), Luis Gordillo (born 1934), Ferran García Seville (born 1949) and Miquel Barceló (born 1957). With his synthesis of figuration and abstraction, Gordillo greatly influences younger Spanish painters.

Andalusian Festival Culture

There is always a reason to hold a festival

»A people that suffers a lot, sings a lot.« This Andalusian saying may provide an explanation for the Andalusians' enthusiasm for »fiestas«, which has become virtually proverbial. When and where these festivals take place can be found in the events calendar on p.98 ff.

Semana Santa

Incense and orange blossoms

Viewed from the outside, Semana Santa, **Passion Week**, is both surprising and confusing. Two fragrances dominate the towns and villages during these days before Easter and introduce an apparent incompatibility of opposites: incense and orange blossoms. The first symbolizes the Passion of Christ; the second expresses the character of festivals and the awakening of spring. **Compassionate suffering** and repentance merge to some extent with an extremely secular **zest for life** and wild abandon.

Procession as teamwork with a burden of hundreds of kilos

The streets of many villages, and naturally of the big cities, are transformed into one great stage for the most magnificent processions. In many places, usually toward the end of Semana Santa, thousands of »nazarenos« parade past with their conical hoods and monk's robes at all hours of the night and day. By now, there are over 50 processions in Seville. The processions are each conducted by a »cofradia«, a **religious brotherhood** of the parish. At the centre of the procession is the »paso« with sculptures of Christ, whole scenes from the Passion and often figures of the Virgin Mary (»virgen«) carried on a platform which usually weighs over a ton. Up to thirty bearers, the »costaleros«, are required for a single »paso«. During the hours-long procession, concealed beneath cloths, they become welded together into a rhythmic body. The skill of the »costaleros« is the focus of everyone's attention – particularly at the beginning of the **procession**. The shrines are carried out through the church portals, some of which are very narrow, and the bearers are applauded when they succeed in not bumping into anything. The Nazarenes then begin to move along with their candles. The beating of drums and Easter hymns (»marchas«) accompany the processions.

Things change when the Madonna, portrayed as a queen, emerges. These shrines (»paso de palio«) are decorated all over with burning candles, flowers and chased silverwork, also often adorned with a majestic canopy. The Madonna figure is enveloped in an up to 3m/ 10ft-long train of costly fabrics embroidered with precious items, and, with all the luxury, literally presents a counterpoint to the suffering Christ. The Mother of God is fashioned as a child-like figure of a girl (Spanish: **»virgen«**), with a realistic Baroque face, which is emphasized through glass eyes and tears. The crowds celebrate their »virgen« at the top of their voices with calls of »bonita«, praise her beauty and drink wine in her honour.

»Romerías« – a Festive Procession of Cheerful Pilgrims

A »romería« is celebrated at least once a year in almost every Andalusian village. This pilgrimage named after Rome usually leads to a »santuario«, a small chapel or church set in the open countryside that had been erected there because of an apparition of the Virgin Mary or another miracle. The pilgrimage to ▶El Rocío has gained renown outside Spain.

A »romería« in every village

Having arrived after the pilgrimage at the »santuario«, camps are set up and paella prepared over an open fire. Usually on the same evening, Mass is celebrated as the religious climax, during which the pilgrims devote themselves to worship and the adoration of the figure of the Virgin Mary. For the rest of the night, however, it is »fiesta« time. Then there is plenty of sumptuous eating, drinking and dancing until the early hours.

Pilgrimage, worship and festival

The »Feria« – the Major Summer Festival

Andalusia's »ferias« almost always have their origins in the cattle markets held since the 19th century. Once a year the farmers in the towns and villages gathered to offer their animals for sale. Today though, this reason for the »ferias« has almost disappeared. The »fiesta« character is foremost, even if the festival costumes and the »señoritos« on horseback still reflect the colourful atmosphere of bygone days.

Origin

IN SEARCH OF EL DUENDE

In Jerez de la Frontera there is a professorial chair for »Flamencologia«; the specialist literature on the subject fills whole bookcases, and everyone in Andalusia has something to say about flamenco. Nevertheless, it is almost impossible to get a clear answer to the question of what flamenco is, what constitutes the »arte« of a dancer or singer – it is easier to find out what flamenco is definitely not.

Flamenco is not »merely« music, dance and singing. For the connoisseur it is the expression of an attitude to life. The **sources that formed the character of flamenco** are as varied as the history of Andalusia itself. Moorish influences, elements of Byzantine liturgical music and the structures of medieval romances have all been traced. One thing is certain: the Andalusian gypsies, the **Gitanos**, have had the greatest influence on flamen-

co. To this day the best flamenco artists come from gypsy families. About 200 years ago they established the original form of modern flamenco, which was danced and above all sung in family circles in those times. In the early 20th century flamenco moved out beyond its ethnic base, was performed at festivals and spread in the 1920s through the **cafés cantantes**. There are flamenco schools in all Andalusian cities, and even abroad –

The Gitanos, gypsies, look down on castanets. For a »bailaora«, a true dancer, they can never substitute the rhythmic clapping of her fellow musicians, the »toque de palmas«.

including in Japan! – where enthusiastic learners discover how to express its rhythms and movements in song and dance.

Flamenco is not folklore

It would be wrong to regard flamenco as a folk dance, as folklore, even though **commercialization** has produced more and more music and dance rhythms that are borrowed from flamenco – and have hardly anything in common with its original character. Flamenco is more than this; it is an art form, at which few attain perfection.

El cante jondo

There are no less than 30 types of song, not all of which can be danced to, but which all originate in the provinces of Andalusia: the bulería comes from Jerez and the alegría from Cádiz, while the malagueña is mainly sung in Málaga. Whether they tell of joy or pain, all of these forms have one thing in common: **el cante jondo**, the intensity of feeling of the music and song. The themes are taken from everyday life: love, pain, a lost son, a failed harvest, happiness, finding a friend, subjects that are sung in a language rich in imagery but at the same time simple and intense. The same applies to dance.

The **staccato of boots** expresses anger and pride, the beguiling **movements of the hands** and fingers tenderness and courtship. Just as the listeners are at one with the emotions of the singer and sometimes feel a tremor run through them that is released at the end of the song with a liberating, many-voiced »olé!« onlookers experience of the movements of the dancer in their own bodies. When this happens, flamenco transcends the boundaries of song and dance and finds its »duende«, its demon, as the writer Federico García Lorca put it.

While in smaller places only one large colourful tent is set up, whole **tent quarters** spring up in the large cities. Many of the »little houses« are not open to everyone. In these, members of the upper crust mingle amongst themselves.

A stage for self expression

The great Spanish thinker, Ortega y Gasset, spoke of the »tendency of Andalusians to dramatize themselves and to be actors playing themselves«. The »ferias« are the perfect stage for this phenomenon. In the morning, the members of the »great families« of Andalusia promenade down the lanes between the rows of tents on their elegant, highly bred horses: the men with wide-brimmed »sombreros« and in short bolero jackets and, behind them on the horses' croups, the ladies in flamenco dresses laden down with frills and flounce bring to life the **world of the big landowners**.

Bullfighting

Andalusia is hard to imagine without bull fighting and no »feria« is complete without it (►Baedeker Special p.370).

Dancing in the flamenco »Sevillana« costume will draw attention.

Moorish Life in Andalusia

Moorish Urban Culture

The Moors were present in Spain for almost eight centuries and produced **one of the most flourishing cultures**, which also had a significant influence on the history of European civilization and which, for the Middle Ages, demonstrated an amazing tolerance. Muslims, Christians and Jews lived together in al-Andalus without any great conflict. Although Islam was the dominant religion, the new rulers forced neither the Christians nor the Jews to convert – a special tax was merely levied on them.

In the first years after the invasion, the Muslims and Christians even shared the same places of worship. In a certain way, this culture, which was far superior to the Christian West in terms of the thirst for scientific knowledge, state organization, way of life and civilized refinement, was in fact the result of the close exchange between precisely these three religious and cultural circles. The scholars of Moorish Spain had assimilated the philosophies of ancient Greece, produced the best mathematicians of their time, developed complicated irrigation systems and perfected the production of paper. The legacy of this unique culture lives on today, above all in Andalusia, in the big cities as in the smallest villages – not only in the monuments there, but also in the alleyways of the old towns, in the »patios« of the houses, in the small »plazas« of the city districts and even in some of the habits the Andalusians have which are obviously Moorish in origin.

Tolerance as the basis of an advanced culture

The Moors in Spain built their cities similarly to those in North Africa and in the Near East. The centre of the city was the walled-in **»medina«** with the main square, the Alcázar that served as the residence of the caliph, and the central mosque. The outer districts were situated beyond the walls that were locked at night. Such was the case in Córdoba. The paved main streets led from the inner city to the city gates. The rest of the public lanes formed a labyrinth of small squares and alleyways that altered in size and direction every few yards, or ended abruptly. A city's importance was measured by the number of its city gates. The »medina« of Córdoba had seven of them and no less than 21 suburban districts enveloped the city core. There were a total of almost 500 smaller mosques in the city. The big cities had enclosed sewage systems, an abundance of wells with drinking water and public baths. Córdoba, during the time of the caliphate with its 300,000 inhabitants, had almost 800 wells – at the time it was Europe's most densely populated and most modern city. **Industries and trade** were organized into guilds and these usually grouped together in one street or district. Many lanes in the old towns of Andalusia are named after guilds: for example »Calle Lin-

Early urban architectural culture

It stays cooler in narrow lanes – on the Albaicin in Granada.

eros« – the street of the linen weavers; and »Calle Armas« – the street of the armourers.

The lanes were built narrow so that the unbearable hot summer sun could not shine in. From the outside the houses looked plain, almost poor, and provided little information about the social status of the people living in them. They were built with two floors and even the poorer houses had a **patio** that allowed light and air to enter and that was the **centre of the family life**. The bedrooms were on the lower floor and only a narrow staircase led up to the floor above – which was reserved for the women. Niches used to store household articles were built into the cooling walls that were up to three feet thick. Cabinets, chairs and tables were unknown to the Moors. Everything took place on the carpets upon the tiled floors. Clothing was stored in trunks.

»Siesta« in summer, »Brasero« in winter

It is known from the poetry and songs of the time that life slackened during the summer months around midday. The oppressive heat forced the people to withdraw to »patios« shaded by cloths and plants. Public life first began to pulsate again after sunset, but then lasted late into the night. The summer days were divided in two in al-Andalus and it is still so today – this is the natural and historical explanation of the oft quoted Spanish »siesta«. Despite the mild climate, a source of warmth was necessary in the winter. In the finer houses that had baths, hot water was channelled under the floors through ceramic pipes. The poorer people had large bowls of metal or clay in which charcoal glowed.

Moorish-Arab Bath Culture

Washing as a ritual

The Moors treasured cleanliness in the house, clothing and body. Undoubtedly, one of the reasons for the **great cultural value placed on hygiene** was the ritual washing before prayers in the mosques. In the finer houses, the »bathroom« was an extremely important, aesthetically and opulently decorated room often containing a bath tub carved from a block of marble. The palaces, on the other hand, had their own baths, as can be seen today, for example, in the Alhambra in Granada.

Finally, there were public bathhouses. It is estimated that 10th-century Córdoba had 600 hundred such facilities, which were available to all levels of the population – this is equal to a bathhouse for every 500 inhabitants. The structure of the bathhouses was imitative of the **Roman baths**.

◄ Public bathhouses

In the morning, the men were allowed in; in the afternoon, the women. First of all came the immersion in a pool of hot water, then in one with warm water and finally cold water. Soap, »âle«, and towels were available. **Masseurs** offered their services. The walls and floors were often lined with colourful tiles or even marble, and frequently they could be heated with hot-air pipes.

There were even reports from Córdoba of a »beauty institute«. The distinguished Cordobans were able to practice handling blades, pastes and waxes to remove body hair and were introduced to the use of toothpastes and »toothbrushes« fashioned from plant roots – in the 10th century! After bathing, the body was heavily perfumed.

The restored baths in Jaén give an impression of how highly regarded bodily hygiene and culture were in al-Andalus. In contrast, in the Christian West water was an element that, for moral reasons, only seldom came into contact with the human body; this applied far into the modern age. In re-Christianized Spain, church officials immediately set themselves against the »immoral« use of the bathhouses.

Christian prudery prohibited bath culture

! Baedeker TIP

Bathe like a caliph

... in Córdoba's Hammam, which is set up like a Moorish bath and can be found between the Mezquita and Plaza del Potro. Reservations are necessary (Corregidor Luis de Cerda, 51; tel.: 957 48 47 46)

Moorish Science and Technology

The consistent support of science led to a **wealth of discoveries and knowledge**, which in part was only again taken up in the Renaissance.

The country's valley basins were very fertile, but water was scarce. The Moors perfected the Roman technique of agricultural irrigation by boring deep wells and channelling the water to the fields through underground canal systems. Huge bucket-wheels driven by the flow of the rivers conveyed the water to the higher-lying areas, where it was then channelled through canals to the fields. If the power of a river was unusable, mules were used to drive the bucket-wheels.

Irrigation technology and windmills

The pious guidelines of the builders in inscription friezes on the walls in the Alhambra.

Some such wells, called »norias«, are still to be seen today on the Castilian plateau.

Wind was used for windmills that could be adjusted to the wind direction. In **Vejer de la Frontera** some of them still exist.

The constant perfecting of the manipulation of water led to some absurd inventions, such as **hydraulic robots**; figures of clay and bronze with a system of cables, counter-weights and valves inside that were installed in some palaces as **»dumb waiters«**. By pressing on a lever, they poured out drinks, offered towels or made other movements.

Cooling of drinks But the mosttechnologically difficult problem to overcome was the heat. There was a type of »refrigerator« for food. Ice dealers would collect snow in the winter in the mountain regions near Granada, compress it in deep rock crevices and sell the **ice** in the cities. Bulbous jugs of porous fired clay were used to cool drinks. Some of the water was able to »sweat« through the porous walls of the filled vessel and evaporate, producing the cold necessary for cooling.

Weapon technology A chapter in the dark side of human inventiveness also goes back to al-Andalus. During the century-long fight against the Christians, the armies of Moorish Spain were the **first in Europe to use cannons** on the battlefield.

Progressive medicine One of the mostadvanced sciences was medicine. Diagnostic procedures, based on Hippocrates, were improved and **surgical operations** performed. Anaesthesis, disinfection and the suturing of wounds with strands of gut were widely practiced procedures. Doctors such as **Averroes** dissected corpses and so formulated theories about the human organism. The studies of Abulcasis (10th century) were translated into several languages. This text was still serving the medical students of the Renaissance as the basis for their research and treatises in the 16th century.

Libraries An extensive paper industry and a high regard for the written word produced libraries, some of whose books survived the fall of the Moorish culture.

The Other Side of the Coin

It is deceptive however to concentrate only on the high level of civilization. Seen as a whole, the living standards of the simple classes in society were lower than in the Near East. Wheat was the basic foodstuff and only through the consumption of lentils, chick-peas and beans was it possible to meet the required amount of protein. **Meat was a luxury item**.

Meagre diet

The slave trade also flourished. Boys and women were carted off as spoils of war from the attacks on Christian territories and sold in the markets. Galician women were especially popular as **concubines** for the harems. Black Africans were coveted for their physical strength as **slave labourers**.

Slave trade

Despite a generally constituted jurisdiction based on the Qu'ran, the people were frequently at the mercy of the judges' arbitrary use of power. During his reign, Abd ar-Rahman II was forced to dismiss no less than eleven of the highest judges (»qádí«) for being guilty of violating the Qu'ran.

Judicial insecurity

Repeatedly, there were fundamentalist movements that restricted liberal thought or considered the living standards of the elite to be »illegal« according to the Qu'ran. The end of the reign of the Caliphate of Córdoba was brought about by a **civil war** fomented by fundamentalist Berber groups. The library of over 400,000 volumes that Al-Hakam II had built up was censored and thousands of books went up in flames, long before the Christian Inquisition.

Fundamentalism

Famous People

From which Andalusian port did Columbus start his voyage to the New World? Who took modern Spanish lyric poetry to new heights? Who is known as the flamenco guitar god? Here are some short biographies of people who have left their mark on Andalusia.

Abd ar-Rahman I (731–788)

Abd ar-Rahman I was born in Damascus, but was forced to flee from **Emir of Córdoba** the city in the year 750, the sole survivor of the massacre of the Umayyads at the hands of the Abbasids. Travelling by way of Morocco he came to al-Andalus, where in 756 he founded the Emirate of Córdoba which was independent of the caliph of Baghdad; the emirate later became the caliphate. His battles against the armies of Charlemagne in 778 in Roncevaux Pass are recorded in the *Song of Roland*. As Emir of Córdoba, he ordered the construction of the magnificent **mosque** there.

Abd ar-Rahman III (889–961)

Al-Andalus experienced its **political and cultural flowering** under **Caliph of** Abd ar-Rahman III who was from 912 the Emir, and from 929 the **Córdoba** self-proclaimed Caliph of Córdoba, and thus a rival of the Caliph of Baghdad. He drove the Christian kingdoms of León and Castile back across the Ebro and in 951 forced them to pay tribute. He defeated the Fatimids in North Africa and ruled over northwestern Maghreb.

Almansur (940–1002)

Almansur, whose whole name was Abu 'Amir Muhammad ibn Abi **Grand vizier** 'Amir al-Ma'afiri, was for over twenty years the **sovereign ruler** in al-Andalus, although his formal position was »only« that of grand vizier of Caliph Hisham II. His title, Almansur bi-llah (Arabic for »victorious by grace of God«), and his epithet, the »Scourge of Christianity«, characterize this man, who again spread the domination of Islam over almost all of the Iberian Peninsula more than two hundred years after the Moorish invasion. Almansur was born near Tolox in what is today the province of Almería. Prefect of a province under Caliph al-Hakam II, he rose under al-Hakam's son, Hisham II, to become administrator of the realm in 976. He became grand vizier in 979 and soon reduced Hisham II to insignificance. He ruled the caliphate from **Medina Azahara** and expanded it once again far into the north in over 50 military campaigns. He conquered Barcelona in 985 and Santiago de Compostela in 997. He died during one of his campaigns in the fort of »Medina Selim«, today's Medinaceli.

Averroes (1126–1198)

Averroes (Abu l-Walid Muhammad; also Ibn Rushd) was born in **Scholar** Córdoba, the scion of a Muslim family of legal scholars, and was a **judge** in Seville and a **personal physician at the court of the Almohads** in Morocco. Besides writing legal works and a general medical

← *Paco de Lucia revolutionized flamenco guitar playing.*

encyclopaedia, he gained importance as the quintessential **commentator on Aristotle** of the Middle Ages and as founder of Averroism, philosophical teachings named after him that permanently influenced Latin-Christian and Jewish philosophy. Averroes interpreted the Aristotelian teaching of the existence of a prevailing intuitive reason (»nous«) in all mankind and of the eternity of the world as a »thinking intelligence« independent of human existence. This view of the world was effective for him in terms of the Qu'ran. Following his lead, numerous Christian and Jewish theorists attempted to prove the compatibility of their religion with philosophy. Among the opponents of Averroism were Albertus Magnus and Thomas Aquinas. Averroes died in 1198 in Marrakech.

Boabdil (died 1527)

King of Granada It is not known when the last king of Granada, Abu 'abd-Allah Muhammad XII, known to the Christians as Boabdil or »el rey chico« (»the Little King«) was born. It is certain that he was the son of King Muley Hassan and his wife Aisha. His adolescence was marked by the disputes between his father and his father's lover, the Christian Soraya, on the one hand, and his mother and the **Abencerrage family** on the other. They wanted to raise Boabdil to the throne, but Muley Hassan learned of the conspiracy and had his mother and son imprisoned in Comares tower on the Alhambra. They were able to escape, however, and flee to Guadix. A short time later, a revolt ended Muley Hassan's reign and in 1482 Boabdil ascended to the throne. After he had defeated the Christians at Loja and Ajarquía, he besieged Lucena in 1483 but was captured and taken to Córdoba. The Catholic monarchs forced him to accept **subjugation**. His uncle, Abu abd-Allah Muhammad el Zagal, attempted to unite the Moors against the advancing Christians and forced Boabdil to side with him. The Catholic monarchs interpreted this as a betrayal and as a consequence they attacked Loja in 1486. Once again Boabdil was taken prisoner and once again he was forced to accept subjugation and, in addition, stand against El Zagal, whom he defeated with the support of the Christians. Despite that, in 1490 the Christians demanded the forfeiture of Granada. When Boabdil rejected this, they accused him again of breaking their agreement and the **siege** began. On 2 January 1492, the **Catholic monarchs** entered into the city. Boabdil left his homeland on 6 January and withdrew to the Alpujarras, but he was driven out again in 1493 and found refuge with the King of Fez in Morocco. He fell in battle in service of the king in 1527.

Camarón de la Isla (1950–1992)

Flamenco singer José Monge Cruz was a slight, blonde, seemingly nondescript **Gitano** from Isla del León, San Fernando, in the province of Cádiz, which is why his uncle called him »Camarón«, after the almost transparent little crabs that are fished out of the Atlantic off the coast of Cádiz. The son of a blacksmith first performed as a flamenco singer at the age of eight and as early as this first performance the experts recognized that he could bring expression to the »duende« like no other. He began an unparalleled career that made him the **greatest »cantaor« of this day and age** and earned him the national prize for singing of the Jerez de la Frontera School of Flamenco Art in 1975. At first he stuck to traditional singing, especially during the congenial

!   *Baedeker* TIP

Soy Gitano

»I am a Gitano« – the title of the album that appeared in 1989 for which Camarón de la Isla received his first gold record. The album released in 1980, *La leyenda del tiempo*, was crucial in defining his style.

collaboration with the guitarist **Paco de Lucía**. Later he allowed elements of jazz and rock to be incorporated into his music and created what he called »flamenco rock gitano«. He was one of the few Gitanos also to gain recognition in the world of the »**payos**«, the non-Gitanos, but he always remained true to his roots. 50,000 people followed the coffin at his burial in his native village.

Manuel de Falla (1876–1946)

The composer Manuel de Falla was born in Cádiz and lived from 1914 in Granada. His roots in Spanish folk music clearly shape his most important works, the opera *La Vida breve* (1905) and the ballet *El Amor brujo* (1915). He additionally wrote numerous songs and pieces for the piano. In 1939, Manuel de Falla moved to Argentina, where he died in Alta Gracia. He is buried in the **cathedral** of the city of his birth, Cádiz.

Composer

Federico García Lorca (1899–1936)

Federico García Lorca, along with other poets of the »Generation of '27«, strove to raise **modern Spanish poetry** to a last high point before the outbreak of the civil war. He was born in Fuente Vaqueros in the province of Granada, studied philosophy, literature and law, stayed in New York and Cuba from 1929 to 1930 and in 1931 took over the direction of the »La Barraca« touring company, which brought Spanish classics to the stage in the provinces. His own dramas – the best known are *The House of Bernarda Alba* and ***Blood Wedding*** – are often set in Andalusian surroundings. A major theme of his poetry was also his **native Andalusia**, its landscape and culture, its myths, and the passion of its people, especially that of the »Gitanos«, expressed above all in *Romancero gitano*. Federico García Lorca was murdered by Falangists in Viznar shortly after the start of the civil war on the 19th of August 1936.

Poet

Through oranges and olives
Flows the river Guadalquivir.
The two rivers of Granada
Cascade from snow to wheat.
O' love that left, not to return!

The river Guadalquivir
Has a beard of grenade crimson.
Lament and blood
Are the two rivers of Granada.
O' love, departed on the winds!

Seville has a waterway
for sailing ships -
But on the waters of Granada
Lonely sighs are all that row.
O' love that left not to return!

Wind in groves of oranges,
high tower, Guadalquivir.
Darro and Genil are little towers,
Ended already at the pools.
O' love, departed on the winds!

Who would say the water bears
Cries flickering as will o' wisps!
O' love, gone not to return!
No, bear orange blossoms,
Bear olives, Andalucia,
Down to your two seas.
O' love, departed on the winds

Federico Garcia Lorca
Little Ballad of the Three Rivers
(1931)

Washington Irving (1783–1859)

Writer

It is only thanks to the American writer Washington Irving, born in New York, that the interest in the **Alhambra** in Granada, and with it Spain's Moorish legacy, was awakened in Europe at all. After several years in Scotland – visiting Walter Scott – as well as in Germany, Irving came to Spain in 1826 where he stayed for three years.

In 1829, he undertook a journey from Seville to Granada and lived there for four months on the Alhambra in the chambers of Charles V. He wrote down his impressions in the account of his journey *The Alhambra*, which was published in 1832. The book had a great effect on his contemporaries and more and more travellers came to Granada. Irving returned to Spain as his nation's ambassador once again from 1842 to 1845.

Isidore of Seville (around 560–636)

Church scholar

Isidore, born in Cartagena, was named Bishop of Seville in the year 600. He is regarded as one of the last Western Church Fathers who

was influential down into the high Middle Ages through his writings such as *Sententiarum libri tres*, a textbook about ethics and dogmatics. Furthermore, he wrote chronicles and historical works such as *Historia Gothorum*, a history of the Visigoths, and an encyclopaedia of knowledge with his 20-volume *Etymologiae*. But he also showed himself to be anti-Semitic and sowed the seeds of the pogroms with his sermons and his work *De fide catholica contra Iudaeos*.

Juan Ramón Jiménez (1881–1958)

Juan Ramón Jiménez is considered the most significant representative of Spanish **modernism** and had a determining influenced on the direction taken by the subsequent generation of writers. He was born the son of a wine dealer in Moguer. His life was marked by depressive phases and illnesses that appear in his work as strong emotional impressions. He often drew on the landscape and motifs common to his native land. His first great success was the novel published in 1917, **Platero y Yo** (*Platero and I*), the story of a little donkey in his hometown of Moguer. In 1951, Jiménez moved to Puerto Rico. In 1956, he received the **Nobel Prize in Literature**.

Poet

Christopher Columbus (1451–1506)

The seafarer Christopher Columbus originally came from Genoa and in 1476 moved to the Portuguese capital of Lisbon. There he investigated the possibility of reaching India by sea that had been spoken of since antiquity, but the crown showed no interest. So he went to Spain where, in the monastery of La Rábida, he was given a letter of recommendation by the father confessor of the Spanish Queen, Isabella. He sealed a contract with her that ensured the planned sea voyage, bestowed on him the rank of grand admiral, and made him viceroy of any territories discovered; in addition, he was guaranteed 10% of the proceeds of the endeavour. On 3 August 1492, the caravels the *Niña*, the *Pinta* and the *Santa María* left the harbour of Palos de la Frontera on the Andalusian Atlantic coast. On 12 October, sailors sighted the island of Guanahani in the Bahamas; later they reached Cuba and Haiti. This was followed by three further voyages from Andalusian ports: from Cádiz, Columbus sailed to the Lesser Antilles, to Puerto Rico and Jamaica (1493–1496); sailing from Sanlúcar de Barrameda, he reached the north coast of South America (1498–1500); and again from Cádiz he sailed to Honduras and Panama (1502–1504). That he had not reached wealthy India but rather a supposedly uncultivated land inhabited by savages that held no prospects of economic exploitation, however, caused disappointment in Spain. As a consequence, Columbus was denied success during his lifetime – even the lands he discovered were named after someone else, the Italian Amerigo Vespucci. Not even his place of burial is certain – although both Seville and the capital of the Dominican Republic, Santo Domingo, claim to have his grave.

Maritime explorer

Bartolomé de Las Casas (1474–1566)

The Dominican monk Bartolomé de Las Casas, the »Apostle of the Indies«, was born the son of a merchant in Seville. He travelled to Cuba in 1502, where he witnessed such terrible treatment of the Indians that he championed them from then on. He undertook four-

»Apostle of the Indies«

teen voyages to the New World to study the situation of the indigenous peoples. He converted the impressions he gained into practical suggestions that he presented to Charles V, among others. Tragically, he prompted the importation of slaves from Africa because he considered them to be physically more robust – which he later bitterly regretted. When all of his efforts were to no avail, he withdrew in 1523 for ten years to the Dominican monastery of La Hispaniola (Cuba) and wrote two treatments of the history of the West Indies. After he had instigated Spanish soldiers in Nicaragua to desert in 1539, he was ordered back to Spain. He wrote what is probably his most famous work in the following four years, *Brevísima relación de la destrucción de las Indias occidentales* (*A Brief Account of the Destruction of the Indies*). He achieved the promulgation of the »New Laws« in 1542, which were supposed to ensure extensive protection for the Indians but which were recalled shortly afterwards in 1545. In 1543, he returned to America as bishop of Chiapas, Mexico. By 1547, however, he was back in Spain. In 1550, he once again took a position against his opponents in a famous debate in Valladolid, Castile. Bartolomé de las Casas died in Madrid without ever seeing America again. The site of his grave is unknown; there is also no monument in remembrance of him in Spain. In Central America, however, he is greatly revered to this day.

Paco de Lucía (born 1947)

Guitarist   Paco de Lucía, born Francisco Sanchez Gomez in Algeciras, is justifiably described as the **most important flamenco guitarist of the present day**. Possessing a magnificent playing technique, he is equally impressive as guitar soloist or accompanist of singers, most of all the legendary **Camarón de la Isla**. Pushing his musical boundaries, he has also worked together with jazz greats like Al DiMeola, Larry Corryell and John McLaughlin. He wrote the music for Carlos Saura's film *Carmen*.

Moses Maimónides (1135–1204)

Scholar   Born in Córdoba, Moses Maimónides (Rabbi Mose ben Maimon, called Rambam) was the intellectual and for a time also the official head of the Jewish community in Egypt. He studied astronomy, philosophy and medicine. In 1148, he was forced to flee the persecution of the Almohads in Andalusia. In 1167, he arrived in Egypt where he became the personal physician of the son of Sultan Saladin and five years later the head of the Jewish community. Maimónides wrote medical treatises, but his chief work is a commentary on the first record of Jewish religious law, the *Mischna*, which he codified in his *Mischne Tora* (*Repetition of the Torah*), which has been binding for centuries. His major work, *More Nevuchim*, in which he refers to the deeper meaning of revelation being ascertainable only through philosophy, influenced Christian scholasticism, namely Albertus Magnus and Thomas Aquinas.

Manolete (1917–1947)

Manuel Rodríguez Sánchez, known as »Manolete«, scion of a bull-fighting family from Córdoba, was the **most popular torero of his day**. Beginning in 1940, after having trained for ten years, he triumphed in all of the great arenas of Spain and Latin America and was lauded by the »aficionados« for his calm fighting style. He invented a new pass that was named »la manoletina« in his honour. His career and indeed his life came to an end in Linares during a fight with the bull »Islero«, when he was impaled on the bull's horns during a corrida. Many of Manolete's personal effects are on display in the bullfighting museum of Córdoba.

Torero

Pablo Picasso (1881–1973)

Pablo Picasso, a painter, sculptor, graphic designer and ceramicist born in Málaga, is considered the **most important artist of the modern age**. After his first years of training with his father, he studied at the academies of Barcelona and Madrid, moving to Paris in 1904. His early work, at first defined by seemingly melancholy pictures, was divided into blue and rose periods according to the dominantly used colours. With his epoch-making key work, ***Demoiselles d'Avignon***, completed in 1907, he created the prerequisites for **Cubism**. He returned to depicting figures after the First World War and moved closer to the Surrealists. The main subjects were now cycles of illustration following antique texts, works that dealt with the Spanish Civil War – for example, ***Guernica***, one of his most famous paintings – as well as pictures of bullfighting and portraits. After the Second World War, Picasso worked intensively with ceramics and graphics. His work in total exhibits a sense of sovereignty in dealing with art history, with his own history and with the greatest variety of artistic media and techniques; the uniqueness of his work is founded not least in the latter. He died in Mougins, France.

Artist

Mariana Piñeda (1804–1831)

She is considered a folk hero in Spain, honoured in many songs, poems and pictures. Federico García Lorca immortalized her in his drama of the same name. Mariana Piñeda came from a mésalliance between an aristocratic naval captain and a farm worker. At the age of 14, she met and fell in love with a much older man, a supporter of Liberalism. Being an adherent of liberal ideas and voicing the related demands during the time of the Restoration under the reign of the absolutist ruler Ferdinand VII was extremely dangerous. When Piñeda's husband died after a few years, she was left alone with two small

Liberal revolutionary

children. Despite that, she hunted down the injustices in her country, exposed suppression and force and got herself into great difficulties. In 1828, she helped a convicted revolutionary to flee and from that point on was under surveillance by the police. She was finally arrested and after steadfastly refusing to give in to the judge's sexual demands or reveal the names of her liberal conspirators, she was sentenced to death and strangled with the garrotte.

Seneca (around 4 BC to AD 65)

Poet and philosopher

Lucius Annaeus Seneca was born in Roman Córdoba, the son of the rhetorician Seneca the Elder. After being trained in rhetoric and a stay in Egypt, he was made quaestor under Caligula. Empress Messalina had him exiled to Corsica in 41 BC, from where he was called back by Empress Agrippina to tutor her son Nero. During the initial years of his reign, Seneca was Nero's closest confidant, but Nero turned more and more away from him until finally the emperor suspected Seneca of being involved in the Pisonian conspiracy and forced him to commit suicide.

The manner of the Stoics was for Seneca the ideal form of human existence; his major philosophical works are *Epistulae morales ad Lucilium* and the *Naturales quaestiones* with scientific discussions and moral reflections. As a tragedian, he was basically interested in showing the fatal consequences of human passion.

Trajan (53 –117)

Roman emperor

Marcus Ulpius Traianus, born in Itálica in the Roman province of Baetica, was the first emperor of Rome to come from a province. In the year 98, he assumed power over the world empire that reached its maximum extent through his campaigns in Dacia (which approximates to today's Romania), in Arabia in the year 106 and, in war against the Parthians from 114 to 117, with the conquest of Armenia, Assyria and Mesopotamia. Trajan's column still proclaims today the conquests of Dacia in Rome on the Forum Traianum. Trajan died in Selinus in the province of Anatolia.

Diego de Silva y Velázquez (1599–1660)

Painter

Velázquez, a student of Pacheco de Río born in Seville, was the most important Spanish painter of the 17th century. His artistic development can be divided into three periods. Influenced by Caravaggio, he painted religious subjects and Andalusian stereotypes in his early Sevillian period. In 1623, he was summoned to Madrid, where he painted a portrait of Philip IV and soon rose to be **court painter**. The impression made by the art of Titian and Tintoretto during his first stay in Italy from 1629 to 1631 changed his painting, producing often less flattering portraits of the royal family in bold colours, and

Velázques immortalized himself on the left edge of the famous group portrait »Las Meninas«.

one of his major works, *Las Lanzas* (***The Surrender of Breda***, 1634/35). His second trip to Italy from 1649 to 1651 again influenced his style through his development into one of the precursors of Impressionism, who captured the fleeting impressions of light and colour on canvas. But he didn't give up portrait painting. One of his most famous works was created in 1656, **Las Meniñas** (*The Maids of Honour*), in which he portrays the members of the royal family posing for the painting and above all himself, peeking out from behind the canvas. The **Museo de Bellas Artes in Seville** possesses the most important collection of his paintings in Andalusia.

Practicalities

WHAT ARE THE SPECIALITIES OF
ANDALUSIAN CUISINE? WHICH
ANDALUSIAN CRAFTS ARE
WORTH BUYING? WHERE CAN
YOU SEE AUTHENTIC FLAMENCO?
READ IT HERE – IDEALLY
BEFORE THE JOURNEY!

Accommodation

Rural Tourism

Those wishing to spend their holidays in a rural environment can choose from nearly 500 officially approved »casas rurales«, offering a kind of tourism that is gentle and close to nature. The generic term **»turismo rural«** covers small and larger holiday homes, hostels, plus smaller and larger countryside hotels, most of which use historic rural buildings that are furnished in a simple but snug fashion and lie in scenic countryside.

! *Baedeker* TIP

Be a caveman ...

... without the smoky air, freezing cold, and darkness – it's possible in Galera. Here you can rent one of 24 cave dwellings for 1 to 8 people, complete with kitchen, bath or shower, and fireplace from 49 € per night (for booking and information: Casas Cueva, C. Cervantes 11, E-18840 Galera, tel. 958 73 90 68 or 958 73 90 32 or www.casa-cuevas.es).

Camping

The approximately 100 Andalusian camp sites are heavily frequented during the peak tourist season. They are concentrated on the coast in particular. Booking in advance is recommended.

The Federación Española de Campings publishes the four-language **camping guide** »Guía Oficial de Campings«, which can be purchased at petrol stations and bookshops or ordered from the address below.

Wild camping is generally forbidden, yet spending a night at a car park or lay-by is usually allowed; it is advisable, however, to enquire beforehand whether a local or regional prohibition exists.

The filling of gas cylinders brought into the country is prohibited in Spain. Campers should therefore have their equipment fitted for Spanish connections. The appropriate valves (regulador) are available in shops, at plumbers, and at some petrol stations.

Youth Hostels

Many larger and medium-sized towns have youth hostels where younger tourists can find accommodation at little cost.

In general, the hostels are available from July to September to members of national youth hostel organizations affiliated with the International Youth Hostel Federation. In most cases, Spain's youth hostels are open from 7am to 11pm.

Hotels and Paradors

Spain's hotel industry distinguishes between hotels (H, with restaurant), Hoteles-Apartamentos (HA, with cooking facilities in the

INFORMATION AND ADDRESSES

INFORMATION ON RURAL TOURISM

▶ **Red Andaluza de Alojamientos Rurales (RAAR)**
Apartado de Correos 2035
E-04080 Almería
Tel. 950 26 50 18
Fax 950 27 16 78
E-Mail: info@raar.es
www.raar.es
Booking service:
Tel. 902 44 22 33
(in Spanish, English, German and French)

CAMPING INFORMATION

▶ **Federación de Campings y Ciudades de Vacaciones**
San Bernard, 97–99
E-28015 Madrid
Tel. 914 48 12 34

ADDRESSES CAMPING (A SELECTION)

▶ **Almería: La Garrofa**
N 340, km 108/68 mi
Tel. 950 23 57 70
Open: all year;
situated at the beach.

▶ **Almúñecar: Nuevo Camping La Herradura**
Paseo Andrés Segovia
Tel. 958 64 06 34
Open: all year; close to the beach in the west of the bay.

▶ **Las Alpujarras/Órgiva: Camping Órgiva**
Just over a mile south of the city centre, between the city and the Río Guadalfeo
Tel. 958 78 43 07
Open: year-round
Small site with pool and restaurant.

Price categories

■ The hotels recommended in this travel guide in chapter »Sights from A to Z« are divided into the following price categories:
Luxury: over €180 / £125
Mid-range: €120–180 / £85–125
Budget: €60–120 / £40–85
(double bedroom per night without breakfast)

▶ **Las Alpujarras/Trevélez: Camping Trevélez**
Less than a mile south on the GR-421 direction Busquístar
Tel. 958 85 87 35
Open: year-round;
with restaurant.

▶ **Antequera: El Torcal de Antequera**
About four miles south of the city direction El Torcal and Villanueva
Tel. 952 11 16 08
Open: all year
Equipped with pool.

▶ **Aracena**
In a valley just over one mile east of the town, and 500m/550yd north of the N-433 (direction Corteconcepción)
Tel. 959 50 10 05
Open: all year.

▶ **Cabo de Gata**
Just over one mile north on the minor road from Ruescas
Open: all year,
with pool and restaurant.

▶ **Córdoba: Camping Municipal El Brillante**
Avenida del Brillante, 50

The Renaissance patio in the parador in the Palacio Condestable Davalos in Úbeda is perfect for daydreaming.

Tel. 957 28 21 65
Open: all year;
large pool, bus stop.
About half a mile north of the centre (towards the parador on the road to Villaviciosa).

Granada: Camping Sierra Nevada

Avenida de Madrid, 107/Circunvalacion, Salida 126
Tel. 958 15 00 62
Open: March–Oct,
well-equipped
Two miles north of the centre, close to the bus station.

Ronda: El Sur

Carretera de Algeciras, km 1.5
Tel. 952 87 59 39
Open: all year
On the road to Algeciras, 1.5 mi south of the city centre, bungalows available for let, restaurant, pool, bicycle hire, and a beautiful view of the town.

Seville: Villsom

Ctra. N IV, km 554,8/345 mi
(exit: Ctra. Isla Menor)
Tel. 954 72 08 28
Open: all year
The campsite, equipped with pool, lies on the western edge of Dos Hermanas, 12km/7.5mi south of Seville's city centre (with bus connection into the city).

Sierra de Cazorla, Segura y Las Villas: Camping Cortijo

Camino de San Isicio, s/n
(approx. 1mi from Cazorlas' centre)
Tel. 953 72 12 80
Open: March–Nov
Rurally situated beneath fruit trees on a slope – Cortijo means farm; basic facilities, small pool.

Tarifa: Camping Torre de la Peña

Carretera Nacional 340
km 78/48 mi

Tel. 956 68 49 03
Open: all year
8km/5mi from Tarifa; well-equipped site with rocky beach and great view to Africa.

INFORMATION ON YOUTH HOSTELS

▶ **Red Española de Albergues Juveniles**
Barquillo, 15A, 1 G
E-28004 Madrid
Tel. 915 22 70 07
Fax 915 22 80 67
www.reaj.com
E-Mail: info@raej.com

BOOKING YOUTH HOSTELS IN ANDALUSIA

▶ **Instalaciones y Turismo Joven**
Miño, 24
E-41011 Sevilla
Tel. 902 51 00 00
www.inturjoven.com

ADDRESSES OF YOUTH HOSTELS (SELECTION) (ALBERGUE JUVENIL)

▶ **Almería**
Isla Fuerteventura, s/n
Tel. 950 26 97 88
In Zapillo near the beach; shared accommodation.

▶ **Cabo de Gata/San José**
C. Montemar, s/n
Tel. 950 38 03 53
Open: April–Oct
shared accommodation.

▶ **Córdoba**
Plaza Judá Levi
Tel. 957 29 01 66
In the Judería.

▶ **Granada**
Avenida Ramón y Cajal, 2

Tel. 958 28 43 06
Located outside west of the university, near the stadium; double bedrooms only.

▶ **Málaga**
Plaza de Pio XII.
Tel. 952 30 85 00
Rooms with varying amenities.

▶ **Marbella**
C. Trapiche, 2
Tel. 952 77 14 91
On the northern edge of the old town, with swimming pool.

▶ **Seville**
C. Isaac Peral, 2
Tel. 954 61 31 50
Outside town; bus number 34 goes there from Puerta de Jerez and from Plaza Nueva.

▶ **Paradores de Turismo**
Requena, 3
E-28013 Madrid
Tel. 915 16 66 66
Fax 915 16 66 57
E-Mail: info@parador.es

Budión lies in the middle of the Alpujarras.

rooms, often also with a restaurant or café), Hostales (HS, basic and often without restaurant), and guesthouses (P).

The showpieces of Spanish hotel industry are the **paradors**, established at significant tourist points, mainly **in historic buildings** such as Moorish palaces, medieval castles, or ancient monasteries. These national hotels are comfortably and tastefully furnished, have superbly trained staff, and often also exquisite restaurants serving dishes of the region. For the most part they are somewhat more affordable than »normal« hotels in the same category, and often have more to offer. Timely booking is advised.

Hotels The hotels are rated with stars: 1 star stands for accommodation with at least a sink in the room, 2 stars for rooms with bathroom, 3 stars for telephone and TV in addition, plus hotel restaurant, 4 stars for convenience and luxury, 5 stars for luxury. The highest category is 5 stars with the addition GL (»Gran Lujo«). As this classification has limitations as a clue to pricing, merely the price range is given here. Prices vary considerably according to season. They can climb to twice the normal amount during festivals or for instance during the Easter week, however, they can also be adjusted downwards in less well-frequented periods, if one asks about it before booking. As a rule, the price contains neither breakfast (2.50 – 12 €) nor VAT (IVA). The following prices serve as a guide for a double bedroom; single rooms are 20–30% below that.

Arrival · Before the Journey

How to Get There

By air **Scheduled flights** to Málaga and Gibraltar are available from London (British Airways), but the »no-frills« airlines normally offer a better deal to destinations in the south of Spain. Flights with Iberia via Madrid are also an option. It is worth looking at the wide range of **charter flights** that are offered from many airports, in particular to Málaga and Almería, but also to Seville and Jerez.

By car From the ferry ports at Santander (from Plymouth) and Bilbao (from Portsmouth) or from the French border crossing at Irún, it is a long but straightforward day's journey to Andalucia via Burgos and Madrid. If driving from the south of France along the Mediterranean coast, take the AP7/A7 route, leaving the A7 to take the A92N to Granada and Malaga. There are motorway tolls in France and Spain.

Those who like travelling by train and don't mind the long journey By train
may travel via Paris – Madrid – Córdoba – Seville using the high-speed train AVE from Madrid to Seville.

The main lines are run by the **state railway RENFE** (Red Nacional de los Ferrocarriles Españoles). Andalusia's rail network is not very dense, making train journeys time-consuming. In compensation, the prices are fairly low. The RENFE web site indicated below gives information on many special tariffs and discounts. The high-speed train **AVE** (Tren de Alta Velocidad) runs between Madrid and Seville in a good two hours. Another high-speed train, the **Talgo 200**, services the routes Madrid – Málaga, plus Madrid – Cádiz, and Madrid – Huelva.

Eurolines **buses** leave for Málaga and Seville from Paris and many other cities. In continental Europe, but for travellers from the UK and Ireland, this method of travel is normally no cheaper but definitely much slower than a low-cost flight.

> **! Baedeker TIP**
>
> **Al-Andalus Express**
>
> For a special treat with the atmosphere of the »good old days« of rail travel, book a 6-day trip on the luxury train Al-Andalus (between March and November) from Seville via Córdoba and Granada to Jerez de la Frontera or vice versa. The fare includes city tours and meals in the cities mentioned, admission to festivals and events, plus dinner and accommodation on the train (information and booking in travel agencies; www.andalusexpreso.com).

Andalusia Rail Network

⏵ GETTING THERE

AIRPORTS

▸ **Almería**
Aeropuerto de Almería
(8km/5mi to the east in the
direction of Níjar)
Tel. 950 21 37 00
Transport connection: bus no. 14

▸ **Jerez de la Frontera**
Aeropuerto de Jerez de la Frontera
(8km/5mi to the north-east)
Tel. 956 15 00 00
Transport connection: taxi

▸ **Málaga**
Aeropuerto Internacional
de Málaga Pablo Picasso
(8km/5mi to the south-west)
Tel. 952 04 88 38
Transport connection: train service Málaga – Fuengirola half-
hourly between 5.45am and
11.45pm; bus

▸ **Seville**
Aeropuerto de San Pablo
(12 km/7.5 mi to the east)
Tel. 954 44 90 00
Transport connection: bus

TRAIN INFORMATION IN LONDON

Rail Europe Travel Centre
178 Piccadilly
London W1V 0BA
Tel. 0870 8 37 13 71
www.raileurope.co.uk

TRAIN INFORMATION IN SPAIN

▸ **RENFE**
Tel. 902 24 02 02
www.renfe.es (Spanish)

GETTING THERE BY BUS

▸ **Eurolines**
Bookings online and in UK
through National Express
Tel. 087 05 80 80 80;
www.eurolines.com and
www.nationalexpress.com

Entry/Exit Requirements

Papers   Visitors from EU countries require a valid identity card or passport
for entry. Children under 16 require a children's passport, or must
be registered in their parents' passport. Those planning a **trip to Morocco** require a passport in all cases.

Vehicle   The national driving licence and vehicle registration certificate of ci-
documents tizens of EU states are recognized and must be carried; the international insurance card is required in the event of damage or loss. Vehicles without an EU number plate must be marked with the sign of
their nationality.

Pets   Those planning to take pets along with them require an official
veterinary **health certificate** not older than two weeks, as well as cer-
tification of anti-rabies inoculation in English and Spanish. The in-

noculation must date back at least 21 days, yet may not be older than twelve months prior to entry.

Movement of goods for private purposes is largely duty free within the area of the European Union. Certain restrictions on quantities apply (e. g. for visitors over 17, 800 cigarettes, 10 litres of spirits, and 90 litres of wine). In the case of spot checks by the authorities, confirmation is required that the commodities are truly for private use only.

Customs regulations

Health Insurance

The statutory health insurances must also reimburse fees for doctors' services abroad in the EU. The precondition is that the doctor concerned with treatment is presented with the European health insurance card. (Since 01/01/2005 this has superseded the E111 form for EU citizens; a replacement certificate must be issued for those without such a card.) In many cases, a part of the medical costs or. expenditures for particular medicaments must be paid by the patient, even with this card. Where applicable, the health insurance at home may reimburse the costs on production of receipts.

Statutory health insurances

The conclusion of an additional travel health insurance is certainly recommended for travellers from non-EU countries and should also be considered by EU citizens, as costs for medical treatment and medications are usually paid in part by the patient, and costs for possible return transportation are not borne by the statutory health insurances at all.

Private travel health insurance

Beaches

The Andalusian coast stretches for 836km/520 mi along the Mediterranean Sea (**Costa del Sol**) and the Atlantic Ocean (**Costa de la Luz**). An enjoyable beach holiday is guaranteed, especially as many beaches have showers and beach bars.

Beach holiday

The most important beaches are supervised; and their current status is shown with coloured flags:
green = bathing is unrestricted
yellow = bathing is dangerous
red = bathing is prohibited.

Beach warning service

The beaches are kept clean by the communities along the entire Costa del Sol, and at the larger resorts of the Costa de la Luz.
In the 1990s, following growing complaints, beach resorts along the

Quality of the beaches

Summer, sun, sand and a strawberry daiquiri – the sweet life on the beach at Nerja on the Costa del Sol.

Costa del Sol in particular took measures to regenerate the beaches and improve the environmental situation. For example new promenades were built, and the construction of sewage plants was enforced. The **blue flag** of the Foundation for Environmental Education in Europe (FEEE) flies at many beaches, indicating clean water and a good infrastructure. It is awarded to the communities upon application, a procedure that environmental associations criticize. Thus the absence of a blue flag by no means implies that the beach is bad. Information on all beaches marked by the blue flag is obtainable on the internet at www.fee-international.org.

The Spanish ministry of the environment has a **complaint hotline** set up during the summer season where shortcomings of and complaints about beaches with the blue flag can be reported (Mon–Fri 9.30am–3pm, tel. 900 17 15 17). Information on all beaches and their water quality, updated weekly, can be obtained at tel. 900 21 07 63. The Spanish- and English-speaking telephone service is staffed from 8am to 3pm during weekdays in the summer months.

Mediterranean coast

The **western Costa del Sol** (Costa de Málaga) is characterized by **large tourist centres** such as Torremolinos, Marbella, Fuengirola and Estepona, where the beaches are well-kept, yet often overcrowded.

The beaches of the eastern Costa del Sol, between Rincón de la Victoria and Castell de Ferro, lie partly in rocky bays and consist mostly of fine gravel sand. The **coast of Almería** has about 45 beaches. Whereas **mass tourism** prevails to a large extent at the bay of Almería, delightful, **little-frequented natural beaches** can be found, especially to the east of Cabo de Gata.

The **coast of Huelva** possesses with the Playa de Castilla, among others, a large beach of **fine, white sand**. However, the water quality in the direct proximity of Huelva leaves much to be desired.

Children in Andalusia

As a rule, Andalusians very tolerant of children. They are welcome in hotels, cafés, bars and restaurants. Often even the smallest Andalusian children romp around at midnight; to compensate they nap for a few hours afternoons during the greatest heat! Older children will certainly have fun in the theme parks at (**Isla Mágica** in ►Seville) or in the aqua parks and the vivarium at Estepona (Selwo Aventura). Great excitement is guaranteed during a visit to **Mini Hollywood** near ►Almería, where Westerns are filmed.

 CHILDREN'S ADDRESSES

THEME PARKS
WILDLIFE PARKS

► **Reserva Natural**
in Castillo de las Guardas
60km/37mi northwest of Seville
Opening Hours:
daily from 10.30am to 7pm
Visitors can see elephants, rhinoceroses, and giraffes during a tour on foot, by car or with a small train.

► **Crocodiles Park**
C/Cuba, 14
Torremolinos
Opening hours: daily from 10am until late afternoon
As the name implies – a park full of crocodiles.

► **Selwo Aventura**
Autovía Costa del Sol, at km 162.5mi
At Estepona
Opening hours:
Feb–Nov 10am–6pm
A blend of funfair and zoo.

AQUA PARKS

► **Aquopolis**
Opening hours:
June–August daily 11am–7pm
(July, August until 8pm)
Situated in the east of Seville; bus number 55 stops right in front of the main entrance.

► **Aqua Tropic**
Paseo Marítimo at
Playa de Velilla
Almuñécar

ℹ The four big hits for kids

- Seville: »Isla Mágica«, swoosh through waterfalls, discover lost temples, experience naval battles (see photo)
- At Estepona: »Selwo Aventura«, a successful blend of funfair and zoo
- At Almería: »Mini Hollywood«, a film set for filming Westerns, with shows
- Granada: »Parque de las Ciencias«, most popular museum of Andalusia

Opening hours:
June, Sep daily 11am–6pm
July, Aug 11am–7.30pm
Situated right at the beach.

▶ **Selwo Marina**
Parque de la Paloma
Benalmádena
Opening hours:
Feb–Nov
daily 10am–6pm
Water park with popular
dolphin shows.

MUSEUMS FOR CHILDREN

▶ **Aventura Minaparque**
Plaza Ernest Lluch,
Minas de Riotinto
Opening hours: daily

10.30am–3pm, 4–7pm
A walk through the mining museum, a visit to Europe's largest open pit, and a train ride along the Río Tinto.

▶ **Parque de las Ciencias**
Avda. del Mediterráneo, s/n
Granada
Opening hours:
Tue–Sat 10am–7pm,
Sun 10am–3pm
closed in the second half of September
Hands-on science museum: natural sciences for touching and trying out.

Drugs

Spain is deemed to be one of the main channels through which hashish (»chocolate«) from North Africa and cocaine from Latin America reach the EU by the ton – the drug mafia is often faster than the police. Drug trafficking is especially prevalent in the large cities and sea ports, in particular in Málaga, Cádiz and Algeciras.

Be warned: the possession of drugs is heavily penalized. Also beware of accepting »small packages for friends« from new-found acquaintances to take home, or to take from the North African exclaves Ceuta and Melilla to Spain, as there is danger of being used as a courier in this manner.

Electricity

The Spanish power supply network runs on 220 volts alternating current. The large hotels usually have useable European standard plugs; visitors from the UK or USA should bring an adapter with them.

Emergency

 USEFUL TELEPHONE NUMBERS

CENTRAL NUMBER
► **Tel. 112**
Call this emergency number to reach doctors, the fire brigade, and the police around the clock in Spanish or English.

► **Guardia Civil (traffic police)**
Tel. 062

► **Local police**
Tel. 092

BREAKDOWN SERVICE
►Transport

Entertainment

Flamenco festivals take place all year round in Andalusia (www.andaluciaflamenco.org). Tablaos where authentic flamenco is most likely to be offered are listed here. And as not only flamenco in particular, but also Andalusian nightlife in general puts people in the mood for going out, the cities' hotspots are mentioned here.

 ADDRESSES FOR GOING OUT

ALMERÍA
Music bars are located around C. San Pedro.

► **Irish Tavern**
Plaza González Egea
Bar with terrace seating.

► **La Clásica**
Poeta Villaespesa, 4
Salsa and pop in the courtyard.

► **Peña El Taranto**
Tenor Iribarne
Authentic flamenco, mostly weekends.

ARCOS DE LA FRONTERA

▸ **Peña de Flamenco de Arcos**
Plaza de la Caridad, 4
Tel. 956 70 12 51
Flamenco.

CÁDIZ

In the old town people meet in C. Zorilla on Plaza de la Mina before midnight, with bars and pubs all around. In winter the meeting point moves somewhat to the east around Plaza San Francisco/C. Rosario. On weekends, young people go out to the Punta San Felipe peninsula north of Plaza España until the morning hours. In summer, from midnight on, there is a lot going on around Plaza Glorieta – at Paseo Marítimo there are plenty of discos und bars; and C. General Muñoz Arenilla is also well-frequented in winter.

CÓRDOBA

The English newspaper »Córdoba in ...« has up-to-date information on nightly events.
There is an active scene in the new town, mostly in C. Cruz Conde north of Plaza de las Tendillas, as well as around Avenida Tejares and Avenida Gran Capitán.

Partying is usually done in front of the bars, not inside.

▸ **Tablao Cardenal**
C. Torrijos, 10
Tel. 957 48 33 20
The tablao opposite the Mezquita offers classic flamenco open-air from 10.30pm.

GRANADA

Night owls go to the streets north of the cathedral, for example to C. Granada. There are several discos and bars on C. Pedro Antonio in the west of the city centre; on weekends a lot is happening to the west of Plaza Nueva.

▸ **El Camborio**
Camino del Sacromonte
From midnight people party at this »in« dancing location with a garden terrace and a view of the Alhambra.

▸ **Zambra Gitana La Rocío**
Sacromonte, 79
Tel. 958 22 71 29
The visitor can experience a flamenco show in a whitewashed den with an intimate atmosphere around 10.30pm every day.

HUELVA

In summer, revellers go to Punta Umbría. There are pubs on C. Concepción, C. Berdigón, and Avda. Pablo Rada to the north of Plaza de los Monjas. It is also very lively around Plaza de la Merced and Plaza Dos de Mayos.

JAÉN

Several nice old bars with flair are located northwest of the cathedral on C. Cerón and on the streets Arco del Consuelo and Bernardo López. Tapas bars entice on the C. Nueva. The actual nightlife, moreover with live music, happens more around the station and university.

JEREZ DE LA FRONTERA

The places to go on weekend nights in Jerez are near the bullring, along the streets Pastora and Cádiz, and around Plaza Canterbury.

▶ **Tablao Lagá de Tio Parilla**
Plaza del Mercado, s/n
Tel. 956 33 83 34
The tablao offers good flamenco shows from 10.30pm – instead of an entrance fee, guests pay a stiff price for the first drink after the beginning of the show.

MÁLAGA

The nightlife is lively on Plaza de la Merced and north of the cathedral, the streets C. Granada and C. Beatas, as well as in the area around Plaza Uncibay and in Malagueta, south of the bullring. Additionally in summer things happen on the coast in the suburb Pedregalejo, and on its high street Juan Sebastián Elcano.

MARBELLA

At night a lot goes on in the centre of Marbella around Plaza Puente de Roda, C. Pantaleón, and the Plaza Africa. People party on Avda. Ramon y Cajal, and at the marina Puerto Deportivo. The not-quite-so-young amuse themselves around C. Camilo José Cela. Discos are a little distance outside, mostly at luxury hotels: in summer, about ten kilometres/six miles in the direction of Málaga, people go to the disco »Oh! Marbella« at the hotel Don Carlos. The beautiful and the wealthy

Nightlife in Málaga is also colourful.

meet at La Notte on Camino de la Cruz between Marbella and Puerto Banús. The largest disco on the Costa del Sol, Dreamers, is reached via the first exit in Puerto Banús. The jet set meets in the exclusive luxury bars of the millionaires' port Puerto Banús. The tourist information offices provide a Spanish/English event guide, *Guía Marbella – Día y Noche.*

SEVILLE

In Barrio Santa Cruz try the buzzing pub districts of C. Mateos Gago and C. Argote Molina, as well as around Plaza de la Gavida and Plaza del Salvador. There is often live music around Plaza Alfalfa and along Alameda de Hércules (the alternative scene

You have to be in the right place at the right time to experience an authentic flamenco – the Adalusian heart first really begins to beat in intimate groups after the show.

meets at Habanilla Café, and there are rock concerts at Fun Club), as well as on C. Tarifa. The bars around Plaza de Toros offer a nice view of the Guadalquivir. In summer, nightlife mainly occurs on the eastern shore side between Puente de Triana and the La Barqueta bridge.

► Antigüedades
C. Argote de Molina, 10
Music bar, furnished with paintings and sculptures.

► Blue Moon
C. J. A. Cavestany, s/n
Live jazz on the weekend (closed in August).

► El Choza
Ricardo Palma, 133
Tel. 954 63 08 26
Open irregularly from May to Oct.
José Domínguez offers »real« flamenco in his house.

► La Carbonería
Levíes, 20
Tel. 954 56 37 55
Live music in the evening, often flamenco, too.

► La Imperdible
Plaza San Antonio de Padua, 9
Lively café bar with many events, including. live jazz, and flamenco on Wednesdays.

► Los Gallos
Plaza Santa Cruz, 11
Tel. 954 21 69 81
Daily flamenco shows at 9pm and 11.30pm at the most famous tablao of the city (further tablaos ►Seville).

► Teatro de la Maestranza
Paseo de Cristóbal Colón, 22
Tel. 954 22 65 73
The theatre, just 100 yards away from the bullring, stages operas, and jazz and classical concerts.

Etiquette and Customs

As a rule, the Spanish are polite people, and this politeness also pervades their daily actions. They enjoy discussing things extensively, listen patiently to the opinions of others, and of course also try to convince others. They are not sparing of word or gestures, yet never adopt a know-all attitude. If, for example, someone in the office claims, »Our new colleague is called Pedro«, then nobody would contradict directly and say: »No, no, he's called José.« The more elegant, Spanish answer would be: »José or Pedro?« If a request, a desire, or a demand has to be objected to, then things get difficult for the polite Spaniard. Even then, they will never give a brusque »No!«. For example: a stranger in some small place asks the owner of his guest house for the nearest car rental. His host knows, of course, that none exists far and wide, yet will never say it like that, but instead remark: »That will be difficult.« In plain language however, that means: »You can forget it!«

Invitations are extended quickly and gladly, yet only very rarely to another's house. Bars or restaurants serve as an alternative. However, people do not stay long, but prefer to move on quickly to the next place. Spaniards do not like going out by themselves, preferring small or larger groups. If someone brings a friend along to the evening get-together, then he is quickly integrated and immediately belongs. This also applies to foreigners – there are few inhibitions. Yet no one who is bid farewell with a »Call me sometime« should expect a deeper friendship. It is not necessary to comply with such a request right the next day.

Payment of bills in bars or restaurants is handled as follows in Spain: one person always pays for all. If a group passes through several bars, then everyone gets a turn. It is not done to sort out fussily who paid what; **generosity** is the order of the day. A foreigner may find it hard to get a turn at paying in a Spanish group, as somebody else is always faster.

Another rule applies in restaurants: never join a stranger at a table. A question such as **»Is this seat taken?«** is not asked. Yet guests also never sit down without asking at a free table. As a basic principle, they stop in the restaurant foyer. Within seconds, the maitre d' arrives, asks for the number of persons and suggests tables. The guests are then shown to the chosen seats and handed the menu.

The **bill** is requested very casually in restaurants. It arrives on a small plate, the waiter disappears again. Someone casually picks up the bill, glances at it, and places either a credit card or a few notes onto the plate. The waiter will return equally casually and take the plate with him with a murmured »gracias«. After a while he comes again, slides the plate with change to the payer with a repeated »gracias«. The payer ignores this for a few seconds longer, pockets the change, and leaves a certain amount lying on the plate as a tip. Only once the entire table has left the restaurant does the waiter pick up the plate with the tip one last time.

Festivals · Holidays · Events

PUBLIC HOLIDAYS

▶ **1 January**
Año Nuevo (New Year)

▶ **6 January**
Reyes Magos (Epiphany)

▶ **28 February**
Día de Andalucía (for the national referendum on home rule)

▶ **19 March**
San José (St Joseph's Day)

Menacing – hooded men during Semana Santa

▶ **1 May**
Día del Trabajo (Labour Day)

▶ **24 June**
San Juan (St John the Baptist's Day; name day of the king)

▶ **29 June**
San Pedro y San Pablo (St Peter and St Paul's Day)

▶ **25 July**
Santiago (St James' Day)

▶ **15 August**
Asunción (Assumption of the Virgin)

▶ **12 October**
Día de la Hispanidad (Discovery of the Americas)

▶ **1 November**
Todos los Santos (All Saints Day)

▶ **6 December**
Día de la Constitución (Constitution Day, Spanish national day)

▶ **8 December**
Immaculada Concepción (Immaculate Conception)

▶ **25 December**
Navidad (Christmas)

MOVEABLE FESTIVALS

▶ **Viernes Santo (Good Friday)**
▶ **Corpus Christi (Corpus Christi)**

CALENDAR OF EVENTS

The meaning and nature of the festivals in Andalusia are described in detail in the chapter Art and Culture (►p.60).

JANUARY

► Granada
Granada remembers the final expulsion of the Moors in 1492 with »Día de la Toma« (2 January).

► Almerímar
Romería de la Virgen del Mar: sea pilgrimage (first Sunday in January).

FEBRUARY/MARCH

► Cádiz / Málaga
Carnival is celebrated exuberantly with processions, floats, and bull runs.

HOLY WEEK (SEMANA SANTA)

Holy Week is marked throughout Andalusia. Particularly worthwhile are the events in:
Aguilar de la Frontera
(especially on Good Friday)
Almuñécar
Antequera
Arcos de la Frontera
Baena (especially from Wednesday to Good Friday)
Cádiz
Castro del Rímo (especially at daybreak of Good Friday)
Córdoba
Granada
Huelva
Jaén
Jerez de la Frontera
(especially on Wednesday)
Málaga
Montilla
Motril

> ### *i* Seven great festivals
>
> - Cádiz (February): »Carnaval« here is deemed to be the wildest in Andalusia
> - Seville (Holy Week): »Semana Santa«, with the most impressive processions of all
> - Córdoba (May): »Festival de los Patios«, the most beautiful, flower-bedecked patios
> - El Rocío (Pentecost): »Romería del Rocío«, one of the most high-spirited pilgrimages
> - Nerja (July): »Summer festival«, music and ballet in the cave
> - Sanlúcar de Barrameda (August): »horse racing« along the beaches (!)
> - Ronda (September): »Fiestas de Pedro Romero«, festival with corridas and more

(especially from Wednesday to Holy Saturday)
Osuna
Ronda
Seville (the ne plus ultra of Semana Santa)
Úbeda
Utrera

EASTER

► Arcos de la Frontera
Encierro de Aleluya (bull run in the street; Easter Sunday).

► Vejer de la Frontera
Fiesta del »Toro Embolao« (popular bull run in the street; Easter Sunday).

APRIL

► Andújar
Romería de la Virgen de la Cabeza (pilgrimage, last Sunday in April).

▶ **Seville**
Feria de Abril (begins two
weeks after Easter)

MAY

▶ **Córdoba**
Cruces de Mayo (on the first
weekend in May; altars with May
crosses are set up in the streets, in
front of which dances and celebrations take place in the evening)
Festival de los Patios Córdobéses
(in the week following the first
weekend in May; the most beautiful patio is chosen)

▶ **Granada**
Cruces de Mayo (May Crosses;
first weekend in May).

▶ **Jerez de la Frontera**
Feria del Caballo (horse fair).

▶ **El Puerto de Santa María**
Feria de Primavera (spring festival;
21–25 May).

▶ **Sanlúcar de Barrameda**
Feria de la Manzanilla (sherry
festival; last week in May).

Pentecost

▶ **El Rocío**
Romería del Rocío
One of the most significant pil-
grimages in Spain (▶Baedeker-
Special p.362).

JUNE

▶ **Granada**
At the end of June (until July) the
International Festival of Music and
Dance begins with concerts in the
palaces of the Alhambra.

▶ **Ronda**
Romería de la Virgen de la Cabeza
(pilgrimage, 14 June).

▶ **Utrera**
Fiestas de San Juan (24 June).

JULY

▶ **Cabra**
Romería Nacional de los Gitanos
(gypsy pilgrimage; on a Sunday in
July).

▶ **Nerja**
Summer festival (2nd half of July;
music and ballet in the Cuevas).

AUGUST

From August on, most of the
Ferias begin, originally cattle-
market days that are always
coupled with bullfights.

▶ **Aguilar de la Frontera**
Feria real (6–10 August).

▶ **Alcalá de Guadaira**
Feria (first weekend after 15
August).

▶ **Algeciras**
Feria (15 August).

▶ **Almería**
Feria (22–31 August).

▶ **Almuñécar**
Feria (middle of August).

▶ **Antequera**
Feria (18–25 August).

▶ **Huelva**
Feria (Festival of Columbus; first
week in August).

▶ **Linares**
Feria (Corridas de Toro; 27 August
to 1 September).

▶ **Málaga**
Feria (1st half of August).

► **Sanlúcar de Barrameda**
Horse racing on the beaches.

SEPTEMBER

► **Carmona**
Romería de la Virgen de Gracia
(pilgrimage, first Sunday in September).

► **Granada**
Romería del Albaicín (pilgrimage,
29 September).

► **Jerez de la Frontera**
Fiesta del Vino (Grape Harvest
Festival).

► **Lora del Río**
Romería de la Virgen de Setefilla
(Pilgrimage, 8 September).

► **Montilla**
Fiesta del Vino (Grape
Harvest Festival; beginning
of September).

► **Ronda**
Feria y Fiestas de Pedro
Romero.

► **Tarifa**
Feria (first Sunday in
September).

OCTOBER

► **Almodóvar del Río**
Feria (first Sunday in October).

► **Jaén**
Feria de San Lucas
(around 18 October).

Nowhere is the suffering during Holy Week more splendid than in Seville.

Food and Drink

Mealtimes In Spain, lunch is usually not before about 1.30pm, and people have dinner at 9pm at the earliest. Restaurants normally offer hot meals in the afternoons from 1pm, in the evenings from 9pm.

Meals Breakfast (desayuno) is usually taken at a bar. It mostly consists of some coffee and a piece of toast, or a small cake or **churros** (lard pastry). Hotels at tourist locations offer a more comprehensive breakfast, or a buffet. Lunch (comida or almuerzo) and especially dinner (cena) are all the more generous, and the Andalusians like to take a lot of time for it: three, or even four courses are the order of the day.

Much olive oil and garlic are used. The typical spices of Andalusian cuisine, such as pepper, cinnamon, nutmeg, cumin and saffron date from Moorish times. Andalusia is famous for its deep-fried fish, seafood, crustaceans, shellfish, air-dried ham, gazpacho and egg dishes. Tapas are offered in small bowls in all bars (▸ Baedeker Special p.104; ▸choosing see Language, Menu).

Dishes

Egg dishes **Tortilla**, an omelette made of eggs and potatoes that can be varied in many different ways, is a Spanish classic. **Revueltos**, scrambled eggs, are a common dish. They are served almost everywhere with all kinds of vegetables or seafood. **Huevos a la flamenca** are eggs that are poured raw over tomato slices, sausage, ham, potatoes and various vegetables, and heated in the oven.

! | *Baedeker* TIP

Salmorejo

If you like gazpacho, definitely try the delicious Córdoban variation called Salmorejo, a thick soup that is garnished with ham and egg, and served refreshingly cool in many restaurants.

Gazpacho Gazpacho is an **Andalusian speciality typical** of the hot summer, a soup made with oil, garlic, tomatoes, bell peppers and cucumbers. It is served cold and in countless variations.

Fish dishes In Andalusia, there is naturally a wide variety of fish dishes, yet other seafood can also almost always be had fresh, such as king prawns, crayfish and crabs. The **best crustaceans and shellfish of the Andalu-**

sian coast can be found in the province of Cádiz. Gambas de Huelva are especially good and fresh, as they are not caught with a drift net. The Andalusian fried fish (pescado frito), which is sold at the deep-fried take-away is no less famous. The **trout** of the Sierra Nevada is also renowned.

Meat dishes

Cocido andaluz is a stew made of various ingredients, especially chick peas, pieces of meat, potatoes, beans and several other vegetables. Kidneys in Jerez wine (riñones al jerez) and oxtail (cola or rabo de toro) are also **worth a try**. Spicy black pudding (morcilla) is a speciality of the province of Jaén, and is preferably served warm.

The **air-cured hams** of Andalusia are a delicacy. The addition »jamón ibérico de bellota« guarantees that the ham originates from free-range pigs from the »cerdo ibérico« race, which feed on **acorns**, a practice

that comes at a price. »Jamón serrano« is indeed also air-cured, yet may also originate from pigs from feedlot operations. The hams from **Jabugo** (province of Huelva) and **Trevélez** (province of Granada) are unsurpassed. They are eaten in proper style, thinly sliced and above all, sliced by hand.

Vegetables

Andalusian cuisine makes use of many vegetables such as tomatoes, bell peppers, cucumbers, artichokes, and onions. Spinach fromJaén (espinacas al estilo de Jaén), cazuela de habas verdes (bean stew), and habas con jamón (beans with ham), a speciality from Granada, are among the **traditional dishes**.

Fruits

There are abundant orange, tangerine and lemon trees in Andalusia. Figs, dates, almonds and pine nuts are obtainable everywhere, too.

Desserts and cake

Sweet biscuits are very popular as dessert, as well as for snacks in-between. Most types can be traced back to **Moorish origins**. Flan (a pudding with caramel sauce) and sweet egg yolk are often offered as afters. Fruits and ice cream cakes (tarta helada) form an alternative. One **very rich fried speciality** is called churros con chocolate: choux pastry that are dipped in hot chocolate and mainly eaten for breakfast.

Drinks (bebidas)

Apart from the usual refreshing drinks, freshly squeezed fruit juices is often served. The **most popular mineral water** comes from Lanjarón in Sierra Nevada.

THE ART OF EATING TAPAS

When people think of tapas, bars immediately come to mind. Some bars offer at least five specialties of the house with ingredients fresh from the market, from strips of cheese and pickled olives on air-cured ham and little fried squid to small kidneys in sherry and baked mushrooms.

The people come and go in Andalusian bars, ordering in leisure under a roof of hams, engage in a little small talk and usually do not linger for long. Tapas are traditionally eaten standing at the bar, not seated. Small dishes with two to three savoury and tasty appetizers are displayed in a long row on the bar counter to be served with beer, sherry or wine. They cannot fill you up nor are they meant to, they simply make the drink, the conversation, life, more enjoyable and help keep a clear head. Tapa thus denotes not the kind of food but the amount. They can also be ordered as a ración (portion) for several persons, however, or as a media ración (half a portion) for one person. Where the term tapa comes from is not undisputed. More than likely it denotes the piece of bread or slice of sausage that was set

»The fate of a bar depends on the reputation of its tapas.«

on wine glasses as a lid (tapa) to protect against dust and flies in the 18th century in Andalusian bodegas, originally in Seville. But one thing is certain; tapa means a dish that accompanies a drink. The tapeo, the

tradition of eating tapas, is a matter for the whole family. The Andalusian tapa culture spread over all of Spain in the 1920s after the dictatorship of General Primo de Rivera, who was a confirmed tapa-lover.

What's on offer?

Going out for tapas is a way to bridge the gap before the actual meal, which comes later – at the earliest around 9pm, often not before 11pm. By going from bar to bar and trying a different tapa delicacy each time, it is possible not only to become acquainted with their great variety but in the end to do without the main meal quite easily. Now and then, as is the ancient custom, they are served with the drink without asking and free of charge. The moderate consumption of alcohol, drinking as a social ritual for becoming acquainted and for relaxed togetherness, is closely connected to tapas. Tapas are offered in innumerable forms – depending on the imagination of the kitchen. There are egg and pastry dishes in which lamb's brains and ram's testicles are baked as in tortilla al Sacromonte. Tapas are equally well served in the form of vegetables, fruit and salad; for example, coliflor al ajo arriero (cauliflower mule-driver style) or skewered banana, date and prune. Or as meat dishes like cabrito a la pastoril (kid shepherd style) or callos a la andaluza (tripe pot) and fish dishes like rape al vino blanco y naranja (anglerfish in white wine and orange) and shellfish such as almejas en Jerez (clams in sherry).

Friends meet in a bar and hardly ever invite anyone home, but rather move along together from bar to bar. The tab is always paid by the round, which is added up in chalk on the wooden bar counter – at least in places where marble and aluminium have not yet replaced them.

They are especially delicious in the land of the olive groves.

People enjoy a **café solo** (espresso) after meals or in-between. **Café con leche** (café au lait) is preferred for breakfast; **café cortado** is coffee with little milk.

Beer, for example San Miguel or Mahou, has meanwhile become more popular than wine. To get draught beer, order **»una caña«**.

Brandy is served after the meal, usually from Jerez de la Frontera or El Puerto de Santa María, or an aniseed liquor.

Wine and sherry ▶ Baedeker Special p.308

Restaurants and Bars

A vast number of restaurants also serve international cuisine in the tourist centres and larger cities. If authentic and **typical Andalusian dishes** are desired, then it is often better off in the homely taverns in smaller towns or the countryside.

The bar is one of the **centres of life** in Spain. Even village often have several. People meet here for breakfast, a lunch break, for a game of dominoes in the afternoon with coffee, beer, a »fino« or anis, and in the evening they go from bar to bar sampling the tapas.

Light snacks, other than **tapas**, are »bocadillos« – rolls or baguettes with ham, sausage or cheese – and sandwiches.

Health

Pharmacies   Pharmacies (Spanish: **farmacias**) in Spain are identified by a green cross on a white background. They are normally open Mon–Fri 9.30am–1.30pm and 4.30–8pm, as well as Sat 9am–12.30pm. Pharmacies providing emergency service are listed in each pharmacy on the **»Farmacia de Guardia«**, and in the newspapers.

Medical care   Medical care is available everywhere; though in rural, remote areas might it take longer to get to a doctor. Contact the accident and emergency unit (**urgencia**) of the nearest hospital in acute cases.

Health insurance   ▶Arrival · Before the Journey

Information

 USEFUL ADDRESSES

INTERNET

► **www.spain.info**
Web site of the Spanish
tourist office.

► **www.andalucia.org**
Web site of the Andalusian
tourist office.

► **For further internet addresses**
see Media

IN CANADA

► **Spanish Tourist Office**
Bloor Street West 2-Suite 3402
Toronto, Ontario M4W 3E2
Tel. (01) 416 961 3131
Fax 416 961 1992
E-Mail: toronto@tourspain.es

IN UK

► **Spanish Tourist Office**
2nd floor, 79 New Cavendish
Street
London W1W 6XB
Tel. (207) 48 68 077
Fax (207) 48 68 034
E-Mail: londres@tourspain.es

IN USA

► **Spanish Tourist Office**
Fifth Avenue 666-35th floor
NY. 10103 New York
Tel. (212) 265 88 22
Fax 265 88 64
E-Mail: nuevayork@tourspain.es

► **Spanish Tourist Office**
Wilshire Blvd. 8383 - Suite 960
Beverly Hills California 90211
Tel. (1323) 658 71 95

Fax 658 10 61
E-Mail: losangeles@tourspain.es

IN ANDALUSIA

There is a distinction between
municipal tourist offices, mostly
called Oficina de Turismo, and
regional offices of the Andalusian
government (Oficina de Turismo
de la Junta de Andalucía) –
addresses ►Sights from A to Z.

► **National directory assistance**
Tel. 901 30 06 00
Here the opening hours of museums and sights, hotels etc. are
available in English.

CONSULATES IN ANDALUSIA

► **Australia**
Consulate in Seville
Calle Federico Rubio 14
Tel. 954 22 09 71

► **Canada**
Consulate in Malaga
Plaza de la Malagueta 2, 1st floor
Tel. 952 22 33 46

► **United Kingdom**
Consulate in Malaga
Edificio Eurocom
Calle Mauricio Moro Pareto 2
Tel. 952 35 23 00

► **United States**
Consular Agency in Seville
Paseo de las Delicias 7
Tel. 954 23 18 85

Language

The staff of larger hotels and restaurants usually speak English quite well. There might be communication difficulties in smaller towns in the heartland.

In Spanish the vowels a, e, i, o, u, are **pronounced** openly and distinctly. Long vowels (as in boot, path) don't exist, and a closed e and o (as in rate, boat) equally so.

SPANISH LANGUAGE GUIDE

At a Glance

Yes./No.	Sí./No.
Maybe.	Quizás./Tal vez.
All right./Agreed!	¡De acuerdo!/¡Está bien!
Please./Thank you.	Por favor./Gracias.
Thank you very much.	Muchas gracias.
My pleasure.	No hay de qué./De nada.
Sorry!	¡Perdón!
Pardon?	¿Cómo dice/dices?
I don't understand you.	No le/la/te entiendo.
I only speak a little …	Hablo sólo un poco de …
Could you please help me?	¿Puede usted ayudarme, por favor?
I would like …	Quiero …/Quisiera …
I (don't) like that.	(No) me gusta.
Do you have …?	¿Tiene usted …?
How much is it?	¿Cuánto cuesta?
What time is it?	¿Qué hora es?

Greetings and Meetings

Good morning!	¡Buenos días!
Good afternoon!	¡Buenos días!/¡Buenos tardes!
Good evening!	¡Buenos tardes!/¡Buenos noches!
Hello!	¡Hola!
My name is …	Me llamo …
What is your name, please?	¿Cómo se llama usted, por favor?

Fresh fish in the market hall in Jerez

How are you?	¿Qué tal está usted?/¿Qué tal?
Fine, thanks. And you?	Bien, gracias. ¿Y usted/tú?
Goodbye!	¡Hasta la vista!/¡Adiós!
Bye!	¡Adiós!/¡Hasta luego!
See you soon!	¡Hasta pronto!
See you tomorrow!	¡Hasta mañana!

On the Road

left/right	a la izquierda/a la derecha
straight ahead	todo seguido/derecho
near/far	cerca/lejos
How far is it?	¿A qué distancia está?
I would like to rent … .	Quisiera alquilar …
… a car	… un coche.
… a boat	… una barca/un bote/un barco.
Excuse me, where is …	Perdón, dónde está …
… the train station, please?	… la estación (de trenes)?
… the bus station, please?	… la estación de autobuses/ la terminal?
… the airport, please?	… el aeropuerto?

Breakdown

My car has broken down.	Tengo una avería.
Could you please send me a breakdown truck?	¿Pueden ustedes enviarme un cochegrúa, por favor?
Is there a garage nearby?	¿Hay algún taller por aquí cerca?
Where is the nearest petrol station, please?	¿Dónde está la estación de servicio/a gasolinera más cercana, por favor?

I would like… litres of …	Quisiera … litros de …
… regular petrol.	… gasolina normal.
… super./ …diesel.	… súper./ … diesel.
… unleaded./ …leaded.	… sin plomo./ … con plomo.
Please fill up.	Lleno, por favor.

Accident

Help!	¡Ayuda!, ¡Socorro!
Warning!/Look out!	¡Atención!/¡Cuidado!
Please, quickly call …	Llame enseguida …
… an ambulance.	… una ambulancia.
… the police.	… a la policía.
… the fire brigade.	… a los bomberos.
Do you have bandages?	¿Tiene usted botiquín de urgencia?
It was my (your) fault.	Ha sido por mi (su) culpa.
Give me your name, please, and your address.	¿Puede usted darme su nombre y dirección?

Food

Where can I find …	¿Dónde hay por aquí cerca …
… a good restaurant?	… un buen restaurante?
… restaurant that is not too expensive?	… un restaurante no demasiado caro?
Please book a table for us this evening for 4 people.	¿Puede reservarnos para esta noche una mesa para cuatro personas?
Here's to you!	¡Salud!
Could I have the bill, please!	¡La cuenta, por favor!
Did you enjoy your meal?	¿Le/Les ha gustado la comida?
The food was delicious.	La comida estaba écelente.

Shopping

Where do I find …	Por favor, dónde hay …
… a market?	… un mercado?
… a pharmacy?	… una farmacia?
… a shopping centre?	… un centro comercial?

Accomodation

Could you please recommend me …?	Perdón, señor/señora/señorita. ¿Podría usted recomendarme …
… a hotel	… un hotel?
… a guest house	… una pensión?

I have booked a room.	He reservado una habitación.
Do you still have ...	¿Tienen ustedes ...
... a single bedroom?	... una habitación individual?
... a double bedroom?	... una habitación doble?
... with shower/bath?	... con ducha/baño?
... for a night?	... para una noche?
... for a week?	... para una semana?
What does the room cost with ...	¿Cuánto cuesta la habitación con
... breakfast?	... desayuno?
... half board?	... media pensión?

doctor

Could you recommend me a good doctor?	¿Puede usted indicarme un buen médico?
I have ...	Tengo ...
... diarrhoea.	... diarrea.
... a temperature.	... fiebre.
... a headache.	... dolor de cabeza.

Bank

Excuse me, where is ...	Por favor, dónde hay por aquí ...
... the bank, please?	... un banco?
... the bureau de change, please?	... una oficina/casa de cambio?
I would like to exchange dollars for euros.	Quisiera cambiar ... dollar en euros.

Post

How much does ...	¿Cuánto cuesta ...
... a letter ...	... una carta ...
... a postcard ...	... una postal ...
to England cost?	para Inglaterra?
stamps	sellos
telephone cards	tarjetas para el teléfono

Numbers

0	cero	5	cinco
1	un, uno, una	6	seis
2	dos	7	siete
3	tres	8	ocho
4	cuatro	9	nueve

10	diez	40	cuarenta
11	once	50	cincuenta
12	doce	60	sesenta
13	trece	70	setenta
14	catorce	80	ochenta
15	quince	90	noventa
16	dieciséis	100	cien, ciento
17	diecisiete	200	doscientos, -as
18	dieciocho	1000	mil
19	diecinueve	2000	dos mil
20	veinte	10 000	diez mil
21	veintiuno(a)		
22	veintidós	1/2	medio
30	treinta	1/4	un cuatro

Restaurant/Restaurante

desayuno/almuerzo/cena	breakfast/lunch/dinner
camarero	waiter
cubierto	place setting, cutlery
cuchara/cucharita	spoon/coffeespoon
cuchillo	knife
lista de comida	menu
plato	plate
sacacorchos	corkscrew
tenedor	fork
taza	cup
vaso	glass

Tapas

albóndigas	meatballs
boquerones en vinagre	small anchovies marinated with vinegar
caracoles	snails
chipirones	small squid
chorizo	spicy pepper sausage
ensaladilla russa	Russian salad
jamón serrano	dried ham
morcilla	black pudding
pulpo	squid
tortilla	potatoe omelette

Entremeses/Starters

aceitunas	olives

anchoas	anchovies
ensalada	salad
jamón	ham
mantequilla	butter
pan	bread
panecillo	rolls
sardinas	sardines

Sopas/Soups

caldo	consommée
gazpacho	cold vegetable soup
puchero canario	stew
sopa de pescado	fish soup
sopa de verduras	vegetable soup

Platos de huevos/Egg-dishes

huevo	egg
duro	hardboiled

In the relaxed daily routine, there is time for one or even two cervezas, a tapa and a chat.

pasado por agua	softboiled
huevos a la flamenca	eggs with beans
huevos fritos	fried eggs
huevos revueltos	scrambled eggs
tortilla	omelette

Pescado/Fish

ahumado	smoked
a la plancha	grilled on a hot iron plate
asado	fried
cocido	boiled
frito	baked
anguila	eel
atún	tuna
bacalao	dried cod, codfish
besugo	bream
lenguado	sole
merluza	hake
salmón	salmon
trucha	trout
almeja	river mussel
bogavante	lobster
calamar	calamari
camarón	shrimp
cangrejo	crab
gamba	prawn
langosta	crayfish
ostras	oysters

Carne/Meat

buey	beef, ox
carnero	mutton
cerdo	pork
chuleta	chop
cochinillo, lechón	suckling pig
conejo	rabbit
cordero	lamb
ternera	veal
vaca	beaf
asado	roast
bistec	steak
carne ahumada	smoked meat
carne estofada	pot roast
carne salada	salted meat

fiambre	assorted cold cuts
jamón	ham
lomo	sirloin or chine
salchichón	hard cured sausage
tocino	bacon
pato	duck
pollo	chicken

Verduras/Vegetables

aceitunas	olives
cebollas	onions
col de Bruselas	Brussels sprouts
coliflor	cauliflower
espárragos	asparagus
espinacas	spinach
garbanzos	chickpeas
guisantes	peas
habas, judías	beans
lechuga	lettuce
patatas	potatoes
patatas fritas	chips
pepinos	cucumbers
tomates	tomatoes
zanahorias	carrots

Condimentos/Spices

aceite	oil
ajo	garlic
azafrán	saffron
mostaza	mustard
pimienta	pepper
sal/salado	salt/salted
vinagre	vinegar

Postres/Desserts

bollo	sweet roll
dulces	confectioneries
flan	flan
helado	ice-cream
mermelada	jam
miel	honey
pastel	cake

queso . . . . cheese
tarta . . . . gateau

Frutas/Fruit

cerezas . . . . cherries
chumbos . . . . prickly pears
dátiles . . . . dates
fresas . . . . strawberries
higos . . . . figs
limón . . . . lemon
mandarinas . . . . tangerines
manzana . . . . apple
melocotón . . . . peach
melones . . . . cantaloupe
membrillo . . . . quince
naranjas . . . . oranges
nueces . . . . nuts
pera . . . . pear
piña . . . . pineapple
plátano . . . . banana
sandías . . . . watermelons
uvas . . . . grapes

Special Items

bocadillo . . . . roll
chorizo . . . . red pepper sausage
churros . . . . choux pastry fritters
migas . . . . croutons

Drinks

agua mineral . . . . mineral water
con/sin gas . . . . fizzy/still
aguardiente . . . . liquor
amontillado . . . . medium dry sherry
anís . . . . aniseed liqueur
Brandy . . . . brandy
cerveza . . . . beer
café con leche . . . . café au lait
café solo . . . . espresso
café cortado . . . . with little milk
fino . . . . dry sherry
horchata . . . . almond milk

leche	milk
la Manzanilla	camomile tea
oloroso	sweet sherry
té	tea
vino	wine
blanco/tinto	white/red
rosado	rosé
dry/sweet	seco/dulce
zumo	fruit juice

Literature

Rafael Alberti: *Lost Grove*. University of California Press 1981. Alberti describes his youth in Cádiz in this novel.

Novels and stories

Federico García Lorca: *Blood Wedding*. A & C Black 2006. Drama in three acts about a family tragedy at Rodalquilar on the Cabo de Gata.

Théophile Gautier: *A Romantic in Spain*. Interlink Publishing 2001. The French author's account of his journey through Andalusia in 1840 is a classic of travel literature, a book that at times is surprisingly current, sharp-tongued, and spirited.

Ernest Hemingway: *Death in the Afternoon*. Scribner Classics, 2003. Not exactly a book about Andalusia, but it is a literary standard about bullfighting from the viewpoint of the aficionados. With a narration about Ronda.

Juan Ramón Jiménez: *Platero and I*. Dover Publications; 2004. The Nobel Prize winner from Moguer, province Huelva, philosophizes with his donkey.

i Suggested books

- Gerald Brenan *South of Granada*
- Ernest Hemingway: *Death in the Afternoon*
- Washington Irving: *Tales of the Alhambra*
- María Rosa Menocal: *Ornament of the World*

James A. Michener: *The Drifters*. Fawcet Books, 1986. Young people from around the world travel to Torremolinos – after all, the sun shines there all the time... A narrative worth reading about the emotions of young people in the escapism and optimism of the hippy era, about a generation, for whom the search for the meaning of life was more important than prosperity and middle-class security.

Marianne Barrucand and Achim Bednorz: *Moorish Architecture in Andalusia*. Taschen 2002 A book that really whets the appetite for a trip to the south of Spain.

Gerald Brenan: *South of Granada*. Penguin Books, 1992.
Brenan lived in the Alpujarras village Yegen from 1920 to 1934 and describes a way of life that is now lost.

Titus Burckhardt: *Moorish Culture in Spain*. Fons Vitae 2001. A classic account of the subject, illuminating background for a trip to the region.

Richard Fletcher: *Moorish Spain*. University of California Press, 2006. A readable book, much of it about Andalusia

Washington Irving: *Tales of the Alhambra*, Editorial Everest, 2005
Literary classic of the Alhambra literature, written by the American author Washington Irving after a long stay in the decaying Alhambra in 1832. With this work he renewed international interest in this architectural jewel.

María Rosa Menocal: *Ornament of the World*. The subtitle tells it all: How Muslims, Jews and Christians Created a Culture of Tolerance in Medieval Spain Littel, Brown and Company 2003.
The Yale professor writes about old Andalusia in a knowledgeable and entertaining manner.

Hugh Thomas: *The Spanish Civil War*. Penguin Books 2003. Lengthy account but a great work of historical writing and enjoyable to read

Mark Williams: *The Story of Spain* Santana Books, 2000. Fairly concise overview of Spanish history

Media

Newspapers International newspapers are available in Andalusia, in particular at the tourist centres along the Costa del Sol; usually a day after publication, sometimes even on the same day. Away from the coast, and in cities such as Seville or Granada, it can be a matter of luck.

Television The national Spanish television (Radio Televisión Española, RTVE) offers two programmes (La primera, La 2); the commercial broadcasters include Antena 3, Telecino, and the pay-TV channel Canal Plus. Getting a taste of one these programmes in the many bars is unavoidable, as the TV often runs non-stop. A number of English-speaking channels can be received via satellite.

⏵ USEFUL INTERNET ADDRESSES

► **www.andalucia.com**
Everything, absolutely everything about Andalusia. In Spanish and English.

► **www.andalucia.org**
The website of the Andalusian tourism centre covers a lot: information on sights to visit, places for swimming and diving, hotels, directories of golf courses, yacht marinas, and casas rurales ...

► **www.juntadeandalucia.es**
Website of the Andalusian government, also with a good tourism section.

► **www.alandalus-expreso.com**
Informative, nicely designed web site on round trips with the luxury hotel-train Al-Andalus Expreso (English).

► **http://cvc.cervantes.es**
The online window to the Spanish language, literature, and culture.

► **www.icom.museum/vlmp/ spain.html**
Internet addresses of Spain's most significant museums (E., Sp.).

► **www.mma.es**
Spanish ministry of the environment: directory of Spanish beaches and nature reserves.

► **www.parador.es**
This provides comprehensive information on the paradors, shows the individual buildings, palaces or castles, and is a portal for booking.

► **www.sherry.org**
Everything about sherry.

Money

Since 1 January 2002 the **euro** has been the official currency in Spain, as in twelve other states of the European Union.

Cash machines (ATMs) are provided with multilingual operating instructions. Withdrawals can be made from these using a bank card or established credit cards in conjunction with a PIN.

Banks, hotels, car rentals, many restaurants, and shops accept the usual **credit cards**, especially Visa and MasterCard. In the event of loss of credit cards, the relevant credit card organization should be notified immediately.

i Exchange rates

- 1 € = 0.68 £
  1 £ = 1.47 €
  1 € = 1.35 US$
  1 US$ = 0.74 €

- Latest rates: www.oanda.com

Post · Communications

Postage | The postage for postcards and standard letters up to 20g is 0.51 € within Europe (also to non-EU countries); foreign mail goes into the letter box labelled »extranjero« (abroad).

Stamps | Post offices and tobacco shops (»estancos«) sell stamps (»sellos«) as well as bus tickets and phone cards.

Opening hours | The **post and telegraph offices** (Correos y Telégrafos) are open Mon–Fri 9am–2pm and Sat 9am–1pm.

Telephone cards | Telephone cards are sold in branch offices of the telephone company »Telefónica«, and in tobacco shops (»estancos«).

Mobile phone | When using a mobile phone (»móvil«) not registered in Spain to phone a Spanish number, the country code +34 or. 00 34 must be entered before dialling a telephone number.

▶ DIALLING CODE AND DIRECTORY ASSISTANCE

DIALLING CODES

▶ **To Spain from other countries:**
Tel. 0034 or +34

▶ **From Spain to other countries**
International access code 00 followed by the relevant country code (44 for GB, 1 for USA, etc

When calling the above mentioned countries from Spain, the 0 of the respective local dialling code is not dialled.

DIRECTORY ASSISTANCE

▶ **National and international**
Tel. 003

Prices · Discounts

Citizens of the European Union get free admission to many national museums and archaeological sites upon presenting their identity card. Children also benefit from discounts on admission fees, or even have **free admission** to many museums and sights.

Children under four have **free rides** in Spanish trains, and children ages four to eleven pay only 60% of the standard price.

The **table d'hôte** is usually the cheapest option when eating and drinking.

WHAT DOES IT COST?

Main course
from €6

3-course menu
from €15

Glass of wine
from €2.50

Café solo
from €1.50

Simple double room
from €40

Beer (half litre)
from €1.20

Shopping

Opening Hours

Banks are open Mon–Fri 9am–2pm, Sat 9am–1pm. Most banks are closed on Saturdays during the summer. Branches with longer opening hours can be found at shopping and holiday centres as well as at stations and airports. Most shops are open from Mon–Fri 9am or 9.30am to 1.30pm and from 4.30pm or 5pm to 8pm; Sat 9am–1pm. As Spain has no fixed closing times, some supermarkets and shops open outside the opening hours given above, including Sundays, particularly at tourist centres. **Banks** ◄ **shops**

Arts and Crafts

Andalusia produces many traditional Spanish arts and crafts items, and much more. However, expect much higher prices at the tourist centres and in large cities than in the provinces from which the products originated.

i Time for a shopping spree

- Úbeda: Alfarería Tito, novel ceramics (p.189)
- Córdoba: Espaliu, oriental-looking silver jewellery (p.219)
- Granada: Eduardo Ferrer Lucena, leather bags and accessories (p.259)
- Jerez de la Frontera: Casa del Jerez, sherry of all brands, plus arts and crafts (p. 305)
- Seville: Artesanía Textil, stoles, shawls, table linens – all hand-knotted (p.385)

The Moorish heritage lives on, particularly in Granada. Besides rare woods and ivory, shells are worked, too. **Inlays**

Every Andalusian province has its own centre of pottery production. Almería province: Albox, Níjar, and Vera. **Pottery**

Córdoba province: Bujalance, La Rambla, Lucena, Montilla.
Granada province: Cúllar de Baza, Granada, Guadix.
Huelva province: Aracena, Cortegana.
Jaén province: Alcalá la Real, Andújar, Arjonilla, Bailén, Martos, Úbeda.
Seville province: Triana-quarter in Seville.

Basketry Almería province: Alhabía and Níjar.
Cádiz province: Medina Sidonia and Jerez de la Frontera.

Wrought ironwork Grilles, candlesticks, and also bedsteads are made primarily in the provinces of Cádiz (Cádiz, Arcos de la Frontera, Sanlúcar de Barrameda) and Jaén (Jaén, Úbeda Torredonjimeno).

Lampisteria Ornate **lead glass lamps** are a speciality of Granadan craftsmen. Tin lamps, also from Granada, are a more traditional type.

Leather Córdoba province: Cordovan leather. from Belalcázar.
Huelva province: products of morocco leather and shagreen from Ubrique, shoes from Valverde del Camino.

Granada is known for its guitar-makers – Bellido in Calle de Molinos.

Flamenco guitars are manufactured in Granada, for example in Cuesta de Gómerez, and also in Málaga and Córdoba.

Beautiful silver jewellery can be found in Córdoba.

Mantillas from Granada and the Mantones de Manila (Seville), beautifully embroidered silk fringed shawls, are popular.

Cádiz province: hand-woven woollen blankets from Grazalema.
Granada province: colourful blankets from the Alpujarras.
Almería province: hand-woven carpets from Níjar.

Food and Drink

The best **hams** of Spain are made in **Trevélez** in Granada province, and in **Jabugo** in Huelva province. The term »**Jamón Ibérico de Bellota**« denotes the especially fine and very expensive ham produced from pigs fed on acorns.

Wines, sherry and brandy from Jerez de la Frontera and Sanlúcar de Barrameda (Cádiz), as well as Montilla (Córdoba) and Málaga are popular (► Baedeker Special sherry p.308).

Tortas, Cabello de Ángel (angel hair), Polverones and other sweet temptations are a deeply **Moorish heritage**, which are made not only in many pastelerías, but also often by nuns.

> ## ! Baedeker TIP
>
> ### Sampling
>
> It goes without saying that the olive oil in Baena should be sampled. The right place to do this is the oil mill of the Nuñez de Prado family on the Avenida Cervantes, which has been in existence since the 18th century. Visitors here can learn about the manufacture of cold-pressed oil at anytime, and then purchase the wonderful liquid gold (opening hours: in summer: Mon–Fri 8am–1pm; in winter: Mon–Fri 9am–1pm and 4–6pm, Sat 9am–1pm; tel. 957 67 01 41).

Sport and Outdoors

Sports

Anglers find rich fishing grounds both on Andalusia's coasts and in the rivers and lakes of the Sierra Nevada and Sierra de Cazorla. A fishing licence is required. This is issued by the Andalusian ministry of the environment and is available for a fee (approx. 8 €) at every branch of the Caja Rural de Andalucía savings bank. Handling time is at least a week, but the paying-in slip is normally accepted by the fishing clubs, as well.

Climbing The Sierra Nevada and the Sierra de Cazorla are excellent for **climbers and hikers**. Many of the firms and booking centres of the »casas rurales« offer guided hiking and other activities in nature (▶ rural tourism).

With over 60 golf courses Andalusia provides optimum conditions for **golfing**; the Costa del Sol alone accounts for 30 facilities, and has meanwhile acquired the byname **»Costa del Golf«**. The tourist offices have information.

As **home to thoroughbred Andalusian horses**, Andalusia is of course an ideal place for **riding holidays**. A large number of organizers and riding centres offer a wide selection. Here again the tourist office issues information.

Sailing Andalusia's Mediterranean coast possesses 22 marinas, some of them very modern. Up to now, the Atlantic coast has taken second place – it makes different demands on **yachtsmen** – but in recent years steps have been taken to establish mooring facilities for **pleasure craft** there as well. There are now 18 marinas and buoy mooring locations.

The exclusive golf course with an ocean view in Sotogrande is one of the best in all of Europe.

⏵ INFORMATION SPORTS

ANGLING

► Federación Andaluza de Pesca Deportiva
León Félipe, 2
Apartado de Correos 157
E-04080 Almería
Tel./fax 915 15 17 46
www.fapd.org

CLIMBING / HIKING

► Federación Andaluza de Montañismo
Camino de Ronda, 101
Edificio Atalaya
E-18003 Granada
Tel. 958 29 13 40
www.fedamon.com

GOLFING

► Real Federación Española de Golf
Capitán Haya, 9 – 5
E-28020 Madrid
Tel. 915 55 26 82, fax 915 56 32 90
www.golfspainfederacion.com

► Federación Andaluza de Golf
Sierra de Grazalema, 33
E-29016 Málaga
Tel. 952 22 55 90, fax 952 22 03 87
www.fga.org

RIDING

► Escuela de Arte Ecuestre
Carretera Nacional N 340, km 159
E-29680 Estepona
Tel. 952 80 80 77
www.escuela-ecuestre.com
Riding schools and arenas.

► Real Escuela Andaluza del Arte Ecuestre
Avda. Duque de Abrantes, s / n
E-11408 Jerez de la Frontera
Tel. 956 31 96 35
Fax 956 31 80 14

www.realescuela.org
Courses in Andalusian horseman-ship.

► Equitrail
Heroes de Toledo, 30
E-41000 Sevilla
Tel. 954 66 37 11
Riding trips lasting several days on the routes of Al-Andalus.

► Equiberia
E-05635 Navarredonda de Gredos
Tel./fax 920 34 83 38
www.equiberia.com
Equiberia organizes riding trips lasting several days, following in the tracks of the pilgrims of El Rocío, and around the Coto de Doñana.

SAILING AND MOTORBOATING

► Real Federación Española de Vela
Luis de Salazar, 9
E-28002 Madrid
Tel. 915 19 50 08
Fax 914 16 45 04
www.rfev.es

► Real Federación Española de Motonaútica
Avda. de América, 33
E-28002 Madrid
Tel. 914 15 37 69
Fax 915 19 04 69
www.rfemotonautica.org

ADVENTURE SPORTS

► Amatur
Apartado de Correos 46
Avda. Los Alcornocales, 44
E-11180 Alcalá de los Gazules
Tel. 956 41 30 05
www.amatur.net

Skiing **Europe's southernmost skiing area**, the Sierra Nevada, offers ample opportunity for winter sport from November to the end of May. Sol y Nieve is the most important stop.

Tennis There are numerous tennis courts all along the Costa del Sol. Many hotel resorts have their own courts.

Surfing Windsurfers and surfers find good conditions off the Atlantic coast in particular. The surfing area at **Tarifa** off the coast of Cádiz is internationally renowned.

Adventure The **Agency Amatur** provides more adventurous sports such as white sports water sports, climbing, caving, hang-gliding and paragliding, ballooning, riding excursions, plus accommodation in »casas rurales«.

Time

During the winter half-year (end of October to end of March), Central European Time (CET) applies to Andalusia, and in the summer half-year (beginning of April to end of October) summer time applies (CET + 1 hr). This is **one hour ahead of Greenwich Mean Time**.

Tipping

A service charge is generally included in the bill (all-inclusive pricing); nevertheless, hotel staff, waiters, taxi drivers and others expect a tip, which should be about 5–10% of the total amount. In bars and restaurants the tip is left on the small plate after paying.

Transport

Roads Use of **motorways** (autopistas) is **subject to tolls** (peaje). The autovias, **expressways** similar to motorways, can be used **free of charge**.

The numbered **national routes** (Carreteras Nacionales; N-...) are also good-quality roads. Crawler lanes have normally been built for trucks on inclines, where they have not yet been extended to four lanes as autovías.

The **country roads**, likewise numbered, (carreteras autonomas; A... or abbreviation of the province), are also in good condition, provided they constitute major connections. Unnumbered secondary roads can hold surprises, however, and turn out to be **dirt roads**.

USEFUL ADDRESSES

AUTOMOBILE CLUBS

▶ **Real Automóvil Club de España (R.A.C.E)**
José Abascal, 10
E-28003 Madrid
Tel. 915 94 74 00
www.race.es

▶ **Real Automóvil Club de Andalucía**
Avda. Eduardo Dato, 22

E-41002 Sevilla
Tel. 95 463 13 50 or 95 463 13 54
Further branch offices of the R.A.C.E. are located in Almería, Cádiz, Córdoba, Granada and Málaga.

BREAKDOWN SERVICE

▶ **R.A.C.E.**
Tel. 902 30 05 05

Unless absolutely necessary, **avoid driving into cities**, particularly into old town centres, where streets are often very narrow. The one-way systems make car trips into the cities complicated and lengthy.
In most cities **parking** in spaces marked in blue is **subject to fees**, and **prohibited** in spaces marked in yellow. Fees are paid to attendants, or at parking ticket machines.

In cities

Urban: 50kmh/31mph; non-urban: 90kmh/55mph
On roads with at least two lanes in each direction: 100kmh/62mph
On motorways: 120kmh/74mph
Cars with caravan: 70kmh/43mph; on motorways: 80kmh/49mph

Maximum speed limits

Traffic in Spain **drives on the right** – as in the rest of continental Europe. The wearing of **seat belts** is compulsory for front and back seats. The **legal drink-drive limit** is 50mg of alcohol per 100ml of blood.
Fines of up to 600 € may be levied for **using a mobile phone in the car** without a hands-free set.

Traffic regulations

When **turning left** outside towns, there are separate lanes on larger roads that first veer to the right and then cross the main road (raqueta).
When **overtaking**, first the left indicator, then the right one is used during the entire procedure. Overtaking is prohibited on hill brows and roads with a clear view of less than 220yd/200 m.
In Spain, it is permissible to use only **parking lights** on well-lit roads (except on expressways and motorways). Replacement bulbs must be carried. **Towing** is prohibited using private vehicles.

Special regulations

In the event of a breakdown or an accident, the vehicle must be marked with two warning triangles, one in front of the car and one

Roadside assistance

behind it. Those displaying only one triangle are liable to fines up to 90 €. Additionally, it is compulsory to wear a reflective vest. Emergency telephones are placed at regular intervals along the motorway. When driving a rented car, contact the car rental office immediately in the event of a breakdown. The Policía Municipal helps in towns, and the Guardia Civil de Tráfico outside towns.

Rented cars At the international car rental companies, lower budget vehicles are available from 18 to 30 € per day, depending on term of lease. Numerous smaller local car rental firms often undercut these prices considerably. Offices of the international car rental companies are situated in all larger towns, as well as at the airports of Almería, Jerez de la Frontera, Málaga, and Seville.

Travellers with Disabilities

Andalusia is exactly a pioneer in terms of service for the disabled, but the situation is improving. Most large hotels, plus paradors and youth hostels, as well as establishments along the motorways are disabled-friendly. The major problem is the local public transport – buses and trains are usable for wheelchair users only with great difficulty; however, most taxi drivers are helpful. Disabled toilets are also scarce.

▶ USEFUL ADDRESSES

IN SPAIN

▶ **ECOM
(Federation of Spanish private organizations for the disabled)**
Gran Vía de las Corts
Catalanas 562 principal, 2a
E-08011 Barcelona
Tel. 934 51 69 04
The federation provides information on holidays and establishments throughout Spain.

▶ **Centro Estatal de Minusválidos Físicos**
Luis Cabrera, 63
E-28002 Madrid
Tel. (0034) 914 44 36 00
Fax 914 13 19 96

www.cocemfe.es
A brochure on disabled-friendly hotels can be obtained.

UNITED KINGDOM

▶ **RADAR**
12 City Forum, 250 City Road,
London EC1V 8AF
Tel. (020) 72 50 32 22
www.radar.org.uk

USA

▶ **SATH (Society for the Advancement of Travel for the Handicapped)**
347 5th Ave., no. 610
New York, NY 10016:
Tel. (21) 4 47 72 84
www.sath.org

When to Go

Moderate temperatures and lots of sunshine make spring and autumn the **best time to go**; September and October are particularly favourable with agreeable air and water temperatures, and stable weather conditions right up to the second half of October. On the Costa del Sol the visitor is spared autumn showers the longest. July and August can only be endured to some degree right on the coast. In winter, Andalusia enjoys almost consistently pleasant day temperatures and lots of sunshine. This climate results in the early **almond blossom**, which starts as early as the end of January.

! *Baedeker* TIP

Knowing when

Tourists travelling in spring be warned: April is often surprisingly cool and unstable, due to frequent encroachment of cold air into the western Mediterranean. The weather is more stable in March, and also much warmer from May onwards.

The blossoming almond trees give the wide countryside a spring-like splash of colour.

Tours

ALONG THE SUN COAST OR THROUGH OLIVE GROVES INTO THE INTERIOR? TO THE WHITE VILLAGES OR THE CRAGGY MOUNTAINS? MAKE YOUR TRIP A PILGRIMAGE – AS FULL OF LIFE AS THIS ONE IN MOCLÍN – TO THE MOST COLOURFUL SITES IN ANDALUSIA!

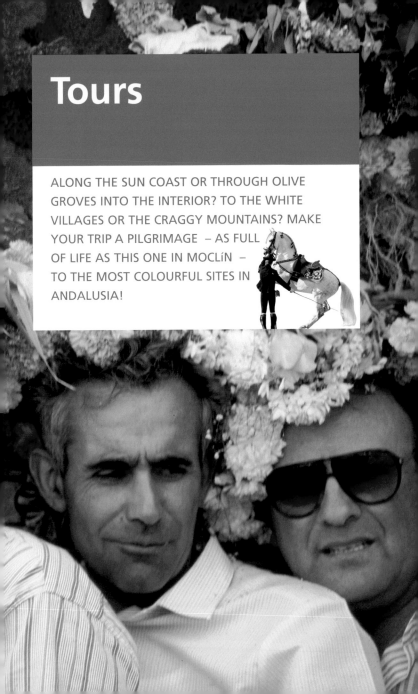

TOURS THROUGH ANDALUSIA

Are you wondering where to go? Our suggestions for tours reveal some particularly beautiful and exciting routes and tips for the best destinations.

The castle of Velez-Blanco in the wide-open spaces of the Sierra de Maria

Flamenco
A dance like life –
joy and pain lie close
to one another.

Architecture
The magnificent dome of
the Mihrâb Neuvo in the
Mezquita in Córdoba

© Baedeker

★★ Úbeda

★★ Baeza

★★ Medina   TOUR 3
Azahara   ★★ Córdoba   ★ Jaén

★ Écija

★★ Sevilla   ★★ Carmona

Priego de Córdoba

★ Guadix

★★ Granada   TOUR 4

★★ Coto de Doñana   TOUR 1   ★ Almería

★ Sanlúcar   ★ Arcos de la   ★★ Ronda   ▲ Málaga   ★★ Sierra Nevada
Frontera

★★ Jerez   Medina
Sidonia
★ Cádiz   ★ Vejer   ★ Marbella

TOUR 2

Coto de Doñana
…60 species of birds can be
…bserved in the national
…ark of the same name.

Dream beach
There are kilometre-long
beaches with fine sand to be
enjoyed on the Costa de la
Luz – like here near Isla
Cristina.

Generalife
Once the private park of the
kings of Granada, today
everyone can enjoy its shade
– and waterworks.

Travelling in Andalusia

Fun at the beach, enjoyment of nature and cultural delights of the highest order; in Andalusia you don't have to do without anything, because it can all be nicely packaged together. In the morning, an excursion into the **Moorish past**, in the afternoon, a hike in **secluded countryside** and in the evening, a **dip in the ocean** to cool off – this is certainly possible if you pick the right place as a base. It depends to no small extent on how you travel to Andalusia. Because most holidaymakers arrive by charter flights, which are downright cheap and take only about three hours from the UK and most other parts of Europe, it makes sense to present Andalusia's holiday regions according to the airports; travel by car takes two to three days, and the rail journey is equally long (▶Practicalities, Arrival).

Arrival in Málaga: Costa del Sol

Málaga, Andalusia's second-largest city, is the traffic hub of the Costa del Sol. The »sunshine coast« reaches from Tarifa in the southwest to the province of Málaga's eastern border. Its nucleus, the coastline from Málaga to Estepona, is **Europe's largest continuous resort area**. If you are neither a beach-lover nor a party-goer but are seeking peace and quiet, this coast is not for you because the **night life** is just as important as the **beach life**, and there is no lack of discos, nightclubs, restaurants, bars, fiestas and every conceivable kind of beach entertainment.

It gets quieter further away from the coast into the mountainous hinterland. Just a few miles from the beach there are pretty little hotels or holiday cabins perfect for a **relaxing holiday with excursions** to towns like Ronda or Antequera. Granada is not to be missed; an overnight stay there is recommended. The Costa del Sol is also **Europe's golfing paradise**. Many hotels have their own golf courses and offer golfing holidays (▶ Practicalities, Sport and Outdoors). The strip of coastline east of Málaga belonging to the province of Granada is called **Costa Tropical**. Building eyesores have been avoided here for the most part, and this is still the **most beautiful and pristine** part of the sunshine coast, even though the coastline is steep and the beaches therefore smaller. Tourism around the main city, Almuñécar, is on a smaller scale.

Arrival in Jerez de la Frontera: Costa de la Luz

Jerez de la Frontera is **the most convenient airport** for a holiday on the Costa de la Luz. Even if there are a few new resorts like Matalascañas or Novo Sancti Petri, it is fortunately still a far cry from the conditions on the western Costa del Sol. Costa de la Luz remains a destination for everyone who wants to enjoy sun, sand and sea **without disco and entertainment hype**. **Fantastic beaches** (totalling 265km/165mi) with fine sand are inviting places for a swim in the Atlantic. Water-sports enthusiasts, mainly surfers, consider the iso-

All the happiness in the world on the back of a horse – most of all on the beach of Tarifa

lated coves to be unmatched. **Nature lovers** are attracted to the Coto de Doñana National Park and the Sierra de Grazalema.

Culture fans will find what they are looking for in Cádiz on the coast and inland in Jerez de la Frontera, in the »pueblos blancos« and above all in Seville, which is not far from the sea. The hinterland is the country of the big landowners, who cultivate sherry, Manzanilla and olives, as well as breeding fighting bulls and horses – which makes it ideal for a **holiday on horseback** (▶ Practicalities, Sport and Outdoors). When looking for a place to stay, it is best to remember that although the beaches

? **DID YOU KNOW …?**

- The southern Atlantic coastline of Spain between the Río Guadiana estuary on the Portuguese border and the headland of Tarifa on the Straits of Gibraltar is called the »Coast of Light«, because it is almost always inundated by brilliant sunshine.

north of the Guadalquivir are great, they are located inconveniently if you want to get to the southern Costa de la Luz because there is no bridge over the river mouth, necessitating very long detours by way of Seville.

A holiday on the Costa de Almería is **pretty much off the beaten track** (170km/106mi from Almería to Granada). Instead, there is

Arrival in Almería: Costa de Almeria

countryside like nowhere else and some of **Andalusia's best beaches** because they are not overcrowded – particularly around Cabo de Gata. Nowhere else in Andalusia is the presence of Africa felt more strongly than here, where it rains just about 25 days a year. The brown and occasionally rugged rocks punctuated by volcanic hills have but a sparse covering of vegetation. This countryside is protected by law. The tourist infrastructure is accordingly relatively undeveloped – no huge concrete hotels or tourist resorts, but rather smaller hotels and isolated bungalow parks on the edge of villages. Only San José has grown a little larger, but is still a pleasant place to stay. Things are a lot different on the coastline west of Almería. It is a **major destination of package tourism**, which means that hotel and bungalow complexes tower over the usually well-tended beaches, and behind the hotels there is often a sea of plastic: the greenhouses. Costa de Almería does not offer much culturally, but all the more of the great outdoors. Wonderful day trips can be taken from every coastal town into the Sierra de Alhamilla or the mountains of the Alpujarras, where the climate is so mild that the Moors already cultivated citrus fruit there. Sierra de Alhamilla looks **like the Wild West** – literally, because there are three Wild West movie towns that draw the crowds today and Western films are occasionally still shot here.

Northeast Andalusia and the Guadalquivir basin

Two regions remain where a **seaside holiday** is not possible and no airports are close. The part of northeast Andalusia that essentially encompasses the region of Jaén is well worth discovering. The **largest olive-growing area on earth** is something for people who enjoy **wide, archaic-looking landscapes**, who seek outdoor adventure (in the Sierra de Cazorla) or who have a taste for **magnificent Renaissance cities** like Baeza or Úbeda. **Córdoba**, the old capital of the caliphate, is a must, even though it is in the Guadalquivir basin, which has a small disadvantage for tourism: this place is not called »**Andalusia's frying pan**« for nothing. It is not unusual for the thermometer to climb over 40°C/104°F here between June and September!

Mobility

If you don't want to spend your whole vacation on the beach but also want to experience something of Andalusia, then there is no good alternative to **hiring a car** (from €150 per week, ▸ Practicalities, Transport) or having your own car. On the other hand, the bus network is so dense that all the interesting sites can be reached without a problem. In most seaside resorts, the local organizers offer **bus trips** into the interior, for example, to Granada. Andalusia by rail **cannot be strongly recommended** because the railway network is not very dense. It is more than likely that the train station is located miles outside the village you want to visit. One exception is the **Al-Andaluz Express** (▸ Baedeker tip p.87).

Travel time and tours

To see a lot of Andalusia, allow 14 days for a grand tour (▸Tour 1). A three week stay would be ideal in every respect. Then it is possible to plan a week or more at the **seaside** and have a week or two to **explore the country**. A tour from the Costa del Sol could then include three of Andalusia's main attractions with two nights each in Granada, Córdoba and Seville. Cádiz, Seville, and Jerez de la Frontera can be reached comfortably from the southern Costa de la Luz. A **tour of the white villages** of Sierra de Grazalema is an absolute must. If you feel like undertaking something after a week on the beach at Costa de Almería, begin the following week with a trip to Granada in the Alpujarras (one day), spend a day there and on the third day, after visiting Jaén, Baeza and Úbeda, stay overnight in Jaén. On the return trip to Almería there is still time to see the cave-dwellings in Guadix. If you have just a week's time, choose between a beach holiday and culture. In the latter case, there are two main alternatives; after arriving in Málaga, the tour already mentioned above to Andalusia's three main attractions or a leisurely tour through the white villages (► Tour 2).

Chequered white villages on mountains ridges in the hinterland – it is cool inside their walls.

Tour 1 Andalusia in Three Weeks

Length of the tour: 995km/620mi

Giralda
»The tower sleeps standing and the cathedral lying down because the Giralda is life and the cathedral is faith.« (Fernando Villalón)

✶✶ Medina Azahara

140 km/87

15 km/ 9mi

7

6

✶✶ Córdoba

✶ Écija

64 km/40mi

8

✶✶ Sevilla

9

55 km/ 34mi

10

38 km/ 24mi

✶✶ Carmona

Medina Azahara
Legendary palace city of the caliph of Córdoba

90 km/56mi

Costa de la Luz
Coast of light – Look forward to the sea and the warm wind over the sandy beach.

125 km/78mi

✶✶ Coto de Doñana

11

✶ Málaga

1

12

25 km/ 16 km

✶ Sanlúcar

13

✶✶ Jerez

40 km/25mi

14

✶ Cádiz

✶✶ Ronda

16

40 km/ 37mi

17

59 km/ 37mi

✶ Marbella

56 km/ 35mi

15

✶ Vejer

132 km/82mi

Cádiz
Washed by the Atlantic from three sides – the oldest city in Europe

This tour touches the sightseeing highlights of Andalusia and can be covered in three weeks. If only two weeks are available, leave out Jaén and the surrounding area, northern Costa de la Luz and Coto de Doñana.

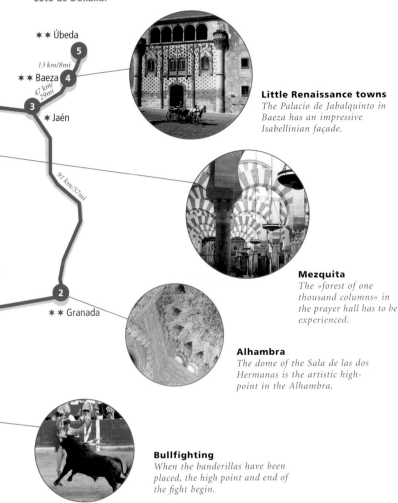

✶✶ Úbeda

5

13 km/8mi

✶✶ Baeza

4

47 km/ 29mi

3

✶ Jaén

91 km/57mi

2

✶✶ Granada

Little Renaissance towns
The Palacio de Jabalquinto in Baeza has an impressive Isabellinian façade.

Mezquita
The »forest of one thousand columns« in the prayer hall has to be experienced.

Alhambra
The dome of the Sala de las dos Hermanas is the artistic high-point in the Alhambra.

Bullfighting
When the banderillas have been placed, the high point and end of the fight begin.

From Málaga to Granada The starting point is ❶ ✳ **Málaga**, where a day can be spent seeing the cathedral, the Alcazaba and the Picasso sites. Drive north on the N-331 from the metropolis on the ✳ **Costa del Sol** to ✳ **Antequera** for a tour of the prehistoric megalith burial sites and a hike in the ✳✳ **El Torcal** mountains as well. (Antequera's parador is comfortable, inexpensive, conveniently located accommodation, but not particularly stylish.) The A-92 motorway crosses through the Vega of Granada to the old Moorish city of ❷ ✳✳ **Granada**, the first highlight of the trip. Try to stay here at least two days – three would be better – in order to enjoy the Alhambra (order tickets ahead! see p.262), the cathedral and the old town in a leisurely manner and perhaps undertake an excursion into the ✳✳ **Sierra Nevada**.

✓ **DON'T MISS**

- Granada: visit to the Nasrid Palace in the Alhambra in the evening, Albaícin, stop for coffee on Plaza Nueva
- Jaén: cathedral, castle. Arab baths
- Baeza and Úbeda: Renaissance pearls
- Sierra de Cazorla: hiking, riding, Jeep safaris through wild mountain scenery

Jaén and the northeast Plan to stay the next couple of nights in Jaén – perhaps in the splendid parador in the fortress – which can be reached from Granada by going north on the N-323. Just the trip there through the endless groves of olive trees is an experience. Once in Jaén, tour the cathedral, the Moorish quarter and the imposing castle. Do take a day trip to the Renaissance cities of ❸ **Jaén**, ❹ ✳✳ **Baeza** and ❺ ✳✳ **Úbeda** (105km/65mi round trip). Nature lovers will find a side trip from Úbeda into the ✳✳ **Sierra de Cazorla** (55km/35mi) rewarding.

From Jaén to Seville Now head from Jaén to Córdoba, either first to the north by way of Andújar and from there in a westerly direction on the N-IV, or – even better – straight through the land of olives on the A-316 and the A-306, which joins the N-IV a few miles outside Córdoba. ❻ ✳✳ **Córdoba** is also worth a stay lasting a couple of days. It has the Mezquita, one of the largest mosques on earth and the largest old town of any Spanish provincial city. The old caliphs' town can be used as a base for excursions into the wine-growing district of Montilla-Moriles around Lucena (about 75km/47mi) and above all to the once-forgotten residence of the caliphs, ❼ ✳✳ **Medina Azahara**, (15km/9mi). The N-IV runs right across the Guadalquivir plain, passing through ❽ ✳ **Écija**, the city of Baroque bell towers, and ❾ ✳ **Carmona**, with its old town and Roman necropolis, to ❿ ✳✳ **Seville**, the capital of Andalusia. This city on the Guadalquivir offers magnificent attractions; sights to see of the first order like the cathedral and the Alcázar, the old town and the Triana quarter with its pulsing nightlife, the gardens and parks on the river and Isla Mágica amusement park on the former EXPO grounds. There are also worthwhile destinations in the surrounding area, including the ruins of the Roman town of ✳ **Itálica** (10km/6mi), the castle of Alcalá de Guadaira (20km/12mi), the northern part of the ✳✳ **Costa de la Luz** with its beaches strung out around Huelva; and Moguer, the ✳ **La Rábida monastery** and Palos de la Frontera, which are closely associated with the voyages of Columbus (91km/57mi to Huelva); and finally a one-day trip into ⑪ ✳✳ **Coto de Doñana** National Park (90km/56mi to El Acebuche visitor centre).

South of Seville, ✳ **Jerez de la Frontera**, the capital of sherry and Andalusian horsemanship, can be quickly reached on the A-4 motorway. ⑫ ✳ **Sanlúcar de Barrameda**, the city of Manzanilla, is only a few miles out of the way, while the attractions further south are the city of sherry, ⑬ ✳✳ **Jerez**, followed by the clear light of the old port of ⑭ ✳ **Cádiz**. The stretch of the N-340 south of Cádiz along the Costa de la Luz with its coves and beaches swept by the eternal wind is the refreshing part of this tour after the trip through the interior. Recuperate in ⑮ ✳ **Vejer de la Frontera**, a »white village« close to the coast, or in the surfers' mecca of ✳ **Tarifa** with its lively nightlife – where a side trip to ✳✳ **Gibraltar** can be taken – before starting the somewhat taxing drive along the A-369 through San Roque, Castellar de la Frontera and Jímena de la Frontera into the ✳ **Serranía de Ronda** (alternative route: take the A-382 and A-372 out of Jerez via ✳ **Arcos de la Frontera** to Ronda). It is worth spending two days in ⑯ ✳✳ **Ronda**, perched breathtakingly above a deeply carved out gorge, to explore the town and the surrounding mountain countryside. The last leg is on the A-376, which crosses the Sierra Bermeja and runs along the Costa del Sol back to Málaga, passing through the holiday resorts of ⑰ ✳ **Marbella**, Fuengirola and Torremolinos.

From Seville back to Málaga via the Costa de la Luz and Ronda

The Giralda and the Torre del Oro shine out into the Sevillian night.

Tour 2 The »White Villages«

Start D 9

Length of the tour: about 250km/155mi

The »white village« route (»Ruta de los Pueblos Blancos«) touches the hill country and mountain landscape of southwest Andalusia. Outstanding cultural monuments take second place to the colourful combination of beautiful scenery sprinkled with villages of white-washed houses, each inviting visitors to stroll through narrow lanes. But don't be fooled by the term »village« – many have long since grown into small towns.

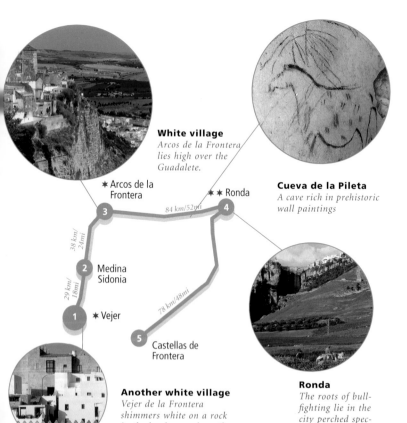

White village
Arcos de la Frontera lies high over the Guadalete.

Cueva de la Pileta
A cave rich in prehistoric wall paintings

* Arcos de la Frontera

** Ronda

84 km/52mi

3

4

38 km/24mi

2 Medina Sidonia

29 km/18mi

78 km/48mi

* Vejer

5 Castellas de Frontera

Another white village
Vejer de la Frontera shimmers white on a rock in the landscape above the Rio Barbate.

Ronda
The roots of bullfighting lie in the city perched spectacularly above a gorge.

The journey begins in ❶ * **Vejer de la Frontera**, high on a hill in the vicinity of Cabo de Trafalgar. The A-393 heads north here to ❷ **Medina Sidonia**, an old noble seat in the middle of Andalusia's bull-breeding region. Take a detour into the interior to experience another typical village, Alcalá de los Gazules (40km/25mi round trip). Leaving Medina Sidonia, continue north to ❸ * **Arcos de la Frontera**. Majestically enthroned on a rock above the Río Guadalete, it is often called the most beautiful of the »white villages«.

From Vejer de la Frontera to Arcos de la Frontera

One of the most pleasant legs of the tour begins here; on the A-372 across the * **Sierra de Grazalema** through fields of sunflowers, grain, olive groves and copses of oak. Lying at the foot of this mountain is El Bosque, the centre for hiking tourism in protected countryside. The narrow road winds up to the pass of Puerto del Boyar, where there is a spectacular view, and down again to Grazalema, nestled on the slopes under the towering El Reloj crag. An alternative to the drive over the pass is the equally beautiful but somewhat longer detour on the A-373 from El Bosque to Ubrique in the south and from there along the A-375 to Grazalema (about 40km/25mi). To see a really attractive »white village«, take a side trip to Zahara de la Sierra north of Grazalema (about 50km/30mi round trip). The next destination after Grazalema is ❹ ** **Ronda**, sensationally built around the Río Guadiaro gorge. Before the town, a small, narrow road branches off at La Quinta to * **Cueva de la Pileta**, a cave lying high in the mountain with fascinating prehistoric paintings. It is worth staying a little longer in Ronda to also undertake excursions to two »white villages« captivatingly set in the rocky countryside: * **Setenil** and * **Olvera**. More than a few people live there in perfectly comfortable cave dwellings.

Through the Sierra de Grazalema to Ronda

✔ **DON'T MISS**

- Arcos de la Frontera: fine dining in the parador
- Sierra de Grazalema: hiking, riding tours
- Zahara de la Sierra: impressive castle
- Ronda: wonderful setting, Moorish old quarter, bull fights
- Beaches of Costa de la Luz: Zahara de los Atunes, Canos de Meca, Chiciana, Tarifa, Mazagón, Conil de la Frontera
- Beaches of Costa del Sol: Marbella, Nerja

After touring Ronda, head out to the south on the A-369. The road passes by groves of olive trees and oak and through picturesque villages before it reaches Jímena de la Frontera, from where it heads directly south. A narrow cul-de-sac branches off near Almoraima to the quaint fortified village of ❺ **Castellar de la Frontera** with its 13th century Moorish fort. The coast of Africa is visible from here on a clear day. After taking this detour (about 15km/9mi round trip), continue south. The junction with the N-340 / E-15 presents the choice of either going west to ** **Costa de la Luz** on teh Atlantic Ocean or east to * **Costa del Sol** on teh Mediterranean Sea.

From Ronda to the Costa del Sol

Tour 3 Tour of the caliphate

Start H 7

Length of tour: about 180km/112mi

This route runs west on the N-432 from Granada to Córdoba, combining all the most significant Andalusian Moorish cities. It goes through the heartland of the caliphate, and time and again includes side trips to smaller places where, upon closer inspection, much Moorish heritage remains to be discovered.

5 ✷✷ Córdoba

61 km/38mi

Olive groves
They alternate with fabulous open country-side.

Baena

4 31 km/29mi

28 km/17mi

Alcalá la Real

3

2

Priego de Córdoba

Mezquita
This horseshoe gate once led into a mosque's holiest of holies – the mihrâb.

51 km/32mi

Sierras Subbeticas
The stretch of land sparkles green, blue and silver.

✷✷ Granada **1**

Alhambra
Moorish pièce de résistance of world architecture

✓ DON'T MISS

- Granada: evening visit to the Nasrid palace in the Alhambra, Albaícin, coffee break on Plaza Nueva.
- Baena: centre of olive oil production with a Moorish old town.
- Priego de Córdoba: Baroque church with a fountain.
- Zuheros: castle from Moorish times.
- Sierras Subbéticas Nature Park: hiking.
- Córdoba: Mezquita and Judería; eat in Pepé de la Judería or in El Rincón de Carmen, both in Calle Romero; flamenco in Tablao Cardenal.

This is the case with the first stop after ❶ ✷✷ **Granada**, **Moclín**, on a side road out of Puerto López. Here the proud border fortifications of the Nasrid rulers of Granada and the Casa del Pósito, a Renaissance granary, can be visited. It is worth taking yet another detour from here to see a Mudejar-style parish church in the smaller fortified village of **Colomera** (20km/12mi). ❷ **Alcalá la Real** on the N-432 has many old churches and the next impressive castle, Castillo de la Mota, which, together with the destroyed castle of Castillo de Locubín, once dominated the pass over the rugged sierras. The castillo of Alcaudete is also worth seeing.

Before driving directly on to **④ Baena** with its Gothic parish church, it is worth taking a trip on the A-333 into the **Sierras Subbéticas** Nature Park (80km/50mi) with its many caves and springs.

③ Priego de Córdoba is also worth a visit and an overnight stay. Then continue on the A-340 through Carcabuey and Cabra and along the A-316 to **Zuheros** (with the Cueva del Cerro de los Murcié-lagos), whose castle has the most beautiful setting on this excursion. The N-432 can be reached again from there and not far down it is **Castro del Río** with its picturesque lanes and churches. Besides the Moorish-inspired cuisine, on this leg of the journey it is worth taking note of the famous olive-wood furniture. Finally, after travelling by way of Espejo through wide **fields of sunflowers and olive groves**, the tour ends in **⑤ ✳✳ Córdoba**.

> **!** *Baedeker* TIP
>
> **Devotional singing**
> The brotherhood of the parish church of La Aurora in Priego de Córdoba processes every Saturday around midnight through the streets to honour the patron saint of their church with songs.

Zuheros has a castle in a breathtaking location, on a sheer rock.

Tour 4 Through the Sierra Nevada

Start H 7

Length of tour: about 400km/250mi

This is the route for nature lovers. It leads to Spain's highest peak, through bleak volcanic tuffstone landscape, to Europe's only desert and finally to an old region of terraced countryside cultivated by the Moors in the Alpujarras.

Guadix
City of the cave dwellings

Lacalahorra
The Renaissance fortress lies between the green of the plateau and the blue of the sky.

✱ Guadix

55 km/
34 mi

Lacalahorra

18 km/
11 mi

✱✱ Granada

96 km/60mi

46 km/
29mi

Lanjaron

90 km/56mi

✱✱ Sierra Nevada

✱ Laujar
de Andarax

65 km/
40mi

✱ Almería

Sierra Nevada
Conquering the summit of Pico de Velata is something to be proud of.

Alpujarras
The mountains are named after the goddess of light.

Almería
The Alcazaba of Almería is the second largest Moorish structure in Europe after the Alhambra in Granada.

It is possible to go on a day trip from  ✶✶ **Granada** along Europe's highest mountain pass road (A-395) through the ski areas and get right up close to Pico de Veleta (3428m/11,247ft), the highest peak of the ✶✶ **Sierra Nevada** and Spain (round trip 88km/ 55mi). Driving up to the pass, 9km/5.5mi outside Granada turn into a small connecting road that runs along the Río Aguas to Dúdar and Quéntar. There is a fantastic view of the summit of the Sierra Nevada all along the drive from La Peza to ❷ ✶ **Guadix** with its interesting cathedral, but in fact the **cave dwellings**, typical of this area, are the real attraction. If the more arduous way was chosen to get here instead of the A-92, then an overnight stay in Guadix is recommended. Continue the next day along the A-92 across the Marquesado de Zenete plateau where there are tempting side trips to pretty villages – don't miss the Renaissance fortress of ❸ **Lacalahorra**. In Huénejar the **Arab baths** are worth stopping for; in Fiñana a small mosque has survived in almost its original state. Past Gádor is the junction with the N-340/E-15 leading to ❹ ✶ **Almería**. Plan an overnight stop here to allow time for a drive into the Sierra de Alhamilla or to Cabo de Gata.

From Granada to Almería

✔	DON'T MISS
■	Granada: evening visit to the Nasrid palace in the Alhambra, Albaícin, coffee break on Plaza Nueva
■	Sierra Nevada: Spain's highest peaks
■	Guadix: cave dwellings
■	Lacalahorra: Renaissance fortress in a pristine setting
■	Almería: Alcazaba, in the vicinity, little Hollywood
■	Cabo de Gata: desert and sea
■	Las Alpujarras: terraced landscape high in the mountains
■	Trevélez: try serrano ham

The Río Andarax accompanies the drive back to Granada through the ✶ **Alpujarras**. This is the region of the Morisco revolt of the 16th century. It retained a **Moorish character** long after the Reconquista. Mulberry trees were cultivated in its mild climate and today the people still grow vegetables, citrus fruits and wine in **terrace gardens** here. The route leads along the A-348 from Gádor to Alhama de Almería and ❺ **Laujar de Andarax**. A side trip to see the source of the Río Andarax river is possible from there. Further on, are **Juviles** with its stunningly beautiful Mudejar church, **Trevélez**, at 1480m/4,855ft the highest settlement, known for its delicious »jamón serrano« (air-cured hams), and **Capileira**. Then descend deep into the valleys of the southern slopes of the Sierra Nevada and back to Granada through Órgiva, ❻ **Lanjarón** – a good place to stay the night – and Durcal.

Through the Alpujarras

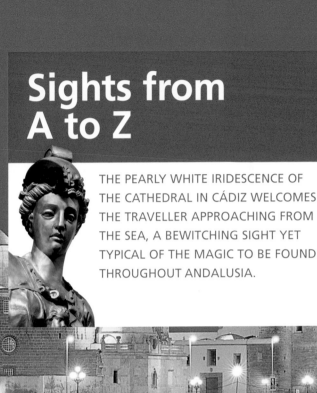

Sights from A to Z

THE PEARLY WHITE IRIDESCENCE OF THE CATHEDRAL IN CÁDIZ WELCOMES THE TRAVELLER APPROACHING FROM THE SEA, A BEWITCHING SIGHT YET TYPICAL OF THE MAGIC TO BE FOUND THROUGHOUT ANDALUSIA.

✳ **Los Alcornocales**

(Parque Natural de los Alcornocales)

D 8/9

Province: Cádiz

The Los Alcornocales nature reserve that stretches between the rock of ▶ Gibraltar and the ▶ Sierra de Grazalema is well worth a visit for nature-lovers because of its diverse vegetation and its rich variety of bird species.

Flora and fauna The mountainous nature reserve covering 1700 sq km/660 sq mi in the westernmost foothills of the Betica Cordillera is **one of the world's largest cork oak forests**. Some truly majestic specimens grow at higher altitudes. The forests form the basis of the region's

 VISITING LOS ARCORNOCALES

GETTING THERE

Jimena de la Frontera, near ▶Algeciras, and the village of Alcalá de los Gazules are the best gateways into the nature reserve. The park can be explored by car from the A 375 that runs right across the middle of it from Alcalá de los Gazules into the Sierra de Grazalema in the direction of Ubrique. The A 369 between Castellar de la Frontera and Gaucí is the road to take for a look at the eastern edge of the reserve.

INFORMATION

Calle los Pozos, s/n
E-11180 Alcalá de los Gazules
Tel. 956 41 31 83/08
Fax 956 41 33 71
www.alcornocales.org

Misericordia s/n
E-11330 Jimena de la Frontera
Tel. 956 64 05 69
Opening hours:
Mon–Fri 11am–1pm, 4–6pm,
Sat, Sun 10am–1pm

The information offices can provide information about hiking and accommodation in the region.

WHERE TO EAT AND WHERE TO STAY

▶ **Moderate**
La Almoraima
In Castellar de la Frontera
Tel. 956 69 30 02
A good tip for wild game dishes and traditional cooking. Provides hotel accommodation at the edge of the Los Alcornocales nature reserve.

▶ **Budget**
Posada La Casa Grande
C. Fuente Nueva, 42
E-11330 Jimena de la Frontera
Tel. 956 64 05 78
Accommodation with a family atmosphere. The owners also run the La Cuadra tapas bar next-door.

cork industry. Once a tree's layer of cork bark is 7 to 10 cm (3 to 4 inches) thick, which occurs about every 9 or 10 years, it is ready to be harvested and processed. In addition, the acorns serve as the main diet of the Iberian wild boars that roam free in the forests. Besides cork oak, other plants that thrive here include holly, wild olive trees, hawthorn and bracken. Among the **most characteristic trees** are a species of oak related to the Portuguese oak that grows on shady and moist slopes and tends to be strongly overgrown with epiphytic plants,. The wild animals of the Alcornocales include not only wild boar, but red deer, roe deer, otters, mongooses, griffon vultures and booted eagles, lizards and fire salamanders, plus many other reptiles and amphibians.

Algeciras

E 9

Province: Cádiz   **Altitude:** 15m/49ft
Population: 101,900

Algeciras lies near the southern tip of the Iberian peninsula on the western side of the bay of Algeciras across from ►Gibraltar. The city is highly important as a ferry port to ►Ceuta and Tangiers in North Africa. It is used annually by close to 3.4 million travellers, particularly during the summer months when Moroccans working in Europe cross the strait to spend their holidays at home.

Algeciras is anything but beautiful, so that most people only take it in as a stop-over on the way to North Africa. The proximity to Morocco also lies behind the fact that the rate of drug offences in Algeciras is higher than anywhere else in Spain. Do not under any circumstances bring drugs (»chocolate«) in any form or amount back from Africa and do not procure any in Algeciras – the punishments for this are severe. It was the Moors who re-established the Roman port of Portus Albo in 713 and named it Al-Gezîra al-Khadrâ (»Green Island«). It was conquered in 1344 by Alfonso XI (Alfonso the Just) but was retaken by Mohammed V of Granada in 1368 before being wiped out by the Christians a year later.
When Gibraltar was captured by the British in 1704, Spanish emigrants from there began to resettle the town.

Gateway to North Africa

> **! Baedeker TIP**
>
> **Trip to Morocco**
> The proximity to Africa is evidenced by the lively activity in the harbour and it might just arouse the urge to take a trip to Morocco. The crossing to Tangiers takes only about two hours. Among the companies offering day-trip excursions, including a tour of the city, is Viajes Transafric, Avda. la Marina 4 (tel. 956 65 43 11; remember your passport) and the price is around €45.

▶ VISITING ALGECIRAS

INFORMATION (OFICINA DE TURISMO)

C. Juan de la Cierva, s/n
E-11207 Algeciras
Tel. 956 57 26 36, fax 956 57 04 75

WHERE TO EAT

▶ Moderate

① *Montes*
Juan Morrison, 27
Tel. 956 65 42 07
Far from sophisticated, but authentic and always full. Tapas from the same kitchen are served in the accompanying bar at the corner of C. Castellar.

Los Remos

In San Roque
Finca Villa Victoria, s / n
Crta. de Gibraltar, tel. 956 69 84 12
»Muy sofisticado«, say the purists, but the cuisine is indisputably among the finest and tradition has not been sacrificed in the face of international influences.

WHERE TO STAY

▶ Luxury/Mid-range

San Roque Club Suites Hotel
In San Roque, Ctra. N-340, km 126,5
Tel. 956 61 30 30
Fax 956 61 30 12, 100 rooms
www.sanroqueclub.net
Luxury in one of Andalusia's largest fincas. The core of the hotel is the old manor house surrounded by an exquisite Andalusian garden. It also includes a first-class restaurant.

▶ Mid-range

② *Hotel Reina Cristina*
Paseo de la Conferencia, s/n
Tel. 956 60 26 22
Fax 956 60 33 23, 188 rooms
Romantic, colonial-style hotel south of the harbour, set in the middle of a park. The hotel has had a series of illustrious guests including Sir Arthur Conan Doyle and Federico García Lorca.

▶ Budget

① *Al Mar*
Avda. de la Marina, 2
Tel. 956 65 46 61
Fax 956 65 45 01, 192 rooms
The hotel is next to the harbour and the view across the Bay of Algeciras with its refineries and oil tanks is not exactly idyllic.

What to See in Algeciras

Plaza Alta
In the 18th century, the city began to spread out from around Plaza Alta, the city's main square, lined with palms and decorated with fountains. The churches Nuestra Señora de Europa and Nuestra Señora de la Palma date from that time.

In 1906, the conference of Algeciras was held in the **Casa Consistorial** (the old town hall built in 1897), a result of the First Moroc-

---

! *Baedeker* TIP

Shopping under a roof of steel

The centrally located market hall in C. Nuestra Señora de la Palma is ideal if you are shopping for a picnic. It features an interesting steel structure designed by the engineer Eduardo Torroja.

Algeciras *Plan*

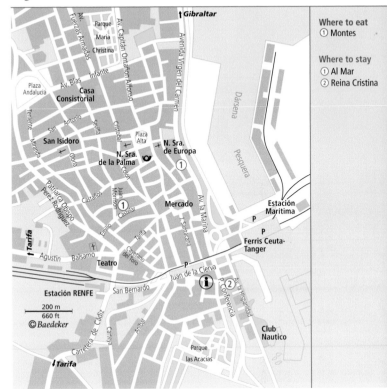

Where to eat
① Montes

Where to stay
① Al Mar
② Reina Cristina

can Crisis (1905/1906), in the course of which **Kaiser Wilhelm II** made a point of visiting Tangiers.

The Germans were trying to frustrate French colonial policies in North Africa and gain influence in Morocco. Despite that, the treaty of Algeciras eventually gave joint control over Morocco to France and Spain.

Parts of the **Merinid baths** dating from the 13th or 14th century were found in the city centre in 1996 and have since been moved to the Parque María Cristina. The remains of walls and floors as well as parts of a sewer system can be seen.

Parque María Cristina

The city museum in the Parque las Acacias offers information about the history of the city. Do not miss room IV where the Merinid baths on display illustrate the **domestic hygiene of the time** (opening hours: Mon–Fri 10am–2pm, 5pm to 8pm, Sat 10am–1pm).

Museo Municipal ☉

Algeciras has a unique backdrop for a city, the Rock of Gibraltar.

Around Algeciras

La Línea dela Concepción

La Línea de la Concepción is the border town leading to the British dominion of ►Gibraltar. The village has a bullfighting museum and a museum featuring works by the local-born artist Cruz Herrera.

✳ Castellar de la Frontera

A small road branches off the A 369 to ►Ronda at Castellar Nuevo 10km/6mi outside Algeciras and follows a route lined with cork oak, eucalyptus and carob trees to Castellar de la Frontera, a **walled, fortified village amid a rocky landscape**. Many of the families living there were forced to move to Nuevo Castellar in the 1970s because the new Embalse de Guadarranque reservoir had a disastrous effect on harvest yields. Subsequently, the abandoned village was discovered by artists, artisans and drop-outs. For the time being, the village still feels like a picturesque and secluded paradise behind its ancient defensive walls, but it is attracting an increasing number of foreign as well as Spanish holidaymakers. Castellar is also known for its **flamenco festival**, which takes place in August.

Jimena de la Frontera

To the east of the ►Los Alcornocales nature reserve and 12km/7mi north of Castellar lies Jimena de la Frontera, a sleepy village clustered around the ruins of a Moorish castle. The present tourist office is in the restored, 15th-century Iglesia de la Misericordia. Information is available from there regarding tours of the **Cueva de Laja-Alta** to the northwest of Jimena de la Frontera, where cave paintings some 3,000 years old have been discovered.

✶ Almería

L 8

Province: Almería
Population: 168,000

Altitude: 16m/52ft

The broad Gulf of Almería with its long, enticing beaches spreads along the southeastern corner of Andalusia. Only a few miles inland, the bare peaks of the Sierra de Gádor to the west and the Sierra Alhamilla to the northeast rise above the coastal strip. The most southerly point of Spain is marked by the ►Cabo de Gata.

Almería, the capital of the province, is lively and friendly but not spectacular. Its greatest attraction for tourists is the beautifully restored Alcazaba, **Andalusia's largest Moorish castle**.

Friendly provincial capital

Almería Plan

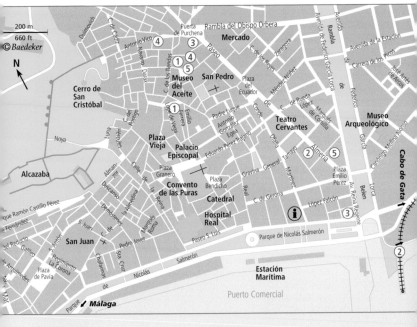

Where to eat
① Casa Puga
② Club de Mar
③ El Alcazár
④ Restaurante Valentín
⑤ Taberna Asador Calle Mayor

Where to stay
① AM Congress
② Costasol
③ Gran Hotel Almería
④ La Perla
⑤ Torreluz IV

There is a captivating view of the city and the harbour from the Alcazaba.

The province of Almería is not rich. There is little industry. On the other hand, the sun shines 320 days of the year on average, so that vegetables can be grown under plastic on a major scale across the plains around the provincial capital. First-time visitors may be put off by the plastic foil cloches stretching endlessly into the distance. The wretched housing of the day labourers – mostly North African immigrants – does not leave a good impression either. Nevertheless, the province is continuing to win more and more fans thanks to the fabulous, and not yet overcrowded beaches, along with the pristine natural landscape that can be found primarily in the eastern part of the region around the cape. The coast westwards of Almería, on the other hand, has surrendered to mass tourism. The airport lies 8km/ 5mi east of the city and is Andalusia's second busiest for charter flights after Málaga.

History The southern tip of the Iberian peninsula is an area with a culture that dates back to ancient times, since it is a **nexus of sea routes** from North Africa to Europe and from the eastern Mediterranean to the Atlantic. One of the most significant archaeological sites for the

▶ VISITING ALMERÍA

INFORMATION (OFICINA DE TURISMO)

Parque Nicolás Salmerón/corner of Martínez Campos, E-04004 Almería
Tel. 950 27 43 55, fax 950 27 43 60
Airport Tel. 950 29 29 18
www.dipalme.org;
www.aytoalmeria.es

WHERE TO EAT

▶ Moderate

① *Casa Puga*
Jovellanos, 7
The bar is legendary for its tapas, both in terms of quality and quantity.

② *Club de Mar*
Muelle de las Almadrabillas
Tel. 950 23 50 48
Gourmet restaurant in the marina with fish specialities and a classy atmosphere.

④ *Restaurante Valentín*
Tenor Iribarne, 19
Tel. 950 26 44 75
Fish dishes in myriad variations.

▶ Inexpensive

③ *El Alcázar*
Tenor Iribarne, 2
Tel. 950 23 89 95
Typical marisquería offering fried fish and seafood.

⑤ *Taberna Asador C. Mayor*
C. General Segura, 17
Delectable tapas and choice meat from the grill.

WHERE TO STAY

▶ Mid-range

③ *Gran Hotel Almería*
Avda. Reina Regente, 8
Tel. 950 23 80 11
Fax 950 27 06 91
www.granhotelalmeria.com
E-mail: reservas@grandhotel almeria.com, 117 B.
Finest hotel in the city with the usual services and amenities for this price range.

⑤ *Torreluz IV*
Plaza Flores, 3
Tel. 950 23 43 99
Fax 950 28 14 28
www.torreluz.com, 105 rooms
Modern hotel near the Alcazaba that is also linked with two other cheaper hotels with two and three stars.

Portomagno
In Aguadulce
Paseo Marítimo, s / n
Tel. 950 34 22 16
Fax 950 34 29 65, 383 rooms
Beach hotel with all the extras including a golf course.

Baedeker recommendation

▶ Budget

Tapas in Almería
One excellent place for a tapas break in the old part of Almería is the Bodeguilla de Ramón in C. Padre Alfonso Torres, a quiet lane near San Pedro church.

▶ Budget

① *AM Congress*
Tenor Iribarne, 15
Tel. 902 23 49 99
www.amhoteles.com
Nicely furnished and comparatively low-priced hotel.

② *Costasol*
Paseo de Almería, 58
Tel. / fax 950 23 40 11

The hotel is located between the harbour and the city centre and provides a great breakfast.

④ *La Perla*
Plaza del Carmen, 7
Tel. 950 23 88 77
Fax 950 27 58 16
The best rooms face the plaza. The oldest hotel in the city has maintained its charm.

Playacapricho
In Roquetas de Mar
Urb. Playa Serena H-10
Tel. 950 33 31 00

Fax 950 33 38 06, 331 rooms
Large facility with indoor swimming pool and garden.

SHOPPING

C. de las Tiendas is the main shopping zone along with the many little side streets around it. A morning market is held in C. Aguilar de Campo at Paseo de Almería.

EVENTS

Feria
Celebrations for 10 days and nights at the end of August with music and bullfighting.

Beaker people culture is at Los Millares, 25km/16mi north of Almería. The Phoenicians also settled here, followed by the Greeks, the Carthaginians and after them the Romans, who built up an important harbour by the name of Portus Magnus. After the Visigoths came the Moors, under whom the city flowered and gained the name Al-Mariyya, which roughly means **»mirror of the sea«**. Under Abd ar-Rahman III, it was an important port for the caliphate. After that regime disintegrated, it became the capital of a taifa that was mightier than Seville and included Murcia, Jaén, Córdoba as well as parts of Granada. However, this too was short-lived and Almería deteriorated into a nest of pirates. Alfonso VII succeeded in conquering the city in 1147, but ten years later, the Christians had to pull out again and it was not until 1489 that an uncle of the last ruler of Granada handed over Almería to the Catholic Monarchs. An earthquake destroyed major parts of the city in 1522 and in 1567 expelled Moslems once again appeared before the gates, but they were defeated. As of the 19th century, ore mined in the surrounding area was shipped from here. The cultivation of vegetables began after the decline of mining in the 1980s.

✳ ✳ Alcazaba

🕐
Opening hours:
May–Sept
10am–2pm and
5–8pm, Oct–April
9.30am–1.30pm
and 3.30–7pm

On the summit that towers above the Barrio de la Chanca to the west of the town, hardly visible from the town centre but well signposted, is the enormous Alcazaba, Europe's second largest Moorish building after the Alhambra in ▶ Granada. It was built in the 10th century under Abd ar-Rahman III, enlarged by Almansur, further expanded between 1014 and 1028 by Jairán, the first ruler of the taifa, and finally extended once again by the Catholic Monarchs. The rebuilt

Alcazaba of Almería Plan

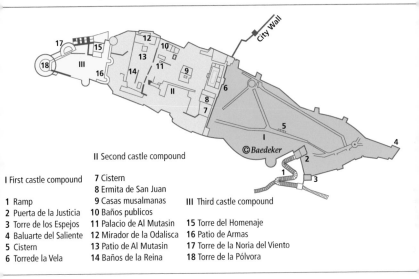

II Second castle compound

I First castle compound

1 Ramp
2 Puerta de la Justicia
3 Torre de los Espejos
4 Baluarte del Saliente
5 Cistern
6 Torre de la Vela

7 Cistern
8 Ermita de San Juan
9 Casas musalmanas
10 Baños publicos
11 Palacio de Al Mutasin
12 Mirador de la Odalisca
13 Patio de Al Mutasin
14 Baños de la Reina

III Third castle compound

15 Torre del Homenaje
16 Patio de Armas
17 Torre de la Noria del Viento
18 Torre de la Pólvora

area of the fortress encompasses more than 35,000 sq m/9 acres and more than 20,000 people could take refuge within its walls. Three walls crowned with battlements follow the contours of the hill and enclose three castle compounds at varying heights. A steep, zig-zagging ramp leads up from the ticket box and through the Puerta de la Justicia into the first compound area, which once sheltered refugees during sieges or concealed defenders readying to break out. It has been transformed nowadays into a very pretty park traversed by streams. Here stands the Torre de la Vela, erected under Carlos III. Its bell was used to sound alarms but also announced curfew and watering times. There is a **fantastic view** from here of the Saliente bastion in the east jutting out from the town like the bow of a ship. The oldest part of the grounds is in the second castle yard. This was where the palace of the Moorish rulers once stood, accompanied by a mosque with a cistern beneath it, although little remains today except for the foundation walls. It is still possible to take a tour inside the cistern. There are a few modest items of the Islamic past on display. The Christians built the upper enclosure as a self-contained fortress. Three mighty towers are grouped here around the parade courtyard; the four-sided Gothic Torre del Homenaje with the coat of arms of the Catholic Monarchs, the Torre de la Noria del Viento (windmill tower) and, on the west point, the Torre de la Pólvora (powder tower) with some of the old cannons. The Torre del Homenaje includes the Centro Andaluz de la Fotografía, the Andalusian Centre of Photography, which has an ever-changing exhibition program.

◀ Tours

The monumental Moorish castle, the Alcazaba, towers over Almeria.

City wall   From the junction between the first and second castle compounds, the fortified city wall built under Jairan descends down into the la Hoya valley and climbs back up to the Cerro de San Cristóbal across from the Alcazaba. The Knights Templar built the **Castillo de San Cristóbal** on the adjoining hill and four large towers of the castle are still standing. The giant statue of Jesus was put up in 1928.

La Chanca   The barrio of La Chanca (Arabic: »tuna net«) that spreads up the hill beneath the castle is home to many Gitanos or gypsies. They are unlikely to appreciate it if their impoverished living conditions are taken for a tourist attraction.

Town Centre

The palm-covered Parque de Nicolás Salmerón extends alongside the ferry harbour. At the far eastern end, the old ore-hauling railway crosses high over the street at a dizzying altitude.

Parque de Nicolás Salmerón

Just before the bridge, the Rambla de Belén forks away and a little further along, the Paseo de Almería turns off it. This is a good place to stroll, shop or visit one of the street cafés. Among the conspicuous buildings in the street are the seat of the civil government, once a casino, and the magnificent buildings associated with it, the Teatro Cervantes and the Círculo Mercantil. Behind them is the **Basílica de la Nuestra Señora del Mar**, dedicated to the city's patron. An appearance of Our Lady is said to have taken place on the beach in 1502. The market hall is located to the right of the Paseo.

Paseo de Almería

The grand Plaza de la Catedral can be reached by going to the left of the Paseo. The cathedral is a **typical fortified church** with four formidable corner towers, tower-like apses and a fringe of battlements. It also served to protect against pirate attacks. Diego de Siloé built it after the earthquake of 1522 between 1524 and 1543 on the site of a mosque known as the Friday mosque. The main portico and the Puerta de los Perdones, both by Juan de Orea, appear less bulky with double columns richly decorated with statuary and finished off with the coat of arms of Charles V. The **choir stalls**, once again carved in walnut by Juan de Orea (1558), are an outstanding work of art in the interior. Their unusual relief figures depict, alongside clergy und saints, a worker, an official and a female Moor as well. Also notable are the »Listening Christ« in the axis chapel of the choir (Bishop Villalán, the founder of the church, is also buried there), an Annunciation by Alonso Cano in the Capilla de la Piedad to the left, as well as a statue of Saint Indalecio – the patron saint of Almeria – a work by Francisco Salcillo, to the right of the choir crest.

✴ *Cathedral*

A little way past the archbishop's palace is the pretty, arcaded Plaza Vieja (Plaza de la Constitución) where the city hall is situated. C. de las Tiendas, formerly the main axis of the city, goes all the way to Puerta de Purchena at the northern end of Paseo de Almería. Just before it is the 16th-century **Santiago el Viejo** church with its 55m/180ft-high Romanesque tower and a magnificent portal with the figure of St James as a slayer of Moors, again created by Juan de Orea. The church furnishings were destroyed in 1936 during the civil war. A little further up beyond the church, some 11th-century **Moorish cisterns** can be viewed (opening hours: Mon–Sat 11am–1pm and 7–9pm).

Plaza Vieja

🕐

The Museo del Aceite de Oliva in C. de las Tiendas (no. 15) off C. Real is dedicated to all aspects of **olive oil**. For a small fee, some of

Museo del Aceite de Oliva

⏱ the different kinds can also be sampled (opening hours: Mon–Fri 10am–1pm, 5.30–8pm, Sat mornings only).

San Pedro It is only a stone's throw from the olive museum to Plaza San Pedro. The church was built on the foundations of the walls of a mosque in 1494. The present structure with frescoes by Fray Juan García dates from 1795.

Museo Arqueológico Almería's archaeological museum is currently without a home. Parts of the collections are on display in the Biblioteca Francisco Villaespasa (C. Hermanos Machados) and in the Archivo Histórico (C. Infanta). Precise information can be obtained from the tourist office.

Around Almería

Western Costa de Almería The western Costa de Almería (eastern part ▶Mojácar) is the **prime destination for the package tour industry**, which means numerous hotels and bungalow complexes tower up behind long and mostly excellently tended beaches are. More often than not, directly behind them is a plastic sea of greenhouses. There is no dearth of pools, parks, sports centres, supermarkets and discos in Aguadulce nor in neighbouring Roquetas de Mar. **Almerímar** aims at a different clientele with its luxurious complex built where nothing stood before, almost a city in itself, and its large golf course. Weekend sailors are welcome to anchor here at one of the 1,100 berths in Andalusia's second-largest yacht marina.

Los Millares
⏱
Opening hours:
Tue–Sat 9am–4pm
The archaeological site at Los Millares to the northwest of Almería, accessed via the A-92 and A-348, is **of such major importance** that the cultural era between the Stone Age and the Copper Age is named after it. Here, high above the valley of Río Andarax in the desert-like Sierra de Gádor, between 2,500 and 1,500 BC lived a people who produced pottery beakers of a distinctive bell-shaped design and buried their dead in megalithic tombs. From Los Millares, continue travelling on the A-348 down into the **green, fertile terraced countryside** of ▶Alpujarras.

✱ Sierra Alhamilla

Europe's only natural desert The bare hilltops of the Sierra Alhamilla rise to the northeast of Almería up to a height of over 1,500m/5,000ft. Europe's only natural desert can be explored as part of a day trip by car. Buses also go to the western theme towns.

Wild west towns The sandy brown landscape with its sparse vegetation is instantly reminiscent of the southwestern USA. This fact did not escape the attention of some film producers, and in short order the sierra became a location for shooting wild west films, since production costs were

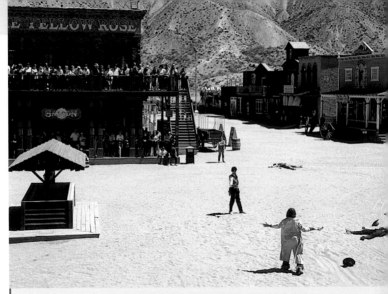

Cowboys, colts, cancan – high-noon and the audience is right there.

considerably cheaper here and there were plenty of potential film extras available. It was not only a host of spaghetti westerns that were filmed here; soon major U.S. productions were also coming to Spain and bringing with them stars like Clint Eastwood, Lee van Cleef and Burt Lancaster. Even scenes from ***Lawrence of Arabia*** (the storming of Aqaba by the Bedouins) and ***Indiana Jones*** were shot here. After film production rolled back, the Western town sets were opened as tourist attractions. The largest and most professional among them is »**Mini Hollywood**« (opening hours: daily 10am–9pm), north of Almería, just after the A-370 forks off from the A-92. Every day a **bank robbery and a gunfight** are played out between the saloon, bank, hotel, jail and gallows, etc., (daily noon, 5pm, June–Sept also 8pm). The can-can is also performed in the saloon (daily 1pm, 4pm, June–Sept, also 7pm), and there is also a parrot show (daily 11am, 3pm, 6pm), a quite respectable zoo, as well as a vintage car and carriage museum. The more modest »Texas Hollywood« is further along the road to Tabernas and, on the A-92 in the direction of Guadix, lies »Western Leone«.

A little way beyond the sleepy village of Tabernaswith the ruins of a Moorish castle enthroned on the hill above it, the A-349 branches off from the A-370 northward towards the solar power facility of the International Energy Agency, IEA (signposted »Plataforma solar«). Some 4km/2.5mi along the road, hundreds of mirrors can be seen to the right, following the course of the sun, focussing the light and reflecting it onto an 80m/260ft-high receiver, where it is transformed into energy.

★
Solar power
plant

Sorbas ✴

Further along the A-370 comes Sorbas, a village known for its red **pottery** with a very lovely and cosy plaza screened by acacias. The eastern edge of Sorbas plummets precipitously down into the Río de Aguas – the houses clinging to the rock at a height of 40m/130ft over the gorge. For cavers, theKarst de Yesos de Sorbas east of Sorbas include a **subterranean labyrinth of caverns**. Natur Sport Sorbas, tel. 950 36 47 04, provide guided tours with the necessary equipment provided.

Karst caves ▶ ✴

Over the Sierra to Níjar ✴

The motorway to Almería has a junction at Sorbas. However, a much more attractive return drive follows the A-370 back another 9km/ 5.5mi and then the AL-102 across the Sierra. A narrow, winding stretch, but amid **stunning scenery** that leads through the former mining village of Lucainena de las Torres , where some old ore-smelting furnaces can still be seen. The road finally ends up in **Níjar**, high above the sea of plastic that covers the plains of Almería. The village is widely known for its **pottery and woven carpets** offered for sale in many shops along the main road. The small plaza with the village church is at the highest point of the village.

Sierra de los Filabres

During the drive along the A-370, the Sierra de los Filabres mountain range is constantly visible to the north. There, atop the 2168m/ 7113ft **Calar Alto** are the five domes of the German-Spanish **observatory, the largest of its kind in Europe**. The clear air at that high altitude allows a clear view of the starry cosmos virtually all year round, but only for the astronomers. Normal tourists can nevertheless enjoy the **fantastic view** of the mountains and coastline.

Almuñécar · Costa Tropical

H 8

Province: Granada
Population: 21,500

Altitude: 24m/79ft

Almuñécar is the chief city on the Costa Tropical, as the stretch of the Costa del Sol that lies within the province of Granada has come to be called in recent years. Here, the »sun coast« is still at its most beautiful and natural. Architectural eyesores like those on the coastline around ▶ Málaga have been avoided for the most part until now.

Capital of the Costa Tropical

Sugar cane, avocados and mangos thrive in this precipitous coastal landscape with its almost tropical climate and the cultivation and processing of these crops, along with tourism, form the major sources of income for the population. As is the case with many places along the Costa del Sol, Almuñécar was also founded by the Phoenicians (Sexi). The town has a very important place in the history of

▶ VISITING ALMUÑÉCAR • COSTA TROPICAL

**INFORMATION
(OFICINA DE TURISMO)**
Palacete de la Najarra, Avda. de
Europa, s/n, E-18690 Almuñécar
Tel. 958 63 11 25, fax 958 63 50 07
www.almunecar.info

WHERE TO EAT
▶ **Moderate**
Horno de Cándida
Orovia, 3
Tel. 958 63 46 07
A real bargain! The restaurant belongs
to the school of hotel management
and is situated in an old bakery in the
old part of town. It offers exquisite
cooking at very reasonable prices.

▶ **Inexpensive**
Boto's
Playa San Cristóbal
Tel. 958 63 30 79
Restaurant on the beach.

WHERE TO STAY
▶ **Budget**
Casablanca
Plaza San Cristóbal, 4
Tel. 958 63 55 75
Fax 958 63 55 89, 35 rooms
The fancifully Moorish-looking hotel
with its large balcony is very conven-
iently situated across from Playa de
San Cristóbal in the vicinity of the
ornithological and botanical gardens.

Helios
Paseo San Cristóbal, s/n
Tel. 958 63 44 59
Fax 958 63 44 69
The hotel is on the sea and features
comfortable rooms and a pool.

EVENTS
Jazz en la Costa
Two-week jazz festival in mid-July.

Andalusia – it was here that Abd ar-Rahman I, the **founder of the Emirate and later Caliphate of Córdoba**, landed in 755 after his flight from Damascus.

What to See in Almuñécar

The remains of a Moorish castle built on Roman foundations are, as always, impressive. It was captured by the Christians in 1489, ex-panded in the 16th century and in 1808 suffered major damage at the hands of Napoleon's soldiers. A tour leads through the baths, cis-terns, the remains of the Nasrid palace and to the city museum (opening hours: Tue–Sat 10.30am–1.30pm, 6.30–9pm, Sun 10.30am–2pm).

Castillo de San Miguel

Not far from the castle is the archaeological museum in the **»Cave of the Seven Palaces«**, a multi-chambered, vaulted complex of Roman origin. Along with burial objects from the necropolis of the city, the Egyptian urn of Pharaoh Apophis I (16th century BC) is a valuable rarity (for opening hours see Castillo).

★ **Cuevas de Siete Palacios**

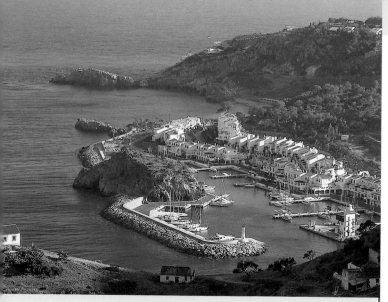

Almuñécar is the chief city of the steep coastal landscape of Costa Tropical.

Parque Ornitológico A number of tropical birds are housed below the castle in a shady bird park (opening hours: daily 11am–2pm, 5pm–7pm).

Parque del Majuelo Close to the ornithological park in the Parque del Majuelo botanical gardens there are also remains of a Phoenician fish factory from the 5th century BC that was famous in antiquity for its »garum«, a fish paste widely used as a condiment.

Beaches The Peñon del Santo projects out into the sea and beaches stretch out on either side of it, the most beautiful being Playa de San Cristóbal, west of the rock.

Around Almuñécar

La Herradura West of Almuñecar lies the crescent-shaped bay of La Herradura, sheltered by the rocky promontories of Cerro Gordo and La Punta de la Mona. A **mountain road offering one fabulous view after the other** winds its way to Marina del Este, where there is a pebble beach that is a meeting place for many scuba divers. A small yachting marina has also been established there.

Salobreña 14km/9mi to the east along the coast road is the resort of Salobreña, picturesquely set on a mountainside and dominated by a Nasrid castle. It is popular with the residents of Granada who like to meet in the beach restaurants Casa Emilio and El Peñon on Sundays for some tasty fish dishes.

Motril follows just a few miles further to the east. It is worth seeing the churches of La Encarnación and Nuestra Señora de la Cabeza. The latter stands in the ruins of a Moorish castle that was home to the mother of Boabdil, the last king of Granada. The sugar cane processing plant Nuestra Señora del Pilar with its fully preserved steam engines, and which was in operation until 1994, is **Andalusia's most important industrial monument**.

Motril

Passing through La Calahonda, a fishing village transformed into a resort with fantastic beaches, the road eventually reaches Castell de Ferro, dominated by a Moorish tower. The village lives from fishing, vegetable cultivation and, in the summer thanks to its long beaches, also increasingly from tourism.

Castell de Ferro

✳ Las Alpujarras

Province: Granada, Almería

The Alpujarras, lying south of ► Granada and the ► Sierra Nevada boast a mountain landscape stretching across the provinces of Granada and Almería that is occasionally barren but nonetheless thrilling and is blessed with a marvellous climate.

The Berbers settled here as early as the 8th century and built up a lucrative silk industry in the 10th and 11th centuries. After losing Granada in 1492, all of the Moors withdrew to remote villages until they were finally driven out in 1568 after several bloody revolts. A couple of families, though, were forced to stay by the new Christian settlers to maintain the **cleverly devised irrigation systems and terrace gardens**, in which grain, olives, citrus fruits and vegetables grew and which are still farmed to this day. The low-ceilinged stone houses of the Alpujarras with their cylindrical chimneys are typical of Moorish architecture. The houses are first covered with wooden laths and reed mats, then by flat stone slabs. A mass of grey clay is then spread over them providing them with a waterproof, all-purpose terrace. The Alpujarras were rediscovered by writers and hikers at the

Typical stone house architecture in the Alpujarras

▶ VISITING LAS ALPUJARRAS

INFORMATION (OFICINA DE TURISMO NEVADENSIS)

In Pampaneira, C. Verónica, Plaza de la Libertad
Tel. 958 76 31 27
This is the place for information about hiking trails through the mountains. They can also arrange for guides for treks, excursions on horseback and climbing tours.

WHERE TO EAT

► Moderate
La Fragua
In Trevélez, San Antonio, 4
Tel. 958 85 86 26
www.hotellafragua.com
Pork specialties are of course served in this restaurant in a village famous for its ham, but tasty lamb dishes feature on the menu as well.

► Inexpensive
Ibero
In Capileira, Parra, 1
Tel. 958 76 34 13
Family run hotel with low-priced traditional fare.

WHERE TO STAY

► Budget
Villa Turística de Bubión
In Bubión, Barrio Alto, s / n
Tel. 958 76 39 09
Fax 958 76 39 05, 136 rooms
This hotel combines a traditional Alpujarras style of living with modern amenities. The owner offers an attractive tour and recreation program.

Las Terrazas
Plaza del Sol, 7
Tel. 958 76 30 34
Fax 958 76 32 52
Simple hotel with three terraces and mountain panorama; bicycle hire.

Finca Los Llanos
In Capileira, Ctra. de Sierra Nevada
Tel. 958 76 30 71
Pleasant hotel on the edge of town.

Alcazaba de Busquistar
In Laujar, Crta. Orgiva-Laujar
Tel. 958 85 86 87
Fax 958 85 86 93
Featuring large, farmhouse-style furnished rooms, pool; pony hire.

---

beginning of the 20th century and the book **South from Granada** by the British writer Gerald Brenan was instrumental in making them known to a wider public.

Drive through the Alpujarras

Lanjarón Head south from ►Granada, initially along the N-323. After 39km/ 24mi, the A-348 branches off to Lanjarón, a mountain health resort where **one of Spain's best-known mineral springs** bubbles up to the surface.

Valle del Poqueira From there, a narrow, winding road branches off after Lanjarón at Órgiva and descends deep into the Valle del Poqueira. Three **char-**

The Alpujurras near Bubión with a mountain panorama and picturesque villages suitable for the movies

ming villages are lined up here in the shadow of the Veleta, any one of which is a good starting point for hikes. Many **weaving mills** producing colourful blankets and rugs (»jarapas«) are sited here too. On the edge of the **mighty Poqueira gorge** lies Pampaneira with its delightful Plaza de la Libertad, where the tourist office has detailed hiking maps at the ready. At the parish church in Bubión there is an Alpujarran house on display furnished with numerous objects typical of the region (Casa Alpujarreña; opening hours: Mon, Wed–Fri 10am–2pm, Sat, Sun 11am–2pm, 5–7pm). Above Bubión is Capileira, at an altitude of 1436m/4711ft, it is the highest altitude village in the Valle del Poqueira region. It even has a museum of popular art. The

◀ Pampaneira

◀ Bubión and
Capileira
🕐

The GR-421 climbs through Pitres, Pórtugos and picturesquely nestling Busquístar up to an altitude of 1476m/4842ft to **Trevélez**, the **highest village in Spain**. Some of the best ham in the country is produced in the shadow of the giant Sierra Nevada mountains – on sale in more than just a few stores.

> ## ❗ *Baedeker* TIP
>
> ### Online in the mountains
> For a pleasant break, try Café Morisco's invitingly secluded garden terrace in Bubión. They even have internet access there for sending e-mails to loved ones at home.

The A-348 can be reached again near Narila and the road then leads on to Yegen. A plaque there marks the house where **Gerald Brenan** lived from 1920 to 1934 and wrote about the life of the villagers in

Yegen

his book *South from Granada*. The A-348 meets the A-347 about 25km/16mi beyond Yegen. It travels southward through Berja down to the coast.

La Alpujarra almeriense

Going north, the road gradually gains height via some sweeping hairpin bends and crosses the »Alpujarra almeriense«. The main town in the region is **Laujar de Andarax**, at one end of which is the source of the Río Andarax. Other sights to be seen include the remains of an alcazaba and the La Encarnación Church, built on the ruins of a mosque burned down during the Moriscan uprising. After his defeat of 1492, the last Moorish king, **Boabdil**, is said to have settled here initially, but he was soon forced to move on to Morocco. From Laujar de Andarax the road mostly follows a route high above the valley of Río Andarax, from Ohanes through a **delightful terraced landscape** and through villages in wonderful settings to the thermal spa of Alhama de Almería. From there, it is another 30km/19mi to ▶Almería.

Andújar

G 5

Province: Jaén
Population: 35,800

Altitude: 211m/692ft

The town of Andújar, located in the north of the province of Jaén on the right bank of the Guadalquivir, is the centre of Andalusian olive oil production and known for its earthenware, »alcarrazas« or »jarras«, that feature motifs of flowers or shapes of grotesque figures. Fighting bulls are also bred here.

History

Not far from the present town, near Los Villares, there was once an ancient Iberian settlement called Illiturgi, the actual origin of Andújar. The Moors set up strong fortifications around Andújar and after the Christians conquered it in the 13th century, they made it their first outpost in Andalusia.

What to See in and around Andújar

Plaza de España

At the peaceful centre of the town is Plaza de España that is separated into two parts by a yellow and white painted gatehouse. Around it there are some pretty houses, the town hall and the church of San Miguel, which has some beautiful carvings inside.

Santa María la Mayor

Andújar's most important attraction is the church of Santa María la Mayor, slightly to the north of the plaza. It is a Renaissance building with a Plateresque façade that is somewhat plain but does contain two valuable masterpieces; *Christ on the Mount of Olives* by **El Greco** in the second chapel off the left-hand aisle and the *The Immaculate Conception* by Pacheco. A choir screen by Master Bartolomé and a manuscript by Juan de la Cruz are also among its treasures. The Mudejar bell tower is not attached to the church, which may support a theory that it was fashioned out of the minaret of a former mosque. The **Parque Natural Sierra de Andújar** spreads out to the north and east of Andújar, an unspoiled piece of **nature amid the wild and romantic Sierra Morena**. The Río Jándula runs through it and opens up into two lakes. Wandering through the oak and pine forests are fallow deer, wild boar, lynx and even wolves. Eagles and vultures still nest in the most remote areas. A good starting place for a hiking tour is the village of **Las Vinas**, 15km/9mi northeast of Andújar, where there is a visitor centre (main office in Andújar, Cercado de Ciprés, Tel. 953 50 02 79). Amidst the **quiet solitude of the mountains** lies the Santuario de la Virgen de la Cabeza, which venerates a martyress said to have been sent to »Illiturgi« by Saint Peter. This veneration peaks during the pilgrimage on the last Sunday in April. According to legend, the virgin is said to have appeared to a shepherd in 1227 and ten years later the construction of the chapel began. The former Gothic church was totally destroyed in the Spanish Civil War and rebuilt afterwards. From these heights there is an **awe-inspiring panoramic view**.

ANDÚJAR

INFORMATION (OFICINA DE TURISMO)

Ayuntamiento, Plaza de España, 1,
E-23750 Andújar
Tel. 953 50 82 00, fax 953 50 82 07

EVENTS

Romería de Nuestra Señora de la Cabeza

On the last Sunday in April many pilgrims make a pilgrimage to the shrine of Andújar's patron; along the way there are many fabulous views of the countryside.

✳
◄ Santuario de la Virgen de la Cabeza

✳ Antequera

F 7

Province: Málaga
Population: 40,200

Altitude: 577m/1893ft

Antequera is the main town on the plateau of the same name where the Río Guadalhorce has its source and lies between the rugged Sierra del Torcal and areas dominated by agriculture.

Even though Antequera's architecture may create a somewhat random impression, there are a surprising number of Renaissance and Baroque churches in the old town, often mixed with Mudejar elements. This and the evidence of prehistoric settlement make Ante-

Churches and megalithic tombs

Antequera lies with its proud Moorish castle at the foot of the Sierra del Torcal.

quera a very worthwhile place to visit, although it remains largely devoid of tourists. The burial chambers in the immediate locale are evidence that there were once megalithic settlements there. Under the Romans it was called Anticaria and was of quite some importance, but it was the Moors who built the site up into a great fortress until it was captured in 1410 by Ferdinand »of Antequera«, king of Aragon.

What to See in Antequera

Alcazaba The 14th-century alcazaba, thought to have been built on top of a Roman fort, towers atop a hill overlooking the eastern part of town. The entrance is through the Arco de los Gigantes, erected in 1585 to honour Philip II and adorned with the town's coat of arms. Two sections of wall and the great Torre de Papabellotas with its Baroque topping have survived from the castle.The church of Santa María la Mayor was built within the fortress in the 16th century. It is a Plateresque church with a Renaissance façade that imitates a Roman triumphal arch, while the interior was finished off with a Mudejar artesonado ceiling. Next to it, the remains of a Roman baths have been excavated. The castle garden offers a beautiful view of the **Peña de los Enamorados**, »Lovers' Rock«, with its distinctive profile that is reminiscent of a Red Indian. Its name is derived from a legend about the daughter of a Moslem city governor and her Christian lover who threw themselves from there to their death when her parents would not agree to a marriage.

★
Real Colegiata de Santa María la Mayor ▶

▶ VISITING ANTEQUERA

INFORMATION (OFICINA DE TURISMO)

C. Infante Don Fernando, 90, Edificio San Luis, E-29200 Antequera
Tel. / fax 952 70 81 34 / 35
Plaza de San Sebastián, 7
Tel. / fax 952 70 25 05
www.aytoantequera.com

WHERE TO EAT

▶ Moderate

La Espuela
Plaza de Toros
Tel. 952 70 34 24
The specialty of the restaurant in the bullfight arena is, of course, oxtail ragout.

Noelia
Alameda de Andalucía, 12
Tel. 952 84 54 07
Refined Mediterranean and regional cuisine.

WHERE TO STAY

▶ Budget

Parador de Antequera
Paseo García del Olmo
Tel. 952 84 02 61
Fax 952 84 13 12
E-mail: antequera@parador.es
www.parador.es, 55 roomsModern, but very pleasant and inexpensive parador for a stopover, lovely garden.

Nuevo Infante
Infante Don Fernando, 5
Tel. 952 70 02 93
Fax 952 70 00 86, 18 rooms
Small, reasonably-priced hotel, quite centrally located beneath the castle.

EVENTS

Real Feria de Agosto
Harvest festival in August with bullfighting and fair.

The 17th century church, El Carmen, can be reached by leaving the fortress and turning to the right, then bearing left and right again. It was built between 1583 and 1633 and was once part of a Carmelite convent. The simple façade is in contrast to the Baroque interior and the Churrigueresque wooden retable of red pinewood bearing scenes carved by Antonio Primo.

Nuestra Señora del Carmen

From the Arco de los Gigantes head downhill to the left through the Cuesta de Judas to Plaza San Sebastián with its fountains. Here stands an 18th-century brick church of the same name. The nave dates to the 16th century; the main façade is richly decorated in the Plateresque style. Backed against it is the whitewashed **Iglesia de la Encarnación** dating from the 16th century with its beautiful artesonado ceiling.

San Sebastián

From San Sebastián, C. Encarnación descends slightly to a plaza that opens up to the right and includes the Baroque Palacio Nájera, which contains the municipal museum. Standing out among the objects on display are the marble head of the Venus of Antequera and a

Museo Municipal

bronze ephebe, a Roman copy of a Greek original from the 1st century AD (opening hours: Tue–Fri 10am–1.30pm, 4–6pm, Sat 10am–1.30pm, Sun 11am–1.30pm).

Museo Conventual de las Descalzas

This museum is on the plaza of the same name housed within the convent of the Discalced Carmelite nuns and dedicated to **sacred art**. Among the art works that are particularly worth seeing are the sculptures by Pedro de Mena and Pedro de Roldàn, as well as a painting of St Theresa by Luca Giordano (opening hours: Tue–Fri 10.30am–2pm, 5–7pm, Sat, Sun 10am–12.30pm).

Palacio Consistorial

C. Infante Don Fernando, the main shopping street of the city, begins at Plaza de San Sebastián. On the right hand toward its northeastern end lies the Palacio Consistorial with its gorgeous inner courtyard, formerly a monastery cloister, with columns made of marble from the Sierra del Torcal. Adjacent to the palace is the church of **Nuestra Señora de Los Remedios**. It contains a magnificent retable by Antonio Ribera.

More churches

The Iglesia San Zoilo (Plaza de Abastos) belongs to the monastery complex founded by the Catholic Monarchs. The late Gothic church has a wooden Mudejar ceiling and elaborate plaster work was added in the 17th century. The inside of the Iglesia de Belén (1628–1709; C. Belén) is a prime example of the exuberance of Andalusian Baroque.

★★ Dólmenes de Antequera

With the megalithic tombs of Cueva de Menga, Viera and El Romeral, Antequera possesses three prehistoric grave sites that are among the **best preserved and most impressive of their kind** (opening hours: Tue 9am–3.30pm, Wed–Sat 9am–6pm, Sun 9.30am–2.30pm). The **Cueva de Menga and Cueva de Viera** passage graves are built right into the hill. The entrance is on the left-hand side, right next to a petrol station on the main road leading out of town toward Granada. The first grave has been dated to be from the 3rd millennium BC and is aligned to the course of the sun on an east-west axis. The whole grave has a total length of 25m/82ft and is up to 3m/10ft high. A passage supported by three pillars opens up into the oval burial chamber that consists of 15 megalith blocks. These blocks support immense stone slabs, one of

Prehistoric passage graves

The work of millennia – the fissured stone formations of El Torcal

which is thought to weigh 180t. One of the blocks of the left-hand wall has symbol-like drawings on it. The Cueva de Viera dates back to about the same time but is considerably smaller. A passage formed by stone slabs leads to an almost cubical burial chamber. The **Cueva del Romeral** can be found by travelling a little further from the town in the direction of Granada as far as the N-331 junction and then turning left toward Córdoba. It is also from the 3rd millennium BC and consists of a 24m/80ft passage leading to two chambers.

Around Antequera

About 10km/6mi south of Antequera on the C-3310 in the direction of Villanueva de la Concepción is the entrance to the El Torcal Nature Reserve (information centre opening hours: daily 10am–5pm). The jagged mountains are a **fantastic karst mountainscape** that the processes of upfolding, storm and rain have created out of the porous limestone over the course of millennia. Currently only one (green) marked hiking trail covering a distance of 1.5km/1mi and lasting about 45 minutes leads through the area.

✸ ✸
Parque Natural de El Torcal
🕐

Southwest of the Torcal mountains, the Río Guadalhorce slices from the north down through the mountain range in a 3km/2mi-long gorge that is up to 400m/1300ft deep. This **spectacular rocky land-**

✸
Garganta del Chorro

scape, the Garganta del Chorro, otherwise known as the Desfiladero de los Gaitanes, is a big attraction to hikers and climbers. North of the gorge, the river has been dammed to create four reservoirs; the most beautiful of them being the Gaitanejo reservoir. Griffon vultures and the occasional golden eagle also make their homes in the gorge. A good starting point for any exploration is El Chorro railway station (trains to and from ▶ Málaga), which can be reached from Antequera via the A-343 and MA-226. It is not advisable to try crossing over the gorge because the only route, the so-called Caminito del Rey, a stomach-churning walkway built at a dizzying height into the rock wall, has partially collapsed and is officially closed. Sneaking through the train tunnel in the gorge is illegal and yet still popular. A section of the gorge can be accessed from the El Chorro camp site. A hike around the reservoir lakes affords some **good views of the gorge** and it is also possible to look down into the gorge from the higher altitude of the Tajo de la Encantada that can be reached via Bobastro. There is an information centre at the southern end of the Guadalteba-Guadalhorce reservoir that offers further information (opening hours: daily 9am–8pm). The **ruins of Bobastro** (narrow road out of El Chorro) are evidence of a Mozarabic hill fort constructed in the 9th century by the rebel Ibn Hafsun, who had converted to Christianity. This was his headquarters during his resistance against the Umayyad and he had himself buried in the church there when he died in 917. Abd-ar Rahman III captured Bobastro in 927 and had the whole place destroyed.

Laguna de la Fuente de Piedra

Laguna de la Fuente de Piedra, near the village of the same name 18km/11mi northwest of Antequera, is **one of the last major breeding grounds for pink flamingos in Europe**. The birds gather in their thousands in spring on this salt lake that covers 13,000 ha/50 sq mi and stay to raise their young until August/September. The lagoon itself is fenced in, but there is a 20km/12mi path leading around the lake that provides observation points at regular intervals (bring binoculars). Besides flamingos, it is also possible to catch sight of Kentish plovers, black-winged stilts, cranes, gull-billed terns, storks, herons and perhaps even an osprey (information centre on the northeast corner of the lake, opening hours: Tue–Sun 10am–2pm, 4–8pm, Oct–March 4–6pm).

Archidona

Archidona, 15km/9mi northeast of Antequera, served the Carthaginians as a base during the Punic wars. A must to visit is the **Ermita de la Virgen de Gracia** with its lovely view of the surrounding countryside. It was once a mosque that was remodelled into a church at the end of the 15th century and possesses a baptismal font that was a gift from Isabella the Catholic. The centrepiece of town is the unusual octagonal Plaza Ochavada that was laid out in the 18th century by Francisco Astorga and Antonio González following a French model.

✶ Aracena

Province: Huelva
Population: 6,300

Altitude: 732m/2402ft

The mountain village of Aracena nestles in the midst of olive trees, fig and almond orchards amid the Sierra de Aracena at the extreme northwest tip of Andalusia.

Due to its climate, Aracena is a popular climatic spa. Local artisans typically create pottery but the processing of cork also provides many here with a livelihood. Sculptures from contemporary Andalusian artists are displayed everywhere throughout the centre of village.

Climatic health resort

 VISITING ARACENA

INFORMATION (OFICINA DE TURISMO)

Plaza de San Pedro, s/n
E-21200 Aracena
Tel./fax 959 12 82 06

Centro de Interpretación del Parque Natural
Plaza Alta
www.sierradearacena.org
Information is available about the Sierra de Aracena y Picos de Aroche nature reserve half-way up to the fortress.

WHERE TO EAT

► Moderate
La Despensa de José Vicente
Avda. Andalucía, 53
Tel. 959 12 84 55
This restaurant is considered one of the best in town.

Montecruz
Plaza San Pedro
Tel. 959 12 60 13
The speciality of the house is dishes of wild game. A nice view of the castle can be had from the upper room of the restaurant.

WHERE TO STAY

► Mid-range
Finca Valbono
Crta. Carboneras, km 1
Tel. 959 12 77 11
Fax 959 12 76 79
The ideal place for a holiday in the country. This finca outside the town offers holiday cottages and a hotel with five rooms and 20 apartments, including sports facilities, a pool and a riding stable.

► Budget
Los Castaños
Avenida de Huelva, 5
Tel. 959 12 63 00
Fax 959 12 62 87
A hotel located near the caves with a restaurant and a nice view.

EVENTS

Feria de Agosto
Music, dancing, bullfighting and fireworks in the third week of August.

Romería de Nuestra Señora de los Angeles
Pilgrimage around 7–9 September.

The jewel of Spanish gastronomy – the Jabugo ham (jamón ibérico)

History The Romans were already taking an interest in the natural resources of this area in the first century. In the Middle Ages, Sancho of Portugal took the town from the Moors, but was forced to relinquish it to Castile in 1267. Alfonso X turned over Aracena to the Knights Templar, who erected a castle. Only the ruins of it remain today.

What to See in Aracena

Iglesia del Castillo On the castle hill amidst the ruins stands the late Gothic Iglesia del Castillo (Nuestra Señora de los Dolores), a Knights Templar church. It was built upon a mosque and the plinth of the minaret (12th century) today supports the bell tower. There is a terracotta tomb inside the church from the 16th century where the prior Pedro Vázquez is buried.

Cabildo Viejo On Plaza Alta beneath the castle is a 15th-century storehouse, the Cabildo Viejo, that houses an exhibition about the region as well as the tourist office. Taking pride of place opposite is the Iglesia Nuestra Señora de la Asunción that dates back to the 16 and 17th centuries.

Gruta de las Maravillas ✳ The Gruta de las Maravillas extends over 1200m/4000ft inside the castle hill; an **absolutely beautiful limestone cave with stalactites and stalagmites** featuring twelve chambers and six lakes, in which the stone and crystal formations are reflected in glorious colours. The entrance to the cave can be found together with a modest mineral museum at the Ermita de San Pedro (tours daily: 10.30am– 1.30pm, 3–6pm).

The convent of Santa Catalina, the church of which was once a synagogue, is attractive because of its portal and late Gothic interior.

Convento de Santa Catalina

Around Aracena

Although Jabugo, 16km/10mi west of Aracena, possesses no tourist attractions, it is known far beyond Spain's borders. It is the **centre of the ham industry** , where the delicious air-cured hams that bear the name »pata negra« are produced from the semi-wild pigs living in the oak forests of the Sierra. Although the countryside round about Jabugo was declared a national park in 1989 (Parque Natural de la Sierra de Aracena y Picos de Aroche), most of the area is in private hands and is off-limits to hikers.

Jabugo

Almonaster la Real lies 27km/17mi west of Aracena. The **castle complex is of Moslem origin** and includes a mosque from the 10th century, which has integrated the remains of an earlier Visigoth structure, such as the lintel in the entrance area. It is noticeable that the church of San Martín includes some typical elements of the Manueline style of nearby Portugal; columns twisted like strands of rope and ornamentation richly decorated with shells and crabs. For a splendid view of the Sierra and the village, go to Mirador de San Cristóbal (outside the eastern entrance to the village).

Almonaster la Real

Located 42km/26mi west of Aracena is **Aroche**. It was »Aruci Vetus« in Roman times. The Moors built a defensive wall on the Roman foundations. The Castillo de las Armas, also dating back to that time, has an inner court that serves as a bullfighting ring and houses an archaeological museum. For something more curious, visit the **Museo de Rosario** at the entrance to the village. It has 1,300 rosaries on display.

The mining district of Río Tinto begins south of Aracena, a desolate, scarred landscape, barren of vegetation. The Río Tinto river lives up to its name in that it really is tainted red from the eroding ore. Río Tinto and Nerva are the main centres of the copper mining district that was mined as early as Iberian and Roman times. From 1873 to

Río Tinto copper mines

Copper and iron colour the Rio Tinto red – but the goats don't care.

1954 it belonged to the British Río Tinto mining company. A great deal can be learned about its history in the **Museo Minero**. The main attraction is a reconstruction of a Roman mine and a luxurious railway carriage that belonged to a maharajah, although it was originally built for Queen Victoria in 1892 in Birmingham on the occasion of a royal visit to India. It was transported to Río Tinto for a visit by Alfonso XIII. On the edge of town is the Barrio Bellavista with its Victorian houses and a Presbyterian cemetery and church built for the British employees of the mining company. Two miles north of Río Tinto is a Roman burial site, the **Necrópolis de la Dehesa** from the 2nd century, that is open for tours. At the giant Parque Minero it is possible to see at how ore was mined up until the end of 2001. Two **railway excursions** of various lengths travel along the Río Tinto in Victorian cars to Corte Atalaya, which is **Europe's largest opencast mine** and descends to a depth of 330m/1100ft (information and tickets at the ticket office in the Museo Minero; opening hours: daily 10am–3pm, 4–6pm).

Parque Minero near Aracena ►

✳ Arcos de la Frontera

D 8

Province: Cádiz
Population: 27,900

Altitude: 185m/607ft

Arcos is without a doubt one of Andalusia's most beautiful »white villages«. To find out why, just take a walk through the maze of steep, winding lanes in the old part of town, the layout of which is obviously Moorish.

Classic example of a white village

For the best view of Arcos de la Frontera, approach it from the east. Houses like little white cubes cling in a semi-circle to the rock wall **160m/525ft above the Río Guadalete**, and out of the tangle of houses jut the towers of the main churches.

History

The Carthaginians and later the Romans, who called their settlement Colonia Arcensis, made use of the strategic location on the top of

► VISITING ARCOS DE LA FRONTERA

**INFORMATION
(OFICINA DE TURISMO)**
Plaza del Cabildo s/n
E-11630 Arcos de la Frontera
Tel. 956 70 22 64
Fax 956 70 09 00
www.ayuntamientoarcos.org

WHERE TO EAT
► Expensive
El Convento
Marqués de Torresoto, 7
Tel. 956 70 32 22
The best restaurant in town has a
delightful patio.

► Inexpensive
Círi de la Unión
Boticas, 6
Tel. 956 70 31 07
Plain, inexpensive, regional fare.

WHERE TO STAY
► Moderate
Parador de Arcos
Plaza del Cabildo
Tel. 956 70 05 00
Fax 956 70 11 16
E-mail: arcos@parador.es
www.parador.es, 24 rooms
A stylistically authentic recon-
struction of the Casa del
Corregidor offering a wonderful
view of the old town.

► Budget
Cortijo Faín
Crta. Arcos – Algar, km 3
Tel. 956 23 13 96
Fax 956 23 19 61,
10 rooms
Elegant 17th-century Andalusian
country house with plenty of style,
surrounded by olive trees and bou-
gainvilleas.

La Casa Grande
C. Maldonada, 10
Tel. 956 70 39 30
www.lacasagrande.net
Family hotel in the old part of town
with a view as fine as that from the
parador.

Parador de Arcos
Plaza del Cabildo
Tel. 956 70 05 00
Fax 956 70 11 16
E-mail: arcos@parador.es
www.parador.es, 24 rooms
A faithful reconstruction of the
Casa del Corregidor offering a
wonderful view of the old
town.

Baedeker recommendation

► Budget
Marqués de Torresoto
Marqués de Torresoto, 4
Tel. 956 70 42 56
Fax 956 70 42 05, 15 rooms
The former palace of the Marqués
de Torresoto, dating from the 17th
century, offers reserved, stylish rooms
and an unforgettable breakfast in the
patio arcade.

EVENTS
Semana Santa
With a bull run on the open streets on
Easter Sunday.

Feria de San Miguel
Dance competition and
bullfighting in honour of the
town's patron saint on
29 September.

Arcos de la Frontera towers up high on the north slope of the river Guadalete.

the rocks to keep a watch over wide swathes of the countryside. As of the 11th century the town was called Medina Arkosh and had become the capital of a taifa. After 1250, the town came to be called Arcos and was part of Ferdinand III's Christian kingdom; but the population remain Moslem until 1264 when, under Alfonso X, they were driven out after a revolt against Christian domination.

What to See in Arcos de la Frontera

Plaza del Cabildo

Plaza del Cabildo is the town's highest point and at the same time the centre of the old part of town. The observation terrace on the plaza offers a **breathtaking view of the landscape far below**. The town hall stands at the southwest corner alongside a castle of Arab origin that was completely rebuilt in the 15th century (now under private ownership). The Casa del Corregidor opposite, a 16th-century magistrate's residence, is now given over to Arcos' own parador, and to the right of the entrance is its bar offering a splendid view.

Santa María de la Asunción ►

The most impressive building on the plaza is the Basilica Menor de Santa María de la Asunción with its massive square tower that soars above all the neighbouring buildings. The tower and the portal zone were created in Baroque, whereas the nave is primarily 16th-century work that replaced an earlier church, which was itself erected on the foundation of the original Friday mosque. The finely worked west portal is a **splendid example of the Plateresque style** of the 16th century. In the sanctuary, take a look at the late Gothic fan vault as well as the 17th-century high altar retable with the theme of Mary's assumption. The oldest part of the structure is the apse behind it with elements in the Mudejar style. In the second chapel to the right stands a statue of the town's patron, the »Virgen de las Nieves«.

San Pedro

Santa María's neighbour, San Pedro, was built on the remains of a Moorish fortress. The members of both communities spent decades feuding with each other in a most unchristian manner. The squabble was only settled by a papal dictum in the 18th century. The late Gothic interior holds a fine high altar retable from the 16th century and shows Saints Peter and Jerome. Saint Ignatius and the Virgin Mary are to the left and right of them, as depicted by Francisco Pacheco, the tutor of Diego Velázquez.

A walk through the old town reveals several aristocratic palaces from the 16th and 17th centuries including the Renaissance façade of the Palacio de Mayorazgo right next to the church of San Pedro, the Convento de la Encarnación with its Plateresque portal and the Palacio del Marqués de Torresoto which has a patio in the street of the same name. The Gothic-Mudejar façade of the Palacio del Conde de Aguila from the 15th century in the Cuesta de Belén is the oldest in the town. **Old town**

Around Arcos de la Frontera

Bornos, about 10km/6mi northeast of Arcos alongside the reservoir of the same name, grew around a Moorish castle that gained its current appearance primarily in the 15th and 16th centuries. The church of Santo Domingo de Guzmán with its late Gothic and Baroque features is also worth seeing. Beyond the town centre are the remains of the Roman settlement »Clarissa Aurelia«. The CA-402 leads from Bornos to **Espera**, where there is a very well-preserved Moorish castle. **Bornos**

Villamartín, 9km/5.5mi east of Bornos, was spaciously laid-out in the 16th century with churches and palaces of nobles. That there were settlements here already in prehistoric times is shown by the dolmen of Alberite, 4km/2.5mi south of the village, dated at around **4000 BC**. **Villamartín**

✳ ✳ Baeza · Úbeda

I 5/6

Province: Jaén

Almost hidden in the northeast of Andalusia and some miles apart, two architectural pearls of the Renaissance slumber practically untouched by mainstream tourism: the towns of Baeza and Úbeda. The drive there is certainly worthwhile because the once prosperous citizens had magnificent palaces built for themselves that have survived almost unchanged, creating a unique, wholly Renaissance townscape. The architect Andrés de Vandelvira was especially active in this region.

Baeza

Altitude: 790m/2592ft

Population: 17,700

History

The Visigoths expanded the former Roman settlement Beatia to the extent that it became a bishopric. Under the Moors it was for some time the capital of a taifa, until Ferdinand III entered it victorious in 1227 and made the place **one of the most important bases for the Reconquista of Andalusia**. Baeza gained a university in 1542. Its first rector was Juan de Ávila, and Juan de la Cruz also worked there. Baeza experienced its greatest flowering in the 16th century when it was a border town and trading centre between Mancha in Castile and Andalusia.

! *Baedeker* TIP

Oil, oil, everywhere

Baeza is one of the main centres of east Andalusian olive oil production. Oil from the region can be purchased in the Casa del Aceite (Paseo de la Constitución, 9). How it is produced, what can be made from it and the cultural history of the olive tree are all told in the Museo de la Cultura del Olivo in the Hacienda de la Laguna. A pleasant hotel and a restaurant also belong to this 17th-century country estate in which, naturally, almost everything is prepared with olive oil. To get there take the A-316 toward Jaén, turn right after about 9km/5.5mi beyond Puente del Otopo and drive about another 2km/1.5mi (museum opening hours: Tue–Sun: summer 10.30am–1.30pm, 4.30–7pm; winter 10.30am–2pm, 4–6.30pm; hotel information: http://rgo.net/lalaguna).

Baeza lies surrounded by fields of olives and grain and by vineyards high above the valley of the Río Guadalquivir. The **Plaza del Pópulo**, Baeza's meeting place and the site of its most beautiful Renaissance ensemble, can be seen on the right directly at the edge of the old town. The **Fuente de los Leones** fountain in its centre is adorned with four lion figures from the Roman ruins of Cástulo near Linares and an Iberian-Roman statue of a woman. She is said to represent Imilce of Castillo, the wife of the Carthaginian general Hannibal.

✳ Antigua Carnicería ▶

The Antigua Carnicería stretches away to the left of the fountain. The former meat market was built in the middle of the 16th century and is now an historical archive. In today's terms, its **features are astounding** for a building with such a mundane purpose. It has a gallery and an unusually large and magnificent coat of arms belonging to Charles V.

✳ Casa del Pópulo ▶

The Plateresque Casa del Pópulo on the east side of the plaza is by no means overshadowed by the meat market in terms of beauty. Behind the six double doors on the ground floor, chamber clerks once produced documents for the court that sat in session on the upper floor. Today, Baeza's tourist office occupies the building.

Next door to the right of the Casa del Pópulo are the **Puerta de Jaén city gate** and the triumphal arch, the **Arco de Villalar**, that was erected in 1521 to commemorate the crushing of the revolt of the »comuneros«. The »comuneros« were several Castilian cities that had

The elegant Isabellinian façade of the Palacio Jabalquinto

joined together under the leadership of Juan de Padilla and demanded more rights from Emperor Charles V.

Up the steps to the left of Casa del Pópulo and then on further to the left is Plaza Santa Cruz. Almost the whole length of C. Beato Avia along the way to Plaza Santa Cruz is taken up by the front of the **Antigua Universidad**, which was founded as a university in 1542 and converted into a grammar school in 1875. A portal crowned by a medallion depicting the Holy Trinity forms the entrance to the inner court where there stands a simple monument to the poet **Antonio Machado**, who was a French teacher at the school from 1912 to 1919 and died in exile in France in 1939. The **most impressive building on the plaza** is the Palacio de Jabalquinto constructed at the end of the 15th century by Juan Guas and Enrique Egas for the Countess of Jabalquinto and Benavente. The Isabelline façade is without parallel. Its dressed blocks like cut diamonds and its Gothic buttresses are flanked by two large columns that broaden towards the top into small pulpits at the apex, a feature characteristic of Andalusia. The palace encloses a pretty patio and possesses a monumental Baroque stairway. It is worth taking a look at some of the late Gothic frescoes in the late Romanesque **Santa Cruz** church across from the palace that gives the plaza its name. Next to the church is the museum of the Santa Cruz friars whose order was founded in 1540.

Plaza Santa Cruz

✶ ✶
◀ Palacio de
Jabalquinto

🕐
Opening hours:
Tue–Sun
10.30am–1.30pm,
4–6.30pm

▶ VISITING BAEZA

INFORMATION (OFICINA DE TURISMO)

Plaza del Pópulo, s/n, E-23440 Baeza
Tel. / fax 953 74 04 44, www.baeza.net

WHERE TO EAT

▶ Expensive

① *Andrés de Vandelvira*
San Francisco, 14
Tel. 953 74 81 72
The finest regional cuisine is served in the gallery around the cloister of the Iglesia de San Francisco. Baeza's culinary specialty comes from the sea, but dried due to the distance; and is called Bacalao (dried cod) al estilo de Baeza.

▶ Moderate

② *Juanito*
Avda. Arca del Agua, s / n
Tel. 953 74 00 40
www.juanitobaeza.com
The restaurant is known for its authentic Jaén province cooking.

▶ Inexpensive

③ *La Góndola*
Portales de Carbonería, 13
Meat from the grill served beneath the Paseo de la Constitución arcades.

WHERE TO STAY

▶ Budget

① *Confortel Baeza*
Concepción, 3
Tel. 953 74 81 30
Fax 953 74 25 19
Modern hotel with a Renaissance patio.

② *Hospedería Fuentenueva*
Avda. Puche Pardo, 11
Tel. 953 74 31 00
Fax 953 74 32 00
www.fuentenueva.com, 12 rooms
Lovingly decorated, the hotel is in a former women's prison. It also puts on art and craftwork exhibitions.

③ *Juanito*
Avda. Arca del Agua, s / n
Tel. 953 74 00 40
Fax 953 74 23 24
www.juanitobaeza.com, 37 rooms
Family business with a garden terrace on the edge of the city. The cooking in the restaurant is authentic to the Jaén province.

④ *Hostal El Patio*
Conde Romanones, 13
Tel. 953 74 02 00
Small hotel in the old part of town with a combined living area and patio.

EVENTS

Romería del Cristo de la Yedra
On 7 September, music, dance and the friars' parade accompanied by decorated carts and riders on horseback.

Plaza Santa María It is only a few paces from there to Plaza de Santa María, dominated by the cathedral, although a fairly weathered fountain in the form of a triumphal arch bearing the coat of arms of Philip II also stands out.

✳ **Cathedral** ▶ The Gothic Santa María cathedral was erected on the foundations of a former mosque on the south side of the plaza and remodelled in 1567 and 1593. The Puerta de la Luna in the west is still Moorish

Baeza *Plan*

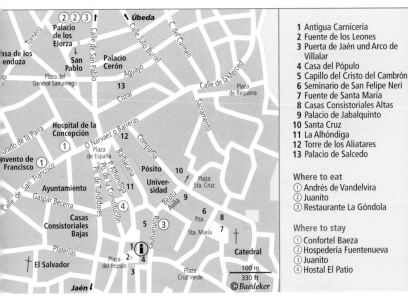

1 Antigua Carnicería
2 Fuente de los Leones
3 Puerta de Jaén und Arco de Villalar
4 Casa del Pópulo
5 Capilla del Cristo del Cambrón
6 Seminario de San Felipe Neri
7 Fuente de Santa María
8 Casas Consistoriales Altas
9 Palacio de Jabalquinto
10 Santa Cruz
11 La Alhóndiga
12 Torre de los Aliatares
13 Palacio de Salcedo

Where to eat
① Andrés de Vandelvira
② Juanito
③ Restaurante La Góndola

Where to stay
① Confortel Baeza
② Hospedería Fuentenueva
③ Juanito
④ Hostal El Patio

while Puerta del Perdón, spanning a lane in the south, exhibits a Gothic style. Andrés de Vandelvira helped to fashion the interior and it is worth looking at the **Capilla Mayor** with its stellar vault and the elaborate, fully gilded retable with its spiral columns. The masterly rendering of the choir screen is by Bartolomé de Jaén, who also fashioned the screen in the Capilla del Sagrario to the right of the Capilla Mayor. The six-sided, wrought-iron pulpit was made in 1580 and shows the apostles Paul and Andrew as well as four former bishops of Baeza. Some arches from the former mosque are included in the cloister. Connected to the cathedral are the **Casas Consistoriales Altas**. They were built at the end of the 15th century and bear the coats of arms of Joanna the Mad and Philip II. Across the way, the seminarians immortalized themselves in bull's blood on the façade of the former Seminario Conciliar San Felipe Neri – today the international Antonio Machado University.

Head back from the cathedral past Plaza del Pópulo to Paseo de la Constitución, the centre of Baeza. Its northern end is marked by Plaza de España with the Torre de los Aliatares clock tower, named after a Moorish tribe. **La Alhóndiga** can be seen on the east side of the paseo, the former grain market hall with its triple-arched gallery. It is connected at the back to an old, beautifully decorated granary (el pósito), which directly supplied the market hall. On the west side of the paseo is the **Casas Consistoriales Bajas**, which was built at the

Paseo de la Constitución

beginning of the 17th century as a town hall and was specifically provided with a balcony so that high-ranking guests could follow the festivities on the plaza below.

Calle de San Pablo

There are also **beautiful palaces** along the Calle de San Pablo that leads off to the north from Plaza de España: first the Gothic Palacio de los Condes de Garcíez with an inner courtyard and a double portico, then the castle-like Palacio Cerón and Casa Acuña, and finally Casa Cabrera with its Plateresque façade.

Ayuntamiento

To the west of Paseo de la Constitución the main place of interest is the town hall (Ayuntamiento) on Paseo Cardinal Benavides. It was built in 1559 as a courthouse and prison and is captivating with its lovely balconies, decorative rosettes and magnificent coats of arms including that of Philip II.

Santa María del Alcázar y San Andrés

The church of Santa María del Alcázar y San Andrés a bit to the west of the town hall is is consecrated to the patron saint of the city. Its chancel was designed by Vandelvira, and the **nine Gothic panel paintings** that depict themes from the New Testament in the local folk tradition are particularly worth seeing. It was in this church that Ferdinand III brought into being the order of the »200 Archers of the Lord of Santiago« that, despite its name, especially venerated Saint Andrew and Saint Isidor. They were feared enemies of the Moors. Only nobility from around Baeza were admitted to membership.

Úbeda

Population: 32,500   **Altitude:** 748m/2454ft

The Andalusian Salamanca

Baeza was impressive enough, but Úbeda, 9km/5.5mi further to the northeast, definitively surpasses its sister city with the harmony of its old town and the number of its Renaissance buildings, which has earned it the nickname »The Andalusian Salamanca«. Add to that the fact that the city is ideally suited as the starting point for an excursion into the ▶Sierra de Cazorla and that extremely beautiful pottery and objects fashioned from esparto grass can be purchased in the barrio of San Millán in the old town, for example, and Úbeda is clearly not to be missed.

History

The Moors called the place »Obdah«, fortified it and developed it to a first period of prosperity. Following the Christian conquest in 1234, some noble families living there, like the Los Cobos and the Molinas, rose to be among the most powerful families in Spain. They reached the apex of their influence in the 16th and 17th centuries and the city profited too, as they attempted to outdo each other in the grandeur of their palaces.

▶ VISITING ÚBEDA

INFORMATION
(OFICINA DE TURISMO)
Palacio Marqués de Contadero, Baja
del Marqués, 4, E-23400 Úbeda
Tel. 953 75 08 97
Fax 953 79 26 70

WHERE TO EAT
▶ Expensive
② *Parador Restaurante Nacional del Condestable Dávalos*
Plaza de Vázquez de Molina
Tel. 953 75 03 45
Regional recipes with fresh ingredients in a 16th-century palace.

▶ Inexpensive
① *Barbacoa*
San Cristóbal, 17
Traditional dishes and home-baked bread from wood-burning ovens.

WHERE TO STAY
▶ Mid-range
① *Alvar Fánez*
C. Juan Pasquau, 5
Tel. / fax 953 79 60 43
Luxurious old town hotel with a charming patio and a pleasant observation terrace.

▶ Budget
② *María de Molina*
Plaza del Ayuntamiento, s/n
Tel. 953 79 53 56
Fax 953 79 36 94
www.hotel-maria-de-molina.com
The hotel is in a 16th-century palace on the town hall plaza with a patio and restaurant/bar.

③ *Palacio de la Rambla*
Plaza del Marqués, 1
Tel. 953 75 01 96
Fax 953 75 02 67, 8 rooms
One of Spain's most beautiful inns.

The 16th-century palace is laid out around a Renaissance patio; the spacious rooms are outfitted with wicker furniture and pottery from the local region and from Portugal with a sure sense of style. The aristocratic owners live under the same roof.

Baedeker recommendation

▶ Mid-range
④ *Parador de Úbeda*
Plaza Vázquez de Molina, s / n
Tel. 953 75 03 45
Fax 953 75 12 59
E-mail ubeda@parador.es
www.parador.es, 31 rooms
Unbeatable location right in the historic centre in the Renaissance palace of Conde de Dávalos with a fantastic patio.

SHOPPING

The main shopping streets are C. Mesones and C. Otopo Cobos, plus the streets between Plaza de Andalucía and the Hospital de Santiago.

Alfarería Tito
Plaza del Ayuntamiento, 12
Shop with original pottery.

La Casa del Aceite
C. Juan Montilla, 3
Some of the region's best olive oil can be purchased here.

EVENT
Semana Santa

Fiesta de San Miguel
Celebrated since 1234 at the end of September with fireworks, bullfighting and street festivals.

Úbeda Plan

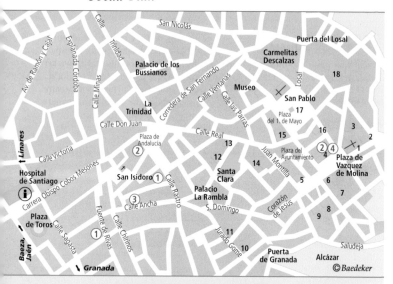

1 El Salvador
2 Hospital del Salvador
3 Palacio de los Cobos
4 Parador del
  Condestable Dávalos
5 Palacio de las Cadenas

6 Antiguo Pósito
7 Palacio de Mancera
8 Cárcel del Obispo
9 Santa María de los
  Reales Alcázares
10 Casa de las Torres

11 Palacio de Medinilla
12 San Pedro
13 Palacio de Guadina
14 Palacio de Vela
  de los Cobos
15 Ayuntamiento viejo

16 Casa de los Salvajes
17 Monumento a
  San Juan de la Cruz
18 Oratorio de San Juan
  de la Cruz

Where to eat

① Barbacoa
② Parador de Úbeda

Where to stay

① Alvas Fánez
② María de Molina

③ Palacio de la Rambla
④ Parador de Úbeda

✶ ✶
Plaza de Vázquez de Molina

✶
Palacio de las Cadenas ►

Nowhere else is Úbeda's former greatness more manifest than on Plaza de Vázquez de Molina, the main square at the edge of the hill upon which the old town is built as it falls abruptly towards the Guadalquivir basin. The alcázar once stood over this precipice; today there is a great view from here out over the groves of olive trees and the Sierra de Cazorla. The eastern corner of the plaza is dominated by the Palacio de las Cadenas (Palace of Chains) and is nowadays the site of the town hall and tourist information office. The noted architect Andrés de Vandelvira built it for Don Juan Vázquez de Molina and chose a different form of column for each of the three storeys – Corinthian at the bottom, Ionic in the middle and Caryatid at the top. Two lions holding a shield guard the entrance. The name of the palace is explained by the chains enclosing the forecourt. On the

The relief-adorned main façade of El Salvador →

ground floor, the **Museo de la Alfarería** exhibits a cross-section of Spain's traditional pottery in its four rooms and naturally places the focus on local and Andalusian products (opening hours: Tue–Sun 10am–1pm, 4–7pm, Sat 10am–2pm).

The church of **Santa María de los Reales Alcázares** across from the Palace of Chains was built on top of the main mosque and instead of a bell tower has two slender bell supports. Inside there are magnificent Gothic chapels and Renaissance choir screens by Bartolomé de Jaén to admire. The cloister, once part of the mosque, has an atmosphere all its own and was remodelled into the Gothic style. Next door to the Santa Maria on the left stands the **Cárcel del Otopo**, the former bishop's prison, now the courthouse. To the left is where the Marqués de Mancera, the viceroy of Peru, had his city palace built in the 16th century.

Sacra Capilla del Salvador ►

The most outstanding building is the Sacra Capilla del Salvador on the northern side, a masterpiece of Renaissance architecture that was designed by Diego de Siloé, Andrés de Vandelvira and Alfonso Ruiz and was built in the first half of the 16th century. It was financed by Francisco de los Cobos, a state secretary to Emperor Charles V, who is buried in the crypt. The main façade, adorned with reliefs, is flanked by two low, round towers. An allegorical depiction of faith and justice as well as the Los Cobos and Molina coats of arms can be seen on the arch over the entrance portal, above which is a towering image of Christ the Saviour framed by Saint Peter and Saint Paul. The retable, decorated solely with the figure of Christ, stands behind a splendid choir screen beneath the high dome of the Capilla Mayor. It is the last remaining figure of a group of statues called the *Transfiguration of Christ* by Alonso de Berruguete that was destroyed by fire in 1936 during the civil war. The sacristy, in which some church silver is stored, was marvellously fashioned by Vandelvira. Next, to the right behind the church, is the Hospital del Salvador, an excellent example of the various forms of column design used in the Renaissance. The façade of Francisco de los Cobos' palace is still standing to the left behind the chapel. Also to the left of the church is the Parador Condestable Dávalos, a two-storey Renaissance palace with three beautiful patios named after Fernando Dávalos, a general of the Castilian king, Juan II.

Casa de los Salvajes

C. Horno Contado leads away to the left from in front of the Salvador to Plaza del Primero de Mayo. Here the Casa de los Salvajes can be seen on the left. Its name translates as the »House of Savages«, so named because above the beautifully-worked portal are two »savages« wearing skins and holding the coat of arms of the house's owner, Francisco de Yago, the bishop's chamberlain.

Plaza del Primero de Mayo

The Plaza del Primero de Mayo that comes next on the tour was once the market place, bull ring, and the place of execution for those convicted by the Inquisition. In its centre stands a memorial cross for Juan de la Cruz, the mystic and companion of Saint Theresa of Ávila. To the left is the town hall (Ayuntamiento viejo) built in the 16th century.

San Pablo ►

San Pablo overlooks the northern side of the plaza, a building from the time of the Reconquista with an apse from 1380. After the Capilla del Salvador, it is the most remarkable church building in the city. A figure of the Apostle Paul is placed on the middle pillar of the Isabellian main portal from 1511, while above it angels float around the Virgin Mary. A fountain was set into the outside wall in 1559 and decrees were once proclaimed from a niche to the left of the portal. Worth taking a look at on the inside are the Plateresque Capilla del Camarero Vago by Vandelvira and the marvellous grille work.

Museo Arqueológico

The Casa Mudejar, Úbeda's archaeological museum, displays its treasures in C. Cervantes that leads away from the church portal.

The Palacio Condestable Davalos is today a parador.

The mystic, Juan de la Cruz, died in 1591 in Úbeda. A chapel was erected in the 17th century over the house where he passed away, which is now a museum displaying relics and personal objects once belonging to the saint. The chapel is at the end of C. Juan de la Cruz that leads off from the northwest side of the plaza.

Oratorio y Museo de San Juan de la Cruz

The city's elegant shopping boulevard, C. Real, can be reached by taking C. Marqués de Molina from the southern corner of Plaza Primero del Mayo. Branching off from C. Real is C. Juan Montilla with another beautiful Renaissance palace, the **Palacio de Vela de los Cobos**, which has a series of arcades on the upper storey that run around the corner. On the next street to the left is the **Monasterio de Santa Clara**. It was founded in 1290, but except for the Mudejar gate of the monastery chapel, its appearance is Baroque. Next along C. Real is the Palacio de Guadiana and on the alley that branches off from there is the church of **San Pedro** which has Romanesque origins although it was faced with a Renaissance façade in the 17th century. Finally, you come to **Plaza de Andalucía**, the traffic hub of the town. The Torre del Reloj (clock tower) stands here, built in the 16th century on top of the old town fortifications.

Calle Real

Somewhat outside the city centre, spread out along C. Otopo Cobos west of Plaza de Andalucía, is the Hospital de Santiago, a large, plain Renaissance structure with an arcade patio that Vandelvira began in 1565 and in which he died ten years later. There is also a museum there dedicated to the **subject of Passion Week**. More **Renaissance palaces** can be found by heading south away from Plaza de Andalucía on C. Rastro. Palacio de Rambla is on Plaza del Marqués, and Palacio de Medinilla is on C. Jurado Gome that branches off from the plaza; followed by Casa de las Torres, an exquisite urban palace with a Plateresque portal and a filigreed balustrade. This building was also once occupied by the Condestable Dávalos. Finally, winding up at Plaza de San Lorenzo, there is a church of the same name and Puerta de Granada, a well-preserved part of the fortification ring.

Hospital de Santiago

Around Úbeda

Vandelvira's buildings
Andrés de Vandelvira also left behind evidence of his architecture in the villages round about Úbeda. 10km/6mi west of Úbeda in the village of Canena is a Moorish castillo that he remodelled into a palace with a beautiful court. Sabiote, situated 9km/5.5mi to the northeast on the edge of a plateau, has a large Moorish castillo and a Carmelite convent as well as a church he designed. Finally, take the N-322 in a north-easterly direction past Torreperogil – a pretty village with picturesque streets – to Villacarillo, where he created the impressive church of **La Asunción**, one of the province's most important works of the Renaissance.

Iznatoraf
The mountain village of Iznatoraf can be reached by driving on past Villacarillo and taking a short mountain road to the left. Iznatoraf's parish church from 1602 is a beautiful example of country Renaissance architecture. There is a magnificent view of other villages and mountains from here. If the mood takes you, drive on to the pretty village of Villanueva del Arzotopo, where Juan de la Cruz used to live, and then on to Beas de Segura, which is dominated by a mighty castle. Saint Theresa of Ávila founded a convent for Discalced Carmelite nuns here.

✶ Cabo de Gata

(Parque Natural del Cabo de Gata-Níjar)

L 8

Province: Almería

Nowhere in Andalusia is the presence of Africa felt more strongly than in Cabo de Gata, jutting out into the sea southeast of ►Almería. This has nothing to do with cultural heritage but rather with the prevailing climatic conditions that characterize the countryside. Here, in the extreme southeast of Spain, it rains scarcely 25 days a year.

Nature and bathing
The hot, dry climate leaves its impression on the landscape. The brown and occasionally rugged rocks punctuated by volcanic hills only have a sparse covering of vegetation that includes esparto grass, gorse, agave, prickly pears, European fan palms and a grove of date palms here and there, sprinkled among whitewashed houses facing the azure of the sea – **echoes of North Africa**. Fan palms, seldom taller than half a metre/two feet, along with the Cretan date palm, are, by the way, the only palm species native to Europe. Esparto grass is used to produce wicker chairs, handbags and baskets – such as can be found on sale in Níjar and other places in large numbers. The lo-

At Cabo de Gata, the most south-eastern point of Spain has been reached.

cal animals are mostly birds and reptiles; including among the more rare species, the trumpeter finch, Bonelli's eagle, thekla larks, flamingos, sandpipers, pied avocets, snub-nosed vipers and geckos. Scorpions also live here. This unique and still relatively unspoiled countryside belongs in administrative terms to the district of Níjar near Almería (▶p.164) and is under conservation protection as the Parque Natural Cabo de Gata-Níjar. The tourist infrastructure is consequently somewhat undeveloped – no huge concrete hotels or tourist resorts, but rather isolated bungalow parks on the edge of villages and more modest hotels. Only San José has grown a little larger. Anyone spending their holidays here is probably looking to **experience nature**, mainly involving hiking and cycling, and will be able to bathe on beaches that are among the most beautiful in Andalusia, if only because they are not yet overcrowded.

What to See in the Cabo de Gata region

The cape can be reached from Almería by travelling on the well-sign-posted secondary road that runs parallel to the west coast. It skirts the fishing village of San Miguel de Cabo de Gata, behind which the extensive **sea-water salt flats** begin. They are still being worked. In the neighbouring village, La Almadraba de Monteleva , mountains of salt are piled up in the salt works near an abandoned fortified church – simultaneously providing a habitat for large colonies of flamingoes and stilts that can be observed from a hut (with a coin-operated telescope) situated to the left of the road at about the halfway point. To the right of the road, the long Playa de Cabo de Gata stretches along the coast.

West coast

◀ Cabo de Gata

After La Almadraba the road winds up the mountainside until, beyond one tight bend, a fantastic view of the **cape with the lighthouse** suddenly unfolds ahead. Although the name Cabo de Gata literally means »Cape Cat«, it is actually a corruption of Cabo de Agata, which means »Agate Cape«. There is a breathtaking view from the platform beneath the lighthouse down to the volcanic rocks below, some of which bear names like »Las Sirenas«. A hiking trail leads from the cape along the top of the cliffs to San José.

East coast

Anyone wishing to travel by car to San José will have to retrace the route back from the lighthouse to the road that goes through Ruescas and El Pozo de los Frailes, where there is an old restored wooden watermill (»noria«) powered by a donkey. **San José** lies further south on the seashore. It is the largest holiday resort on the cape, a not unpleasant mixture of fishing port, yachting marina and holiday village. If you fancy swimming, though, forget the beach to the left of the town and go 2km/1.5mi west along the bumpy road to the beautiful **Playa de los Genoveses** – over a kilometre (1,100 yards) in length,

Beaches ▶

▶ VISITING CABO DE GATA

The bizarre coastline of Cabo de Gata has wonderful, secluded beaches.

50m/150ft wide, light-coloured sand, really shallow and yet with proper waves. Just as beautiful, but with black sand and only about 350m/400yd long is the Playa del Monsúl, 2 km/1.5mi further on, which is adjacent to the Playa de Media Luna. Back in El Pozo, take the turn-off to **Los Escullos**, which detours around the highest summit on the cape, the 493m/1,617ft-high Cerro del Fraile. Los Escullos is a holiday village with a lovely beach beneath a bizarre rock arch and a fort from the 18th century. It is followed by La Isleta del Moro, a tiny fishing harbour with a small holiday village and a pleasant bar. After that, the road climbs up to **Mirador de la Amatista**, from where there is a stupendous view of the whole east coast. The hilltop behind Mirador offers a view far into the valley of **Rodalquilar**. Things are rather quiet these days in the former mining village – the gold mine that can still be seen on the slopes was not abandoned un-

✳
◀ Mirador de la
Amatista

til the 1960s. Its beach, El Playazo, can be reached over a bumpy dirt road 3km/2mi to the east that goes by the remains of a former Nasrid castle called Castillo de la Batería. The 18th-century Batería de San Ramón guards the beach itself. Within the same district is a farm called Cortijo del Fraile, where a family tragedy took place in July 1928 that Federico García Lorca used as the basis of his play ***Blood Wedding***.

> ! ***Baedeker* TIP**
>
> **PanPePato**
> The unusual name of the restaurant in the tiny village square of Rodalquilar. They offer – at decent prices – tasty pizzas and Andalusian dishes like rabbit stew, accompanied by a cheerful and relaxed atmosphere when young and old, tourist and locals meet in the evening at the plaza (tel. 950 38 97 03).

Once out of Rodalquilar and beyond the turn-off to the holiday resort of Las Negras, the road winds its way up between steep gorges then quickly drops down onto the plain of Almería where the view gives way to the familiar sea of plastic cloches. Despite that, the route is worth taking because it leads via Campohermoso and the N-340 to the very pleasant resort of Agua Amarga in the north of the Cabo de Gata nature reserve. It has a well-tended, sandy beach and nice bars right behind it and there are more beautiful bays to the south. The Playa de los Muertos joins it to the north beyond Mesa de Roldán.

✳
Agua Amarga

★ Cádiz

C 8

Province: Cádiz
Population: 143,100

Altitude: 4m/13ft

The port of Cádiz is famous for its magnificent location spread out on a shell limestone rock rising out of the sea at the end of a promontory 9km/5.5mi long that projects out into the Bay of Cádiz on the Atlantic Ocean (►photo pp. 148/149). A fresh breeze constantly wafts through the streets making a stay in midsummer pleasant and providing a shimmering, clear light in the city, which earned it its nickname »una tazita de plata« (»little silver cup«). Lord Byron even got carried away and claimed that Cádiz is »the Siren of the Ocean«.

»Una tazita de plata«
Mighty walls up to 15m/50ft high protect the city from the waves. The **tidal differential** here is almost 2m/6ft 6in (at spring tide it is as high as 3m/10ft). The high, white flat-roofed houses with their characteristic glazed balconies (»miradores«) and the parks with planted gardens of palms endow the city with a charm all its own. The lack of space on the peninsula led to towering blocks of flats being erected in the new part of town, so that the long drive into the city through the residential and industrial areas gives a rather unpromising impression. The inner city, enclosed by a fortified wall, therefore appears all the more pleasant with its spacious plazas and narrow lanes, mostly laid out in the 18th century. Today, Cádiz is one of Spain's most important ports with large **wharves** and **refineries** in its outlying areas. Fishing and **fish canneries** are also of importance.

Europe's oldest city
Cádiz is not only the oldest city on the Iberian peninsula, but also in Europe. The earliest archaeological finds, though, only date back to the 8th century BC. The Phoenicians founded Cádiz in around 1100 BC as a storage facility for tin and silver from Tartessos on the island that was not yet connected to the mainland in those days. They gave it the name Gadir (»fortress«) and built a temple to their god Melqart – later equated with the hero Hercules – on the island now called Sancti Petri. The Carthaginians occupied Gadir around 500 BC and from there pushed up into the south of Iberia. The city fell to the Romans during the Second Punic War and with its new name, Iulia Augusta Gaditana, the city flowered under Roman rule. Greek scholars studied the tides here, which were like nothing they had ever seen. Giditanian dancers, the »puellae gaditanae«, were coveted as slaves and even the cooking was famous. **Ancient mythology** assumed the **entrance to the underworld** to be nearby. Scholars like Plato and later Pliny believed this to be the site of the sunken

Cádiz *Plan*

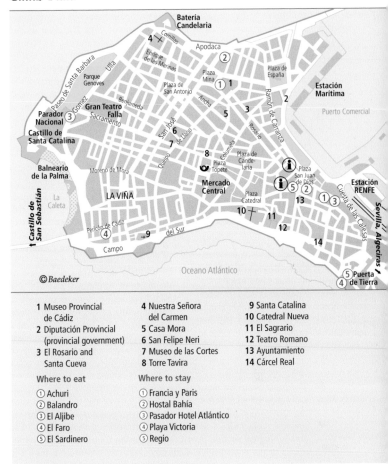

1 Museo Provincial de Cádiz
2 Diputación Provincial (provincial government)
3 El Rosario and Santa Cueva
4 Nuestra Señora del Carmen
5 Casa Mora
6 San Felipe Neri
7 Museo de las Cortes
8 Torre Tavira
9 Santa Catalina
10 Catedral Nueva
11 El Sagrario
12 Teatro Romano
13 Ayuntamiento
14 Cárcel Real

Where to eat
① Achuri
② Balandro
③ El Aljibe
④ El Faro
⑤ El Sardinero

Where to stay
① Francia y Paris
② Hostal Bahía
③ Pasador Hotel Atlántico
④ Playa Victoria
⑤ Regio

Atlantis. After the Visigoths, the Moors captured the town, until the harbour, now called »Jezîrat Kádis«, was attacked by the Normans in 844 after which sank into insignificance. Resettlement only began after Alfonso X had taken the city in 1262. With the discovery of the New World – **Columbus** sailed from here on his second and fourth expeditions – Cádiz rose to become the most important port for the silver fleet after Seville. This attracted English competition, however. In 1587 **Sir Francis Drake** sank a fleet anchored in the roads and in 1596 the Earl of Essex destroyed over a third of the city. But Cádiz recovered and in 1717, after Seville had dropped out of contention

◄ Port to the New World

Stronghold of
liberalism ►

due to silting of the Guadalquivir, it was granted the privilege of trading with the colonies. In 1805, the Spanish-French fleet that was subsequently destroyed by **Admiral Nelson** at **Cape Trafalgar** set sail from here. The French were unable to take Cádiz during the Spanish War of Independence, which enabled the Cortes in the city to assemble in 1810 and in 1812 and proclaim a **liberal constitution**, »La Pepa«; although it was abolished two years later under Ferdinand VII. The patriots in Cádiz proclaimed the constitution again eight years later, but this only lasted a short time because the French troops of the Holy Alliance crushed the patriots in the »Battle of Trocadero«.

What to See in Cádiz

The train station and harbour lie behind Puerta de Tierra, which is where the ferries to the Canary Islands embark. The tour of the city begins here, on the Avda. Ramón de Carranza. To the left of where this palm-studded avenue begins is Plaza de San Juan de Dios with the stately city hall (**Ayuntamiento**), built in 1799 and remodelled in 1861. The broad **Plaza de España** at the end of the harbour boulevard provides the backdrop for a mighty monument in remembrance of the Cortes first convened in Cádiz between 1810 and 1812. The province government building stands on the north side of the plaza.

! **Baedeker** TIP

A boat cruise ...

through the Bay of Cádiz opens up a whole new perspective of the city with its fortifications facing the sea. In July and August, the »Cabo Leiras« sets sails at 8am and 7.45pm from the Estación Marítima for a 90-minute tour. (INFORMATION tel. 956 25 00 99). The »Vaporcito« crosses the bay in 45 minutes to ►El Puerto de Santa María.

★
Plaza de Mina

★
Museo Provincial
de Cádiz

🕐
Opening hours:
Tue 12.30–8.30pm,
Wed–Sat
9am–8.30pm, Sun
9am–2.30pm

★ ★
Zurbarán paintings

►

The most beautiful plaza in the inner city is Plaza de Mina, luxuriantly planted with palms and greenery. One of the buildings houses the Museo de Cádiz (Museo de Bellas Artes y Arquéológico) that has various collections on display. On the ground floor, the **archaeological section** provides information about the earliest settlements in the region of modern-day Cádiz, the Phoenician founders of the city and much more. Of particular interest are two anthropomorphically shaped sarcophagi depicting a man with a curly beard and a woman with very fine facial characteristics that were found in Punta de la Vaca and date from 400 BC. Other rooms cover the Roman town of Iulia Augusta Gaditana from various points of view, including burial techniques, sculpture (there is a large statue here of Emperor Trajan from Bolonia), trade (model of a boat), everyday life, religion, domestic arrangements and work. The **collection of paintings** on the first floor is the most important in Andalusia after the Museo de Bellas Artes in ► Seville. The centrepiece of the museum is a collection of 18 works by Zurbarán in room 2, including *The Ecstasy of St Bruno*, *The Vision of St Francis of Assisi*,

▶ VISITING CÁDIZ

GETTING THERE

There are two ways to get to Cádiz. The more interesting is via Puerto Real on the N-IV bridge over the Bay of Cádiz with the city visible from afar. The other route goes around the bay by way of San Fernando. Both routes lead onto the access road that passes through the new town as far as Plaza de la Constitución, where it ends in front of the Puerta de Tierra that was built in 1755. The best way to explore the old town is on foot.

INFORMATION (OFICINA DE TURISMO)

C. Calderón de la Barca, 1
E-11003 Cádiz
Tel. 956 21 13 13
Fax 956 22 84 71
Plaza San Juan de Dios,
Edificio Amaya
Tel. 956 24 10 01
Fax 956 24 10 05
www.infocadiz.com

ASOCIACIÓN DE GUÍAS

Tel. 956 83 77 91 and 660 67 45 97
Four-hour walking tours (also in German or English) are on offer. Excursions to Morocco can be booked here as well.

PARKING

Do not try to drive in the inner city. There are car parks at the entrance to the old town, at the train station, in the Cuesta de las Calesas and along the promenade.

WHERE TO EAT

▶ Expensive

④ *El Faro*
San Félix, 15
Tel. 956 21 10 68
www.elfarodecadiz.com
One of the best restaurants in Andalusia, especially when it comes to fish and seafood.

▶ Moderate

① *Achuri*
Plocia, 15
Tel. 956 25 36 13
Achuri is a restaurant steeped in tradition. Basque and Andalusian cooking are combined here to perfection; e.g., in the stockfish recipe »Bacalao al andaluz«.

② *Balandro*
Alameda de Apodaca, 22
Tel. 956 22 09 92
The whole, rich diversity of fish and shellfish is proffered.

③ *El Aljibe*
Plocia, 25
Tel. 956 26 66 56
From simple tapas to sophisticated fish cuisine.

▶ Inexpensive

⑤ *El Sardinero*
Plaza San Juan de Dios, 4
Tel. 956 28 25 05
Andalusian and Basque cooking on the city's main plaza across from the city hall.

WHERE TO STAY

▶ Mid-range

③ *Parador Hotel Atlántico*
Avda. Duque de Nájera, 9
Tel. 956 22 69 05
Fax 956 21 45 82
E-mail: cadiz@parador.es
www.parador.es, 97 rooms
Modern parador on the edge of the old town with a fabulous view of the ocean, also providing parking spaces, garage and swimming pool.

④ *Playa Victoria*
Glorieta Ingeniero La Cierva, 4
Tel. 956 27 54 11
Fax 956 26 33 00
Modern and comfortable hotel located in the old town, with pool.

On horseback to the feria

► **Budget**
① *Francia y París*
Plaza San Francisco, 2
Tel. 956 21 23 19
Fax 956 22 24 31
www.hotelfrancia.com, 57 rooms
Quiet and charming old town hotel.

② *Hostal Bahía*
C. Plocia, 5
Tel. 956 25 90 61
Fax 956 25 42 08
Bright and well kept.

⑤ *Regio*
Avda. Ana de Viya, 11
Tel. 956 27 93 31
Fax 956 27 91 13, 40 rooms
Not in the old town but in the newer agglomeration on the busy access road, but it is cheap, practical and only 50m/55yd away from the beach.

SHOPPING

The shopping zone spreads out between Plaza de las Flores and C. San Francisco and on C. Columela along with its side streets. In addition, there is a covered market with a wide choice of merchandise.

Hecho en Cádiz
Plaza Candelaria
Culinary items and handicrafts produced in the province of Cádiz.

Mercado Central
C. Libertad
Masses of succulent delicacies.

EVENTS
Carnival
In Spain only the Canary island of Tenerife celebrates its carnival more exuberantly than Cádiz. If you want to experience it at first hand, then it is best to book accommodation well in advance or, better yet, settle for an outlying area. For ten days – from the last Thursday before Lent to the first Sunday after Ash Wednesday – a state of chaos exists with the streets full of parading »murgas«, groups of costumed people singing satirical songs and performing sketches. There is a huge parade on the Sunday before Lent (www.carnavalcadiz.com).

Semana Santa

Ciudad de Cadiz
Folk festival in the Parque Genovés at the beginning of July.

Feria de los Angeles
Music and dance in July/August.

Whitsun Festival, *Angel with Incense* and a series of portrayals of Carthusian monks from the Carthusian monastery in ►Jerez de la Frontera. Among the other important artists represented are **Murillo** (*The Stigmatization of St Francis*, *Ecce Homo*) and **Rubens** *The Holy Family*); in addition, there are Classic and Romantic works, portraits, painting of the 16th century (Luis Morales; Pedro de Campaña), historicism and paintings by artists from Cádiz. Finally, the top floor is dedicated to Andalusian puppet theatre, which is cultivated particularly in Cádiz.

✱
◄ Puppet theatre

Across Plaza San Francisco and past the Iglesia de Rosario (with sculptures of San Servando and San Germán, the patron saints of the city,) is the church of Santa Cueva, which was built in 1783. It was designed as an oval structure with two chapels, arranged one on top of the other. Three of the five lunette window bays in the upper rooms were decorated in 1795 by **Francisco de Goya** with wall paintings (*Wedding Feast at Cana*, *Miracle of the Loaves and Fishes*, *The Last Supper*), rare examples of religious themes by the master.

Santa Cueva

⊙
Opening hours:
Tue–Fri 10am–1pm,
4.30–7.30pm, Sat,
Sun 10am–1pm

Beyond Santa Cueva, the shopping street, C. Columela, turns off to the right. House no. 28 in the pedestrian zone C. Ancha that crosses it represents a wonderful example of civic architecture of the 19th century. Among the things worth seeing at the Casa Mora urban palace, aside from its impressive façade, are an exquisite inner courtyard and a museum with three floors displaying interior decoration from the period.

✱
Casa Mora

The C. Columela leads to the bustling Plaza Topete, also called Plaza de las Flores because of its many flower stalls. Take a break here in either one of the street cafés, the La Marina or the Andalucía, before taking a stroll through the big **market hall** (Mercado Central), adjacent to the plaza at the southern end.

✱
Plaza Topete

C. Londres and C. Nicaragua lead to the Torre Tavira, which was built in 1704 as a watch tower and, at 34m/112ft, is the highest in Cádiz. A **camera obscura** installed on the top floor projects panoramas of Cádiz every half hour. There were once as many as 160 of these towers in the city during the 18th century, allowing merchants to watch over their ships in the harbour (opening hours: mid-June–mid-Sept daily 10am–8pm, mid-Sept–mid-June until 6pm).

Torre Tavira

⊙

C. Santa Inés can be reached by way of C. Nicaragua, where the Oratorio de San Felipe Neri, an oval building from 1671, is located. This is where the Cortes convened in 1812. Decorating the high altar is **Murillo's** painting *The Immaculate Conception* as well as a *Head of John the Baptist* by **Pedro Roldán** (opening hours: Mon–Sat 10am–1pm). Adjoining the chapel to the south is the **Museo de las Cortes de Cádiz**. Along with numerous documents from the time of

Oratorio de San
Felipe Neri

⊙

Colourful and full of the love of life – carnival is celebrated for ten days in Cádiz.

the war for independence, there is also a very large model of the city fashioned out of ivory and mahogany that was made in the 18th century (opening hours: Tue–Fri 9am–1pm, 4pm–7pm, Sat, Sun 9am–1pm).

Hospital deMujeres

The only painting by **El Greco** in Cádiz, the *Ecstasy of St Francis*, is in the chapel inside the Baroque Hospital de Mujeres, along with various other works (Murillo's *Virgen del Carmen*), (opening hours: Mon–Sat 10am–1pm).

Barrio de la Viña

Barrio de la Viña is just made for a stroll without the pressure of sightseeing. It is in the southwestern part of the city centre, where mainly fishermen and dock-workers lived in the 18th century. In the summer, stalls with tastily prepared fish titbits are lined up one after the other on the Tío de la Tiza plaza. Its name comes from the nickname of **Antonio Rodríguez Martiñez**, who defined the basic rules for the carnival in Cádiz.

Beachfront promenades

The promenades on the Atlantic beachfront begin at Plaza de Mina with the Alameda de Apodaca and the adjoining Alameda Marqués de Comillas. At the end of the Alameda stands Nuestra Señora del Carmen (1737–1764), a Baroque church built in colonial style. Across from it is the Baluarte de Candelaría bastion. which was built in the 17th and strengthened in the 19th century. If citizens of Cádiz

★

Parque Genovés ▶

feels the urge to take a walk, they go to the Parque Genovés on the northwestern side of the rock. On the other side of the Castillo de Santa Catalina fortress, they can go swimming in the Bay of **La Caleta** at the city's edge where the nostalgic Balneario de la Palma (1925) is situated. A quay wall stretches from the southern side of the bay far out into the sea towards the Castillo de San Sebastián and the lighthouse. Campo del Sur leads away from the southern quay wall. On its left-hand side stands the former Capuchin monastery, now a psychiatric clinic. **Bartolomé Esteban Murillo** did the last picture he ever painted, *The Engagement of St Catherine*, for the high altar in the church he began in 1639, **Santa Catalina** (entrance through the courtyard). He fell from the scaffolding while working and died of the consequences on 3 April 1682 in Seville. There are other works of his to be seen in the church.

> ! **Baedeker** TIP
>
> ### Fish & Chips
>
> It's a fact: not the English but the fishermen of Cádiz invented battered fish. Try mackerel, for example, in all manner of »freidurías« or in the really quite inexpensive fish restaurants, perhaps on Plaza de las Flores, Plaza de San Juan de Dios or maybe on Plaza Tío de la Tiza.

From the Campo del Sur, there is a view of the choir side of the cathedral with its great yellow dome. Its main entrance faces the city on Plaza de Pio XII. It was begun in 1722 by Vicente de Acero and completed by members of the Cayón family at the end of the 19th century. Its fairly plain main façade, completed in 1789 by Manuel Machucas, is flanked by two large, octagonal domed towers. In the interior of the church (85m/280ft long, 60m/200ft wide) are an impressive, massive pillar and a magnificent 52m/170ft-high dome over the crossing and the high altar that dates from 1862. The mahogany choir stalls by Pedro Duque Cornejo from 1702 were originally planned for the Carthusian monastery on the Guadalquivir island in Seville. Among the side chapels, the Capilla de San Sebastián with a figure of St Bruno is worth seeing. The crypt is below sea level and contains, along with the graves of bishops, the tomb of the composer **Manuel de Falla**, who came from Cádiz but died in Argentina (►Famous People). Right next door, in the cathedral museum, three monstrances are particularly worth a look. One 17th-century **silver monstrance** made by Antonio de Suárez is almost 5m/16ft high, and the »Custodia del Millón« from 1721 is supposedly set with **one million precious stones**. The oldest monstrance has an amethyst cross at the top and was created by Enrique de Arfe, who came from Cologne to Spain in 1506. The museum has some other works by him and by his son Juan. Among the paintings there is a *Crucifixion by Alonso Cano and an Immaculate Conception by Murillo*.

✱ Catedral Nueva

✱ ◄ Museo Catedralicio

☉ Opening hours: Tue–Fri 10am–2pm, 4.30–7.30pm

Adjoining the cathedral is the church of Santa Cruz, the »old cathedral« that originally dates back to the 13th century and, after its de-

Santa Cruz (Catedral Vieja)

Many Gaditanos make their evenings a little sweeter on Play de la Caleta.

struction by the English in 1596, was rebuilt in Renaissance style in 1602. The interior is decorated with paintings and a high altar richly adorned with figures by Saavedra (about 1650). Excavations right behind Santa Cruz have uncovered the **remains of a Roman theatre** (opening hours: Tue–Sat 11am–1.30pm).

Cárcel Real The former royal prison at the end of the Campo del Sur was built by Torcuato Benjumeda at the end of the 18th century as a Classicistic complex clustered around several inner courtyards. Today it is a courthouse.

Beaches Besides the city's beach, other beaches that are good for bathing include the long Playa de Santa María, Playa de la Victoria and Playa de Cortadura that lie parallel to the major access road behind the tower blocks. Playa de la Victoria is supposed to have the finest sand on the Costa de la Luz.

Around Cádiz

San Fernando The port of San Fernando on the southern shore of the Bay of Cádiz was built as Isla de León in the 18th century on the salt marshes where the Romans had once extracted salt and is nowadays a nature conservation area. San Fernando, which was the last refuge of the

Cortes during the Spanish War of Independence, was and is an important **naval base**. Other sights worth a visit are the museum of city history, the observatory built in 1753 that the Spanish navy uses as a base to determine their position, and the Panteón de los Marinos Ilustres, where 52 statues of famous seafarers are on display. San Fernando is the hometown of the great flamenco singer **Camarón de la Isla** (►Famous People).

The Puente Zuazo, a bridge probably of Roman origin, spans the Salinen des Caño de la Carraca and connects San Fernando with Chiclana de la Frontera. The town is well-known for its wine, particularly for its muscatel, and its **puppet factories**, one of which, Marín, also maintains a museum displaying the products (opening hours: Mon–Sat 9am–1pm). The Iglesia de Jesús Nazareno is also worth a visit. Chiclana lives, however, first and foremost from **beach holidays** because it is only a couple of miles to beaches like the 7km/4mi long Playa de la Barrosa that are among the most beautiful on the Costa de la Luz.New urban housing estates owe their existence to them, such as La Barrosa or the community of quality homes, **Novo Sancti Petri**, laid out precisely by a draughtsman's pen and built in the 1990s around a golf course designed by the golfing legend Severiano Ballesteros. Most of the holidaymakers here are Germans. **Sancti Petri** took its name from the island lying off the coast, upon which a famous temple to Hercules/Melqart is said to have stood in ancient times. A now abandoned housing estate for fish factory workers built in the 1940s was also named after it.

Chiclana dela Frontera
⏱

✶ Carmona

Province: Seville
Population: 25,300

Altitude: 248m/813ft

The little town of Carmona sits enthroned on an exposed ridge of a hill in the middle of the Vega de Corbones, one of Andalusia's most fertile strips of land. Its centre is among the most beautiful of the smaller towns of Andalusia – only ►Baeza and Úbeda are prettier. With its vast fields of Roman graves, Carmona possesses a cultural monument of the first order.

The Romans encircled the hill that had already been inhabited in prehistoric times with a wall and gave the settlement the name Carmo. It became an important station on the road from Córdoba (Colonia Patricia) to Seville (Colonia Iulia Romula) and ►Itálica. The main street that crosses through the upper town follows this arterial route. Ferdinand III took the town away from the Moors, who called it Karmuna, and Carmona developed into one of the residences fav-

Small country town steeped in history

▶ VISITING CARMONA

INFORMATION (OFICINA DE TURISMO)

Alcázar de la Puerta de Seville, s/n, E-41410 Carmona
Tel. 95 419 09 55
Fax 95 419 00 80

WHERE TO EAT

▶ Moderate

Molino de la Romera
Sor Angela de la Cruz, 8
Tel. 954 14 20 00
Regional dishes – incl. game – served in the historical ambience of a 15th century oil-mill near the alcázar.

WHERE TO STAY

▶ Luxury

Casa de Carmona
Plaza de Lasso, 1
Tel. 954 19 10 00
Fax 954 19 01 89, 34 rooms
The 16th-century palace of the powerful Lasso de Vega family has been turned into a luxury hotel. It has shady inner courts, Mudejar fountains, arcades, gardens and fabulous architecture.

▶ Mid-range

Parador Alcázar del Rey Don Pedro
Tel. 954 14 10 10
Fax 954 14 17 12
www.parador.es, 63 rooms
A dream of a hotel with architecture inspired by the palace of Pedro the Cruel. At the edge of the old town above the Bétis valley.

▶ Budget

Pension Comercio
Torre del Oro, 56
Tel. 954 14 00 18, 13 rooms
Directly at the Puerta de Sevilla with a pretty patio and a restaurant.

SHOPPING

Cerámica San Blas
Dominguez de la Haza, 18
Handpainted pottery.

EVENTS

Carnival

Romería de la Virgen de Grácia
A pilgrimage on horseback and wagons on the first Sunday in September. Vibrant and colourful.

oured by the rulers; among those who especially liked to come here were Pedro the Cruel and Isabella the Catholic. A great number of aristocratic residences testify to this period.

What to See in Carmona

Puerta de Sevilla The upper part of the town can be entered from the west through Puerta de Sevilla, which is within the fortress wall extended by the Moors. The gate with one horseshoe and three round arches is part of the alcázar de abajo, the lower castle with the Torre del Homenaje and the Torre del Oro. Today, the **tourist information** is housed here, which also means the building can be toured.

To reach the Plaza de San Fernando, the town's main plaza, go a little up the hill from the gate on C. Prim and past the church of San Bartolomé (15th century) on the right. Some of the town houses in Mudejar and Renaissance style around the plaza are worth seeing. Take a look at the courtyard in the Baroque town hall; a Roman mosaic covers its floor.

Plaza de San Fernando

Close by is Santa María church, which was erected on top of an Almohad mosque in the 15th century. The Patio de los Naranjos, the Patio of Oranges, with its horseshoe arch is a reminder of the mosque. Evidence remains of the existence of an even earlier Christian house of worship predating the mosque: a Visigoth column from the 6th century with an engraved calendar showing the name days of the local saints, the oldest of its kind in Spain. A prominent feature inside is the Plateresque high altar, completed in 1559 with Passion scenes by Ortega and Vázquez el Viej. Take a look at the altar in the Capilla del Cristo de los Martirios in the left aisle, recognizable by its magnificent choir screen; it is thought to be Flemish. Capilla de San José y San Bartolomé in the right aisle holds three retables; the one

Santa María

✳
◀ Visigoth calendar

Santa Maria holds the oldest Visigoth calendar in Spain.

on the right is said to be by Pedro de Campaña. Across the Patio de los Naranjos is the entrance to an exhibition of the most beautiful of the church treasures.

Noble palaces

There are three noble palaces from the 17th and the 18th centuries in the immediate vicinity of the church. To the right on the plaza is the Palacio de los Rueda, across the street on the corner is the reddish-brown painted Palacio de los Aguilar (formerly the town hall), and behind the church to the left on C. San José is the Palacio del Marqués de las Torres, today the **town museum** (opening hours: summer daily 10am–2pm, 6.30–9.30pm, winter likewise 11am–7pm; closed Tuesday afternoons).

Convento de Santa Clara

Along the main street past the Convento de las Descalzas is the Convento de Santa Clara on the right-hand side, noticeable by its delicate tower. It was founded in 1460. The church has a series of portraits of saints from the Zurbarán School, some probably by the master himself. The painting on the high altar is by Valdés Leal.

Puerta de Córdoba

Puerta de Córdobahe marks the eastern end of the town. This gate also dates back to Roman times but was remodelled in classical style in the 17th century, when the powerful octagonal towers on the flanks were set on Roman ashlar blocks.

The upper castle, or alcázar de arriba, was on the highest point of the town, on the cliff edge of the town hill. It is also called Alcázar del Rey Don Pedro because **Pedro the Cruel** chose the Almohad castle for his seat. It was here that he imprisoned the mistress of his father, Alfonso XI: Leonór de Guzman, who fled from here to ►Medina Sidonia, where Pedro had her murdered. Today, there is not much remaining of the castle, but a very nice **parador** has been built on the grounds.

! **Baedeker TIP**

Solo with a view

The terrace at the parador offers a panoramic view over the Vega de Corbones – a great place for a café solo.

San Pedro

The first thing that stands out in the lower part of town, west of Puerta de Seville, is San Pedro church (15th–17th centuries), whose tall Baroque tower is reminiscent of the Giralda of Seville. In the exuberantly furnished Baroque interior are several remarkable green ceramic baptismal fonts (around 1500) and the Capilla del Sagrario (1760), whose splendour even exceeds that of the rest of the interior. It is the work of the Sevillian artist Ambrosio Figueroa, who revived here the Moorish tradition of horseshoe arches.

★ ★ Necrópolis romana

The **Roman cemetery** (necrópolis romana), in the lower part of town across from the amphitheatre (C/Jorge Bonsor; follow the

Carmona Necrópolis romana *Plan*

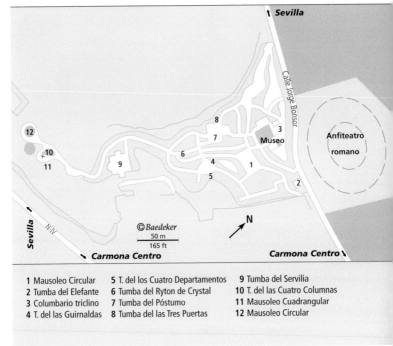

Sevilla

Calle Jorge Bonsor

Museo

Anfiteatro romano

© Baedeker
50 m
165 ft

N

Sevilla
N.V

Carmona Centro   Carmona Centro

1 Mausoleo Circular	**5** T. del los Cuatro Departamentos	**9** Tumba del Servilia
2 Tumba del Elefante	**6** Tumba del Ryton de Crystal	**10** T. del las Cuatro Columnas
3 Columbario triclino	**7** Tumba del Póstumo	**11** Mausoleo Cuadrangular
4 T. del las Guirnaldas	**8** Tumba del las Tres Puertas	**12** Mausoleo Circular

signs), has first place on the list of things to see in Carmonas. The cemetery contains close to 1,000 graves from the 2nd century BC up to the 4th century AD. About 250 of them have been excavated. Many are family tombs, recognizable by wall niches for urns, atriums and triclinia (benches) for the funeral meals. In many cases the remains of wall paintings and plasterwork can still be seen. The dead were usually cremated in crematory chambers that were part of the tombs, but interment tombs have also been found. A **museum** provides information about Roman methods of burial and displays burial objects (pottery, glass, jewellery, and bronze articles), gravestones, altars and sculptures. The large **Tumba del Elefante** is the most remarkable of the tombs. Its name is taken from a well-preserved statue of an elephant, the meaning of which remains, however, a mystery. The tomb consists of several chambers with triclinia (benches) and a stone cistern. The best-preserved wall paintings in the cemetery are to be seen in the **Tumba de Servilia**, including a picture of a lady with a harp. The size of the two-storey tomb indicates that an important family must be buried here. This is corroborated by the large number of burial objects and the life-size statue of one of the

🕐
Opening hours:
mid-June–mid-Sept
Tue–Sat 9am–2pm;
Sun 10am–2pm;
mid-Sept–mid-June
Tue–Fri 10am–2pm,
4pm–6pm,
Sat, Sun 10am–2pm

Family tomb with urn niches in the Roman necropolis

dead found here with the name »Servilia« chiselled into the plinth. The **Tumba del Póstumo** is an example of an interment tomb – though only for the master, because niches for the urns of his slaves are recognizable on both sides of the tomb.

Around Carmona

Marchena

✱
San Juan
Bautista ▶

In the little country village of Marchena, situated 27km/17mi southeast of Carmona, the remains of the medieval town fortification can still be seen. The high altar in the Gothic-Mudejar church San Juan Bautista is of particular interest. In the 16th century Alejo Fernández and his workshop created the panel paintings and sculptures that impressively depict the life of Christ and John the Baptist. Also of great artistic value are the 18th-century choir stalls and the late Gothic side altar with a picture of the Last Supper. The church museum is the proud owner of **nine paintings by Zurbarán**.

Fuentes de
Andalucía

This town, 23km/14mi east of Carmona, possesses a series of notable buildings, primarily Baroque. The ramparts and four towers of a Moorish castle are still standing on the main plaza. The most important church is Santa María de las Nieves, which has double aisles and was built from the 16th up into the 18th century. Its Capilla de la Virgen de Lurdes is lined with 16th-century azulejos. The altar of

San José church (18th century) has two sculptures made for it by Juan de Mesa: *Christ* and *Saint Joseph with Child*.

Villanueva del Río y Minas, located past Lora del Río, 25km/16mi north of Carmona on the Guadalquivir at the foot of the Sierra Morena, developed out of the Roman »Flavium Munigense«, where mining has been going on since ancient times. The impressive Castillo de Mulva can today be seen on the site of the Roman fort. The well-preserved remains of a 4th-century Roman settlement lie outside the town.

Villanueva del Río y Minas

Ceuta

E 10

Province: Cádiz
Population: 7,000

Altitude: Sea level

Ceuta (arabic: Sebta) is one big bazaar. Passengers arriving by ferry are besieged by peddlers offering every kind of ware imaginable. The African port lying closest to Europe at the eastern entrance to the Straits of Gibraltar is a 19.4 sq km/7.5 sq mi Spanish enclave (Plaza de Soberanía) on the Moroccan coast. the El Hacho peninsula is also under Spanish sovereignty. It projects out into the Mediterranean 8km/5mi to the northeast, where the old town of Ceuta occupies an isthmus barely 350m/400yd wide.

For a number of years now, the city and the peninsula have been isolated from Morocco by a formidable barbed-wire fence. This is an attempt to prevent illegal immigrants from entering Spain through Ceuta. Ceuta hardly has any North African character – about 85% of its inhabitants are Spanish citizens; only 8% are Muslims. The city is divided into the walled old town and the new town, which was laid out in 1912 when the north of Morocco was a Spanish protectorate and Ceuta experienced an enormous economic upswing. The decline set in following Morocco's independence in 1956, but Ceuta remains an important centre for fishing, a ferry port and a free trade zone that attracts tourists. Ceuta also has military significance – last put to the test in the somewhat grotesque dispute over the bare Parsley Island west of town when Spanish troops drove out some Moroccan soldiers. Ceuta is also a drug trafficking hub for hashish, which is offered for sale at many places in the city. Do not under any circumstances purchase any!

North African enclave

◄ Drugs

It is thought that Ceuta was an important Phoenician settlement, but the Roman settlement of Septem Fratres, from which both the Arab and the Spanish names were derived, is the earliest of which there is

History

CEUTA

ARRIVAL

Ferries and hydrofoils of various boat companies sail hourly. ▶Algeciras (about 45 min. to 1.5 hr); boats also sail from ▶Málaga to Ceuta.

INFORMATION (OFICINA DE TURISMO)

Calle Edrissis, s/n, E-51001 Ceuta
Tel. 856 20 05 60, fax 856 20 05 65
www.turiceuta.com

WHERE TO STAY

▶ **Mid-range**
Ulises
Camoens, 5
Tel. / fax 956 51 45 40
www.hotelceuta.com, 124 rooms
Most reasonably priced of the city's upmarket hotels.

evidence. It denotes the seven hills of Djebel Moussa, on whose slopes the city was built. After it was taken by the Vandals in 429 AD, it was not until 534 that Emperor Justinian I (527–565) managed to retake it. In 711 the Arabs seized Ceuta, which experienced its golden age in the 13th and 14th centuries as a customs zone, and Morocco's largest place of trade and most important port. In 1415, John I of Portugal succeeded in removing it from Arab control. When Spain and Portugal united in 1580, Ceuta became Spanish. Several attempts by the Arabs to retake it failed, the last in 1860 when it had already become very disreputable as a Spanish penal colony. It was here that Franco prepared the crossing of his troops to Spain in 1936. Morocco still maintains its claim to the disputed territory.

What to See in Ceuta

In the centre of Ceuta on **Plaza de África** stands the church of Nuestra Señora de África. It was built on top of a mosque between 1704 and 1726 and is consecrated to the city's patron saint. The high altar with a statue of the Virgin (16th century) – presumed to be Portuguese – and the church treasures are both worth a look. The cathedral with its two towers rises at the southern end of the plaza. It was built with a neo-classical facade and a black marble portal in 1729 on the remains of the former grand mosque that had served as a church since 1432.

Murallas The massive walls divided by a deep moat just a stone's throw from Plaza de África are the remains of the fortress of El Canderlo, built by the Portuguese in 1530. They recall Ceuta's past as a fiercely fought-over garrison town. The new Museum Revellín de San Ignacio displays art and architecture there.

Museums The **city museum** (Paseo del Revellín 30) displays objects from all eras of the history of Ceuta. Beneath the museum begin 2.5km/1.5mi-long underground passages from the 16th and 17th centuries that were meant to secure the city's water supplies and perimeters. The **Museo de la Legión** south of the city museum on Paseo de

Colón is dedicated to the history of the Spanish Foreign Legion, which maintains a garrison in Ceuta.

This park on the north side of the old town with waterfalls, sculptures and a fake castle was designed by the artist **César Manrique** (1920–1992), who came from the Canary Island of Lanzarote.

Parque Marítimo del Mediterráneo

It is worth taking the 4km/2.5mi trip to the 203m/666ft-high Monte Hacho. It is probably the legendary Mount Abila, which was held to be **one of the Pillars of Hercules** in antiquity. Its counterpart on the European mainland is the Rock of Gibraltar. Drive up the mountain past the lighthouse on the cape – with a fantastic view of Gibraltar and the Rif mountains – to the fortress of Desnarigado where there is a museum describing the history of the garrison of Ceuta. The Ermita de San Antonio, founded in 1593, is also up there.

✳ **Monte Hacho**

✳ ✳ Córdoba

F 6

Province: Córdoba
Population: 310,000

Altitude: 123m/403ft

The most important city in Andalusia after ►Seville lies on a plain gently sloping down to the Guadalquivir at the foot of the Sierra de Córdoba, outliers of the Sierra Morena. Narrow, winding alleyways, small plazas and white-washed houses, usually with their typical pretty patio – Córdoba possesses one of the largest old quarters of all Spanish provincial cities and, in addition, the fantastic Mezquita.

The Moorish character of Córdoba is still tangible, though less so in the Judería – once the Jewish quarter, now taken over by souvenir shops – than in the streets round about. But it is primarily the famous former mosque, today the Mezquita Catedral, that makes the one-time capital of the caliphate a »western Mecca« and the first place to visit in Andalusia. Córdoba is famous for its **silver and leather handwork** that is still produced in many workshops in the old town. Surrounding the city, metal working plants and the electrical goods and food industries have been established in the newer districts. Together with the tourist industry, they are the economic base of the city.

Capital of the caliphate

There was already a settlement here on the bend in the Bétis (Guadalquivir) in ancient Iberian times. It provided the Carthaginian General Hannibal with mercenaries for his military expedition over the Alps. Under the Romans, the village named Colonia Patricia in

History

Highlights *in and around Córdoba*

Mezquita-Catedral
Next to the Alhambra the largest Moorish structure in Europe, containing a world-famous, fascinating Muslim house of prayer and an impressive forest of columns, as well as the magnificently decorated prayer niche (mihrâb).
▶ page 222

The gardens of Alcázar
Park with waterworks and fountains laid out for the Catholic Monarchs in the 15th century
▶ page 229

Judería
The heart of Córdoba with winding lanes full of souvenir and craft shops and antiques dealers.
▶ page 229

Medina Azahara
Ten kilometres (6 miles) to the west lies the old caliphate town legendary for its former splendour, where archaeological excavations have been under way since 1910.
▶ page 332

152 BC rose to become the **capital of the province of Hispania Ulterior**. After being ravaged in the Roman civil war in 45 BC, it alternated with Hispalis (Seville) and ▶ Italica as the capital of the province of Baetica during the time of imperial Rome. In the 4th century AD, it was made the episcopal seat and eventually came under Byzantine domination, which was ended by the rampaging Vandals. When the Visigoth king, Leowigild, entered in AD 572, he found a town without any great significance.

The Umayyad **Abd ar-Rahman I**, who was driven from Damascus in 750 and in 756 became the first Emir of Córdoba, laid the cornerstone for the development of the town into Europe's most outstanding city and its intellectual centre. He introduced new cultivated plants and sophisticated methods of irrigation, started an extensive building program and promoted the sciences. The city was at its peak under Abd ar-Rahman III, who elevated himself to »Caliph of the West« in 929. At this time, the population of Córdoba was probably about 300,000. There were almost 500 mosques, 600 public bathhouses, a number of magnificent palaces, a large Jewish community, 17 universities, abundant libraries and innumerable schools

◀ Highlight of Europe – Moorish Córdoba

← *The view from the Torre de la Calahorra extends from the Roman bridge spanning the Guadalquivir to the Mezquita.*

▶ VISITING CÓRDOBA

INFORMATION (OFICINA DE TURISMO)

Torrijos, 10
(to the west across from the Mezquita),
E-14003 Córdoba
Tel. 957 47 12 35, fax 957 49 17 78

Plaza Judá Levi, s/n
Tel. / fax 957 20 05 22
www.ayuncordoba.es;
www.turismodecordoba.org

WHERE TO EAT
▶ Expensive
① *Almudaina*
Jardines de los Santos Mártires, 1
Tel. 957 47 43 42
www.restaurantealmudaina.com
One of the best addresses in Córdoba, in an historic building with a lovely patio across from the alcázar.

④ *El Blasón*
José Zorilla, 11
Tel. 957 48 06 25
It's hard to leave the tapas to go into the fine restaurant.

⑤ *El Caballo Rojo*
Cardenal Herrero, 28
Tel. 957 47 53 75
www.elcaballorojo.com
Here too it's tempting to stay with the tapas – the lamb kidneys give a good idea of the treats in the restaurant. The cooking here has a Mozarabic touch.

▶ Moderate
② *Casa Pepe »De la Judería«*
Romero, 1
Tel. 957 20 07 44
www.casapepedelajuderia.com
The bar serves tapas of a somewhat more refined sort; in the restaurant fine Cordoban cuisine.

▶ Inexpensive
③ *Taberna Casas Salinas*
Puerto de Almodóvar
Good quality fare served to the sounds of flamenco.

⑥ *El Churrasco*
Romero, 16 (closed Aug)
Tel. 957 29 08 19
Tasty steaks served on a nice patio.

⑦ *Taberna de San Miguel »El Pisto«*
Plaza San Miguel, 1
Tel. 957 47 01 66
Very cosy, old-established tapas bar. The manos de cerdo and rabo de toro are especially good.

WHERE TO STAY
▶ Mid-range
③ *Conquistador*
Mag. González Francés, 15–17
Tel. 957 48 11 02
Fax 957 47 46 77
www.hotel-conquistador.com, 102 rooms
Luxurious and central. The Mezquita can be seen from many of the rooms.

② *Amistad Córdoba*
Plaza Maimónides, 3
Tel. 957 42 03 35
Fax 957 42 03 65, 84 rooms
Luxurious hotel on the city wall in the Judería.

⑦ *Parador de Córdoba*
Avda. de la Arruzafa, s / n
Tel. 957 27 59 00
Fax 957 28 04 09
E-mail: cordoba@parador.es
www.parador.es, 94 rooms

Soberly modern, but very quiet on the edge of town with a very beautiful garden and pool.

Abetos del Maestre Escuela
Avda. San José de Calasanz
Tel. 957 76 70 63
Fax 957 28 21 75
www.hotelabetos.com, 38 rooms
House in colonial style somewhat outside town with a beautiful garden and view.

► Budget
① **Albucasis**
Buen Pastor, 11
Tel. / Fax 957 47 86 25, 15 rooms
Typical house in the Judería, full of unexpected nooks and crannies.

④ **Lola**
Romero, 3
Tel. 957 20 03 05
Fax 957 42 20 63
www.hotelconencantolola.com
Small, charming hotel in the Judería.

⑤ **Maestre**
Romero Barros, 4
Tel. 957 47 24 10
Fax 957 47 53 95, 26 rooms
Maestre, not far from Plaza del Potro, provides better than average comfort at a reasonable price.

⑥ **Mezquita Hotel**
Plaza Santa Catalina, 1
Tel. 957 47 55 86
Fax 957 47 62 19
A 16th-century house across from the Mezquita with flair, a pretty patio and well-furnished rooms.

⑧ **Riviera**
Pl. de Aladreros, 5
Tel. 957 47 30 00
Fax 957 47 41 44
Small, centrally located and still quiet.

⑨ **Séneca**
Conde y Luque, 7
Tel. 957 47 32 34, 12 rooms
Really low-priced, near the picturesque Plaza del Potro, nice patio.

SHOPPING

Córdoba is known for its pottery and handicraft products from goatskin, sheepskin and silver. A good place to shop for fashion in the barrio is between Plaza de las Tendillas and Avenida del Gran Capitán and in the street that connects the two, Conde de Gondomar.

Baedeker recommendation

► Typical Córdoba
In his small workshop, Rafael Varo produces wallcoverings and pictures made of leather in the traditional Cordoban technique (Corregidor Luis de la Cerda, 52; east of the Mezquita). A few paces further is Del Olivo, where it is possible to choose from amongst the finest regional olive oils (San Ferdinand 124 b). Turronarte has typical sweets like pasteles cordobéses, manoletes and suspiros (Medina y Corella 2; east of the Mezquita). There is a wide range of silver and leather in El Zoco, an artisans' market in the Judíos at the Bullfighting Museum.

Espaliu
Céspedes, 12
Exquisite silver jewellery with oriental patterns.

Manuel Reyes Maldonado
Armas, 4
Musicians of note buy their guitars from Manuel Reyes.

Meryan, Lopez Obrero e Hijos
Callejón de los Flores, 2
Leather goods and pottery decorated
with Moorish abstract designs.

PLAZA DE TOROS

Av. de Gran Vía Parque
Tel. 957 23 25 07
The most important fights are in
May.

EVENTS>

Semana Santa

Cruces de Mayo
Holy Crosses of May festival on the
first weekend in May.

Festival de los Patios
In the week following Cruces de Mayo,
the most beautiful flower-bedecked
patio is chosen.

Feria de Mayo
The major fiesta of the city is held
on the last weekend in May on
the opposite bank of the
Guadalquivir.

Guitar Festival
1 June with flamenco, jazz and rock;
guitar greats play at night in the
garden of the Alcázar (www.guitarra-
cordoba.com) – an unforgettable experience!

---

where a vigorous exchange between Christian, Muslim and Jewish scholars took place. Moorish Córdoba had paved and illuminated streets and provided work for a multitude of artisans. It radiated a brilliance that was unequalled in the rest of Europe. Only Byzantine Constantinople and Baghdad, the metropolis of the eastern caliphate, were comparable. But the Caliphate of Córdoba was torn apart by inner conflict and split into several small kingdoms, the »taifas«, in 1031. In succession, the city came under the rule of Seville (1078), the Almora-vids (1091) and the Almohads (1148). In spite of that, during this period, two of the greatest scholars of the high Middle Ages, **Aver-roes** (Ibn Rushd) and **Moses Maimónides** (▶ Famous People) lived

Under the Christians ▶ within its walls. After being taken by Ferdinand III in 1236, Córdoba **slowly faded into obscurity** – thanks to this the old town still has a cohesive appearance, even though many buildings became dilapidated and the fertile campiña turned into a barren steppe. Trade and industry also came to a standstill and it was not until three centuries after the return of the Christians that the resumption of the production of leather wallcoverings revived trade.

famous people Many famous people were born in Córdoba, including the rhetorician Marcus Annaeus Seneca (54 BC – AD 39), the Stoic Lucius An-

---

! Baedeker TIP

Festival de los Patios

Normally, many flower-covered patios remain unseen by the public. Not so during the Festival de los Patios Córdobéses, which is all about picking the most beautiful patio. The exact date is available at the tourist offices in Córdoba. They have maps marking the patios open to the public.

Córdoba *Plan*

1 Palacio de los Marqueses
   de Viana
2 Casa de Fernández de Córdoba
3 Casa de los Villalones
4 Museo Provincial Arqueológico

5 Arco del Portillo
6 Casa de los Marqueses
   del Carpio
7 Posada del Potro
8 Fuente del Potro

9 Museo Provincial
   de Bellas Artes
10 Museo Julio Romero de Torres
11 Museo Taurino
12 San Bartolomé

Where to eat

① Almudaina
② Casa Pepe de la Judería
③ Casa Salinas
④ El Blasón
⑤ El Caballo Roja
⑥ El Churrasco
⑦ Taberna de San Miguel »El Pisto«

Where to stay

① Albucasis
② Amistad Córdoba
③ Conquistador
④ Lola
⑤ Maestre
⑥ Mezquita Hotel
⑦ Parador de Córdoba

⑧ Riviera
⑨ Séneca

naeus Seneca (4 BC – AD 65), the poet Marcus Annaeus Lucanus (AD 39–65); in addition, Averroes (Ibn Rushd, 1126–1198), commentator on Aristotle, Rabbi Moses Maimónides (1135–1204), the poet Luis de Góngora (1561–1627) and Manuel Rodríguez Sánchez (1917–1947), called »Manolete«, the most famous torero of his time.

✳ ✳ Mezquita Catedral

The mosque-cathedral of Córdoba can readily compete in beauty and size with the grand mosques of Mecca and Damascus, with the El-Azhar mosque in Cairo and the Blue Mosque in Istanbul.

When they arrived here, the Moors found a Visigoth church consecrated to Saint Vincent built on the remains of a Roman temple of

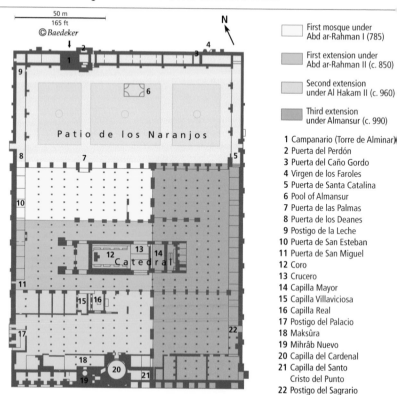

Mezquita - Catedral de Córdoba Plan

50 m
165 ft
© Baedeker

N

Patio de los Naranjos

Catedral

First mosque under Abd ar-Rahman I (785)

First extension under Abd ar-Rahman II (c. 850)

Second extension under Al Hakam II (c. 960)

Third extension under Almansur (c. 990)

1 Campanario (Torre de Alminar)
2 Puerta del Perdón
3 Puerta del Caño Gordo
4 Virgen de los Faroles
5 Puerta de Santa Catalina
6 Pool of Almansur
7 Puerta de las Palmas
8 Puerta de los Deanes
9 Postigo de la Leche
10 Puerta de San Esteban
11 Puerta de San Miguel
12 Coro
13 Crucero
14 Capilla Mayor
15 Capilla Villaviciosa
16 Capilla Real
17 Postigo del Palacio
18 Maksûra
19 Mihrâb Nuevo
20 Capilla del Cardenal
21 Capilla del Santo Cristo del Punto
22 Postigo del Sagrario

Janus. They used it as a mosque but let the Christians continue to use part of it. Abd ar-Rahman I acquired it and had it torn down in order to use the materials to begin building a mosque in 785. Eleven aisles were constructed opening to the Courtyard of the Orange Trees and the mihrâb, the prayer niche directed toward Mecca at the end

DON'T MISS

- Prayer areas – fascinating forest of columns in semi-darkness
- Mihrâb – the prayer niche adorned with millions of colourful mosaic stones
- Capilla Villaviciosa – daring dome construction

of the somewhat larger central aisle. Hisham I had a first minaret put up at the main entrance that no longer exists today. Al-Hakam I surrounded the courtyard with arcades. The aisles were extended to the south under Abd ar-Rahman II from about 830 to 850. Abd ar-Rahman III had the minaret built in 931 that exists today in an altered form and Al Hakam II enlarged the mosque further to its current length of 179m/587ft. The unique »new mihrâb« and the maksûra, the caliph's prayer room, were also built during this expansion. Finally, it was Almansur who extended the mosque to its present width of 134m/439ft by adding eight additional aisles along the whole length of the building to the east so that the prayer space today has 19 aisles and the asymmetrically positioned prayer niche. The Christians hardly touched the length of the mosque; only King Alfonso X had the Capilla Villaviciosa built as the main Christian chapel on the site of the mihrâb from the second building phase. After five aisles had already made way for the first cathedral at the end of the 14th century, there followed one of the most radical changes. In 1523, Bishop Alonso Manrique decided to construct a large cathedral right in the middle of the Islamic prayer space. The town council recognized the danger and threatened with a death sentence anyone who sought to destroy the Moorish structure; but construction began with the consent of the young Charles V under the direction of the architect Hernán Ruiz. A few years later, when the emperor viewed the progress of the construction, he supposedly said to the canons, »If I had known, gentlemen, what you were planning, I would have never allowed it, because what you are building here you'll find everywhere, but what you have destroyed is to be found nowhere on earth.« The construction of the cathedral was essentially completed in 1599. Around this time, the remodelling of the minaret into a bell tower (campanario) also began.

The main entrance on the north side is Puerta del Perdón (pardoner's gate) beneath the campanario. The ticket counter is also here. The Courtyard of the Orange Trees can also be entered by Puerta de los Deanes, Puerta del Virgen de los Faroles, Puerta del Caño Gordo and Puerta de Santa Catalina, a Renaissance gate with a depiction of the old minaret. Of the remaining gates, those that most retain their original Moorish form are Puerta de San Esteban from 855 and Pu-

Outside gates

MEZQUITA

✳︎✳︎ **The former grand mosque of western Islam – one of the largest mosques on earth (175m/574ft long, 130m/236ft wide), today a cathedral (Mezquita Catedral) – is the most significant work of Moorish religious architecture in Spain.**

🕐 Opening hours:
Apr–June Mon–Sat. 10am–7pm, Sun 2–7pm;
July–Oct and March until 6.30pm;
Nov and Feb until 5.30pm;
Dec and Jan until 5pm

① Maksûra
Originally the caliph's prayer room.

② Cathedral
Bishop Alonso Matrique decided in 1523 to erect a large cathedral in the middle of the Islamic prayer hall. With its mixture of Gothic and Renaissance styles, it appears architecturally out of place.

③ Campanario (bell tower)
When the construction of the cathedral was completed around 1599, the conversion of the minaret into a bell tower began. The tower is crowned by a statue of the Archangel Raphael, the patron saint of the city.

④ Crenellated wall
The whole structure is surrounded by a wall 9–20m/30–65ft high on which countless tower-like buttresses stand out and on which the classic decorative elements of Islam — red and white horseshoe arches, ornamental floral and geometric designs and ribbons of Kufic inscriptions are repeated in innumerable variations.

⑤ Water basins
Ritual washings were performed at large water basins, not all of which have survived, before entering the prayer hall that formerly was open to the courtyard.

⑥ Muslim prayer hall
793 columns support the arches with their alternating red and white limestone and brick. Neither route nor direction was prescribed in the Mezquita: each and every spot was its middle point. All places where Muslims perform their prayers are considered equally close to Allah. Back then, light flooded in through the gates that are now walled up, and thousands of little oil lamps provided additional illumination for the hall.

⑦ Mihrâb Nuevo (new mihrâb)
The prayer niche for the prayer leader – which indicates the direction of Mecca – is incomparable and unequalled. It is the holy of holies of the mosque, where the Qur'an rested. The dome, carved out of a single block of marble and symbolizing »the shell of the world«, is covered with floral and geometric patterns, verses from the Qur'an, and mosaics for which Byzantine artists can take credit.

The arcade passages in the Patio de los Naranjos (Orange Tree Court) date back to the 16th century – the orange trees too were first planted by Christians.

⑧ Capilla del Cardenal
Here is where the church treasures are stored. The greatest treasures are a silver monstrance (1510–1516) and a processional cross by Enrique de Arfe, nine statues of saints and an ivory cross by Alonso Cano, as well as Arab manuscripts from the 9th and 10th centuries.

⑨ Arcades
In Moorish times, students and their teachers met under the arcades on the north side of the courtyard for discussions. Doctors gave advice west of the bell tower and the qadi pronounced judgements to the east.

The Pardoner's Gate, where sinners were pardoned, was built under the Campanario in 1377 in Mudéjar style.

View from the cathedral into the mosque; when compared to the artistic skill of the Muslim prayer hall, the cathedral comes out second best.

A horseshoe arch framed by a decorated area composed of millions of coloured mosaic tiles in floral patterns and calligraphic inscriptions leads into the mihrâb, the prayer niche orientated to Mecca.

Masterly craftsmanship reached its apex in the magnificent dome of the Mihrâb Nuevo, which is fashioned in the shape of a blossom.

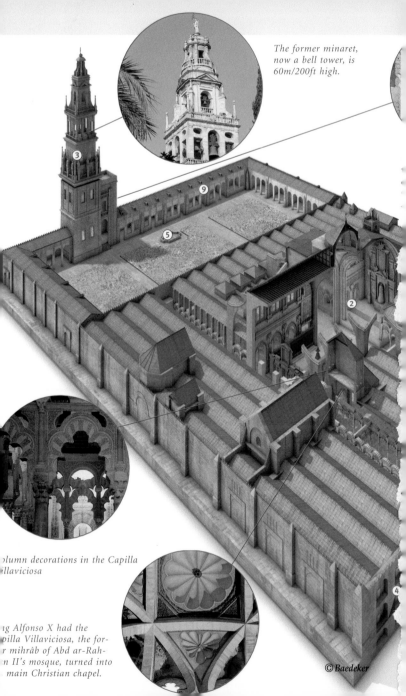

The former minaret, now a bell tower, is 60m/200ft high.

...lumn decorations in the Capilla ...llaviciosa

...g Alfonso X had the ...pilla Villaviciosa, the for- ...r mihrâb of Abd ar-Rah- ...n II's mosque, turned into ...main Christian chapel.

© Baedeker

Miguel. The caliph entered the mosque through Puerta del Palacio, but it was remodelled in Gothic style in the 15th century. Milk was distributed to orphans at Postigo de la Leche.

Campanario

The campanario (Torre de Alminar), rising above Puerta del Perdón and built on the first storey of the old minaret, was given its form based on Herrera style in 1593 by Hernán Ruiz when he encased the minaret.

✳
Patio de los Naranjos

Patio de los Naranjos (Courtyard of the Orange Trees), covered with orange trees and palms, opens out in front of the prayer areas. Puerta de las Palmas, today in the Renaissance style of 1531, is the entrance to the oldest part of the mosque.

✳ ✳
Muslim prayer area

Time and again the attempt has been made to describe the world-famous Mezquita – but the manner in which the **seemingly endless forest of 793 columns in semi-darkness** reveals a different perspective with each step has to be experienced at first hand. The columns of the first section are of jasper, marble and porphyry from Roman and Visigoth buildings in Andalusia and North Africa and were set on bases when necessary to compensate for their varying heights. The character of this part is defined by the four-cornered half-columns topped by round arches on the lower row of horseshoe arches in order to achieve the total height of 11.5m/37ft, resulting in rows of double arches. The beautifully coloured, richly carved timberwork of the old mosque has been revealed at Puerta de las Palmas and between the mihrâbs (prayer niches) orientated to Mecca. The columns in the second phase of building are the first to bear Corinthian capitals. The third phase is recognizable by the fanciful clover-leaf cusped forms in the arrangement of the arches. The section built under Almansur is distinguished by its spaciousness, which allows the rows of arches to appear to their best advantage. A grille on the southwest wall separates the Mihrâb Nuevo from its anteroom – the Maksûra. Even the anteroom has the richest of decoration; particularly the multitude of arch forms, mosaics and ribbons of Kufic script give proof of the masterly skill of the craftsmen, which reached its apex in the **blossom-shaped dome**. The Mihrâb Nuevo (New Mihrâb) is incomparable and unsurpassed. It opens behind a horseshoe arch flanked by two pairs of columns from Abd ar-Rahman II's old mihrâb. A mosaic arch stretches over it with floral ornamentation bordered by an alfiz with bands of Kufic script recounting all the names of Allah.

✳ ✳
Mihrâb Nuevo ▸

Cathedral and chapels

✳
Capilla Villaviciosa ▸

In the 18th century, Francisco Hurtado Izquierdo built the Capilla del Cardenal in which the church treasures are stored next to the mihrâb on the left. The Capilla Villaviciosa across from the Mihrâb Nuevo is the former mihrâb of Abd ar-Rahmans II's mosque. It was converted into the first Christian chapel in the mosque, but its

Byzantine craftsmen created the mosaics of the Mihrâb Nuevo.

Moorish column decoration and the daring construction of the dome are still captivating. Next to it is the **Capilla Real** (14th century), beautifully worked in Mudejar style with faience and plaster facing. It was conceived as a mausoleum for the Castilian kings, Ferdinand IV and Alfonso XI, whose remains were transferred to the church of San Hipólito in 1706, however. The Gothic **transept** serving as choir in the heart of the mosque and the **Capilla Mayor** form a church in its own right. It was built for the most part by Hernán Ruiz, his son and his grandson at the behest of Bishop Alonso Manrique following the demolition of 63 columns. The choir was built between 1523 and 1539, and the chancel between 1547 and 1599. The richly-carved Baroque stalls (18th century) in the choir were created by Pedro Cornejo. There are five paintings by Palomino on the high altar (1618) by Alonso Matías. The two pulpits of mahogony and marble as well as the tomb of Bishop Leopold of Austria are also worthy of note.

✱
◄ Cathedral

Around the Mezquita

Across from the southwest corner of the Mezquita stands the episcopal palace, built in the 15th century on the ruins of the old palace of the caliph and remodelled in 1745. Today it houses the Museo Diocesano, which displays archaeological finds, paintings and religious sculptures from the 13th to the 18th centuries (opening hours: summer Sun–Fri 9.30am–3pm, Sat 9.30am–1.30pm; winter Sun–Fri

Museo
Diocesano

The gardens of the Alcázar refresh the senses with luxuriant displays of flowers and waterworks.

9.30am–1.30pm, 3.30–5.30pm, Sat 9.30am–3pm). San Jacinto church and the Hospital San Sebastián, which contains the congress palace and the **tourist office**, are next to the episcopal palace.

On the Guadalquivir The bank of the Guadalquivir is south of the palace. There on the terrace stands the Triunfo de San Rafael column from 1765 bearing a statue of the archangel Raphael. Puerta del Puente can be seen beneath the terrace standing below street level. It is a Doric triumphal arch, built in the 16th century to honour Philip II, that once served as a bridge gate. On the river bank, also below the terrace, is a restored **Moorish waterwheel** that Abd ar-Rahman II had built in the 10th century.

✳ Alcázar de los Reyes Cristianos To the west lies the Alcázar de los Reyes Cristianos with the Campo de los Mártires in front of its main building, supposedly the place where Christians maryters were executed. The imposing ramparts and towers of the castle in part date back to Moorish times, Alfonso XI, however, started expanding most of it into a military installation with a rectangular groundplan in 1328. It was the royal residence of the Catholic Monarchs during their military expeditions against Moorish Granada. Once a giant Moorish waterwheel turned in front of the alcázar walls, but its creaking disturbed Isabella's sleep and so it was torn down. The castle was the seat of the Inquisition until 1821, and then a prison. The surviving towers include Torre de los

Leones with very beautiful Mudejar work, Torre del Río and Torre del Homenaje, both furnished with remarkable ribbed vaults.

Archaeological finds are on display in the alcázar. Among the best pieces are a Roman sarcophagus from the 3rd century AD with fine reliefs and Roman mosaics (opening hours: Tue–Sat 10am–2pm, 5.30–7.30pm; Sun 9.30am–2.30pm and 9am–3pm in July–Aug).

◄ Museo

Adjoining the main building within the walls are magnificent gardens with fountains, bounded to the west by the remains of the Moorish city wall with the Puerta de Seville. A monument to the great philosopher Averroes was erected outside the walls. The gardens are additionally open in July and August from 8pm to midnight.

★ Gardens

The six-arched Puente Romano over the Guadalquivir was built in about 48 BC after Caesar's victory over Pompey in the Roman civil war. The Moors later erected the present 223m/244yd-long bridge on the foundations. A dilapidated mill dating from Moorish times in the shallow waters of the Guadalquivir presents a picturesque view from the bridge.

★ Puente Romano

The southern end of the bridge is marked by the imposing fortified tower Torre de la Calahorra, erected in 1369 under Enrique II. The museum inside it, Museo Vivo de Al-Andalus, brings Moorish Andalusia to life in an impressive way. Each visitor is given a wireless headset that receives music and the text (also English) appropriate to each room entered. Great philosophers of the time are presented, including **Averroes**, **Maimónides**, **Ibn al-Arabi** and **Alfonso X, the Wise**. Another room is dedicated to medicine, astronomy and geography; the irrigation techniques of the Moors are explained using excellent models and dioramas. Islamic music is explained, and two models of the Alhambra of Granada as well as the mosque of Córdoba as it was in 1236 are shown in further rooms. A **multimedia show** in English presents the history and culture of Córdoba in understandable terms. There is a tremendous view of the old town from the roof of the tower(opening hours: May–Sept daily 10am–7.30pm, Oct–April until 6pm).

Torre de la Calahorra

★ ◄ Museo Vivo de Al-Andalus

★ **Judería**

The Judería, the **old Jewish quarter**, begins north of the Mezquita. Narrow lanes, white-washed houses with inner courtyards full of plants and secluded spots create their own distinct atmosphere that can best be experienced away from the streets directly around the Mezquita where the souvenir shops are lined up one next to the other. The main street, C/Judíos, runs alongside the wall.

Calleja de las Flores, »Flower Alley« decorated with blooms, can be reached by heading away from the northeast corner of the Mezquita on C. Velásquez Bosco and then turning right.

Calleja de las Flores

Maimónides monument	Plaza Maimónides can be reached from the northwest corner of the Mezquita, and a little further on there is a modern monument in memory of the great Jewish scholar on Plaza de Tiberiades.

Museo Taurino

⏱ Opening hours: Tue–Sun 9.30am–1.30pm, 4–7pm

Everything about bullfighting has been gathered in the Museo Municipal Taurino in the Casa de las Bulas on Plaza Maimónides; posters, swords, costumes, the stuffed heads of famous bulls and, above all, tributes to bullfighters from Córdoba like Lagartijo, Machaco, Guerrito, Manuel Benítez (»El Córdobes«) and, first and foremost, Manolete, whose study and sepulchral sculpture are on display. Directly next to the museum is El Zoco, a covered handicraft market.

✱ **Sinagoga**

The synagogue directly opposite is one of Spain's three remaining Jewish places of worship **from the high Middle Ages** (the other two are in Toledo). It shows typical Mudejar decorative elements. Hebraic inscriptions repeat Biblical psalms; one of them on a niche for the Torah scrolls in the east wall names 5075 as the founding date, which corresponds to the year 1315 of the Gregorian calendar. On the south wall steps lead to the women's gallery (opening hours: Tue–Sat 10am–2pm, 3.30–5.30pm, Sun 10am–1.30pm).

> ! **Baedeker TIP**
>
> **Bodega Guzmán**
>
> The best place to take a tapas break in the Judería is Bodega Guzmán across from the synagogue (Judíaos, 9). The house drink is the (bitter) »amargoso montilla«.

Casa Andalusía

⏱

How homes were furnished in Moorish Córdoba and how paper was produced is shown in the 12th-century Casa Andalusía next to the synagogue (opening hours: daily 10.30am–7pm).

Puerta de Almodóvar

The well-preserved Puerta de Almodóvar at the north end of C/Judíos marks the entrance to the former ghetto. Beyond it stands the statue of **Lucius Annaeus Seneca**, the poet, philosopher and tutor of Emperor Nero, who was born in Roman Córdoba. On the way from the gate into town is the 15th-century Casa del Indiano, which has a splendid Mudejar portal.

Rest of the Old Town

The rest of the old town north and west of the Mezquita is a maze of alleyways that developed in the course of the centuries. It imparts a much more authentic feeling of old Córdoba than the tourist-oriented Judería.

✱ **Museo Arqueológico**

The archaeological museum in Casa Paéz, a Renaissance palace on Plaza Don Jerónimo Paéz, is among the finest in Andalusia. Pre-historic finds, Iberian artefacts like a hunting scene from Almodóvar del Río and a figure of a lion, Roman pieces (busts of Germanicus and Commodus, a Mithras altar, mosaics) and early Christian finds including a sarcophagus with almost three-dimensional scenes from the Bible, as well as gold crosses and jewellery from the Treasure of Torredonjimeno are displayed on the lower floor. The Moorish section on the upper floor is the centrepiece of the collection. The valuable objects displayed here are primarily from ► Medina Azahara, the caliphs' residence, including a 10th-century bronze stag with niello inlays (opening hours: Tue–Sat 10am–8.30pm, Sun 10am–2pm).

Plaza del Potro, east of the Mezquita near the riverbank, was the centre of the city and its market place in the 16th century. It takes its name from a small bronze sculpture of a colt from the 16th century. Cervantes once stayed in the old Mesón del Potro inn; today the municipal culture office presents **art exhibitions and concerts** here. The monastery church on the plaza, San Francisco, is richly decorated with paintings by Valdés Leal, Palomino and de Castillo, among others.

The colt gave Plaza del Potro its name.

The Hospital de la Caridad opposite, which was founded by the Catholic Monarchs in the 16th century, today houses two museums. The Museo Provincial de Bellas Artes (museum of fine arts) definitely took a loss after giving up three Goyas and several Riberas, and now the best work it possesses is Valdés Leal's *Virgin of the Silversmiths* and Bartolomé Esteban Murillo's *Immaculate Conception*. In addition many **Cordoban artists** are on display (opening hours: Tue 3–8pm, Wed–Sat 9am–8pm, Sun 9am–3pm).

Museo Provincial de Bellas Artes

Across and past the courtyard is the entrance to the **Museo Julio Romero de Torres**. Torres (1874–1930) was the son of the director of the art museum and made a name for himself painting dark, beautiful women that many dismiss as kitsch, but are none the less

extremely popular in Córdoba (opening hours: May–mid-Oct Tue-–
Sat 10am–2pm, 5.30–7.30pm; mid-Oct–April Tue–Sat 10am–2pm,
4.30–6.30pm; Sun 9.30am–2.30pm).

San Pedro The Moorish apses and two portals still survive in San Pedro (13th
century), east of Plaza del Potro, the church in which Cordoban
Christians gathered to pray during the time of the caliphs. In 1542,
Hernán Ruiz added the Renaissance facade.

✱
Plaza de Past Plaza del Potro to the north is Plaza de la Corredera, which was
la Corredera laid out in 1683 and is completely encircled by arcade houses. It was
also the site of executions and bullfights. The bulls were penned up
ready for their entrance in the Calleja del Torril on the east side.
After a long period of neglect, the plaza was renovated and is once
again the site of a daily market for clothing and handicrafts; Saturday
is the best day.

Templo Romano To the north is the town hall, to the left of which the remains of a
1st-century Roman temple have been uncovered.

✱
San Pablo San Pablo church looms opposite the town hall. It was built in 1241
using material from the palace-city of Medina Azahara. Its nave and
aisles have Mudejar artesonado ceilings and its walls are lined with
azulejos. The Capilla del Rosario originated in Gothic style in 1409
and contains the tomb of the grand master of the Order of Calatrava,
Martín López, while the chancel is decorated in Baroque style. The
vault of the sacristy, on the other hand, is Moorish. A work of art
worth seeing here is the figure group *Virgen de las Angustias by Juan
de Mesa*.

Casa de los Close to the church lies Casa de los Villalones, built in 1560, which
Villalones betrays Italian influence with its triple loggia in the upper storey.

Northern City Quarters

Plaza de Plaza de las Tendillas combines the historical with the bustling side
las Tendillas of Córdoba. The equestrian statue of Gran Capitán Gonzalo Fernández de Córdoba, the fountains and the bars are popular meeting
points after shopping in the stores round about.

Bulvar del C/Conde de Gondomar runs west from the plaza to Bulvar del Gran
Gran Capitán Capitán, the elegant city boulevard lined with bars, cinemas and
shops. About in the middle is the church of **San Hipólito**, to which
the remains of Ferdinand IV and Alfonso XI were brought in 1706
from the Capilla Real in the Mezquita. South of it, in the direction of
the Judería, the remains of a smaller mosque can be seen. The bell
tower of **San Juan** was once its minaret. It still has gemel windows
with horseshoe arches. From the church square in front of San Mi-

guel, north of Plaza de las Tendillas, head along Conde de Torres past the house where the torero Manolete was born and turn right at the corner at the Capucine convent into **Plaza de los Dolores**. Here stands one of **the symbols of Córdoba**, a stone cross with Christ crucified surrounded by eight wrought-iron street lamps, the Cristo de los Faroles, which presents a romantic sight, especially at night. The church holds the most popular Madonna figure of the city, the Virgen de los Dolores, heaped with gold and brocade.

Plaza de los Dolores is the favourite place of many Córdobians,

Further to the north on the northeast side of Plaza Colón towers the eight-cornered, crenellated Torre de la Malmuerta from the 15th century.

Torre de la Malmuerta

East of Plaza de las Tendillas lies the fortress-like church of Santa Marina de Aguas Santas. It was begun shortly after the conquest of Córdoba and stands out because of its massive buttresses. On the church square there is a statue commemorating the bullfighter Manolete, who was born in this quarter.

Santa Marina de Aguas Santas

On the way back to the old town is the Palacio de los Marqueses de Viana, the pompous former city palace of the Viana family with a **garden, twelve patios and 181 rooms** that are filled to overflowing with leatherwork, silver, porcelain, azulejos, furniture and paintings (opening hours: Oct–May Mon, Tue, Thu, Sat 10am–1pm, 4–6pm, Sun 10am–2pm; mid-June–Sept Thu–Tue 9am–2pm; closed first half of June).

✶ **Palacio de los Marqueses de Viana** ⏱

Around Córdoba

In early Christian times, Christians found refuge in the heights of the Sierra de Córdoba. The oldest of today's 13 hermitages was built in the 15th century. They are worth a visit primarily for the beautiful surroundings and the view of the Guadalquivir plains and Córdoba. To reach them drive north out of Córdoba at first in the direction of the parador and then take the road leading to the Arruzafa Nature Park. The hermitages can also be reached from ► Medina Azahara. Once there, take a walk along the very beautiful avenue lined with cypresses and palms to the chapel founded in 1732. A cemetery and a hermit's cottage can be seen in front of it. Below the wayside lies

✶ **Las Ermitas**

the lookout point with a statue of Christ (opening hours: April–Sept Tue–Sun 10am–1pm, 4.30–5.45pm, Oct to March 10am–1.30pm, 3–6pm).

Nobody would travel 25km/16mi west of Córdoba into the hot Guadalquivir basin to **Almodóvar del Río** just to see the village. However, the **castillo** is visible for a great distance towering over the village. With its battlements and mighty towers, it is the perfect **picture-postcard medieval castle**. The Moors erected the castle in the 8th century to control traffic on the navigable Guadalquivir River. It became known as the »plague of the Christians« because it caused the Castilians and Aragonians so much trouble. Ferdinando the Saint captured it in 1240, and it gained its present appearance in the 14th century under Pedro the Cruel who used it to hold his treasures. A ring of ramparts, actually a double ring, encloses the courtyard with its two fountains in the northwest and northeast (opening hours: daily 11am–2.30pm, 4–8pm).

A picture book castle: Almodóvar del Río

Montoro Though a bit out of the way, Montoro, the Roman Epora , can be found by taking the N-IV eastwards through 35km/22mi of cotton fields and olive groves to where it is picturesquely nestled above the left bank of Guadalquivir. It was an important fortress in Moorish times and is **typical for small towns in Andalusia** with its churches, nobles' houses and streets of houses. It is worth taking a stroll through this pretty place, especially around the Plaza de España with its 15th-century church, San Bartolomé, and 16th-century town hall. Take time to look inside the archaeological museum in the former church, Santa María de la Mota. Montoro is also suitable as a starting point for trips into the Parque Natural de la Sierra de Cardeña y Montoro to the north in the Sierra Morena where wolves and lynxes still live.

►see separate entry

Medina Azahara

Costa de Almería

►Almería, ►Cabo de Gata, ►Mojácar

★ ★ Costa de la Luz

A–C 7–9

Province: Huelva, Cádiz

The Spanish southern Atlantic coast between the Río Guadiana estuary at the Portuguese border and the headland of Tarifa on the Straits of Gibraltar bears the name Costa de la Luz (»Coast of Light«), because it is almost always bathed in blazing sunlight.

Despite that, the summers here are not so unbearably hot as in the interior because a **wind**, **the »Poniente«**, constantly blows in from the sea providing a refreshing breeze, at least from Matalascañas up to the Portuguese border. The remaining section of the coast down

»Coast of Light«

Sun on a fine sandy beach, surfing in the fresh ocean breeze and swimming in the Atlantic – the »Coast of Light« provides great pleasure.

to Tarifa, on the other hand, is swept the whole year, often with considerable force, by the dry **east wind**, **the »Levante«** – hardly bearable for »normal« tourists and locals, but for experienced **surfers**, in contrast, a dream. For them, the surfing off Tarifa is among the world's best. Almost all villages on the Costa de la Luz live at least in part from fishing, but tourism is an increasingly important source of income. Even though new resorts like Matalascañas or Novo Sancti Petri have been built from scratch, conditions are still a long way away from those on the Costa del Sol; so the Costa de la Luz remains a destination for all those who want to enjoy sun, sand and sea without being hustled by activity directors. Fantastic beaches (a total of 265km/165mi) with the finest sand, bordered inland by eucalyptus trees and pines, are inviting places for a swim in the Atlantic: Matalascañas between Sanlúcar de Barrameda and Rota, for example, or Chiclana de la Frontera, Barbate or Tarifa. Nature lovers enjoy the unique **Coto de Doñana National Park** which, by the way, divides the coast in two; it takes a long drive around it to get from the north to the south. Tourists seeking culture will get their money's worth inland in cities like Jerez de la Frontera, the »pueblos blancos« and in Seville. The hinterland is the domain of the big landowners, who cultivate wine (sherry, Manzanilla) and olives and breed fighting bulls.

Borderland

The Costa de la Luz also has great historical significance. Cádiz is the oldest city on the Iberian peninsula. Here on the border **between the Christian and Moorish spheres of power** decisive battles were fought, which is why many places bear the additive »de la Frontera« (»on the border«). It was from the ports on this coast that Christoph Columbus started on his expeditions.

Destinations on the Costa de la Luz

►Cádiz, ►Coto de Doñana, ►El Rocío, ►Huelva • Ruta Colombina, ►Jerez de la Frontera, ►El Puerto de Santa María, ►Sanlúcar de Barrameda, ►Tarifa, ►Vejer de la Frontera

✳ Costa del Sol

D–L 8–9

Province: Cádiz, Málaga

For a long time the »Sun Coast« was defined as the whole Andalusian Mediterranean coastline from Tarifa (Cádiz province) to Cabo de Gata (Almería province). As a marketing strategy, the coastline around ►Almuñecar (province of Granada) and around ►Almería were split off and named the Costa Tropical, leaving the strip from Tarifa to the eastern border with the province of Málaga as the Costa del Sol.

The sun shines everywhere on the Costa del Sol,
but only a few beaches are unobstructed like here near Nerja.

The heart of the tourist area, the coastline from Málaga to Estepona, »Sun Coast«
is considered to be **the largest continuous resort area in Europe**.
Up until the 1950s, hardly a traveller strayed this way, but then organized mass tourism discovered the coast where the sun shines 320
days a year. The boom years began that transformed sleepy fishing
villages into hotel cities for tens of thousands and, as tastes changed,
holiday clubs and apartment complexes were added – about 300,000
non-Spanish nationals now live here. The price paid was the disfigur-
ing of the coastal landscape with piles of concrete and the four-lane
N-340 cutting right through villages. The effects of this have been
somewhat mitigated by the construction of the Autopista del Sol toll

road, part of a programme begun in the 1990s to correct previous excesses, including the construction of sewage treatment plants and the redesigning of whole beach promenades. This has made the Costa del Sol indisputably more attractive. Despite that, visitors seeking peace and quiet will not be happy here because the **night life** is just as important as the **beach life**, so that there is no dearth of discos, nightclubs, restaurants, bars, fiestas and all manner of beach entertainment imaginable. Finally, the Costa del Sol is also a **paradise for golfers** – nowhere in Europe are more golf courses concentrated in such a limited space, which the world's best golfers acknowledged by staging the Ryder Cup in Sotogrande, the first time it was held in Europe outside Great Britain. The **mountainous hinterland** is completely different from the coast. There it is possible to escape the hustle and bustle. With its white-washed houses, its agaves and cacti, its slopes covered by pines and olive trees, country estates and cheerful villages, this countryside is a **true image of Andalusia**.

Sights on the Costa del Sol ►Algeciras, ►Estepona, ►Fuengirola, ►Gibraltar, ►Málaga, ►Marbella, ►Nerja, ►Torremolinos

Costa Tropical

►Almuñecar

★★ Coto de Doñana

(Parque Nacional de Doñana)

C 7/8

Province: Huelva, Seville

Numerous migrating birds spend the winter here or take a break on their way to Africa and consort with their fellow birds living here, making the park a unique bird paradise and one of Europe's most beautiful nature reserves.

History The Coto de Doñana National Park lies in the delta of the Río Guadalquivir, bordering it to the east. In the south it extends to the mouth of the river opposite ►Sanlúcar de Barrameda, in the west to the Atlantic and in the north to the A-483 between Matalascañas and ►El Rocío.

This countryside was never much settled – the marshland (marismas) climate was too hostile, with malaria rampant until the middle of the 20th century. The area was of interest almost exclusively as **hunting grounds** (Spanish: coto), which is why it has remained un-

Coto de Doñana Plan

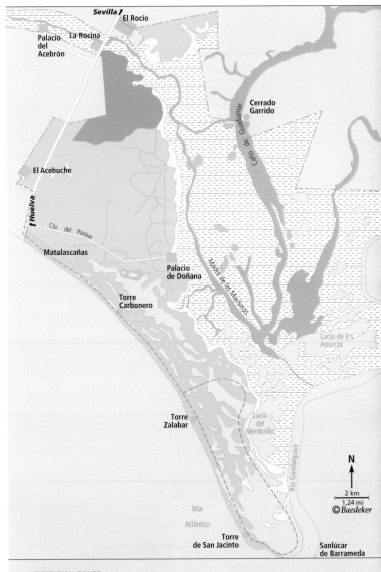

VEGETATION ZONES

- Eucalyptus trees
- Forest and underbrush (›montes‹)
- Shifting dunes
- Stands of pines (›corrales‹)
- Old course of river Guadalquivir (›caños‹)
- Marshes (›marismas‹)
- Transitional zone between marshes and dunes
- Mounds and dry areas (›vetas‹)
- --- Land Rover route

spoiled. Alfonso X, the Wise, was in the habit of hunting here in the 13th century and the dukes of Medina Sidonia, who came into possession of the land, followed his example. The 7th duke, Alfonso Pérez de Guzmán, commander of the Spanish Armada that was destroyed in 1588, erected a **palace** for his wife, Doña Ana, in 1595 in the middle of the present park. Today, it is a research centre. In the course of time, the name »Coto de Doña Ana« became »Coto de Doñana«. The dukes sold the area in 1897 to the sherry baron, William Garvey. Around this time, two British citizens, Abel Chapman and Walter Buck, called attention for the first time to the wealth of nature in Coto, but it was not until the 1960s that conservationists achieved the creation of that national park that opened in 1969 as »Parque Nacional de Doñana« with an area of 37,000 ha/90,000 acres. There followed an expansion in 1978 to 50,000 ha/125,000 acres with additional protected areas amounting to 26,500 ha/65,000 acres close by but not directly part of the park. The park has been a **UNESCO biosphere reserve** since 1994.

Endangered The national park is endangered. The immense rice and fruit plantations surrounding it use up a lot of land and water and toxic substances from the liberal application of fertilizer also reaches the marismas. The greatest catastrophe hit the park in 1998 when 5 million tons of acidic water and mud contaminated with heavy metals flowed into the Río Guadimar and reached right up to the park. Finally, tourism in the form of the Matalascañas holiday resort and its enormous water consumption is a threat to the park. A project planned near Matalascañas with 32,000 beds was stopped. On the other hand, the municipality of Sanlúcar de Barrameda and the Department of Environment approved a luxury holiday centre with golf courses north of the estuary.

Flora and fauna Three eco-systems can be distinguished; the **wetlands** (Doñana Húmedo – marisma in the estuary and lagoons), the **arid region** (Doñana Seco – forest and underbrush) and the **bands of shifting sand dunes** on the coast. The areas flooded for the most part of the year (almajales) are the backwaters of the Guadalquivir (caños),

! *Baedeker* TIP

Take binoculars!
Birdwatching is possible even without a Land Rover tour. The A-483 crosses over an arm of the marisma shortly before El Rocío and the bridge makes a very good observation point, provided you have binoculars. Added to that there is a view of the white houses of the pilgrimage site.

► VISITING COTO DE DOÑANA

PARK ACCESS

Access to the park is tightly regulated and not allowed without the accompaniment of game keepers. El Acebuche Information Centre conducts four-hour tours in Land Rovers; departure: mid-May–beginning of Sept daily 8.30am and 5.30pm, rest of the time daily except Mon 8.30am and 3pm; written or telephone booking with »Sociedad Cooperativa Andaluza Marismas de El Rocío«, Plaza del Acebuchal, 16, E-21750 El Rocío, tel. 959 43 04 32; All-day tours are also offered for groups of eight or more persons. The park can also be experienced on a four-hour boat trip on the Guadalquivir River on the »Real Ferdinand« from Sanlúcar de Barrameda. Stop-overs in Entorno de Doñana on the border of the park, at the Monte Algaida salt-works and the reconstructed marsh village are included. Departure: daily 10am, June–Sept also 5pm, April, May, Oct also 4pm; order tickets in advance at the Fábrica de Hielo Information Centre (tel. 956 36 38 13, fax 956 36 21 96). A one-day horse ride through the marshland can be booked at Doñana Ecuestre, El Rocío, tel. 959 44 24 74. A mile-long trail (»sendero dunar«) leads from the holiday resort of Matalascañas to the first belt of dunes.

INFORMATION CENTRES

The information centres provide comprehensive information about the park and there are short, marked paths on which the animals living there can be observed. The centres are open daily from 8am to 7pm, June–Sept until 9pm.

El Acebuche Information Centre
4km/2.5mi from Matalascañas and 1.5km /1mi from the A-483
Tel. 959 44 87 11
www.parquenacionaldonana.com
Exhibits, audio-visual show, cafétería, souvenir shop, two paths 1.5km/1mi and 3.5km/2mi in length with observation stations.

La Rocina
1km/0.6mi before El Rocío
Audio-visual show, exhibition about Romería del Rocío
(see Baedeker Special p.362),
path 3.5km/2mi.

El Acebrón
7km/4.5mi from La Rocina
Exhibit about charcoal burners, pine-cone collectors and fishermen in the marisma, path 1.5km/0.9mi.

Fábrica de Hielo
Fábrica de Hielo, Sanlúcar de Barrameda, Avenida de Bajo de Guía
Permanent exhibition and observation point (daily 9am–8pm).

WHERE TO STAY
► Mid-range
Parador de Mazagón
In Mazagón, Playa de Mazagón
Tel. 959 53 63 00
Fax 959 53 62 28
E-Mail: mazagon@parador.es
www.parador.es, 43 rooms
Modern hotel in a fantastic location facing the sea, with fabulous beaches, behind it the national park.

Gran Hotel del Coto
In Matalascañas, Sector D, 2. Fase
Tel. 959 44 00 17
Fax 959 44 02 02, 466 rooms
The largest and most expensive hotel

in town. Matalascañas is a not particularly nice-looking new development
with its hotel complexes but offers
every kind of seaside recreation and a
wonderful beach.

▶ Budget
Albaida
Crta. de Matalascañas, km 18,3
Tel. 959 37 60 29
Fax 959 37 61 08
Everything that guests need, directly
on the beach.

El Flamero
Ronda Maestro Alonso
Tel. 902 50 52 00
Fax 902 50 53 00
www.hotelflamero.es,
279 rooms and 52 apartments
Large middle-category hotel.

Los Tamarindos
Avda. Adelfas, 3
Tel. 959 43 01 19, 25 rooms
Small but classy – well furnished
pension.

springs (ojos) and the long, flat lagoons (lucios). In between are
small mounds (paciles) and higher dry areas (vetas).
The **marismas** (marshlands) are influenced by the subterranean
water-level. During the dry season (July–September, lowest point in
August), they lie dry and abandoned; the first **migratory birds** arrive
at the end of September. Seaside bulrush, marsh rush and broad-
leaved cattails are some of the plants that grow here. Ducks (European widgeons, northern pintails, teals, spoonbills and pochards)
find ideal conditions here. Coots, great crested grebes, dabchicks,
purple herons, gull-billed terns, whiskered terns and black terns nest
here in the spring. They are joined by many mud-flat dwellers and
marsh harriers.

Lagoons ▶ The larger lagoons lie parallel to the coastline (Laguna de Santa Olal-
la, Laguna Dulce, Laguna del Taraje), the smaller further inland (Laguna del Moral, de Navazo del Toro, del Sapo, del Brezo and others).
They are lined with cork oak, pine and tree heath; gorse and ferns
provide greenery on the banks. The most important **aquatic
inhabitants** are marsh frogs, European pond turtles and Caspian
terrapins. The endangered red-knobbed coot has its last European
refuge here. Fallow deer and red deer, as well as wild boar visit the
banks; coypu live next to the water.

Cork oak
woodland ▶ Cork oak woods have become rare; one strip of it divides the marismas from Monte de Doñana. These cork oaks are a habitat for **whole
breeding colonies** of grey herons, little egrets, cattle egrets, spoonbills and some white storks. Uninvited guests in the nesting trees are
birds of prey like the common buzzard, red kite, kestrels and jack-
daws. The poisonous snub-nosed viper lives on the ground.

Monte de
Doñana ▶ »Monte« is not the name of a mountain but rather a copse or thick-
et. Monte de Doñana consists of Mediterranean scrub sprinkled with
cork oak. Among others, the philaria (common lime), rosemary, juniper, lavender and white thyme blossom here. The **reptiles** include
the Greek tortoise, the ladder snake, the Montpellier snake and,

Coto de Doñana nursery – whole colonies of storks breed here.

again, the snub-nosed viper. Along with the birds of prey mentioned above, there are magpies, great grey shrikes, nightjars and numerous red hens. The most common mammals are red and fallow deer and wild boar; in addition, weasels, polecats, wildcats und foxes. The small-spotted genet is less common; on the other hand, badgers are numerous and there are great numbers of wild rabbits.Pine trees thrive in the park, particularly in the southern part, and the undergrowth between them is made up of tree heath, rockrose, gorse and pistachio. The pine forests are the biosphere for wood-pigeons, turtle-doves, blackbirds, mistle thrushes, common buzzards, red kites and kestrels; the short-toed eagle and the hobby return each year. The **azure-winged magpie** is very rare and is **almost only to be found here**.

◀ Pine forests

The sand dunes that stretch along the coastline surround pine forests when they advance inland so that these forests stand like islands (corrales) in the sand until they are eventually smothered. The vegetation is very sparse, mainly consisting of beach grass and a scrub called camarina, whose sweet fruit is eaten by birds. The common spiny-footed lizard, the snub-nosed viper and the Montpellier snake are welcome prey for the short-toed eagle and the screech owl.

◀ Dunes

The Spanish lynx (about 25 pairs), smaller than the European lynx and spotted, as well as the snake-eating ichneumon or mongoose, the only representative of this species of viverrid that mostly goose-steps around in family groups, are only to be found in Coto de Doñana. The imperial eagle (about 18 pairs), purple moorhen (the only European breeding colony), white-eyed pochard as well as the ruddy shelduck and the white-headed duck that spend the winters here are all also very rare.

Indigenous species

★ Écija

E 6

Province: Seville
Population: 37,100

Altitude: 110m/361ft

Three things make Écija, located on the left bank of the Río Genil, well known. Its total of eleven church towers lined with azulejo tiles have given it the nickname »city of towers«. The Andalusian and Arab horses that breed here enjoy a nation-wide reputation; and, finally, it is the hottest city in Spain, which justifies its second nickname, »the frying-pan of Andalusia«.

Écija Plan

© Baedeker

Santa Cruz
Convento marroquíes
Convento filipensas
San Pablo y Domingo
Descalzos
Convento de las Teresas
Plaza de Abastos
San Francisco
San Juan
Palacio de Alcántara
Ayuntamiento
Plaza de España
① Palacio de Valhermoso
Santa María
Santa Bárbara
① Palacio de Peñaflor
Palacio de Benamejí
Palacio de Almenara Alta
San Gil
Palacio de Santaella
Palacio de los Aguilar
Convento de la Merced
Santiago
Sevilla, Carmona, ② ↓ ↓ ②

Where to eat
① Bodegón del
② Gallego
③ Las Costillas

Where to stay
① Platería
② Sol Pirola

Roman Astigi, which originated in an Iberian settlement, developed into a very important trading hub thanks to its location on the river. The Moors fortified the town and erected a number of mosques until Ferdinand III drove them out in 1240. The earthquake of 1755 that destroyed Lisbon also toppled many of the church towers that had been made from the minarets. As a result, they were rebuilt in the style of the time – today Écija's tourist asset.

What to See in Écija

Before the dredgers moved in for an underground car park, **Plaza de España** with a fountain and date palms and flowers scattered about, was certainly one of Andalusia's most beautiful squares. During the excavation, however, **extensive archaeological remains** were discovered, so that the plaza has long since been walled up as an excavation site. A Roman bath and two Roman mosaics as well as an extensive Muslim cemetery were found. The plaza can be observed through a **camera obscura** in the tourist information in the city hall on the west side of the plaza (Tue–Sun 10am–2.30pm); a Roman mosaic from the 3rd century AD and the old council chamber are worth seeing in the city hall itself.

⏵ VISITING ÉCIJA

INFORMATION (OFICINA DE TURISMO)

Palacio de Benamejí
C. Cánovas del Castillo, 4
E-41400 Écija
Tel. 955 90 29 33

WHERE TO EAT

▶ **Moderate**

① *Bodegón del Gallego*
C. A. Aparicio, 3
Quality fish and meat dishes.

② *Las Costillas*
Avenida del Genil
Tel. 954 83 39 16

Good fish and meat cuisine and a wide variety of desserts.

WHERE TO STAY

▶ **Budget**

① *Platería*
Garcilópez, 1
Tel. 955 90 27 54, 18 rooms
Decent city hotel.

② *Sol Pirola*
C. Miguel de Cervantes, 50
Tel. 954 83 03 00
Fax 954 83 58 79
Somewhat south of the centre with comfortably furnished rooms.

The cloister of the 18th-century church of Santa María, to the left behind the city hall, holds a sculpture collection with an outstanding marble head of Germanicus.

Santa María

A little south of the church lies the unusually decorated 18th-century Palacio de Benameji with the city museum inside (opening hours: June–Sept Tue–Sun 9am–2pm; Oct–May Tue–Fri 9.30am–1.30pm, 4.30–6.30pm, Sat, Sun 9am–2pm).

✱
Palacio de Benameji

On Plaza de Santiago stands Santiago el Mayor, a church that was begun in the 15th century and remodelled after the earthquake, during which some Mudejar elements were restored. A scallop, the symbol of the pilgrims following the Way of St James, is recognizable above the portal. Among the paintings inside are pictures by Alejo Fernández and Pedro de Campaña, as well as a crucifixion scene by Roldán.

Santiago el Mayor

The Mudejar palace standing behind the town hall dates back to the 14th century and is home to a Carmelite convent, the **Convento de las Teresas**.

Past the Iglesia de la Concepción to the right – it has a splendid artesonado ceiling –is the **Iglesia de los Descalzos**, whose Baroque interior is one of the most beautiful in Écija.

 Baedeker TIP

Bizcochos

The nuns of Convento Marroquíes opposite the Iglesia de los Descalzos are very adept at baking bizcochos (almond biscuits), which they also sell there – do try them!

The tower of San Juan is reminiscent of the Giralda of Seville.

To the north of Plaza de España in **Santa Cruz** church, which was built on the site of a mosque, it is worth taking a look at the 13th-century portrait of Nuestra Señora del Valle and a 4th-century stone Visigoth sarcophagus decorated with reliefs that is used as an altar.

Soaring above the maze of alleyways east of the plaza, the tower of the church of **San Juan** is undoubtedly the most beautiful in the city and reminiscent of the Giralda in Seville.

Behind the church is the **Palacio de Valhermoso** (16th century); its Plateresque facade is on the corner of the building.

✱
Palacio de Peñaflor

Palacio de Peñaflor, across from the Palacio de Valhermoso, particularly stands out among Écija's noble houses. It possesses a stunning facade adorned with 18th-century frescoes and a magnificent portal with straight as well as serpentine columns of rose marble. The marvellous **wrought-iron balcony** that stretches across the whole front of the building on the upper storey is considered to be **the longest in all of Spain**. The exterior Baroque splendour of the palace continues on the inside in the amazing embellishment of the grand stairway and in the patio.

Carmona ►see separate entry

Estepona

E 9

Province: Málaga	**Altitude:** 21m/69ft
Population: 39,700	

Estepona, at the foot of the Sierra Bermeja, is the province of Málaga's most western holiday resort on the ►Costa del Sol. The former fishing village grew considerably during the 1960s with the emerging mass tourism, but managed to maintain its pretty village centre along with a substantial fishing and yacht harbour.

Possibly founded by the Phoenicians, Estepona was inhabited by the **History** Romans, as the baths near Río Guadalmanso testify. It was not until the 15th century that the then Moorish town (called Alexthebuna) fell to the Christians led by Enrique IV.

▶ VISITING ESTEPONA

INFORMATION (OFICINA DE TURISMO)

Avda. San Lorenzo, 1,
E-29680 Estepona
Tel. 952 80 09 13
Fax 952 79 21 81
www.infoestepona.com

WHERE TO EAT

► Expensive
La Posá Dos
C. Caridad, 95
Tel. 952 80 00 29
High-class and pretty, Spanish cooking.

► Inexpensive
Los Rosales
Damas, 12
Tel. 952 79 29 45
Deep-fried fish and seafood – simple, cheap, good.

WHERE TO STAY

► Luxury
Las Dunas
La Boladilla Baja,
Ctra. de Cádiz, km 163,5
Tel. 952 79 43 45
Fax 952 79 48 25
www.las-dunas.com,
76 rooms
An exceedingly luxurious centre for culinary delicacies, beauty cult and relaxation.

El Paraíso
Ctra. Cádiz-Málaga, km 167
Tel. 952 88 30 00
Fax 952 88 20 19
www.hotelparaisocostadelsol.com,
180 rooms
Japanese garden and countless sports activities; sauna, fitness, golf course designed by a U.S. golf pro, Chinese medical centre and the largest heated swimming pool on the Costa del Sol – which all comes at a price.

► Mid-range
Club Marítimo
In Sotogrande, Puerto de Sotogrande
Tel. 956 79 02 00, fax 956 79 03 77
www.hotelmaritimosotogrande.com,
39 rooms
Noble abode on one of the most elegant and bustling yachting harbours on the Costa del Sol with an ocean view from every room.

► Budget
La Malagueña
Raphale, 1
Tel. 952 80 00 11,
14 rooms
Recommendable accommodation in a central location on the main square with balconies facing the plaza.

EVENTS

Fiesta Mayor
The town's biggest fiesta takes place from 4 to 9 July with bullfighting and fireworks.

Fishermen's fiesta Virgen del Carmen
The fiesta of the patron saints with processions on land and water is celebrated on 16 July.

The activities in the fishing and yacht harbour of Estepona can be watched from the cafés and bars in the harbour basin.

What to See in and around Estepona

Estepona

The remains of a Moorish fortress and a medieval watchtower have been preserved in the town. Most of the activity in the old part of town is at Plaza de las Flores and Plaza Arce. The majority of the restaurants are in C. Terraza; there is one bar after the other in C. Real. It is also worth visiting the market hall; early risers can watch the fish auction held every morning in the harbour. Estepona's **town museum** is placed on the edge of an **unusual, elliptic bullring** and has four departments – bullfighting, ancient history, archaeology and local history (opening hours: Mon–Fri 9am–3pm, Sat 10am–2pm).

The beaches totalling 21km/13mi on municipal territory offer a variety of **sports activities**: a sailing club, sea fishing, waterskiing, three golf courses, a riding school, tennis courts and the Pradoworld Aquapark.

Parque Selwo

Adventurous parents and their offspring should not miss Selwo Nature Park, east of Estepona at km 162.5 on the A-49 – not cheap but exciting. More than 2,000 animals live here in the wild, including lions, elephants, tigers and rhinoceros. The grounds are explored on a Jeep tour.

★ Sierra Bermeja

Far away from the busy coast, the hinterland of the Sierra Bermeja has serene places in a countryside marked by cork oak and pine. The white village of Casares is especially pretty in its fabulous location on a mountain ridge only 15km/9mi from the coast and still a world away. Until now, they have been able to keep the bustle of the tourist sites at a distance.

Sotogrande, 23km/14mi to the southwest, is a luxury holiday resort that has grown since 1970 where some of the most beautiful (and exclusive) golf courses on the Costa del Sol are to be found. Taking an example from Miami, its yacht harbour has anchorage right in front of the door. Fish restaurants, bars and cafés are lined up around the harbour basin. The sandy beaches directly to the south are in their natural state and full of flotsam. To the north lies Playa del Puerto – its beach bars are the »in« place with the beach crowd.

! Baedeker TIP

Slow is beautiful

Plan a lot of time for a visit to Genalguacil because, first of all, it takes some while on the winding road through Manilva, Gaucín and Algatocín just to get to the village in the Serranía de Ronda. Secondly, leave time for a leisurely stroll through the lanes where the works of contemporary Spanish artists are hanging or standing. Twice a year the village community invites artists to work here – and leave their works behind.

Fuengirola

F 8

Province: Málaga
Population: 45,000

Altitude: 6m/20ft

Fuengirola lies halfway between ► Marbella and ► Málaga. While the coastline from Marbella to Fuengirola is moderately developed, for the most part with entirely decent-looking bungalow complexes, the real mass tourism begins at Fuengirola, a mecca for beach holidays. Beginning there, one towering hotel follows the other almost without interruption all the way to the gates of Málaga.

What to See in and around Fuengirola

Fuengirola developed from the Roman settlement of Suel, which the Moors named Sujayl and built a castle there. It was conquered in 1485 by the Catholic Monarchs. It cannot be said that Fuengirola is exactly worth seeing, with the exception of the ruins of a castle on the western edge of the town that Abd ar-Rahman III erected in the 10th century. Otherwise, hotel high-rises stand next to no-less monotonous bars, restaurants, souvenir shops, nightclubs and discos. On the other hand, the visitors' entertainment needs are well looked

Fuengirola

VISITING FUENGIROLA

after; 7km/4.5mi of beaches, fiestas and bullfighting when in season, recreational activities from golf courses, yacht harbour and zoo to a large range of courses are enough to keep boredom at bay.

Mijas 9km/5.5mi to the north lies the village of Mijas, praised in Fuengirola as a typical »white village«. Once there, it can be seen that the majority of its white-washed houses are bars, restaurants and souvenir shops run by British, French and German owners, and the »typical Andalusian« touch is hardly authentic. The »burro taxis« fit in with all this – with donkeys decked out with rear-view mirrors, taxi signs and registration numbers, all in accordance with regulations. At any rate, there is a super view of the Mediterranean from the southern slopes of the Sierra de Mijas. The part of the village on the coast, Mijas Costa, has a large water park. Nevertheless, Mijas has a history its own. In the 9th and 10th centuries a Christian king, Samuel I, and his sons ruled the kingdom of Mijas, which was distinguished by religious tolerance, with its predominately Muslim population here in the middle of Muslim territory.

Hinterland Real, typical »white villages« can be seen by venturing out into the hinterland of Mija. Here it is possible to wander around and explore serene places like Alozaina, Casarabonela or Alhaurín el Grande. From Alhaurín, head on to **Coín**, which has four splendid Gothic churches, as well as a bishop's palace dating back to the 16th century. A few miles outside the village stand the remains of a Roman aqueduct.

Gibraltar

E 9

British Crown Colony (dominion)   **Area:** 6.5 sq km/2.5 sq mi
Population: 27,000   **Altitude:** 0–426m/1,397

The »key to the Mediterranean«, the famous rock peninsula of Gibraltar, under British sovereignty since 1704, lies near the southern
tip of the Iberian peninsula. The massive rock that rises straight up
out of the ocean on the east side of the Bay of Algeciras was called Jabal riq by the Arabs; the English call it simply »The Rock«. On
its west slope lies the city, on the east slope the fishing village of
Catalan Bay with the beach of the same name and Sandy Bay.

The Gibraltarians are a mix of people from all parts of the British
Isles, Spain, Portugal and Morocco, and even India. The **jumble of
languages** is accordingly colourful; along with English in all variations and Spanish, there is an English-Spanish mishmash called
»Llanito«. The Rock is an attraction for being a curiosity, a real
British colony in sizzling Spain – replete with pubs and helmeted
policemen – along with duty-free shopping and a fantastic view
across to Africa. Since the withdrawal of the major part of the
British military and the accompanying loss of many jobs, Gibraltar has concentrated on tourism, postage stamp sales, the harbour
and its reputation as a tax haven and financial site – 50,000 companies are registered here. The cur-
rency is the Gibraltar pound,
which has an exchange rate tied to
the British pound. Euros are also
accepted. The airport, whose runway was built in the Bay of Algeciras and is crossed by the road leading to the Spanish border (**traffic
lights!**), has connections to, among
other places, London and Man-
chester. In contrast to Great Britain, they drive on the right-hand
side in Gibraltar!

Key to the Mediterranean

> **!** *Baedeker* TIP
>
> **Hassle-free to Gibraltar**
>
> Do not take a car to Gibraltar! The Spanish
> police often enough subject cars to an extremely
> thorough inspection on the border, causing long
> traffic jams. It is much easier to park in one of
> the multi-storey car-parks directly at the border
> and take the bus or go on foot to Gibraltar.
> Passports or identity cards are needed for entry.

The Strait of Gibraltar, called Fretum Gaditanum or Fretum Hercu-
leum in ancient times, is the vital geographical as well as strategic
link between the Atlantic and the Mediterranean. For the classical
world, the rock named Calpe together with Mount Abyla (Djebel
Musa) on the African side near ► Ceuta were the **»Pillars of Hercules«**, the gateway to the great ocean, which, according to legend,
were created by Hercules' tremendous strength. In AD 711, the
Moors, led by **Tariq**, for whom Jabal Tariq (»Rock of Tariq«) was

*History and
constitution*

named, first set foot on European soil here. It was not until 1462 that the Spanish were able to wrest Gibraltar away from the Arabs again. During the War of the Spanish Succession, British troops under George of Hesse-Darmstadt took the fortress by surprise in 1704. Gibraltar was awarded to the British in the **Treaty of Utrecht in 1713** »for all time«. Since then it has been a **British crown colony** and as such, autonomous in domestic affairs. It is subject to the British crown in matters of foreign policy, defence and internal security. The governor heads the colony, supported by the nine-man Gibraltar Council. The Council of Ministers is chosen by the 15-member parliament.

All attempts by the Spanish to regain Gibraltar, who consider it to be a colonial thorn in their side, both militarily and diplomatically, have been unsuccessful. This has provoked continued harassment at the

▶ VISITING GIBRALTAR

INFORMATION (GIBRALTAR INFORMATION CENTRE)

The Piazza, Main Street, GB-Gibraltar
Tel. (95 67 from Spain) or (0 03 50 from other countries) 7 49 82
18–20, Bomb House Lane (Gibraltar Museum)
Tel. 956 77 42 89
www.gibraltar.gi/tourism, www.gibraltar.gov.uk

WHERE TO EAT

▶ Expensive

① *Bunters*
1, College Lane
Tel. from Spain (96 57) 704 82
Tel. from other countries: (00350) 704 82
Elegant

WHERE TO STAY

▶ Mid-range

② *Rock Hotel*
3, Europa Road
www.rockhotelgibraltar.com
Tel. from Spain
(96 57) 730 00
Tel. from other countries
(00350) 730 00

www.rockhotelgibraltar.com
160 rooms
Flaggship hotel of the crown colony built directly into the rock.

▶ Budget

① *Continental Hotel*
1, Engineer Lane
Tel. from Spain (96 57) 769 00
Tel. from other countries (00350) 769 00
Central location near Main Street; small, respectable hotel.

SHOPPING

All the good things from the island are in Main Street ...

ACTIVITY

Dolphin Watching
Three different species of dolphin live in the Bay of Gibraltar. Boat tours to the dolphins start in the harbour, mostly at Marina Bay (tel. 956 77 19 14) or Queensway Bay.

EVENTS

National holiday
The 10th of September is celebrated in Gibraltar in bikinis and shorts.

border. At least it was agreed in April 2000 not to upgrade Gibraltar's status within the EU. The Gibraltarians have no interest in becoming Spanish – in a referendum in 1967, all of 44 voters out of 12,182 expressed a preference for Spain. Nothing has changed in this majority

Gibraltar *Plan*

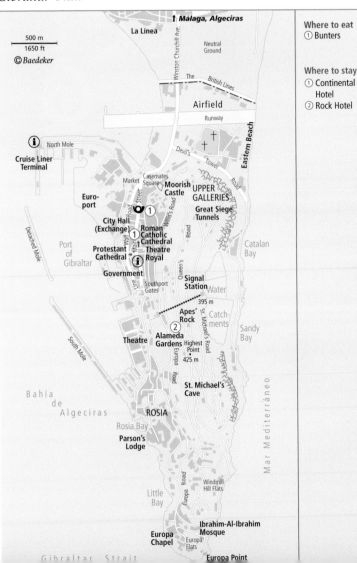

500 m
1650 ft
© Baedeker

↑ *Málaga, Algeciras*

La Linea

Winston Churchill Ave.

Neutral Ground

The British Lines

Airfield
Runway

Eastern Beach

North Mole
Cruise Liner Terminal

Devil's Tower Road

Euro-port

Market
Casemates Square
Moorish Castle
UPPER GALLERIES

Willi's Road

Great Siege Tunnels

City Hall (Exchange)
Wall Road
Main Street
Roman Catholic Cathedral
Protestant Cathedral
Theatre Royal
Government

Catalan Bay

Queen's Road

Line Wall Road
Southport Gates

Signal Station
Water

St. Michael's Road
Catchments

Sandy Bay

395 m
Apes' Rock

Detached Mole

Port of Gibraltar

South Mole

Theatre
Alameda Gardens
Europa Road
Highest Point
425 m

Bahía de Algeciras

St. Michael's Cave

ROSIA
Rosia Bay
Parson's Lodge

Mar Mediterráneo

Little Bay

Europa Road

Windmill Hill Flats

Europa Chapel
Europa Flats
Ibrahim-Al-Ibrahim Mosque

Gibraltar Strait
Europa Point

Where to eat
① Bunters

Where to stay
① Continental Hotel
② Rock Hotel

Spanish fishers off the British rock

situation since then – bad prospects for British-Spanish discussions over a sharing of sovereignty. Spain demands the return of Gibraltar, and for the first time in December 2004, representatives of Spain, Great Britain and Gibraltar held talks.

What to See in Gibraltar

Gibraltar's old town (**North Town**) begins beyond the airport with Casemates Square, dominated on the east by the remains of a **Moorish castle**, which was built in the 8th century and rebuilt by the Almohads in the 14th century. A stone's throw northwest of the castle lies the market and the **harbour**. It was established as early as 1309 and has been noticeably built up in recent years. **Main Street**, which has the most hotels, businesses, pubs and public buildings, goes from Casemates Square past the post office and stock exchange with the the town hall at the back, then on to the Roman Catholic cathedral, a former mosque that was remodelled in Gothic style in 1502. The **Gibraltar Museum** is down Bomb House Lane, which branches off to the right, where, besides everything about the city history, a 30 sq m/320 sq ft model of the rock peninsula from 1865, and a well preserved Moorish bath are also on display (opening hours: Mon–Fri 10am–6pm, Sat to 2pm). On Cathedral Square there is an Anglican cathedral constructed in 1821 in Moorish style. To the right on the south end of Main Street is the governor's palace (The Convent). It was built in 1531 as a Franciscan convent,. The changing of the guard can be seen on Tuesdays at 11am.

Southport Gates at the end of Main Street lead to the Alameda Gardens, Gibraltar's botanical gardens with Trafalgar Cemetery behind it. At the beginning of the gardens are the **cable cars** (cable cars: daily from 9am, last car at 5.15pm, descent 5.45pm) that go up to signal station (395m/1,296ft). The Upper Galleries and Apes' Rock are up there. The fortress, the **Upper Galleries**, was dug into the Rock during the Spanish-French siege from 1779 to 1783. It is still possible to marvel at the cannons in the Great Siege Tunnels and enjoy the fantastic view from the battlements. The Military Heritage Centre also explains more about the history of the fortress. About 150 Barbary apes live on **Apes' Rock or Apes' Den** – the only type of ape to live in the wilds in Europe. Their ancestors were brought over from Africa by British soldiers as pets in the 18th century. Churchill is said to have ordered that the number should never fall below 24. A corporal is detailed to feed these living symbols of Gibraltar. Be careful, as the apes like to bite. The steps along the way from Apes' Rock to **St Michael's Cave** lead up to the Rock's highest point, 426m/1,398ft. St Michael's Cave, the biggest of the 143 caves in Gibraltar has beautiful stalactites and stalagmites. Concerts are also held here in the summer. The Europa Road, a 5km/3mi-long, road on the

Cable cars

Living symbol – the Gibraltar ape (monkey)

heights with beautiful views, runs uphill from Alameda Gardens on the western slope of the Rock between the houses and gardens of the **South Town** and descends again past the fissured rocks of Europa Pass down to Europa Point at the southern tip of the peninsula with its famous lighthouse. There is a stunning view here out onto the Bay of Algeciras, the African coast and Apes' Rock and, in good weather, all the way to the Moroccan Atlas Mountains.

✻ ✻
◄ Europa Point

Parson's Lodge Battery on Rosia Bay, where the »HMS Victory« anchored in 1805 with the body of Admiral Nelson, who was killed at Trafalgar, was built in 1875 and can be toured. One of the two famous 100-ton cannons of Gibraltar still stands on the opposite side of the bay.

Parson's Lodge

🕐
Opening hours:
Daily 10am–6pm

★ ★ Granada

Province: Granada   **Altitude:** 685m/2,247ft 5in
Population: 265,000

»Granada« – the name alone is magic; it brings to mind Arabian nights, the smell of almond and orange blossom and conjures dreams of the wondrous tales of the 1001 nights.

Moorish residence

The former Moorish royal residence, today »just« the provincial capital, lies magnificently at the foot of the Sierra Nevada between two mountain spurs that drop sharply from the fertile Vega of the Río Genil. The northern ridge of the two, Albaicín, is at the same time the older part of Granada, divided by the gorge of the Río Darro, which goes underground in the inner city and empties into the Río Genil by the Alhambra. The wonderful Nasrid palace, the apex of and a unique testimony to Moorish-Arab architecture in Europe, sits enthroned on the Alhambra, shimmering in the red of the sunset. Visitors to Andalusia must see it and its city, as the Moorish poet Ibn Zamrak described in the 14th century:

So come and see.
The city is a lady, a mountain of a woman.
A river shimmeringly encircles her body like a waist belt;
flowerlike, jewels glisten at her throat.

Visitors who approach the city today admittedly search in vain for Lady Granada at first, because they must first suffer the usual faceless concrete suburbs and then find their way through the hectic and noisy inner-city. But anyone who takes an evening stroll over Plaza Nueva or sits in front of a bar along the Río Darro with the majestically illuminated Alhambra as backdrop, or who delights in the panorama of the Moorish residence seen from Albaicín at sunset, will surely agree with Ibn Zamrak – Granada is a city of magical charm, a living university city with friendly people and the unforgettable climax of a trip to Andalusia. For it is said, »Quien no ha vista Granada, no ha vista nada – He who has not seen Granada, has seen nothing.«

History

Granada dates back to the Iberian settlement of Iliveri on the Albaicín, which the Romans rechristened Iliberis and enlarged with the two neighbouring settlements of Quastilla and Garnata. The first Christian council held on the Iberian peninsula was in Iliberis.

Moorish Granada ▶

After the founding of the Emirate of Córdoba, a Berber tribe that settled in the Vega chose Iliberis as its chief town under the name of Elvira. When the Caliphate of Córdoba disintegrated in 1010, the governor, Zari ben Zirí, proclaimed an independent kingdom, a taifa,

► VISITING GRANADA

INFORMATION (OFICINA DE TURISMO)

Corral del Carbón, C. Mariana
Piñeda, E-18009 Granada
Tel. 958 22 59 90 or 958 22 10 22
Fax 958 22 39 27

Generalife, s/n, E-18009 Granada
Tel. 958 22 95 75,
Fax 958 22 82 01
www.granada.org,
www.turismodegranada.org,
www.turgranada.com

TOURIST CARD

Tourist pass »Bono Turistico«
Week-long free entry to museums
and travel on the city buses, all for
€18.

EVENTS

► **Expensive**
④ *Chikito*
Plaza del Campillo, 9
Tel. 958 22 33 64
Federico García Lorca was a guest in
the former Alameda artists' café;
Chikito is now one of the better
restaurants in the city. Andalusian
cuisine.

► **Moderate**
① *Arrayanes*
Cuesta Marañas, 4
Tel. 958 22 84 01
Since you are already in the city with
the largest Islamic population in
Spain, why not try some Moroccan
food in an oriental atmosphere?

⑤ *Galatino*
Gran Vía Colón, 29
Tel. 958 80 08 03
Considered to be one of Granada's
best restaurants.

⑦ *Mesón El Trillo*
Callejón del Aljibe de Trillo, 3
Tel. 958 22 51 82
Exquisite Basque-Andalusian cooking
in a simply wonderful villa with
garden in Albaicín.

⑧ *Mirador de Morayma*
Pianista García Carrillo, 2
Tel. 958 22 82 90
www.alquieriamorayma.com
A pleasurable evening is guaranteed in
this restaurant; enjoy deliciously prepared Granada cuisine in a typical
carmen (villa with garden) in the
Albaicín with a fabulous view of the
Alhambra; flamenco Tuesday from
11pm.

Baedeker recommendation

► **Inexpensive**
③ *Castañeda*
C. Almíreceos, 1–3
(near Plaza Nueva)
Tel. 958 22 32 22
The Bodegas Castañeda are a real institution. Both tastefully decorated pubs – one is
a bodega, the other is a destilería – are a
great place to enjoy an aperitif.

► **Inexpensive**
② *Bodegas La Mancha*
Joaquín Costa, 10
Tel. 958 22 89 68
Large selection of tapas near Plaza
Nueva

⑥ *Horno de Santiago*
Plaza de los Campos, 8
Tel. 958 22 34 76 (closed evenings)
Andalusian food at the foot of the
Alhambra hill.

WHERE TO STAY

▶ Luxury

⑤ *Parador Nacional San Francisco*
Real de la Alhambra, s / n
Tel. 958 22 14 40
Fax 958 22 22 64
E-Mail: granada@parador.es
www.parador.es, 39 rooms
One of the finest, if not the finest parador; unique location in an old Franciscan monastery in the gardens of the Alhambra. Ask for a room with a view of the Alhambra.

▶ Mid-range

① *Alhambra Palace*
Plaza Arquitecto García de Paredes, 1

*Moorish styled
Alhambra Palace Hotel*

Tel. 958 22 14 68
Fax 958 22 64 04
www.h-alhambrapalace.es, 126 rooms
Directly at the Alhambra. Comfortable establishment catering to the Alhambra tourism that started at the beginning of the 20th century; not particularly nice to look at, but a great view of the city and the Alhambra.

**④ *Palacio de
Santa Inés***
Cuesta de Santa Inés, 9
Tel. 958 22 23 62
Fax 958 22 24 65
www.palaciosantaines.com,
36 rooms
16th-century city palace at the foot of the Albaicín with a good view up at the Alhambra

▶ Budget

② *Casa »Los Naranjos«*
Barranco de los Naranjos, 10
Tel. 958 22 51 27
www.granadainfo.com/naranjos
Something different for a change; cave apartments in the Sacromonte quarter.

③ *Los Angeles*
Cuesta Escoriaza, 17
Tel. 958 22 14 23
Fax 958 22 21 25
Pleasant hotel near the Alhambra, all rooms with balcony, pool in the garden.

⑥ *Pensión Rodri*
Laurel de las Tablas, 9
Tel. 958 28 80 43
Well-managed pension in the old part of town.

⑦ *Reina Cristina*
Tablas, 4
Tel. 958 25 32 11
Wonderful hotel near the cathedral.

SHOPPING

Granada is famous for it guitar makers and intarsia artists. The main shopping boulevards are C. Reyes Católicos and Gran Vía de Colón, and it is worth window-shopping in Cuesta de Gómerez (the street of the guitar makers), in Cuesta de Chapiz in the Albaicín, and in C. Real de la Alhambra. The street for antique shops is C. Elvira.

Eduardo Ferrer Lucena
Agua del Albaicín, 19
Leather bags and leather accessories.

Cerámica Al-Yarrar
Sánchez Bernardo, C. Bañuelo, 5
Pretty ceramics.

Taller de Taracea
Miguel Laguns,
C. Real de la Alhambra, 30
Tel. 958 22 90 19
Intarsia woodwork – from tables and cabinets to small boxes and trays.

EVENTS

Semana Santa
Especially on Maundy Thursday, when »Cristo de los Gitanos« is honoured in a pilgrimage to Sacromonte.

Feast of Corpus Cristi
Granada's biggest fiesta with flamenco and corridas lasts a week.

International music and dance festival
Late June / early July – most important Spanish festival for classical and contemporary music and ballet; performances in the Generalife open-air theatre (www.granadafestival.org).

Romería del Albaicín
End of September – pilgrimage goes directly through the Albaicín.

Festival de Jazz de Granada
The mood heats up in November at one of the major European jazz festivals (www.jazzgranada.net).

PLAZA DE TOROS

Av. Doctor Oloriz, 25
Tel. 958 22 22 72
The most important fights are in June.

---

in 1013 and made Garnata its capital. It existed only until 1090 when the Berber Almoravids took over, but they in turn were forced to give way to the Almohads in 1149. Córdoba fell to the Christians in 1236. The surviving Moors retreated to Granada, where in the year 1238 Ibn al-Ahmar of the Beni Nasr tribe founded the Nasrid dynasty as Mohammed I. The Nasrids had to buy peace from Ferdinand III of Castile through tribute payments and military support. Subjugation and constant diplomatic manœuvring, however, were the prerequisites for the golden age of the kingdom that lasted 250 years. The 400,000 inhabitants of the 30,000 sq km/12,000 sq mi kingdom cultivated fruit, vegetables, grain and wine, sought-after goods which were shipped out of Málaga, Granada's harbour. By building the Alhambra in the 14th century, Yûsuf I and Mohammed V made the Nasrids immortal, at least as builders.

Highlights Granada

Alhambra
World Cultural Heritage site and Spain's most visited monument; with the fabulously beautiful palace of the Nasrids, extravagantly decorated rooms and enthralling view from the Torre de la Vela.
▶ page 262

Generalife
Formerly the enchanting park of the kings of Granada, today a shady oasis with splashing water.
▶ page 273

Cathedral
The Catholic Monarchs lie buried in the royal chapel of the most important of Andalusia's four great Renaissance churches.
▶ page 274

Albaicín
Barrio with a view of the Alhambra, where the Moorish history of Granada can best be sensed.
▶ page 278

El Bañuelo
Well-preserved 11-century Moorish baths.
▶ page 278

After the Reconquista ▶
Peace in the last Muslim stronghold in Europe came at an end with the marriage of Ferdinand of Aragón and Isabella of Castile. The Catholic Monarchs declared the expulsion of the Moors to be their primary goal. After the fall of Málaga in 1487, Granada stood alone against the Christian armies, weakened, into the bargain, by the year-long feud between King Muley Hassan and his mistress, Soraya, on the one side and his wife, Aisha, and their son and legitimate heir, Boabdil, on the other. After Muley Hassan's death in 1485, Boabdil ascended the throne as the last Moorish ruler of Granada. In 1491, he abdicated and in the Treaty of Santa Fé ceded Granada to the Catholic Monarchs, who entered the city on 2 January 1492 while Boabdil left it and fled to the Alpujarras.

The downfall of the kingdom was followed by the bloody crushing of the Morisco revolt from 1569 to 1571 and the final expulsion of the Muslims in 1609. The Alhambra fell into disrepair, and it was the American writer Washington Irving who first called attention to this unique cultural monument in 1830. In 1984, the UNESCO declared it to be a »cultural heritage of mankind«. Today, tourism is the most

Granada *Plan*

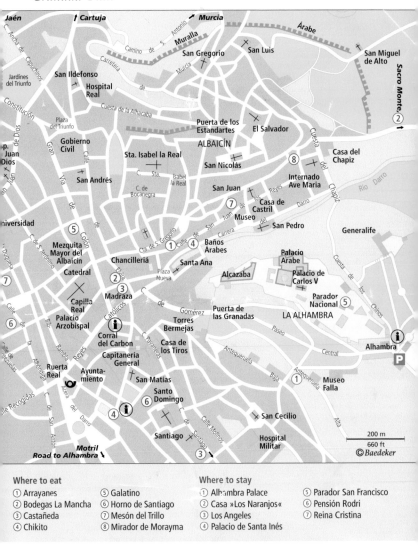

Where to eat
① Arrayanes
② Bodegas La Mancha
③ Castañeda
④ Chikito
⑤ Galatino
⑥ Horno de Santiago
⑦ Mesón del Trillo
⑧ Mirador de Morayma

Where to stay
① Alhambra Palace
② Casa »Los Naranjos«
③ Los Angeles
④ Palacio de Santa Inés
⑤ Parador San Francisco
⑥ Pensión Rodri
⑦ Reina Cristina

import source of revenue in a city where many have again become aware of their Muslim heritage – Spain's largest Islamic community lives in Granada today. They celebrated the opening of their grand mosque on Albaicín in the summer of 2003.

✴ ✴ Alhambra

Access

The main entrance with ticket counters and a large parking lot lies on the extreme east of the hill. To get there, take bus no. 30 or 32 from Plaza Nueva, or by car take Ronda del Sur. Be prepared for a long trek on foot – from Plaza Nueva take Cuesta de Gomérez uphill and then along Paseo Central staying below the Alhambra . Those who already have a ticket can enter at Puerta de la Justicia and avoid the trek to the main entrance.

Buy tickets in advance!

The rush for tickets has become so great that now a **limited number of tickets** are made available. A total of about 8,000 tickets are sold each day, of which only a part are available for sale at the ticket counters. Only the really early birds have a chance at getting a ticket there. It makes sense, therefore, to get tickets in advance (with a surcharge). There are several ways of doing this: from one of the 4,000 Spanish offices of the Banco Bilbao Vizcaya Argentaria (BBVA), by telephoning the BBVA and using a credit card, tel. 902 22 44 60 (from Spain) or 0034 / 913 46 59 36 (from abroad) or by internet at www.al-hambratickets.com. Hotels and camping ground management also provide tickets. Advanced tickets can be picked up at a special counter (Taquilla de Reserva) by presenting a registration number and I.D. Tickets are available in advance for a time period from one day all the way up to one year. There is a limit of five tickets per person. **There are tickets for the morning, afternoon and evening.** They set a half-hour time span within which the Nasrid palace must be entered (though the time for touring is not limited); there are no time limits for the rest of the Alhambra. The tickets are not valid for the museum in the palace of Charles V, however.

❗ *Baedeker* TIP

Alhambra by moonlight

»Who can do justice to a moonlight night in such a climate and such a place?« wrote Washington Irving justly. To stroll in the evening through the illuninated chambers of the Nasrid palace and listen to the soft murmurings of the fountain is indeed an unforgettable expeience.

Not far from Plaza Nueva is **Puerta de las Granadas**, built by Pedro Machuca in 1536 on the site of a Moorish gate and adorned with the coat of arms of Charles V, as well as the symbol for Granada, three pomegranates. Behind it are the Alameda de la Alhambra, the gardens laid out on the Moorish cemetery spreading up the slopes in a ravine between the Alhambra heights and Monte Mauror. Keeping watch on Monte Mauror is **Granada's oldest fortress** , the **Torres Bermejas**, which was erected in the 13th century upon an 8th-century fortress.

✴ Alameda de la Alhambra

Side trip

For a walk through the Alameda, take the path near the gate that forks off to the right and then another path branching off toward

Alhambra and Generalife *Plan*

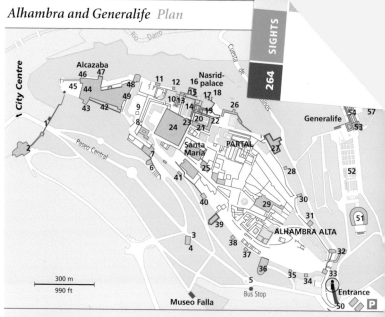

The Alhambra illuminated by the setting sun

Antequeruela Alta through a beautiful villa quarter where the composer Manuel de Falla (1876–1946) owned a house. Unfortunately it is closed for the time being. A little further on is the Convento Carmen de los Martíres founded in 1573. The stroll leads further to a hotel steeped in tradition, the »Washington Irving«, and from there eventually to the main entrance of the Alhambra.

✳ ✳ The Nasrid Palace

Most beautiful palace grounds in Europe

Every visitor to the Alhambra is drawn to the Nasrid palace (Palacio Real or Palacio Árabe), the residence of the kings of Granada and a monument of Arab-Moorish architecture on European soil. The construction work began under Yûsuf I (1333–1354) with the Torre de Comares and the Myrtle Court and was completed for the most part under Mohammed V (1354–1391), who commissioned the Fountain of Lions. Like all Moorish secular buildings, the palace grounds appear unspectacular from the outside. Their artistic significance lies in the rich decorations of marble, fine hardwoods and azulejos, which represent the pinnacle of Moorish craftsmanship. Marble was one of the most important building materials in the palace grounds and was used in columns and floors. The ground plan is a **classic example of Islamic palace construction**, which is divided into three main sections; the Mexuar intended for holding public court and meetings, the royal palace (diwán or seraglio) and the women's chambers (harim or harem). All rooms open onto a courtyard, as had long been usual in Greek and Roman houses.

The low, azulejos-lined Mexuar, the former audience hall and court-room, was converted into a chapel by Charles V. The Moorish decoration suffered in the process, hence Charles V's slogan, »Plus Ultra«, on the walls alongside ribbons of Kufic script. Next to the Mexuar, connecting it to the Myrtle Court, is the **Patio de Mexuar**.

Mexuar

The palace area begins with the Patio de los Arrayanes (Myrtle Court), the former seraglio, which remained undisturbed after the Christian conquest. The long sides of the 37m/122ft by 23m/76ft courtyard are whitewashed, but are pierced by artistically framed gates, gemel windows and niches.

✱ ✱
Patio de los Arrayanes

The southern front is closed off by a building with seven delicate arcades, over which a row of windows and in turn further arcades are arranged. These rooms are connected to the chapel in Charles V's palace. The **Torre de Comares** is on the north side. In front of it is the Sala de la Barca, where the ambassadors gathered for an audience, which was held in the **Sala de los Embajadores** (Ambassadors' Hall). It is one of the richest rooms in the Alhambra thanks to its fantastic cedarwood dome and the or-

 DON'T MISS

- Salón de Embajadores; one of the most delightful rooms in the Alhambra with a magnificent cedarwood dome.
- Patio de Arrayanes; the actual royal palace with a pool framed by myrtle.
- Sala de las dos Hermanas; with the largest of all Arab stalactite vaults.
- Sala de los Abencerrajes; impressive stalactite dome.
- Patio de los Leones; extravagantly designed inner courtyard with the Fountain of Lions.

Nasrid Palace Plan

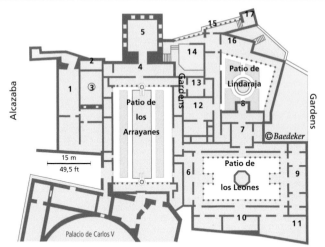

1 Mexuar
2 Cuarto Dorado
3 Patio Mexuar
4 Sala de la Barca
5 Torre de Comares /
   Salón de Embajadores
6 Sala de los Mocarabes

7 Sala de las dos Hermanas
8 Sala de los Ajimeces /
   Mirador de Lindaraja
9 Sala de los Reyes
10 Sala de los Abencerraje
11 Raudas

12 Baños reales
13 Sala de Camas
14 Patio de Cipréses
15 Galería del Peinador
16 Apartments of Charles V
17 Peinador de la Reina

namentation of over 150 different floral and geometric patterns and verses from the Qur'an.

Opening on to Myrtle Court is the Sala de los Mocárabes, which in turn opens to the Patio de los Leones (Lion Court), the centre of the royal winter residence built under Mohammed V with the harem joined to it. From the two pavilions that project at the ends, as well as from the long sides of the court, channels of water run to the Fountain of Lions. In its seemingly archaic simplicity, the Fountain of Lions presents a curious contrast to the exuberant design of the rest of the courtyard. The aura of oriental magic surrounding the Alhambra can be sensed most clearly here in the heart of the palace.

✳ ✳
Patio de los Leones

The Sala de las dos Hermanas (Hall of the Two Sisters) on the north side of the Lion Court, together with the rooms lying behind it, was probably the winter residence of the women. The room with its decorations is the artistic zenith of the Alhambra. The vault, in the form

✳ ✳
◄ Sala de las dos Hermanas

← *The Torre de Comares watches over the Myrtle Court.*

ALHAMBRA

✳ ✳ The name Alhambra is derived from the Arabic »Kala al-Hamra«, which means »Red Mountain«, because its walls and towers shine red in the light of the evening sun. The Alhambra is not only the Nasrid Palace , the most beautiful Arab palace grounds in Europe, but all of the grounds including the Palace of Charles V, the Alcazaba and finally also the garden palace of Generalife.

🕒 Opening hours:
March–Oct daily 8.30am–8pm, Nov–Feb daily 8.30am–6pm; night-time visits (Nasrid Palace only): March–Oct Tue–Sat. 10–11.30pm, Nov–Feb Fri, Sat 8–9.30pm

① Mexuar (1st main section of the palace)
The Mexuar of the Nasrid Palace in the residence of the kings of Granada served for the public administration of justice and for meetings. Charles V remodelled it as chapel.

② Divan or serial
(2nd main section of the palace)
The serail denotes the actual royal palace. The Patio de los Arrayanes (Myrtle Court) with a large pond framed by a myrtle bush hedge is to be found here.

③ Harem
(3rd main section of the palace)
The private life of the monarchs was played out in the women's chambers. In the centre is the Patio de los Leones (Lion Court) with the Fountain of Lions.

④ Patio de Mexuar
Connecting the Mexuar with the Myrtle Court is the Patio de Mexuar. It is lined with marble and azulejos in warm tones that set it apart, which are shown to particular advantage in the Cuarto Dorado (»Golden Room«) and on the façade facing the Myrtle Court.

⑤ Torre de Comares and
Sala de los Embajadores
With its 45m/147ft, the Torre de Comares is the tallest tower on the hill. Audiences were held on the ground floor in the Sala de los Embajadores (Ambassadors' Hall), which measures 11m/36ft square and 18m/59ft in height. The room is one of the most beautiful in the Alhambra thanks to its cedar wood dome and the ornamentation comprising over 150 different floral and geometric patterns as well as verses from the Qur'an. The ruler's throne stood opposite the entrance so that light fell on him from three sides. While those entering saw him only against the light, he could see them clearly.

⑥ Sala de la Barca
Built in front of the Torre de Comares is the hall of seven arcades. Its name is either derived from the boat-shaped artesonado ceiling of cedar wood or from the Arabic word »baraku« (blessing). This is where the ambassadors to the court of Granada gathered before an audience.

⑦ Sala de los Reyes
Five high stalactite domes arch over the room. A rarity here are the three court scenes painted on leather and stretched over wood because Islam normally forbids the representation of figures. A council of ten splendidly-dressed men (thus the name »Hall of the Kings«) can be seen, as well as a hunting scene and the freeing of a girl from the clutches of a savage.

⑧ Tocador de la Reina
The »Queen's Dressing Room « is one of the most charming rooms of the palace. It was laid out as a mirador with a panoramic view and was used by Isabella the Catholic and the wives of Charles V and Philip II.

⑨ Torre de las Damas
More of an »ornamental structure« than a fortress and one of the oldest structures of the Nasrid Palace, it was erected under Mohammed III at the beginning of the 14th century.

⑩ Palace of Charles V
Altogether, the sweeping square with its 83m/272ft sides makes an austere impression, which is reinforced in the inner court, a circular, two-storey structure 31m/101ft in circumference with Doric columns in the first gallery and Ionic in the second. The Maseo de la Alhambra on the ground floor displays numerous Moorish-Arab artefacts, including many from the Alhambra. The Museo Provincial de Bellas Artes on the upper floor presents for the most part artists of the Granada School.

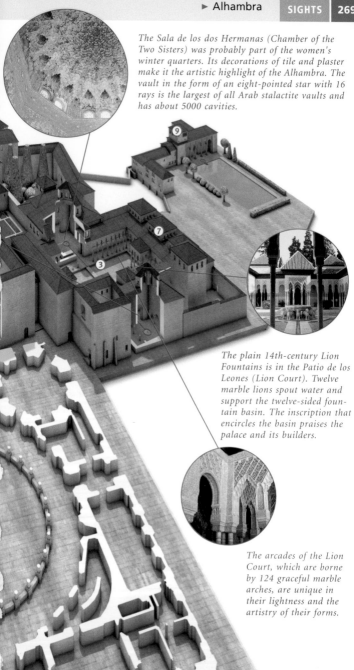

The Sala de los dos Hermanas (Chamber of the Two Sisters) was probably part of the women's winter quarters. Its decorations of tile and plaster make it the artistic highlight of the Alhambra. The vault in the form of an eight-pointed star with 16 rays is the largest of all Arab stalactite vaults and has about 5000 cavities.

The plain 14th-century Lion Fountains is in the Patio de los Leones (Lion Court). Twelve marble lions spout water and support the twelve-sided fountain basin. The inscription that encircles the basin praises the palace and its builders.

The arcades of the Lion Court, which are borne by 124 graceful marble arches, are unique in their lightness and the artistry of their forms.

The Sala de los Abencerrajes takes its name from a family whose leaders – no less than 36 of them – are said to have been murdered here. This was the place where rulers held their winter celebrations. The magnificent eight-sided stalactite dome is the counterpart to the dome of the Sala de los dos Hermanas.

Charles V never lived in this palace, which he built from 1526. It is one of the most important works of High Renaissance architecture outside Italy.

of an eight-pointed star radiating 16 rays, is the **largest of all Arab stalactite vaults**. The room takes its name from the two large identical marble slabs set into the floor. Inscriptions with poems by Ibn Zamrak adorn the walls. Adjoining the Hall of the Two Sisters is the **Sala de los Ajimeces**. Between the two arched windows (ajimeces) in the rear is the Mirador de Lindaraja, a charming projecting alcove with three windows that almost reach down to the floor and provide a view of the peaceful Patio de Lindaraja.

★ ★
Sala de los Reyes ▶

On the east end of the Lion Court lies the elongated Sala de los Reyes (Hall of the Kings or Hall of Justice). The court scenes painted on leather and stretched on wooden domes are a great rarity, because Islam normally does not allow figurative art. The hall is divided into seven sections, and the side rooms are decorated with ceiling paintings from the late 15th century.

★ ★
Sala de los Abencerrajes ▶

Sala de los Abencerrajes can be entered from the southern side of the court. A twelve-sided marble fountain occupies the centre of the hall. The eight-pointed star of a stalactite dome arches above the fountain.

Other Parts of the Alhambra

Patio de Lindaraja

After leaving the Palace of the Nasrids, head down the steps to the left and again left to the former inner palace garden planted with cypresses and oranges, the atmospheric Patio de Lindaraja. It was laid out after the conquest by the Christian kings. The fountain used to stand in the court of the Mexuar.

Patio de Cipréses

The small Court of the Cypresses adjoins the garden. Here there is a gallery leading to the **chambers of Charles V** that the emperor and his wife occupied when he lived in Granada. His son, Philip II, also lodged here. The writer Washington Irving, who is commemorated with a plaque, was a prominent guest here for four months in 1829. The same gallery, which is open toward the slope allowing a nice view of the Albaicín, leads to the **Tocador de la Reina** (»Queen's Dressing Room«) on the upper floor of the Torre del Peinador. At the south end of the courtyard are the baths, (**baños**), an extensive subterranean complex from the time of Yûsuf I.

★
Jardines del Partal

After touring the palace, the **Gardens of the Partal** (Jardines del Partal) with their labyrinth-like paths, waterfalls, ponds and glorious greenery are an ideal place to relax. Rising on the north wall is the **Torre de las Damas**, to its right the Torre del Mihrâb with a discreet prayer room. In the upper gardens (Alhambra Alta) lies the Monastery of **San Francisco**, which has been converted today into **Spain's most luxurious parador**. It was founded in 1495 and held the graves of the Catholic Monarchs before they were moved into the cathedral.

Along the way to the Palace of Charles V is the church of **Santa María**, which was built on the site of the Alhambra mosque. After Granada was handed over, Holy Mass was read in the mosque. The stone columns to the right next to the main portal are a reminder the martyrdom of two Christian in 1397.

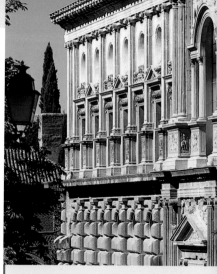

Beginning construction in 1526, Charles V had a palace built on the east side of the Place of the Cisterns, directly on Myrtle Court, which he financed with a special tax levied on the Moors remaining in Granada. It was designed by Pedro Machuca, whose son continued did not complete the work. However, the palace is one of the most significant works of **high Renaissance architecture** outside Italy. An eight-sided chapel was included with direct access to the Nasrid palace, but remained uncompleted. The Museo de la Alhambra displays a large number of Moorish-Arab pieces, many of them from the Alhambra, on the ground floor. The exhibits include glass, pottery, decorative friezes, azulejos and metalwork. The prize pieces are the 1.30m/4ft 3in-high Alhambra Vase (1320), magnificently decorated with leaping antelopes and floral patterns in enamel painting, and a marble ablutions basin, thought to be from Córdoba, depicting lions chasing stags and an eagle, and bearing a later Kufic inscription praising Mohammed V. The Museo Provincial de Bellas Artes on the upper floor mainly presents artists from the Granada school. The outstanding sculptures are the *Burial of Christ* by Jacopo Florentino, *San Juan de Dios* and *Virgin with Child* by Diego de Siloé, as well as a work on the same theme by Roberto Alemán; in addition, works by Pedro de Mena and, as showpiece, the *Triptych of the Gran Capitán*, a work in enamel by the master Léonard Pénicaud of Limoges. Among the painters represented are Fray Juan Sanchez Cotán (*Mary and the Sleeping Infant Jesus*) and Alonso Cano (*Virgin with Child, St Bernard of Siena, Head of Juan de la Cruz*). The »Italian Fireplace Room« (16th century) is hung with tapestries procured for the palace from Genoa and Brussels.

To the west of the Palace of Charles V lies Plaza de los Aljibes, the Alhambra's main square. It was laid out at the end of the 15th century as a military training area. Beneath it are the cisterns that provide the Alhambra with its water.

The Palace of Charles V – High Renaissance in its pure form

✱
Palace of Charles V

◄ Museo de la Alhambra

🕐
Opening hours:
Tue–Sat
9am–2.30pm

◄ Museo Provincial de Bellas Artes

🕐
Opening hours:
April–Sept Tue
2.30pm–8pm,
Wed–Sat
9am–8pm,
Sun 9am–2.30pm;
Oct– March
Mon–Fri to 6pm

Plaza de los Aljibes

Puerta de la Justicia The way through Puerta del Vino, built under Mohammed V, leads down to the imposing Puerta de la Justicia, originally the entrance to the Alhambra. The gate built in 1348 under Yûsuf I, occasionally the site of executions, consists of one large and one small horseshoe arch.

The keystone of the large arch displays a hand, the symbol of the **five basic principles (pillars) of Islam** – the profession that there is only one God, observance of prayer, charity through the giving of alms, abstinence through fasting, and the duty of a pilgrimage to Mecca. A key can be seen on the second arch, a symbol of the keys to heaven bestowed upon the Prophet Mohammed by Allah. Set into the wall on the steps below the gate is a Renaissance fountain, **Pilar de Charles V**.

✳ Alcazaba The wall of the Alcazaba, the oldest part of the Alhambra, runs along the west side of the Plaza de los Aljibes. Mohammed I began in the 13th century with the construction of the palace fortress around the original buildings from the time of the Zirids, of which only the double encircling wall with the powerful towers in the inner ring remain. The most impressive of them are in the entrance wall; the Torre Quebrada and next to it to the right the 25m/82ft-high Torre del Homenaje, in which the commandant lived. Towering up on the north wall is the Torre de las Armas, once the armoury, from which there is a good view of the Darro valley and the Albaicín, and next to it is the Torre de los Hidalgos. There is a view from the south wall, in which the Torre de la Pólvora is set, down to the Jardínes de los Adarves, which were created in the 13th century between the outer and inner walls.

✳ ✳ View from Torre de la Vela ▶ The best view, though, is from the 26m/85ft-high Torre de la Vela above the western outworks (Baluarte). In the 18th century, a belfry was placed on top of the tower, whose bells ring out annually on 2 January, the day the Catholic Monarchs, Ferdinand and Isabella, entered the city. There is a magnificent view of the city from the battlements to the massive cathedral; and in the opposite direction over the courtyard of the Alcazaba with the foundations of the munitions magazines, guards' quarters, baths and prison, behind them Charles V's palace, the towers of the palace complex and, in the distance, the Generalife.

Towers It is possible to take a closer look at some of the towers by walking through the Alhambra Alta, the upper gardens. Torre de las Damas, a fortress tower with an adjoining loggia, water basin and a small mosque, stands east of the palace. Beyond the Torre de los Picos (»Tower of the Points«) are Torre del Candil and the Torre de la Cautiva (»Prisoners' Tower«), which has a small patio and a magnificently decorated main hall. It is followed by the Torre de las Infantas with a richly decorated hall and a platform offering a wide vista. On the east end of the Alhambra hill stands the Torre del Agua with the reservoir for the Alhambra water system. The most interesting feature of the southern part is the tower Puerta de los Siete Suelos (Tower of the Seven Storeys).

✶ ✶ Generalife

The Generalife (Arabic: »Jannat al-'Arif«, the garden of the architect) lying to the east opposite the Alhambra on the slopes of the Cerro del Sol was the **summer residence of the Moorish kings** completed in 1319 under Ismail I. The charm of these grounds is to be found less in the rather unspectacular architecture when compared to the Nasrid palace than in the harmony between the buildings, the gardens and the fountains. Many consider it to be **one of the most beautiful gardens in the world**. A cypress-lined avenue leads to the entrance building (16th century), followed by the Patio de la Acequia planted with laurel and myrtle as well as orange trees, and its fabulous row of fountains, which terminates in the simple residence of the rulers. There is a magnificent view of the Alhambra and the Darro valley from one of the side rooms. Above the building, the floral magnificence continues in more beguiling gardens, grottoes and water gardens, and among them a »water stairway« formed by a series of cascades. An exit here leads to Silla del Moro, an observation point outside the gardens.

»Garden of the architect«

Murmuring water fountains in the Generalife – the Moorish kings knew how to savour the moment.

Around the Cathedral

Catedral Santa María de la Encarnación

The cathedral Santa María de la Encarnación , the **most important of Andalusia's four great Renaissance churches**, rises above the maze of houses in the city centre. Enrique de Egas began it in 1523 in Gothic style, Diego de Siloé carried on in Plateresque in 1525, and in 1561, still uncompleted, it was consecrated. In 1563, Juan de Orea renewed the work, which dragged on until 1703 and eventually ceased without the two planned towers being built. Even the tower that had been begun did not reach its planned height. The west façade (1667) is by Alonso Cano, the relief above the main portal by José Risueño (1717). To the northwest lie the Puerta de San Jerónimo, decorated with sculptures by Siloé, Maeda and others, as well as allegorical figures and the coat of arms of Castile, and the Puerta del Perdón, also by Siloé, completed in 1537. Due to the fact that the choir, formerly in the central aisle, was pulled down in 1929, the eye can rove uninterrupted over the interior of the church. The nave and four aisles, borne by massive clustered pillars, have a total extent of 116m/380ft in length and 67m/220ft in width. The highest point in the interior is the 47m/154ft-high dome of the Capilla Mayor.

Imposing – cathedral from the 16th century

Capilla Mayor ►

Diego de Siloé designed it with two rows of balustrades arranged in a circle 22m/72ft in circumference resting on round arches that open to the choir ambulatory. On the right between the arches stands the statue of St Paul by Alonso de Mena, left the apostle Peter by Martín de Aranda. Paintings by Pedro Atanasio Bocanegra and Juan de Seville (also in the crossing) can be seen in the first balustrade, and above are seven paintings by Alonso Canos with scenes from the life of the Virgin. The windows between and above hold Flemish stained glass from the 16th century. Statues of the Catholic Monarchs by Pedro de Mena are at the pillars of the entrance arch, above them the heads of Adam and Eve by Alonso Cano.

Portal of the Capilla Real ►

In the right aisle stands the closed portal of the Capilla Real, a masterpiece of late Gothic stone masonry designed by Enrique de Egas. It bears the coats of arms of Castile and the Catholic Monarchs, and

Catedral Santa María de la Encarnación Plan

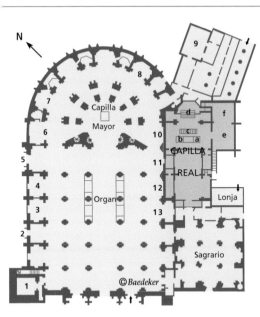

1 Tesoro
2 Puerta de San Jerónimo
3 Capilla de
   N. Sra. del Carmen
4 Capilla de
   N. Sra. de las Angustias
5 Puerta del Perdón
6 Capilla de la Antigua
7 Capilla de Santa Lucía
8 Capilla de Santa Ana
9 Sacristía
10 Altar de Santiago
11 Former entrance
   to Capilla Real
12 Altar de Jesús Nazareno
13 Capilla de la Trinidad

Capilla Real

a Tomb of the
   Catholic Monarchs
b Tomb of Philip the Handsome
   and Joanna the Mad
c Crypt (underground)
d High altar
e Museum
f Sacristy

above are the Infant Jesus flanked by St James and St George the dragon slayer. Left of the portal is a large altar consecrated to the Spanish national patron saint Santiago (James), portrayed in his typical role as a slayer of Moors. A small painting of Virgin of Grace, a present of Pope Innocent III to Queen Isabella, is on top of it. To the right of the portal, the altar of Jesus of Nazareth, laden with gold, holds a few valuable paintings; on the right *St Augustine, Via Dolorosa* and the *Holy Virgin* by Alonso Cano, as well as the *Martyrdom of St Lawrence, The Child Jesus appearing to St Anthony* and, in addition, *Via Dolorosa* by Antonio Ribera, left *St Francis* by El Greco, *Magdalene* by Ribera and a portrayal of Christ by Cano.

The **sacristy**, accessible right of the choir ambulatory through a portal by Diego de Siloé, contains some fine works of art; once again, the works of Alonso Cano stand out. The church treasures can be viewed in the former chapter house in the tower.

The Iglesia del Sagrario, which has a very fine Renaissance baptismal font, was added to the south side of the cathedral between 1705 and 1759. On its north side lies the Lonja, the former stock exchange with loggia, built between 1518 and 1522.

Sagrario and Lonja

★ ★
Capilla Real

The Capilla Real can be reached by way of the loggia. It is the mausoleum of the Catholic Monarchs, erected on the south side of the cathedral under the direction of Enrique de Egas in late Gothic style from 1505 to 1521 upon earlier instructions of Isabella. First upon entering is the anteroom with a copy of a historical painting by Carbonero, the *Surrender of Granada*. An exquisitely beautiful gilded grille (Span: »reja«) by Bartolomé de Jaén divides off the actual mausoleum. The grille bears the coat of arms of Castile supported by lions, next to it the symbols of the Catholic Monarchs, the yoke and arrows. A long series of biblical scenes, crowned by a depiction of the crucifixion, complete the work. Next is the chamber with the tombs of the Catholic Monarchs. To the right, the tomb of Ferdinand († 1516), with sword in hand, and Isabella († 1504), a lion and a lioness at her feet, worked in Carrara marble in 1522 by the Florentine Domenico Fancelli. To the left stand figures by Bartolomeo Ordoñez of Philip the Handsome († 1506) and Joanna the Mad († 1555), daughter of the Catholic Monarchs. The large winged altar with carved biblical scenes by Felipe Vigarny is flanked by the statues of the Catholic Monarchs by Diego de Siloé. Richly decorated reliquary altars by Alonso de Mena (1623) have been placed in both transepts. The famous *Passion Triptych* by Dieric Bouts can be seen in the left transept next to the altar. The mortal remains of the Catholic Monarchs, as well as those of Joanna and Philip and Miguel, the royal couple's grandson and heir to the Portuguese throne, rest in simple lead coffins in the crypt. The sacristy of the Capilla Real contains **personal items of the Catholic Monarchs** including clothing, Ferdinand's sword, crown, and sceptre, and Isabella's reliquary and prayer books. Some outstanding paintings show that the queen was also an intelligent **art collector**: *Christ on the Mount of Olives*, possibly by Botticelli, *Pietà* and *Virgin with Child* by Rogier van der Weyden, *Deposition from the Cross*, *Virgin with Child* and *Lamenting Women* by Hans Memling, another portrayal of the Virgin by Dieric Bouts, *Christ Suffering* by Perugino and *The Apostle John* by Pedro Berruguete. Two outstanding wooden sculptures of the royal couple praying by Felipe Vigarny are also displayed (opening hours: May–Sept daily 10.30am–1pm, 4–7pm, Sun from 11am; Oct–April Mon–Sat 10.30am–1pm, 3.30–6pm, Sun 11am–1pm, 3.30–6pm).

★ ★
Tombs of the Catholic Monarchs ▶

★ ★
Museo ▶

⏱

Madraza

Although the house opposite the Capilla and the Lonja has a Baroque facade and a Castilian coat of arms on it, it is considerably older. It is the **Arab University**, the Madraza, founded in 1349 by Yûsuf I. From 1500, the building was used as the city hall (Casa Cabildo). A prayer room with a mihrâb off the patio remains from the time of the Moors.

Further on past the episcopal palace on Plaza de Alonso Cano is **Plaza de Bib-Rambla**. Enlivened by shops, florists, restaurants and bars and with the Fuente de los Gigantones splashing gaily between trees and kiosks, it is a wonderful place for a café solo.

The **Alcaicería** extends between the plaza and the cathedral, the Moorish market and shopping quarter that mostly dealt in fabrics and burned down in 1843. Rebuilt, it today appears to be more of a collection of souvenir shops and boutiques; but for some, it radiates the atmosphere of an Arab souk.

At the rear of the cathedral lies the Gran Vía de Colón. It meets **Plaza Isabel la Católica**, on which there is a monument from 1892 commemorating the moment Columbus presented his plans to the queen. C. Reyes Católicos, the second most important shopping boulevard after Gran Via de Colón, goes east from the plaza.

A lane branches off to the left from C. Reyes Católicos not far from the plaza toward C. Mariana Piñeda. Here can be seen the horseshoe arch of Corral del

The Alcaicería – just a bit of souk

Carbón, the only surviving **caravanserai** in Spain, a so-called funduq. The building, dating back to the early 14th century, has an anteroom with a stalactite dome and an inner courtyard with a gallery running around it. After the Moors had been driven out, it was used as a storehouse for charcoal dealers, then as a theatre on whose stage Lope de Rueda's dramas were presented and, finally, as a residence. Today it houses, along with **tourist information**, a branch of the state Artespaña, which endeavours to sell upmarket handicrafts.

★

Corral del Carbón

🕐
Opening hours:
Mon–Sat
9am–7.30pm,
Sun 10am–2pm

Casa de los Tiros in the C. de Pavaneras lies across from the military commandant's headquarters not far from Plaza Isabel la Católica. The very plain building was part of the city wall in the 16th century. Its only adornment consists of five figures representing Hercules, Theseus, Jason, Hector and Mercury. In the building the Museo de Artes y Costumbres Populares displays, along with furniture, craftwork, old plans and pictures of Granada, a complete kitchen and two rooms commemorating Washington Irving and Eugenia de Montijo of Granada, who, as Eugénie, became the wife of Napoleon III. The most beautiful room is the Cuadra Dorada with an artesonado ceiling and reliefs.

Casa de los Tiros

◄ Museo de Artes y Costumbres Populares

🕐
Opening hours:
Mon–Fri
2.30–8.30pm

✳ ✳ Albaicín

Old Moorish quarter
The feeling of Moorish times is strongest on El Albaicín, the hill across from the Alhambra heights. It has less to do with spectacular sights than with the **atmosphere and magic** radiating from the narrow and steep alleyways, the angular, whitewashed houses, the patios and churches, but above all by the classic views of the Alhambra – enjoyed best in the afternoon. There are many ways to get up to it; one lane after the other leads up from Plaza Nueva, from Puerta Elvira in the university quarter and from Carrera del Darr. Bus lines 31 and 32 (from Plaza Nueva or Alhambra) drive right into the midst of the Moorish past. Do take a stroll in the evening along Carrera del Darro; this is where Granada lives far into the night – in crowds, loud and happy, partying in the bars and cafés directly beneath the extraordinary backdrop of the illuminated Alhambra.

Plaza Nueva
Plaza Nueva is an elongated continuation of C. Reyes Católicos below the Alhambra hill, with its fountains, bars and restaurants, one of the most popular places to meet in the evening in Granada. Even in earlier times a lot went on here – races, bullfighting, but also executions. The most imposing building on the plaza is the Audiencia (court house). Its design is attributed to Diego de Siloé and it was built between 1531 and 1587. The two-storeyed arcaded courtyard and a monumental stairway with a fine wood ceiling are impressive.

Rio Darro
The Río Darro divides the Alhambra hill from Albaicín. At the northeastern end of Plaza Nueva, where it flows below ground, stands Santa Ana, a Renaissance church erected from 1541 to 1548 to plans by Diego de Siloé with a Plateresque portal and minaret-like tower dating to 1563. This is the beginning of **Carrera del Darro**, one of Granada's oldest streets, as the second bridge over the river testifies – it is still Moorish. Before that, C. Santa Inés branches off to the 16th-century Palacio de Santa Inés, whose Renaissance inner courtyard is decorated with frescoes by Alejandro Mayne, a student of Raphael. Further along on Carrera del Darro is the **Bañuelo** (house no. 31), an 11th-century Moorish bath that still has the changing room and three bath rooms supported by Moorish arches with Visigoth capitals (opening hours: Tue–Sat 10am–2pm). Further on is the church of San Pedro y San Pablo on the right. Across on the left stands **Casa de Castril**, a Renaissance building, whose Plateresque portal was probably designed by Diego de Siloé. The **Museo Arqueológico Provincial** presents there a collection of Moorish artefacts such as painted pottery, glass, jewellery and fabrics (opening hours: Tue 3–7pm, Wed–Sat 9am–7pm, Sun 9am–2pm).

Casa del Chapiz
At the end of Carrera del Darro is Cuesta del Chapiz, which plunges into the uphill maze of streets and alleyways of Albaicín. Right at the beginning, Casa del Chapiz presents a fine example of a well-to-do

Beautiful – the Albaicín, the former Moorish quarter opposite the Alhambra

Morisco residence of the 16th century; it is now the seat of the Institute of Arab Studies.

Heading further on to the left is the Mudejar church of San Salvador, which stands on the site of the former grand mosque of Albaicín and was consecrated in 1499.

San Salvador

Straight ahead is Plaza Larga – an ideal place for a break. From here, a lane goes uphill to San Nicolás church, built in 1525, the heart of Albaicín. From the picturesque plaza in front of the church there is a spectacular and famous view of the Alhambra and the Sierra Nevada – an unforgettable experience, especially at sunset. The new mosque was opened nearby in July 2003. The Belgian painter Max Moreau (1902–1992) lived for 30 years in a house a little below San Nicolás. It is now the **Casa Museo Max Moreau** museum (opening hours: Tue–Sat 10am to 1.30pm, 4–6pm).

San Nicolás

✳ ✳
◀ View of the Alhambra

🕐

A well-preserved section of the Arab city wall (muralla árabe) runs from Plaza Larga down the hill along side Cuesta de la Alhacaba to Puerta Monaitia. A little further down on Plaza del Triunfo stands Granada's former main gate, the Puerta de Elvira, which dates back to the 9th century.

Muralla árabe

San José

The lane facing the Alhambra that runs parallel to the wall leads downhill again past San Miguel Bajo church to Plaza Nueva, going past San José church, whose bell tower is the minaret of a 9th-century mosque and thus one of the oldest Moorish architectural monuments in Andalusia.

Mezquita Mayor del Albaicín

For the first time in 500 years, right next door to San José church and opposite the Alhambra, there is again a mosque. After fighting municipal bureaucracy and neighbours for 23 years, the mosque was built in Andalusian style with funds from Morocco and the United Arab Emirates and finally consecrated in July 2003. The streets below the church have already been transformed in the last ten years into a bazaar full of Arab tea-rooms and restaurants. Around 15,000 Muslims again live among the 265,000 citizens of Granada; about half of them are labour immigrants, the other half students. A group of Spanish Muslims has grown up among the foreign Muslims, about 1,500 converts who have turned their backs on the Catholic church.

! *Baedeker* TIP

Baños Arabes

The Arab steam bath is a place to relax, with its mosaics and splashing water in oriental splendour (Santa Ana, 16, opening hours: daily 10am–midnight, entry on the hour).

Sacromonte

A way leads from Cuesta del Chapiz up the mountain slope and past the former cave dwellings, in which Gitanos have been proven to have lived since 1532, to the former Benedictine monastery Sacromonte (12th century). The remains of the three saints Cecilo, Hiscio and Tesifonte were supposedly found here, which explains the name Sacromonte (holy mountain). Other paths, some of them steep through deeply-cut ravines full of boulders, ascend to the Ermita San Miguel de Alto, high up with a fabulous view all the way to the Sierra Nevada. Sacromonte is considered to be the home of the Gitano culture, where it is said flamenco can be enjoyed in its pure state, though closer inspection reveals that a lot of it is just to dupe tourists.

University Quarter La Cartuja

University

The university quarter in the northwest of the inner city is grouped around the Baroque former Jesuit college in C. San Jerónimo that was taken over in 1759.

✴ Convento de San Jerónimo

Not far away in C. del Gran Capitán is the Convento de San Jerónimo, founded in 1496. The church, which has 18th-century wall paintings, was built between 1496–1547 by Jacopo Florentino and Diego de Siloé as a burial church for the commander of the Catholic Monarchs' armies, Gran Capitán Gonzalo Fernández de Córdoba and his wife. Both kneeling figures flank the high altar with a retablo by Juan de Aragón and Lázaro de Velasco. Sculptures by Diego de Siloé stand in the choir. He also designed the magnificent gate of the patio, which was done completely in Gothic style. The second courtyard appears as a mixture of Gothic, Mudejar and Renaissance styles.

Opening hours: Mon–Sat 10am–1.30pm, 3pm–6.30pm, Sun 11am–1.30pm

✸ San Juan de Dios

One of Granada's most beautiful Baroque edifices, the double-towered church of the Hospital San Juan de Dios, lies a little south.-west above San Jerónimo. The saint after whom it is named holds watch above the entrance portal. St Juan de Dios is buried in the decorated interior behind the retablo by Guerrero. He was the father of the Order of the Brothers Hospitaller and founder of the hospital in 1552.

✸ La Cartuja

The **Carthusian monastery** La Cartuja lies a little over half a mile away in a northerly direction from C. San Juan de Dios (bus lines U and C). The monastery was founded in 1506 on the orders of the Gran Capitán, but only completed after 250 years. The cloister, refectory, church and sacristy remain. The extremely lavish decoration of the interior rooms represents a pinnacle of **Churriguerism**. The refectory and the adjacent rooms leading off from the cloister hold a collection of paintings by Juan Sanchez Cotán and Vicente Carducho. The interior of the church was decorated in **effusive Baroque style**. The central choir is divided by a splendid grille into areas for the monks and for the lay brothers. The ceiling painting is by Pedro Atanasio Bocanegra. Above the sculpture of the Virgin by José de Mora is a seemingly light baldachin (canopy).

Next to the chancel is the Sagrario, a work by Francisco Hurtado Izquierdo, arched over by an imposing dome with trompe-l'œil painting and furnished with paintings by Palomino and Cotán, as well as sculptures by Risueño and Duque Cornejo. The highlight of the tour is the sacristy by Luis de Arévalo, who created lavish plaster ornaments here.

✸ ✸ ◄ Sacristy

Southwest Granada

Huerta de San Vicente

The family of the young **Federico García Lorca** (► Famous People) spent the summer in the Huerta de San Vicente country house. When his father acquired the house, it was surrounded by fruit trees, which have given way to the typical suburb development. Now a rose garden surrounds the house, which is devoted to a **museum**. Part of it still has the original furnishings (bus no. 4 from Gran Via de Colón; opening hours: Tue–Sun 10am–12.30pm, 5–7.30pm).

Parque de las Ciencias

The **Science Park** in Avenida Mediterráneo has nothing to do with Granada's past. It is an **interactive museum** offering hands-on natural science (opening hours: Tue–Sat 10am–7pm, Sun to 3pm).

Around Granada

Viznar

Federico Garcia Lorca was shot in 1936 by Falangists in the village of Viznar northeast of Granada. Today there is a **memorial** here to Lorca and all of the victims of the civil war.

Vega de Granada

A few miles west of Granada on the A-92 lies **Santa Fé**, which was built in the **form of a Roman camp** on the orders of Queen Isabella the Catholic in 1491 to serve as headquarters during the siege of

Monument honouring Federico Garcia Lorca in Fuente Vaqueros

Granada. Three of the original four gates in the rampart have survived. The surrender of Granada was signed here in 1491 and it was here on 17 April 1492 that the queen signed the contract with Columbus for voyages that were to lead to the discovery of the New World. Federico García Lorca was born in **Fuente Vaqueros** to the northwest of Santa Fé. The **house he was born in** is now a museum; a statue in his honour has also been erected there (opening hours: Tue–Sun 10am–1pm, 6–8pm). Next stop is old **Loja**, where the towering ruins of a castle from Moorish times remain. The most interesting evidence of

the Christian era is the church of San Gabriel (16th century) with a portal and dome by Diego de Siloé.

Alhama de Granada

Shortly before Loja, a small side road branches off 26km/16mi to the south to Alhama de Granada, a charming spa whose name means »hot springs«. When the Moors, who enthusiastically took advantage of its healing waters, lost their baths to the Christians in 1482, they lamented bitterly with the cry »Ay de mi Alhama!«, which is a customary cry still used to this day. The springs bubbling out of the earth at a temperature of 45°C/113°F in a Moorish cistern resting on Roman foundations can be viewed in Hotel Balenario (about 1km/0.5mi outside the village). Some secular buildings worth noting are the Casa de la Inquisición with an Isabelline-style façade, the 17th-century former prison on Plaza de los Presos and a granary dating back to the 16th century.

! Baedeker TIP

Fresh trout

If freshly prepared trout served in an idyllic, straw-covered patio sounds irresistible, then don't fail to make a short detour to the Venta Riofrío country inn in the village of Dorf Riofrío a bit south of Loja (tel. 958 32 10 66). There is nothing like a stroll along the inviting river afterwards.

✳ Guadix

17

Province: Granada
Population: 20,300

Altitude: 949m/3113ft

**Off the beaten track of major tourism, yet well within reach of ►
Granada on a day trip, the small town of Guadix lies on the Hoya
de Guadix plateau. The route is enjoyable, leading as it does
through bleak archaic-seeming tuff landscape to one of the largest
settlements of cave dwellings in Andalusia. Pottery is a popular
souvenir from the area.**

Findings from the megalithic culture show that the region was inhabited early. The Romans built Julia Gemelli Acci on an Iberian settlement. Renamed Wadi Ash, from which its present-day name is derived, the city experienced a new peak following the invasion of the
Moors. Only in 1489 did the Catholic Monarchs succeed in wresting
Guadix back from the Moors again. Famous sons of the city are **Pedro de Mendoza** (1499–1537), the **founder of Buenos Aires**, and the
poet Pedro Antonio de Alárcon (1833–1891).

City of cave
dwellings

What to See in Guadix

Begun in 1594 in place of a mosque, the towering cathedral cannot
be missed when driving into Guadix. Diego de Siloé designed its apse
and the chapel of San Torcuato. The tower was completed in the
17th century; Baroque and classical elements were added to the originally purely Plateresque main façade in the 18th century. Striking
Churrigueresque choir stalls can be found inside the church; the museum possesses relics of San Torcuato, goldsmith work, manuscripts,
and paintings.

✳
Catedral

 VISITING GUADIX

**INFORMATION
(OFICINA DE TURISMO)**

Carretera de Granada, s/n,
E-18500 Guadix
Tel. 958 66 26 65, fax 958 66 27 54
www.guadixmarquesado.org

**WHERE TO EAT AND
WHERE TO STAY**

► Budget
Comercio
C. Mira de Amezcua, 3

Tel. 958 66 05 00
Well-kept hotel at the centre, with a
good restaurant.

*Cuevas Pedro Antonio
de Alarcón*
Barriada San Torcuato
Tel. 958 66 49 86
Fax 958 66 17 21, 19 rooms
Those who have always wanted to
spend the night in a cave dwelling can
try it out in Guadix.

Environmentally-friendly living with a tradition in the Barriada de las Cuevas

Convento de Santiago
Built in the 16th century in the Mudéjar style, the Convento de Santiago is reached through a narrow alley to the right of the Plaza Mayor, bordered by arcades. The crest of Charles V can be identified above the Plateresque portal.

Yet probably the most beautiful secular building of Guadix is the 17th-century Palacio de Peñaflor.

Alcazaba
Built of red brick in the architecture typical of the 11th century, the Moorish castle ruin alcazaba lies enthroned above the old town. Remains of its 9th-century predecessor are still preserved in the vicinity.

Barriada de las Cuevas ✳
However, the most interesting sight of the town is without doubt the **district of cave dwellings** Barriada de las Cuevas or Barrio de Santiago. The people in this bizarre »housing area« live in caves dug from the soft loess. Only the whitewashed chimneys and porches are seen, and these do not hint at the often large and well-furnished rooms in the hill. The caves are an almost ideal form of living for the large fluctuations in the climate of this region. Pleasantly cool in summer, they store warmth in winter. The **museum cave** shows what such a cave dwelling looks like. It is at the end of C. San Miguel, at the Ermita Nueva (Cueva Museo; opening hours: Mon–Sat 10am–2pm and 5–7pm, Sun 10am–2pm).

Around Guadix

Purullena
Lying 6km/3.5mi to the west in a tuffstone landscape, Purullena is made up almost entirely of cave dwellings. A row of souvenir shops, restaurants, and bars lines the A-92, yet just a few steps behind it the interesting side of Purullena can be seen.

Bleak earth and endless expanses characterize the Guadix plateau – → the sheep are grazing in front of the backdrop of Lacalahorra castle.

Castillo de Lacalahorra

A hill with a mighty castle constructed in the 16th century looms above Lacalahorra, amidst a very barren-looking landscape south of Guadix (17km/11mi) to the right away from the A-92. The fortress, never used as such, has an elegant Renaissance patio that contrasts with its rugged exterior and the four enormous round towers (sightseeing possible with advance booking, tel. 958 67 70 98). The trip can be continued from Lacalahorra driving south to ▶Alpujarras, or southwest to▶Almería.

🕐 Opening hours:
Wed 10am–1pm,
4–6pm

Baza, near Guadix

It is a journey of 45km/28mi northeast from Guadix to Baza, which would have remained rather insignificant, had an exceptional **Iberian sculpture of a woman, the »Dama de Baza«**, not been discovered here in 1971. It may now be admired at the national museum of archaeology in Madrid. The sights of the town include a visit to the abbey church Santa María (16th–18th century) with its octagonal tower, the alcazaba, and the sparse remains of Moorish baths. Ramblers find a large area for walking in the Parque Natural Sierra de Baza. Continuation of the journey to the town of **Galera**, another 42km/26mi northeast, is recommended for those interested in archaeology, for it was here that the **Iberian necropolis Tutúgi** with 150 tombs dating from the 5th to 3rd centuries BC was discovered.

Huelva · Ruta Colombina

B 7

Province: Huelva
Population: 140,000

Altitude: 56m/184ft

Situated on a peninsula bordered on either side by the Río Odiel and the Río Tinto, Huelva is characterized by industrial activity.

Seaport and industrial city

Measured by its goods turnover, the **commercial port** is one of Spain's largest, primarily due to the loading of ores from Río Tinto and Tharsis, and due to the **petrochemical industry**, which also makes for a correspondingly dramatic environmental situation. Fishing for tuna and sardines, and the fish-canning industry are of further significance. In turn, the province Huelva is one of the **largest European areas for cultivating strawberries**, which are grown here under similar conditions to those of the vegetables from ▶Almería. All this does not necessarily indicate that Huelva is attractive – yet visitors to the surrounding area can follow in the footsteps of Christopher Columbus.

History

Huelva was of great importance for the expeditions of the Genoese Christopher Columbus, who recruited a large part of his crew here. The beginnings of the city most likely lie in a Phoenician settlement, which the Romans took over as Onuba. Some researchers speculate

VISITING HUELVA • RUTA COLOMBINA

INFORMATION (OFICINA DE TURISMO)

Avda. Alemania, 12, E-21001 Huelva
Tel. / fax 959 25 74 03
www.diphuelva.es

WHERE TO EAT

▶ Expensive

Casa Rufino
In Isla Cristina, Crta. de la Playa
Tel. 959 33 08 10
30 years ago, Rufino Zaiño pre-empted nouvelle cuisine with his »Menú Tonteo«. Cultivated even to-day, this succession of courses is »long and slim«: four place settings, eight platos – in view of which guests can cope with an overdose of garlic in the sixth course.

▶ Moderate

① Las Candelas
Carretera de Punte Umbria/Crossing of Aljaraque
Tel. 959 31 83 01
Excellent fish dishes.

② Las Meigas
Avda. de Guatemala, 48
Superb restaurant with fish specialties – prepared in the Basque, Galician and Andalusian style.

▶ Inexpensive

③ Taberna El Condado
Sór Angela de la Cruz, 3
Tel. 959 26 11 23
Tapas bar with atmosphere.

WHERE TO STAY

▶ Mid-range

Parador Costa de la Luz
In Ayamonte, El Castillito
Tel. 959 32 07 00, 48 rooms
Some rooms have a view of the mouth of the Río Guadiana.

Hotel Oasis Islantilla
In Isla Cristina, Ctra. La Antilla
Tel. 959 48 64 22
Fax 959 48 64 21, 479 Rooms
Huge luxury hotel at the beach, with three golf courses nearby.

▶ Budget

① Luz Huelva
Alameda Sundheim, 26
Tel. 959 25 00 11
Fax 959 25 81 10, 107 rooms
Reliable, centrally situated lodgings.

El Paraíso-Playa
Avda. de la Playa, 2 / n
Tel. 959 33 18 73
Fax 959 34 37 45, 34 rooms
Well looked-after, friendly beach hotel in a nice location.

Pato Amarillo
In Punta Umbria, Avda. Océano
Urb. Everluz
Tel. 959 31 12 50, fax 959 31 12 58
E-mail: comercial@hotelespato.com
www.hotelpatoamarillo.com, 120 rooms
Large beach hotel with corresponding amenities.

SHOPPING

Shop after shop lines the pedestrian zone from C. Concepción to C. Berdigón. A department store of the chain El Corte Inglés is on the Plaza de España.

EVENT

Fiestas Colombinas
At the end of July / beginning of August, sailing regattas and bullfights are held to commemorate Christopher Columbus, who embarked on his expedition from Palos in 1492.

Huelva *Plan*

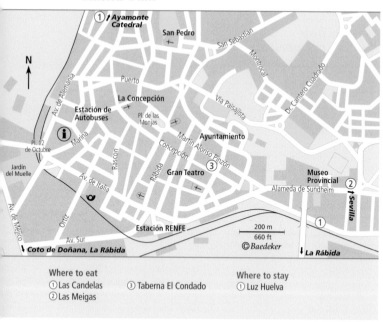

Where to eat
① Las Candelas
② Las Meigas
③ Taberna El Condado

Where to stay
① Luz Huelva

that the legendary Tartessos (Tharsis) of ancient times lies here. Alfonso X wrested the city from the Moors in 1257; Pedro the Cruel gave it as a present to his mistress, María de Padilla, before it came to the dukes of Medina Sidonia in the mid-15th century. The earthquake which destroyed Lisbon on 1 November 1755 also had devastating ramifications for Huelva – it destroyed large parts of the city, so that today there is little to see in terms of impressive sights.

What to See in Huelva

Churches Churches of note are San Pedro (16th century), built over the ruins of a mosque and restored after the earthquake, and La Concepción (16th century), which possesses two small paintings by Zurbarán. The cathedral, which belonged to the La Merced convent (now a hospital) and as such exhibits a somewhat uniform Baroque style, was only consecrated in 1953. The Nuestra Señora de la Cinta (Madonna of the Belt), located 3km/2mi north of the centre was originally built in the Gothic-Mudéjar style. The interior has a Mudéjar coffered ceiling. The magnificent retablo with a painting of the virgin draws attention. Legend has it that Columbus came here to pray before he left on his first voyage of discovery, which is remembered in the ceramic tiles to the right of the altar. The impressive processional image, the »Virgen Chiquita«, is used on 8 September for the Virgen de la Cinta pilgrimage when it is carried from the sanctuary to the Cathedral. Outside is a restored attractive patio with orange trees.

To the east of the provincial museum the Reina Victoria quarter, built entirely **in the style of Victorian working class neighbourhoods** by the English Rio Tinto Mining Company in 1917, is an architectural gem.

Barrio Reina Victoria

At the south end of the city, a martial, 34m/111ft-high monument to Columbus guards the bridge crossing the Rio Tinto at the Punta del Sebo. The sculpture, a work of the American sculptress Gertrude Whitney, was a present from the USA to Huelva in 1929.

Monument to Columbus

Around Huelva

South of Huelva, the delta of the rivers Odiel and Tinto forms an extensive alluvial plain and protected habitat for many bird species, and can be reached by heading in the direction of Punte Umbria. More than 2000 flamingos winter here in Paraje Natural Marismas del Odiel, despite the close proximity to industry, as do wading birds, ducks and spoonbills. Except during winter, the Centro de Visitantes Calatilla organizes tours on foot, by canoe, and by boat (opening hours: Mon–Fri 8am–2.30pm).

Marismas del Odiel

The part of the ►Costa de la Luz that lies to the north of the mouth of the Guadalquivir is easily reached from Huleva. Once the tanks,

Along the Costa de la Luz

The view out onto the great expanse of ocean can be enjoyed on hour-long strolls along the beach at Isla Cristina.

cranes, warehouses and factories in the south of the city have been left behind, the coast road passes miles of sandy beaches, behind which camping sites lie in pine forests. Although many private properties and military prohibited areas block the way to the water, there is access to the sea at two beach resorts: **Mazagón**, which boasts eight miles of beach and the **most sunshine hours on this coast**, and Matalascañas, at the national park ▶Coto de Doñana.

Punta Umbria

On the headland west of the delta, Punta Umbria acts as Huelva's local beach, with beach bars and clubbing till late at night. Boats also come here from Huelva.

Ayamonte

The N-431, leading to the Portuguese border, curves via Gibraleón, and provides several approaches to the beaches of the northwestern Costa de la Luz: El Rompido, La Antilla and Isla Cristina. After 60km/37mi it reaches the Spanish border town Ayamonte, a fishing port of Phoenician origin at the mouth of the Río Guadiana. Apart from mansions, there are also some noteworthy churches, including Nuestra Señora de las Angustias with its beautiful façade, and a Capilla Mayor with a Mudéjar roof. With the opening of the suspension bridge above the wide Río Guadiana delta in September 1991, a road connection between Spain and Portugal was created here for the first time.

Tharsis

An excursion on the A-495 leads from Gibraleón northwest to Alosno, home to fandango. The **mining area of Tharsis** begins here. The name preserves the biblical **Tarshish**, which the Greeks called **Tartessos**. Tharsis is the centre of a mining area in which the Iberians and Romans already mined pyrite and barite. Spain sold the mining rights to the Rio Tinto Mining Company in the 19th century.

Ruta Colombina

Where history was made

At the end of the 15th century, the estuary area of Río Tinto was the scene of events of world history: here **Christopher Columbus** planned and began the undertaking that resulted in the discovery of the New World. The most important historic sites can be discovered along the Ruta Colombina, which leads from Huelva to Moguer via the monastery La Rábida, and Palos de la Frontera.

★
Monasterio de La Rábida
⏱
Opening hours:
Tue–Sat
10.30am–1pm,
4–6.15pm,
Sun 10.45am–1pm

Events began at the monastery of La Rábida, the walls of which gleam from a hill 8km/5mi south of Huelva across the bridge over the Río Tinto. Franciscan monks founded it next to an older church in the 15th century. In 1485, after Christopher Columbus had tried in vain to convince John II of Portugal of his plans, he wanted to try his luck in Spain. On the way there he and his son found a welcome at the monastery and advocates in Father Juan Pérez and Father Antonio de Marchena, the confessor of Queen Isabella. Following long

Monasterio de Santa María de la Rábida Plan

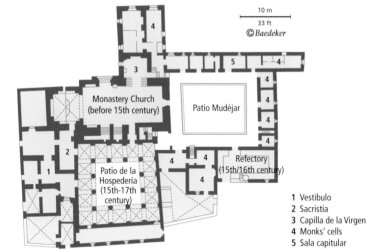

10 m
33 ft
©Baedeker

Monastery Church
(before 15th century)

Patio Mudéjar

Patio de la
Hospedería
(15th-17th
century)

Refectory
(15th/16th century)

1 Vestíbulo
2 Sacristía
3 Capilla de la Virgen
4 Monks' cells
5 Sala capitular

negotiations, Isabella was persuaded to conclude a contract that promised Columbus the means for his expedition, and made him viceroy of the countries yet to be discovered. The monastery offers little in terms of art, yet is still worth seeing as a **memorial to the sojourn of Christopher Columbus,** who is commemorated by a cast-iron cross mounted at the entrance in 1892. Busts of Columbus's two patrons frame the forecourt. The tall column at the exit was erected in 1892 for the 400th anniversary of the discovery of America. The Patio de la Hospedería (18th century) leads into the minster, the oldest part of the complex (14th century). It was rebuilt in the 18th century following the earthquake of Lisbon, and holds its most valuable treasure in the Capilla de la Virgen: the alabaster sculpture of Santa María de la Rábida, created around 1400, to which Columbus and his companions prayed for assistance before departure, and after which the flag ship *Santa María* is named. A cloister in the Mudéjar style is joined to the church, its gallery serving as a museum, with model ships, genuine artefacts from the age of discovery, and portraits. Tables, chairs and other items can be seen in the chapter house, at which Columbus held council with the brothers Pinzón – the captains of the other two caravels– and the two monks. Portraits of personages from the age of discovery decorate the walls; a medallion showing the head of Christopher Columbus, a copy of the original by Guido Mazzoni, is delicate work. The flags of all Latin American countries hang in the Sala de las Banderas, and earth from these countries is kept in the caskets underneath.

✱
◄ Columbus site

As in the time of Columbus – Muelle de las Carabellas

Muelle de las Carabellas ▶ Near the Foro Ibero-Americano below, at the Muelle de las Carabellas lie **replicas of Columbus's three ships**, which can be visited. These, plus a medieval market and an Indian village bring the age of discovery to life. Plants from Spain and Latin America thrive in the botanical garden José Celestino Mutis.

Palos de la Frontera 5km/3mi further east lies Palos de la Frontera, once one of the most important ports for ships travelling to the New World, and the centre of strawberry growing today. On 3 August 1492 Columbus put out to sea from here with the *Santa María*, the *Pinta*, and the *Niña*; this is where he also returned to on 15 March 1493. Hernán Cortés also disembarked in Palos after his trek through Mexico. The brothers Alonso Martín and Vicente Yañéz Pinzón, captains of the *Pinta* and *Niña* respectively came from Palos. A monument near the town hall commemorates Martín; his birthplace can be visited (opening hours: Mon–Sat 10.30am–1.30pm and 5.30–7.30pm, Sun mornings only).

Casa Museo Pinzón ▶

The church **San Jorge**, constructed over a mosque, possesses a beautifully wrought pulpit and azulejo adornment. Columbus and the brothers Pinzón proceeded down to the anchorage, of which nothing can now be seen, through the Puerta de los Novios (Gate of the Betrothed). Somewhat below the choir stands the pump house La Fontanilla, which supplied the ships with water.

Moguer Lying 7km/4.5mi northeast of Palos, Moguer is the last stop on the Ruta Colombina, and of course also has its connection with Columbus, yet its people almost take more pride in the fact that the 1956 **winner of the Nobel prize for literature**, Juan Ramón Jiménez (1881–1958), was born here and raised a monument to his home town with the novel *Platero y Yo* (*Platero and I*). Ceramic plaques with quotes taken from this novel are everywhere in Moguer, and of course a monument honours the author on the square at the town hall. Both his birthplace and the house in which he lived with his life partner, Zenobia Camprubi, can be visited (opening hours: Tue–Sat 10.15am–1.15pm and 5.15–7.15pm, Sunday mornings only). A well belonging to the house is adorned with a figure of the donkey Platero, the »hero« of the novel.

Moguer was one of the main places where Columbus recruited his crew. On returning from his journey, the discoverer spent his first night on European soil in Moguer at the Convento de Santa Clara, and caused mass to be said there. This convent was founded in 1348 and, with its blend of Gothic and Mudéjar elements, is one of the most significant religious structures of Huelva province, not least due to its décor: Mudéjar choir stalls on a plinth of azulejos, a sculpture of the Virgin attributed to Montañés, and an alabaster tomb in the Capilla Mayor with lifelike recumbent figures of the founding family Portocarrero dating from the 15th century. The very beautiful cloister is supported by Mudéjar columns.

◄ Convento de Santa Clara

The painted belfry of the church Nuestra Señora de la Granada (14th to 18th centuries) is reminiscent of the Giralda of ►Seville. A highlight inside is the painting *Adoration of the Magi*, ascribed to Murillo.

◄ Nuestra Señora de la Granada

★ Itálica

C 7

Province: Sevilla   **Altitude:** 20m/66ft

Just 10km/6mi north of ►Seville and west of the N-630 past Mérida near the village of Santiponce lie the ruins of the Roman city of Itálica. It was the first Roman settlement on Iberian soil, and is unique among the Roman remains in present-day Spain in its size and seclusion – even though only the foundation walls have been preserved for the most part.

At nearby Ilipa (now Alcalá del Río) Publius Cornelius Scipio the Elder defeated a numerically superior Carthaginian army under the command of Mago and Hasdrubal Gisco, thereby ousting the Carthaginians from Iberia in 206 BC. He ordered the wounded and veterans to found a settlement at the site of present-day Santiponce, the »vetus urbs« (old town). Thus Itálica became the **starting point for the Latinization of Iberia**. The Roman emperors Trajan and Hadrian were members of two of the original families, favouring their native city with embellishments and founding »nova urbs«, the new city. It

Ruined Roman city with magnificent mosaics

Wonderful mosaic floors have been preserved in Itálica, the first Roman settlement on Iberian soil.

was at its prime in the 2nd and 3rd centuries AD, when it flourished primarily from the wine and olive oil trade. Into the 7th century Itálica was seat of a bishopric, thereafter fading into obscurity. In the 17th century the inhabitants of Santiponce used the houses as raw material to rebuild their village, which had been destroyed by a flood. However, the lower strata remained intact in the process.

Santiponce

The village of Santiponce stands on the remains of the first veteran settlement. A **Roman theatre** that exhibits so-called tabulae lusoriae and carvings is preserved here. The names of horses that ran races in the arena are recorded on them. The fortress-like San Isidoro del Campo monastery, comprising two churches and several courtyards, lies on the southern edge of the village. In 1294 the older of the two churches was founded by Alonso Pérez de Guzmán, referred to as El Bueno, the heroic defender of ▶ Tarifa. Sculptures of him and his wife kneeling by Montañés are placed on either side of the retable, also by Montañés. The second church was founded by Guzmán's son Juan Alonso Pérez, who lies buried with his wife.

✳ **Ruined city of Itálica**

The path leads from the entrance to the **amphitheatre** (anfiteatro), one of the largest-known constructions of its kind, with a 160m/175yd longitudinal axis, a 137m/150yd lateral axis, and seating for 25,000 spectators. Excessive animal hunts and gladiatorial contests took place here, as is documented by a bronze plaque on which the emperor Marcus Aurelius commanded the curtailing of such spectacles (now in the national archaeological museum in Madrid). The cruciform foundations in the

 ITÁLICA

INFORMATION (OFICINA DE TURISMO)

C. La Feria, s/n, E-41970 Santiponce
Tel. 955 99 80 28
Fax 955 99 64 00

Itálica Roman Town Plan

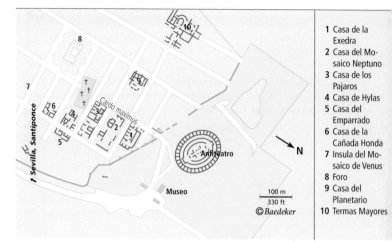

1 Casa de la Exedra
2 Casa del Mosaico Neptuno
3 Casa de los Pajaros
4 Casa de Hylas
5 Casa del Emparrado
6 Casa de la Cañada Honda
7 Insula del Mosaico de Venus
8 Foro
9 Casa del Planetario
10 Termas Mayores

oval's centre served as an animal enclosure and magazine. The rows of seats rise in surrounding tiers, the first row being reserved for patricians, as can still be seen today by the names engraved; the populace sat above (opening hours: April–Sept. Tue–Sat 9am–8pm, Sun until 3pm; Oct. to March until 5.30pm or 4pm).

After leaving the theatre, the paved main road, the cardo maximus, leads to the right up the hill to »nova urbs«. Columns that bore covered walks flank the road. It may be disappointing that so little of the buildings still stands, yet as the base walls have been preserved or rebuilt, the floor plans of the houses can be seen very clearly. Above all, though, the magnificent **mosaic floors** have remained, the most valuable of which have been removed to the archaeological museum in ►Seville.

Precinct

Bird motifs can be seen in the building to the left in front of the cemetery, Casa de los Pajáros. Casa de Hylas lies further to the right in this side street, possessing a geometrically patterned mosaic floor. At the end of this path and to the left is a small incline adorned with a copy of Praxiteles' Aphrodite of Knidos. A path leads back to the main road from here, past Casa del Mosaico de Neptuno, which possesses the most beautiful mosaic decorations: the sea-god Neptune surrounded by dolphins, fish, and mythical creatures; before it a mosaic depicting what is thought to be the labyrinth of Cretan Knossos. The baths of Itálica are situated a little distance outside, slightly down hill and to the right of the main road.

Mosaics, lamps, glasses, coins and a sculpture of Emperor Hadrian as a naked athlete are displayed in the entrance of the museum.

Museo

★ Jaén

H 6

Province: Jaén
Population: 107,200

Altitude: 574m/1883ft

The fact that Jaén, the ancient seat of a bishopric at the foot of Sierra Jabalcuz and Sierra de la Pandera in the northeast of Andalusia, is Spain's olive capital can be seen and smelled: the entire province – the largest uninterrupted expanse of olive groves in the world – is covered with olive trees, and the air is filled with the fragrance of olive pomace.

Spain's olive capital
Certainly the city is much less spectacular for tourists than ►Granada or ►Córdoba, yet after a stroll through its alleyways beneath the truly commanding castle, the visitor can feel its slightly rough, quiet

Jaén Plan

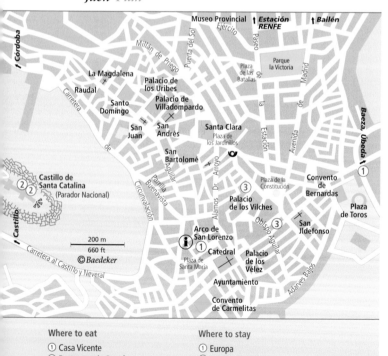

Where to eat
① Casa Vicente
② Restaurant in Parador Castillo de Santa Catalina
③ Río Chico

Where to stay
① Europa
② Parador Castillo de Santa Catalina
③ Xauen

▶ VISITING JAÉN

INFORMATION (OFICINA DE TURISMO)
C. Maestra, 18, E-23002 Jaén
Tel. 953 21 91 16
Fax 953 26 03 32
www.promojaen.es

WHERE TO EAT

▶ Expensive
① *Casa Vicente*
C. Francisco Martín Mora, 1
Fine regional cuisine.

▶ Moderate
② *Restaurant in the Parador Castillo de Santa Catalina*
Tel. 953 23 00 00
Andalusian cuisine is served in the knights' hall of the ancient Moorish castle high above the city. It, is best to order a culinary tour: six hors d'oeuvres and six main courses for two people arrive on the table in small pans.

▶ Inexpensive
③ *Río Chico*
Nueva, 12
Tel. 953 24 08 02
Large selection of tapas and raciones in the bar, restaurant on the second floor.

WHERE TO STAY

▶ Budget
① *Europe*
Pl. de Belén, 1
Tel. 953 22 27 00
Fax 953 22 26 92
Central, quiet, friendly.

③ *Xauen*
Plaza de Deán Mazas, 3
Tel. 953 24 07 89
Fax 953 19 03 12, 35 rooms
Central, well-priced accommodation.

Baedeker recommendation

▶ Mid-range
② *Parador Castillo de Santa Catalina*
Tel. 953 23 00 00
Fax 953 23 09 30
E-mail: jaen@parador.es
www.parador.es, 45 rooms

Among all the paradors the one in the castle of Jaén remains exceptional: high above the city the guest can feel like a knight, even though the rooms are not in the 14th century castle, but in an extension in the same style. The balconies offer an enjoyable and unsurpassed view over the hills of olive. Very good restaurant in the knights' hall.

SHOPPING
C. Roldán y Marín, Paseo de la Estación, and C. de San Clemente are the main shopping streets.

EVENTS
Semana Santa

Feria de San Lucas
Mid-October: the city festival is celebrated for a week – with an end to the season for Spain's best bullfighters, who wish to recommend themselves for engagement in Central and South America.

charm. It is worth taking a short trip into the world of olives. There are particularly beautiful impressions of the landscape in the mountainous area south of the city, and to the east, where the hills roll more gently and olive plantations increasingly give way to corn fields.

History   The Romans who conquered the town fortified by the Carthaginians in 207 BC had more interest in the surrounding silver mines than in olive oil, which is why they named the place Auringis; even today people speak of »silver Jaén«. Under the rule of the Moors, who took over in 712, the town was made capital of a taifa as Yayyan or Geen (»place at the crossing of caravan routes«), following the disintegration of the Cordovan caliphate, and gained its urban character. In 1246 Ferdinand III drove off Ibn al-Ahmar, the founder of the Nasrid dynasty, who withdrew to Granada. From now on Jaén formed a continuously embattled outpost of the Reconquista, and received the honorary title »Most Noble, Famous and Loyal City of Jaen, Guardian and Defender of the Kings of Castile« in 1466. In 1491 the armies gathered here for the conquest of Granada.

The cathedral of Jaén in front of a seemingly endless ocean of olive groves

Catedral de Jaén Plan

1 Puerta Mayor

2 Puerta del Norte

3 Capilla Mayor

4 Capilla de San Fernando

5 Capilla del Santo Rostro

6 Capilla de Santiago

7 Sala capitular

8 Sacristía

9 Capilla de la Virgen
   de las Angustias

10 Capilla de la Virgen
    de los Dolores

© Baedeker

Around the Cathedral

An expertly rendered example of the Spanish Renaissance style, the imposing cathedral stands in an elevated position in the old town on the site of the main Moorish mosque. Its construction was begun around 1500, but the work only progressed more speedily under Andrés de Vandelvira from the mid-16th century, and the final completion was prolonged until the late 18th century. The wealth of statues (17th century) on the façade flanked by two towers are primarily by Pedro and Julián Roldán. Ferdinand III the Saint is in the middle of the balustrade, and to his side are the four evangelists and the four church fathers. The artists portrayed the Blessed Virgin in the tympanum. The north portal by Juan de Aranda also shows the Virgin, this time in prayer. Vandelvira created the south portal.

★
Catedral

The **cathedral interior** is divided into a nave and two aisles of equal height, with a masterly dome by Juan de Aranda over the crossing. The magnificently carved early 16th-century choir stalls are outstanding, with scenes from the Old and New Testament. Master Bartolomé executed the high altar of the Capilla Mayor with a depiction of the Virgin. Three chapels adjoin the east wall behind it. In a shrine of Cordovan goldsmith work, the middle one holds a renowned relic: the **veil of St Veronica**, called Santo Rostro, shown each Friday after mass. Admittedly this cloth, with which the saint wiped the face of Jesus on his way to Calvary, whereby the image of Christ's face was impressed upon the cloth, is one of three in existence (the other two are in Rome and Genoa). Above the shrine stands the Gothic sculpture of Nuestra Señora de la Antigua, which is said to have accompanied Ferdinand III on his crusades; the paintings are by Cellini and

★
◄ Choir stalls

★
◄ Santo Rostro

Titian, among others. An almost gaudy-looking Christ bearing the cross, carried at processions, stands to the left in the Capilla de San Fernando; in the side chapels Capilla de la Virgen de las Angustias and Capilla de la Virgen de los Dolores visitors can see a retable by José de Mora and a depiction of the Mother of Sorrows by Pancorbo, respectively.

Further rooms ▶ To the right of the Capilla del Santo Rostro, in the chapter house, a retable is displayed with a painting by Pedro Machuca. Vandelvira completed the vestry with a coffered barrel vault. Beneath the vestry the cathedral museum displays paintings (by Ribera and others) and religious artefacts, including the large silver Custodia El Vandalino by Juan Ruiz, and a fifteen-armed candlestick by the master Bartolomé de Jaén.

Convento de Carmelitas A little south of the cathedral the original manuscript of Cántico Espiritual by the mystic Juan de la Cruz (St John of the Cross) is kept in the Convento de Carmelitas (Monasterio de Santa Teresa) founded in 1615. Consecrated to St Teresa of Ávila, the convent was the first retreat of Carmelite nuns.

Houses of nobility The Palacio de los Vélez on the east side of the cathedral, and the Palacio de los Vilches somewhat further away, are two beautiful Renaissance palaces, of which there are several examples in the neighbourhood of the church and in the rest of Jaén's old town.

San Bartolomé North of the cathedral toward the Moorish old town lies the church of San Bartolomé, constructed in the 15th century, showing a Gothic ceramic baptismal font and a masterly *Christ on the Cross* by Martínez Montañés.

Monasterio de Santa Clara Adjacent to the church is the Monasterio de Santa Clara (13th century), the city's oldest monastery, possessing a beautiful cloister and a valuable sculpture of Christ, Cristo del Bambú.

✳ La Magdalena

Continue from the convent parallel to the castle to enter the **old town with its Moorish character** , named La Magdalena after its main church. From here narrow alleyways climb steeply up the castle hill.

Capilla de San Andrés Situated at the edge of the old town, this chapel was founded in 1515 by the treasurer to popes Leo X and Clement VII, Gutiérrez González Doncel. Originally it was probably a synagogue. A Madonna of the Andalusian school and a panel of the Virgen del Pópulo can be seen in its Capilla la Purísima; far more impressive, however, is the magnificent choir screen by Bartolomé de Jaén from the 18th century, which depicts which depicts plants and animals.

A little further is the Palacio de los Villardompardo, beneath which **11th-century baths**, the most extensive of the Moorish era in Spain, were discovered in 1913. According to legend, the ruler of Jaén, King Alí, was murdered here by his rival. The baths consist of several rooms with an average width of 3–4m/10–13ft, which are lit and ventilated by shafts formed like eight-pronged stars. The building materials are marble and brick. The changing room was a 14m/45ft-long antechamber. Channels of hot water heated the floor of the steam-bath (al-bayt al Sajun), which is nearly 16m/50ft long. This room merges with a relaxation room (al-bayt al Wastani) of pleasant temperature, measuring about 11 sq m/120 sq ft, at the centre of which a pool is set as if beneath a canopy of horseshoe arches. The last stage of the bath took place in the 11.4m/37ft-long shower room (al-bayt al barid), in which bathers were doused with cold water from earthenware pitchers. The palace also houses a **folk museum and an art museum** (opening hours of baths and museums: Tue–Fri 9am–8pm, Sat and Sun 9.30am–2.30pm).

Palacio de los Villardompardo

✶ ✶

◀ Baños Árabes

🕐

Go past the Convento de Santo Domingo, which stands on the site of the palace of the Arab rulers and is connected with the baths by a subterranean corridor, to La Magdalena church, erected over an Arab mosque and probably the oldest church of the city. It has a late Gothic portal and a valuable retable, and above all a very impressive patio, which still contains the basin for ritual ablutions before entering the mosque. At the church opposite is the Raudal de la Magdalena, a fountain going back to Roman times.

Iglesia de la Magdalena

New Town

Heading east, it is not far from the Plaza de la Constitución down to the city's second largest church, San Ildefonso, completed in the 15th century. A patron saint of the city, the Virgen de la Descenso, is venerated here. Here, too, is the tomb of Andrés de Vandelvira, who made one of the three Renaissance-style portals. The Baroque altar by the brothers Roldán and the Capilla de la Virgen stands out from the décor.

San Ildefonso

Passing the Plaza de las Batallas where a monument commemorates two great battles fought at Jaén (the battle of Navas de Tolosa against the Moors in 1212, and the battle of Bailén against the French in 1808), the Paseo leads to the Museo Provincial. The museum consists of a collection of paintings and sculptures on the second floor (Alonso Cano: *Madonna and Child*; Pedro Berruguete: *Flagellation of Christ*), and an archaeological department on the ground floor. The most interesting pieces are a Roman mosaic, an early Christian sarcophagus from Martos, and Iberian sculptures such as the Bull Fighters of Porcuna. The building also incorporates the 16th century entry to the former corn storehouse, and the façade of the former church of St Miguel.

Museo Provincial
🕐
Opening hours:
Tue–Sat
9am–8pm,
Sun 9am–2pm

★ ★ Castillo de Santa Catalina

🕐 Opening hours:
Courtyard only,
otherwise freely
accessible: daily
except Wed
10am–2pm, 5–7pm

West of the city centre looms a mountain ridge with one of the **most beautiful and impressive fortifications of Andalusia**, Castillo de Santa Catalina, which Ferdinand III conquered in 1246. The best way to get there is by car on the 5km/3mi-long stretch marked Parador Nacional. The Carthaginians built a tower on the hill, but the present-day castle dates back to an Arab fortress which Ibn al-Ahmar expanded to its present imposing size. As Ferdinand captured it on St Catherine's Day it bears her name. Parts of the old fortification walls are visible when coming from the old town. The castle consists of a large forecourt and the mighty Torre del Homenaje, which is connected by battlements to other towers. A vantage point (only for those unafraid of heights) marked by a large cross and jutting out like a ship's bows offers a stunning view over the city and the olive plantations.

★ ★
Vantage point ▶

Around Jaén

La Guardia
de Jaén ▶

The remains of Roman buildings point to the origin of the small town La Guardia de Jaén (11km/7mi southeast); additionally the ruins of an ancient castle are located here, as well as a lovely parish church and cloistered courtyard created by Vandelvira, all that remains of a Dominican monastery founded in the 16th century.

★
Martos ▶

Dominated by two castles, Martos, 20km/12mi west of Jaén, **is the olive capital of Spain** – nowhere else in the kingdom do so many olive trees grow within the communal boundaries. Having developed from the Iberian settlement of Tucci, Martos was wrested from the Moors by Ferdinand III in 1222, and was a vital outpost in the reconquest of Córdoba. The overall impression of the town alone makes a visit to Martos worthwhile: the castle hill rises at its centre, square white houses huddling on it along narrow alleys; the ruins of the Castillo de la Peña de los Carvajales are visible on the rugged rock. The brothers Carvajal were thrown from it to their deaths, despite their innocence, after they had been accused of murdering a favourite of Ferdinand IV. Inside the walls of the second fortress, the citadel, stands the church Santa María de la Villa, built in the 13th century and modified in Gothic style in the 15th century. Its greatest treasures are a Baroque retable and an early Christian sarcophagus dating from the 4th century. The town hall of 1577 and the Renaissance fountain Fuente Nueva of 1580 are also worth seeing.

Alcaudete ▶

Alcaudete, 22km/13mi southwest of Martos, saw many battles, changed hands often and was finally conquered by Ferdinand III in 1245. He gave it to the Order of Calatrava, its remains still dominate the village. Below the fortress are the 15th-century Gothic church Santa María and the grand palace Casa del Almirante.

Jerez de la Frontera

C 8

Province: Cádiz   **Altitude:** 56m/183ft
Population: 181,600

Not far inland from ►Cádiz lies Jerez de la Frontera, world famous as the place of origin of Jerez wine, better known as sherry. Of equal importance is the breeding of thoroughbreds, the epitome of fiery Andalusian horses, at the national stud farm; lastly, Jerez de la Frontera is a centre of flamenco and the cante jondo (►Baedeker Special p.62).

Sherry, horses, and flamenco are combined in three large annual festivals: the **Festival del Flamenco**, the **Feria del Caballo**, and the **Fiestas del Otoño** following the grape harvest. It becomes particularly clear on such occasions that Jerez de la Frontera is a town of aristocratic character, where the sherry barons call the shots.

Sherry, horses, and flamenco

Settling down in Jerez on a mild summer's night with a glass of Amontillado.

▶ VISITING JEREZ DE LA FRONTERA

INFORMATION (OFICINA DE TURISMO)

C. Paul, s/n,
E-11403 Jerez de la Frontera
Tel. 956 35 98 63
Fax 956 33 98 62
www.turismojerez.com

Plaza del Arenal, s/n
Tel. 956 35 96 54/55
A tourist office is also located in the Alameda Cristina on the northern edge of the old town; a good starting point for exploring the sights of Jerez de la Frontera on foot.

WHERE TO EAT

▶ Expensive
Bodega La Andana
C. Moscatel, 4
Tel. 956 30 73 85
High-class cuisine somewhat outside of the centre, known for its fine tapas.

② *Gaitán*
Gaitán, 3
Tel. 956 16 80 21
www.restaurantegaitan.com
One of the most popular and highly praised restaurants in Jerez.

③ *La Mesa Redonda*
Manuel de la Quintana, 3
Tel. 956 34 00 69
Indisputably the best traditional cuisine to accompany sherry in Jerez de la Frontera – be trusting and let the menu entice you.

▶ Inexpensive
① *Bar Juanito*
Pescadería Vieja, 8–10
Tel. 956 33 48 38
This place has the best tapas in the city, a huge selection. The assortment of finos is almost equally large.

WHERE TO STAY

▶ Luxury
③ *Jerez*
Avda. Alcalde Alvaro Domecq, 35
Tel. 956 30 06 00
Fax 956 30 50 01
www.jerezhotel.com, 121 ROOMS
The best hotel in town, amidst beautiful gardens, yet close to the centre.

▶ Budget
① *Doña Blanca*
Bodega, 11
Tel. 956 34 87 61
Fax 956 34 85 86
E-mail: info@hoteldonablanca.com
www.hoteldonablanca.com, 30 rooms
Good, located centrally.

② *El Coloso*
Pedro Alonso, 13
Tel. / Fax 956 34 90 08
www.elcolosohotel.com, 28 rooms
Central and low-priced.

④ *Nuevo*
Caballeros, 23
Tel. 956 34 7 61
Fax 956 33 16 04
Friendly and homely.

BODEGAS

In Jerez, the city of sherry, do not fail to book a tour of a bodega. Many are conducted in English, and they always ending with a tasting:

Bodegas González Byass
Manuel María Gonzalez, 12
Tel. 956 35 70 16
www.gonzalezbyass.es
This bodega, located centrally near the Alcázar also produces a very good brandy.

Guided tours: Mon–Sat mornings and afternoons, Sun mornings only.

Bodegas Domecq
San Ildefonso, 3
Tel. 956 15 15 00
www.domecq.es
The bodegas of this large producer lie behind the cathedral on a spacious site.
Guided tours: Mon–Fri 9am–1pm

John Harvey & Sons
Arcos, 53
Tel. 956 34 60 04
Harvey's cultivates a very British appearance, with stylish vintage cars in the foyer.

Williams & Humbert
Nuño de Cañas, 1
Tel. 956 34 34 06
www.williams-humbert.com
Not far from the bullring, with stables and a garden.

Sandeman
Pizarro, 10
Tel. 956 15 17 00
www.sandeman.com
The storks' nests on top of the warehouse are the symbol of this bodega close to the royal riding school.
Guided tours: Mon–Fri 9am–3pm, advanced booking requested.

Maestro Sierra
Plaza de Silos, 3
Tel. 956 34 24 33
Small bodega near the Alcázar.

Wisdom & Warter Ltd.
Pizarro, 7
Tel. 956 18 43 06
www.wisdomwarter.es
This bodega is also situated near the royal riding school.

SHOPPING

All around C. Larga fashion, crafts (specialty: riding equipment, wickerwork), ceramics, leatherwear and jewellery are on sale. Don't miss the market hall at Plaza Estévez.

Fresh food from one of Spain's oldest market halls

Casa del Jerez
C. Divina Pastora, 1, Local 3, opposite the riding school
Sherry of all brands and a large variety of handicrafts.

EVENTS

Festival del Flamenco
In February / March: information at www.festivaldejerez.com.

Semana Santa

Feria del Caballo
Gymkhana and horse fair in May.

Festival de la Bulería
Festival of Bulería, the Jerez version of flamenco, in September.

Fiestas del Otoño
This includes several festivals from September to October, such as the grape harvest festival and a large horse parade.

Their sweeping bodegas, surrounded by high walls, set themselves apart conspicuously from the rest of the townscape. Grand domiciles in well-tended parks, noble horses and fighting bulls that they breed on their huge estates are shown with great pride, and there is hardly a trace of social responsibility towards the thousands of day labourers who live on the fringes of town, and for whom the grape harvest is the most important source of income.

Lastly, Jerez has also made itself a name in motor sports. 10km/6mi outside the town towards ►Arcos de la Frontera lies the Circuito de Jerez, at which races of the World Motorcycle Championship are held.

History The area between Jerez and the Cabo de Trafalgar was the site of the final battle between the Visigoths under Roderic and the Moors under Tariq in 711. The Muslim victors named the place Seris and upgraded it to a fortress. In 1264 Alfonso X reconquered the city, yet only in 1340 did a further battle at the Río Saladom, from which the Christians emerged victorious, forestall the last invasion from North Africa. Jerez has shared the byname de la Frontera (on the border) with other western Spanish-Moorish frontier towns since 1379.

Old Town

Plaza de la Asunción From Alameda Cristina via C. Tomería go to Plaza de la Asunción with the Plateresque Cabildo Municipal, the former town hall, built by Andrés de Ribera in 1575. The Torre de la Vela, which once served as a signal tower, and the church San Dionisio, built in the Mudéjar style in 1430, also stand on the square. The church has a noteworthy 20m/65ft-high Baroque retable.

San Miguel Begun in 1482, conspicuous for its blue-tiled tower and its three-storey 17th-century west façade, the church San Miguel is reached by going southeast across the Plaza del Arenal; its high altar carries a retable with reliefs by Martínez Montañés and José de Arce (1625) – amongst the paintings of the Zurbarán school a *Divine Countenance* is the outstanding work.

✱ Alcázar A little to the west of San Miguel, an elevated plateau directly at the Bodegas Gonzáles Byass is the site of the alcázar, an impressive Almohad building that has undergone renovations in the recent years. Enter via Puerta de la Ciudad, to discover behind its walls a well-pre-

Jerez de la Frontera *Plan*

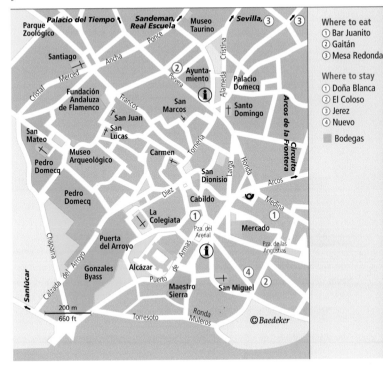

Parque Zoológico
Palacio del Tiempo
Sandeman, Real Escuela
Museo Taurino
Sevilla, ③ ③
Ponce
Santiago
Ancha
Merced
Cristal
Fundación Andaluza de Flamenco
Francos
San Juan
San Mateo
San Lucas
Museo Arqueológico
Pedro Domecq
Pedro Domecq
Chaparra
Calzada del Arroyo
Gonzales Byass
Sanlúcar
Ayuntamiento ②
Porvera
Alameda
Cristina
Palacio Domecq
Santo Domingo
San Marcos
Carmen
Torneria
San Dionisio
Larga
Honda
Arcos de la Frontera
Circuito
Arcos
Diez
Cabildo
La Colegiata ①
Pza. del Arenal
Mercado ①
Pza. de las Angústias
Puerta del Arroyo
Alcázar
Armas
Puerto de
Maestro Sierra
San Miguel
Ronda Muleros
Torresoto
④
②
200 m
660 ft
© Baedeker

Where to eat
① Bar Juanito
② Gaitán
③ Mesa Redonda

Where to stay
① Doña Blanca
② El Coloso
③ Jerez
④ Nuevo

▪ Bodegas

served domed mosque with a restored mihrâb and 14th-century baths. Reconstructed in the Renaissance style, the Palacio de Villavicencio has a **camera obscura** in its tower that produces unusual views of the town.(Hours: May–Sept. daily 10am–8pm, Oct.–April until 6pm.)

From the alcázar the back of the cathedral San Salvador is visible. It was constructed in 1695 to replace a 13th-century church that in turn was built on the foundations of a mosque. The free-standing belfry, the flying buttresses protecting against earthquake damage, the dome surrounded by sculptures, and the beautiful Baroque perron in front of the main façade are remarkable. A valuable baropque crucifix by Juan de Mesa is remains in the vestry; above all, take a look at the **Zurbarán painting** *La Virgen Niña*, a rare depiction of the Virgin as a sleeping child. In September, on the square in front of the cathedral, the annual grape harvest festival begins on the Plaza Encarnación , where the grapes are still pressed in the traditional manner: barefoot.

★ **Catedral**

SHERRY AND ITS RELATIVES

You see them in every bar and eventually, overcome by curiosity, you too order a »copita«, the small glass that narrows at the top allowing the incomparable bouquet of sherry to unfold fully. But be careful not to order »sherry«, because there are many kinds, e.g., a »fino« or an »amontillado« ...

The best known of all Andalusian wines owes its international fame to the British, whose naval hero **Sir Francis Drake** took home a considerable amount of »wine from Jerez«, among other things, from a raid on Cádiz in 1587. The importers soon bought the vineyards in order to produce the sherry themselves, so that today some of the most famous bodegas like **Williams and Humbert** or **Harveys** are still in British ownership. Probably the most famous sherry baron, however, was from France: **Pedro Domecq**, who came to Jerez in 1730.

The sherry triangle

Sherry is cultivated exclusively in the province of Cádiz in a 23,000-hectare (57,000-acres) coastal region formed by the triangle of towns **Jerez de la Frontera, Sanlúcar de Barrameda** and **El Puerto de Santa Maria**. It is only here that the interplay of the chalky soil (»albarizas«) and the mild Atlantic climate fundamental for the quality of sherry works out right. The types of grape grown are **Palomino** for the best finos, and **Pedro Ximénez** and muscatel, used for sweeter wines.

The secret

What really makes a sherry special, however, is the **complicated ageing and production process**. Sherries are not vintage wines (and certainly no distillate as many still believe) but rather a product of a blend of wines of different vintages having the same character. Before being pressed, the grapes are dried in the sun for a number of days – the duration

At a sherry tasting, small amounts are drawn out of the barrel with a venencia. This utensil, a thin rod about eighty centimetres/32 inches long with a cylinder-shaped vessel at its end, allows a sample of the sherry to flow in a high arc into the glass so that the full bouquet of the wine can unfold.

depends on the type of sherry that is desired. The young wine is fortified with brandy to an alcohol content of between 15% and 18% and filled into oak casks or butts, but only filled to a maximum of four-fifths. This allows for a covering of yeast fungus called »flor« to develop on top of the wine, protecting it from oxidation. After the first fermentation, the wine is allotted, according to its type, to separate »soleras«. These are usually five rows of casks with wine of the same character lying on top of each other. The oldest wine is in the lowest row, the youngest on top. Only the wine in the bottom row is bottled. The amount taken is replaced by wine from the next row, and that row is in turn refilled from the row above it and so on. In this way, a wine of consistent character and quality is produced over several years.

Tasting!

No trip to Andalusia is complete without a tasting in a bodega (in this case a sherry bar and not a sherry producer's storehouse)! Finos and amontillados are served ice cold. Only the sweeter wines are drunk at

room temperature. Most people who have tried sherry soon realize that a small glass of fino can be enjoyed on any occasion and not only as an aperitif, especially when there is a small tapa to go with it.

Types of sherry ...

Fino is a light yellow, very dry, slightly acidic and lively wine with an alcohol content of 15% to 17%. It is the most

typical of all sherries and is drunk the most. **Amontillado**, the name given to wine from Montilla, is aged a bit longer than fino, amber coloured, softer, but still has the characteristic bouquet and an alcohol content of 16-18%. An **Oloroso** has a dark golden colour. It is still dry to lightly sweet and gives off a decidedly nutty aroma with an alcohol content of 18% to 20%. **Raya**, of a slightly lesser quality, and the seldom obtainable **Palo Cortado**, are varieties of this. Finally, **cream sherries** are the sweetest and heaviest of sherries, produced from a blend of oloroso and a sweet wine (often muscatel). They have an alcohol content of around 20%.

... and where they come from

Everything worth knowing about sherry can be found out on the internet on the website www.sherry.org. But that is no substitute for the real thing – a tour of the bodega of a sherry producer is a must when visiting Jerez de la Frontera. As a matter of rule they can be visited in the morning as part of a tour (with wine tasting). Do register in advance. Bodegas are not cellars but partially huge halls in which one solera row is stacked on the other (addresses p. 304).

Little brothers

Two other wine-growing regions produce wines very similar to sherry. In the direct vicinity of Sanlúcar de Barrameda grapes are grown for **manzanilla**, a very light, bone-dry fino, which many prefer to the fino from Jerez. Its slightly salty flavour comes from the sea winds blowing through the bodegas; moreover, it is not fortified.

In the 18,500ha/46,000-acre wine-growing region of Montilla-Moriles in the sweltering south of the province of Córdoba – and this is the first great difference to sherry – the grapes grown are primarily the Pedro Ximénez variety. The second difference is in the storage during the maturing

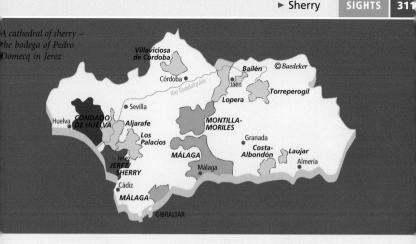

A cathedral of sherry – the bodega of Pedro Domecq in Jerez

process; it is blended according to the solera process not in oak casks but in large earthenware jugs, the »tijanas«. Montilla-Moriles produces the same varieties as Jerez and in addition Pedro Ximénez, which is produced this grape alone; it is very dark and has an alcohol content of 28%.

Cousins

Málaga, a classic dessert wine, comes from the Costa del Sol. The grapes – muscatel and Pedro Ximénez – are grown around Estepona and to the east and north of Málaga on an area of 2,500ha/6,000 acres, but have to be brought to Málaga for processing. This wine is also produced using the solera system, but concentrated grape juice is added to make it sweeter.

The best known Málaga is **Dulce Color**; of a dark amber-like colour, it has an alcohol content of 15% to 23%. The fruity muscatel is also dark with 15% to 20% alcohol.

The light reddish **Pedro Ximénez** is produced only from the grape variety of the same name (16% to 20%).

The lightest in colour and most rare Málaga is **blanco secco**; dry and usually with less alcohol than the rest.

The golden-coloured **Lágrima** is very expensive. Its grapes are not pressed; the must is squeezed out by the pressure of the grapes' own weight.

Finally, 16,000ha/40,000 acres of vineyards are cultivated around Huelva. The same type is produced in the D.O. region of Condado de Huelva as in the sherry regions, though without achieving the same quality. For this reason the area has moved more into the production of house wines, and produces quite good, fresh white wines.

Spirits

Last but not least the sherry triangle also produces spirits. Although the distillates for the **brandies** produced here mostly come from Mancha in central Spain, only what has been aged in Jerez, Sanlúcar or El Puerto de Santa Maria – also using the solera system – may be called »Brandy de Jerez«.

The difference can be tasted and it also has its price – top brandies like **Gran Duque de Alba Oro** from Williams & Humbert or **Hidalgo 200 Solera Gran Reserva** cannot be had for under €50 per bottle.

The stallion of stallions – majestic Andalusians in the Real Escuela Andaluza del Arte Escuestre

Northern and Western Quarters

San Mateo It is not far from the cathedral – cutting along the Bodegas Domecq – to the northwestern neighbourhood and the church San Mateo, which was begun in the 14th century and has a Mudéjar-style chapel.

Museo Arqueológico Near the church the archaeological museum displays as its greatest treasure a Greek helmet from the 7th century BC, evidence of early colonization of the region by the Greeks. Furthermore, Iberian, Roman, Visigothic and Moorish findings are exhibited. The cafeteria on the top floor is a nice place to take a break (opening hours: Tue–Fri 10am–2pm and 4–7pm, Sat and Sun 10am–2.30pm).

Centro Andaluz de Flamenco Past the church San Lucas (14th century) is the Palacio Pemartín on Plaza de San Juan. The 18th-century palace houses the Centro Andaluz de Flamenco. Here, exhibitions, films, performances, and the library teach all you need to know about flamenco; even **dancing and guitar courses** are offered (opening hours: Mon–Fri 9am–2pm). The San Juan de los Caballeros church (15th century) opposite catches the eye with its nine-part apse.

Embedded in a botanical garden, the recipient of several awards, the zoological garden of Jerez is the largest in Andalusia, and one of Spain's finest. A chimpanzee house and a white tiger are the attractions (opening hours: summer Tue–Sun 10am–8pm, winter to 6pm).

Parque Zoológico

The former clock museum La Atalaya was completely re-designed, and now operates as Palacio del Tiempo. However, it continues to show over 300 antique clocks from all over Europe, some of which are extremely valuable. The Misterio de Jerez, an audiovisual show about the wine that made the city so famous, has been added (opening hours: mid June–mid Sept. Mon–Sat 10am–2pm, 6–8pm, mid Sept.–mid June Mon–Sat 10am–7pm, Sun all year 10am–2pm).

Palacio del Tiempo

To the north of the city, the rambling premises of the **Royal School of Andalusian Equestrian Art** stretch along the Avda. Duque de Abrantes. Charles Garnier, architect of the Paris opera house, built the administrative building in the 19th century. 60 of the noblest Andalusian horses are kept in the adjacent stables, and have been used to refine both English thoroughbreds and Lipizzaners. They are bred at the national stud farm nearby. Visitors can tour the stables and the showroom, and can watch the training. The show Cómo bailan los Caballos Andaluces (»how Andalusian horses dance«) in the great hall is the highlight (visits: Nov–Feb Mon, Wed, Fri / March–Oct. Mon, Wed, Fri (cannot be toured on Fridays in August) 11am–1pm; Show: Tue, Thu, in August also Fri noon).

Real Escuela Andaluza del Arte Ecuestre

Around Jerez de la Frontera

A few miles southeast ►Medina Sidonia lies the former Carthusian monastery La Cartuja, founded in 1463, where the cross-breeding of German, Italian, and Andalusian horses resulted in **the Carthusian thoroughbreds race**. The building has a superb free-standing Renaissance gate (1571) and a Gothic church, to which an opulent façade was added in 1667. Sculptures of Carthusian monks stand in its niches, St Bruno uppermost. The famous depictions of Carthusians painted by Zurbarán for the church altar are now in the possession of the department of art of the museum of ►Cádiz.

La Cartuja

Another tip for fans of Carthusian horses: on the Finca Fuente del Suero, also towards Medina Sidonia, located 6.5km/4mi outside of Jerez, **the stud Yeguada de la Cartuja Hierro del Bocado** has specialized in breeding the famous steeds, which can be admired on a guided tour every Saturday around 11am.

Finca Fuente del Suero

Lebrija Lebrija, Roman Nebrissa, 30km/19mi north of Jerez de la Frontera, is the birthplace of Juan Díaz de Solís, the **discoverer of the Río de la Plata** in today's Argentina. The elevated Santa María de la Oliva, founded in a mosque in 1249, and altered several times since, has a prominent place among the churches of the town. Its belfry is reminiscent of the Giralda of Seville; within is a high altar by Alonso Cano, with a sculpture of the saint after which it is named. Further places worth seeing are the hermitage Nuestra Señora del Castillo, founded on the site of a Moorish fort in 1535, and provided with a beautiful coffer ceiling, as well as the Plaza Mayor, surrounded by houses of the nobility. There is a memorial to the **humanist Antonio de Nebrija** (1442–1522) who was born here. He was the author of the first Castilian-Spanish grammar and chronicler to the Catholic Monarchs.

Linares

H 5

Province: Jaén
Population: 58,400

Altitude: 418m/1371ft

The industrial and mining town of Linares lies in the north of Jaén province at the edge of the Sierra Morena and in the middle of a region of copper and lead ore that has been worked since ancient times. Besides mining, Linares lives from the motor industry – the Japanese manufacturer Suzuki produces here.

Linares originated as a suburb of ancient Iberian Cástulo, which was excavated 6km/3.5mi to the northeast. **Imilce, Hannibal's wife**, is said to have come from there.

However, the town gained notoriety throughout Spain due to an incident in 1947: one of the country's most famous toreros, **Manolete**, lost his life during a corrida in the arena of Linares. His nemesis was the bull *Islero*.

▶ LINARES

INFORMATION (OFICINA DE TURISMO)

Plaza de España, s/n,
37760 Linares de Riofrío
Tel. 923 41 60 66
www.ayuntamientodelinares.org

What to See in and around Linares

Although less grand than in the neighbouring Renaissance towns ▶ Baeza and ▶Úbeda, some remarkable palaces from this era have survived in Linares: the Casa Consistorial, the Palacio de los Zambrana, and the Casa de las Cadenas, the mint of Philip VI in the 17th century. The main church dates back to the 12th century and exhibits a fine 16th-century retable; the tower of the former castle leans against the church.

At the Palacio Dávalos-Biedma the archaeological museum features early, Phoenician, Greek, Iberian, Roman and Moorish pieces, including findings from Cástulo. The world-famous guitarist **Andrés Segovia** (1893–1987) was born in Linares; his birthplace is at once museum and tomb (opening hours: mid June–mid Sept Tue–Sun 10am–2pm, mid Sept–mid Jun Tue–Fri 10am–2pm, 4–7pm, Sat and Sun mornings only).

Situated 13km/8mi to the west, **Bailén** offers no sights, yet is of great historical significance. This is where Publius Cornelius Scipio the Elder defeated the Carthaginian Hasdrubal in 208 BC; about 2000 years later, on 22 July 1808, Spanish troops under General

Manolete's last appearance in Linares

Castaños vanquished the French under Dupont, thus inflicting the first defeat upon the Napoleonic armies – a victory of great symbolic value for all of Europe. Castaños is interred at the church La Encarnación.

The N-IV leads from Bailén through never-ending olive plantations to the north into the Sierra Morena. Soon a cul-de-sac turns left to **Baños de la Encina** at the edge of the Sierra de Andújar. Above its

Along the N-IV

picturesque lanes rises the Moorish castle Burgalimar, constructed with its 14 towers and the mighty keep Torre de Homenaje in the 10th century.

Further north along the N-IV lies **La Carolina**, main location of the mining settlements set up by **German and French colonists** whom Charles III brought to the Sierra Morena between 1767 and 1769.

Baedeker TIP

Classical guitar

Naturally classical Spanish guitar music is played in the home town of Andrés Segovia. Information on concerts in the Fundación Andrés Segovia is obtainable under tel. 953 65 13 90 or www.segoviamuseo.org.

The once rich lead mines of the surrounding area have been abandoned; the town itself has some grand houses, the classical church La Concepción, and a Carmelite monastery founded by Juan de la Cruz.

Navas de Tolosa   In the immediate vicinity, 2.5km/1.5mi to the right of the N-IV, lies Navas de Tolosa, likewise a former colonists' village, at which the united armies of the kings of Castile, Aragón and Navarre utterly defeated the Almohads on 16 July 1212, thereby giving the **signal for the final Reconquista**. The N-IV finally winds its way across the »ravine of the falling dogs«, the historic crossing from Andalusia into Mancha; today, the wild countryside is a protected region.

Desfiladero de
Despeñaperros ►

★ Málaga

G 8

Province: Málaga   **Altitude:** 8m/26ft
Population: 528,000

Situated at the foot of Montes de Málaga, Málaga, the second-largest city in Andalusia and economical and cultural centre of the ► Costa del Sol, enjoys sunshine on 300 days of the year.

Hub of the Costa   Most travellers visiting Andalusia see the city at best from a bird's
del Sol   eye view when landing and taking off, for it is the traffic hub of the sunshine coast, from which they are then transferred to the beach re-

View from the mountainside of the city and the Bahia of Málaga

▶ VISITING MÁLAGA

INFORMATION (OFICINA DE TURISMO)

Pasajes chinitas, 4,
E-29015 Málaga
Tel. 952 21 34 45
Fax 952 22 94 21

Alameda Principal, 23
E-29012 Málaga
Tel. 95 21 60 61
Fax 95 22 79 07
www.malagaturismo.com
Additional information offices are at the bus station, train station, and main post office.

WHERE TO EAT

▶ Expensive

② *Antonio Martín*
Paseo Marítimo, 4
Tel. 952 22 21 13
(closed Sun and in July)
In summer there are rows of fish restaurants by the seaside in Pedregalejo suburb – Antonio Martín has top quality.

Tapas, wine and a happy mood in Gorki

③ *Café de París*
Vélez Málaga, 8
Tel. 952 22 50 43
Gourmet restaurant – the young celebrity chef José Carlos García Cortés cooks here.

▶ Inexpensive

① *Antigua Casa de Guardia*
Alameda Principal, 18
Traditional bodega in the government building; best address for Málaga wines and seafood tapas.

④ *El Chinitas*
Moreno Monroy, 4–6
Tapas bar with tradition; select your fish from the pool and have it deep-fried.

⑤ *Gorki*
C. Strachan, 6
Somewhat trendier with excellent tapas and wines.

⑥ *La Cancela*
Denis Belgrano, 3
Tel. 952 22 31 25
Low-priced, tasty, simple fare in the old town.

El Tintero
Playa del Palo II
Tel. 670 60 75 86
In this large beach restaurant in front of Club Náutico in the east of Málaga, guests eat deep-fried seafood that is carried past and presented loudly by the waiter; the bill is calculated by the

marks chalked on the wooden tables. No bookings: just occupy your tables in time.

WHERE TO STAY

► Mid-range

③ *Larios*
Marqués de Larios, 2
Tel. 952 22 22 00, fax 952 22 24 07
www.hotel-larios.com
The highest floor of the upscale hotel offers a view of the cathedral towers; have a cocktail on the roof terrace before sundown.

④ *Parador de Málaga Gibralfaro*
Castillo de Gibralfaro
Tel. 952 22 19 02
Fax 952 22 19 04
www.parador.es, 38 rooms
The renovated parador on the castle hill commands unrivalled views.

⑤ *Parador de Málaga Golf*
Apartado de Correos 324
Tel. 952 38 12 55
Fax 952 38 89 63
E-mail: malaga@parador.es
www.parador.es, 56 rooms
Málaga's second parador– in the regional style, right above the beach – is ideal for golfers as it has its own superb golf course beneath palms.

► Budget

① *California*
Paseo de Sancha, 17
Tel. / Fax 952 21 51 64
Town house with terraces and balconies, not far from the La Malagueta beach.

② *Hostal Pedregalejo*
Conde de las Naves, 9
Tel. 952 29 32 18
Fax 952 29 75 25, 10 rooms
Lovely guesthouse in Pedregalejo suburb, known for its fish restaurants.

SHOPPING

Magnificent fresh foods from sea and land, as well as fashion items, are available on the morning market in C. Marqués de Larios. Naturally the 19th-century market hall presents treasures from the Hoya and from the sea, wine too.
Further shopping areas include the streets around Plaza Flores, Plaza de Félix Sáenz, C. Puerta del Mar, and C. Nueva. The gigantic department store of the El Corte Inglés chain is on the Avenida de Andalucía.

PLAZA DE TOROS

Paseo Reding
Tel. 952 22 17 27
The most important fights are in August.

EVENTS

Carnival
Carnival is celebrated wildly in Málaga.

Semana Santa
Holy Week is truly remarkable in Málaga, for here the largest and heaviest processional altars of all of Spain are carried through the streets – the biggest weighs five tons and has to be shouldered by 260 men! As if that weren't enough, these tronos also get swayed back and forth. Unfortunately the Museo de la Semana Santa has closed indefinitely for remodelling.

Feria
In the first half of August the largest feria of Andalusia takes place with fireworks, music, and dancing; at night celebrations continue on the festival grounds Cortijo de Torres, 4km/2.5mi southwest of the city centre.

Málaga *Plan*

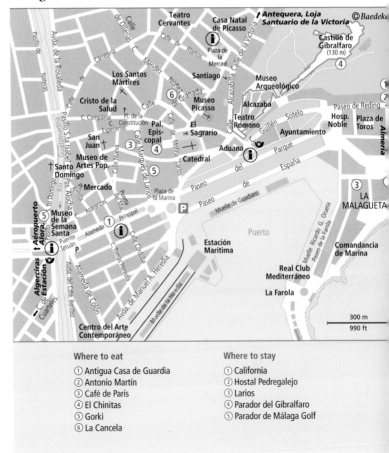

Where to eat
① Antigua Casa de Guardia
② Antonío Martín
③ Café de París
④ El Chinitas
⑤ Gorki
⑥ La Cancela

Where to stay
① California
② Hostal Pedregalejo
③ Larios
④ Parador del Gibralfaro
⑤ Parador de Málaga Golf

sorts. Just about seven million tourists arrive at the airport every year, which can cater for eleven million passengers. And yet Málaga certainly has its charms, even if it cannot compare to the classic destinations ►Córdoba, ►Granada and ►Seville. Its parks and its location on the mountainside sloping down to the Bahía de Málaga, in particular, make a day trip worthwhile and compensate for the faceless suburbs. The west of Málaga is the lush Vega or Hoya de Málaga, where oranges, figs, bananas, sugar cane and cotton thrive. The city is especially famous for its raisins (pasas) and its dessert wines, of which Pedro Ximénez and the moscatel wines Dulce and Lágrimas are particularly well known.

Pedro de Mena (1628–1688), the famous sculptor, lived and died in Málaga; another famous son of the city is the Jewish philosopher and poet Ibn Gabriol (11th century). Nowadays, however, the star of **Pablo Picasso** shines brightest, even though he left the city of his birth when he was 15 (►Famous People). The usually dry bed of the Río Guadalmedina divides Málaga into two large sections: the new town in the west, with rows of high-rises and criss-crossed with wide, busy roads; in the east below the alcazaba is the old town with the cathedral at its centre.

History
Málaga was founded by the Phoenicians, who had a trading centre for salted fish here, which probably explains the city's name: the Phoenician Malaka is derived from »malac«, meaning »to salt«. The Greeks followed the Phoenicians with their colony Mainake in the 8th century BC. The Carthaginians fortified the city, until the Romans conquered it and incorporated it into their empire under the name Malacitanum. After a Byzantine intermezzo came the Visigoths, who were supplanted by the Moors in 711. For a considerable time the city was a small kingdom that did not submit to the emirs of Córdoba. Málaga was at its zenith as the port of the kingdom under the rule of the Nasrids of Granada. In 1487 the troops of the Catholic Monarchs reconquered Málaga. This period saw the construction of many churches, of which over 40 were set alight and destroyed following the proclamation of the republic in May 1931; the city also suffered heavily during the civil war. Málaga`s comeback started with the emergence of tourism on the Costa del Sol.

! **Baedeker TIP**

El Pimpi and Café Central
There is only one place for the true Malageño to have his afternoon coffee or a small glass of wine: El Pimpi on Calle Granada, covering two floors. Mind you, this bar only opens at 5pm; if you want to visit a classic café before then, try Café Central at the Plaza de la Constitución.

Harbour District

★
Paseo del
Parque

There are two particularly striking monuments on Paseo del Parque, Málaga's most beautiful square, adorned with exotic plants and bordered by avenues of palms and plane trees. They portray typical people of Málaga who have now vanished from the streets: the biznaguero, who sold fragrant flowers in spring, and the cenachero, who offered fresh fish. The Fuente de Cisne fountain, created in Genoa in 1560 and originally intended for the Alhambra in Granada, is situated opposite the town hall (1912–1919).

Aduana ►
The classical Aduana, the former customs office to the north side of the paseo, was reconstructed in order to accommodate the collections of the Museo de Belles Artes. For the time being, a selection from the museum is exhibited here including works by Alonso Cano

(*John the Evangelist*), Ribera (*St Francis of Assisi*), Murillo (*St Francis of Paola*), Luis de Morales (*Ecce Homo, Mater Dolorosa*), and Zurbarán (*St Jerome*).

At Plaza de la Marina the paseo merges with Alameda Principal. From there it is not far to the market hall via C. Atarazanas. Apart from the delicacies on sale, the marble gate, Puerta de Atarazanas, is also worth seeing. It is shaped as a 14m/45ft-high Moorish horseshoe arch with Kufic characters and is all that remains of the gigantic shipyard of Málaga built under Abd ar-Rahman III.

Mercado

Old Town

The massive limestone cathedral, one of the most important churches of the Renaissance in Andalusia next to those in ▶Cádiz, ▶Jaén and ▶Granada, was begun in 1528 on the site of a mosque according to plans by Pedro López and Diego de Siloé, and consecrated in 1588. Famous masters such as Enrique de Egas, Andrés de Vandelvira and Diego de Vergara had a part in the construction, which was discontinued in 1783 due to lack of funds. Two towers were to flank the main façade containing three portals, yet only the 86m/282ft-high north tower has been completed. Of the south tower, only stumps of pillars jut above the façade, which is why the cathedral is also called La Manquita – »the one that's missing something«. The 115m/377ft-long and 52m/170ft-high **church interior** is remarkable for its splendid proportions and mighty Corinthian clustered columns. The most prominent piece of church furnishings are the stalls (1647–1660) in the choir (1592–1631) with 103 carved statues, 40 of

Catedral La Manquita

◀ Choir stalls

Catedral de Málaga *Plan*

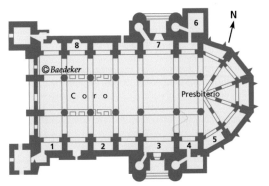

1 Capilla Nueva
2 Capilla del Rosario
3 Puerta del Sol
4 Capilla de N. Sra. de los Reyes
5 Capilla de San Francisco
6 Sacristía
7 Puerta de las Cadenas
8 Capilla del Cristo de la Buena Muerte

© Baedeker

Coro   Presbiterio

which were done by Pedro de Mena, who from 1658 continued the work of Luis Ortíz and José Micael, the originators of two and ten statues of the apostles respectively. The modern altar in the Capilla Mayor bears scenes of the Passion from 1580. Of the side and ambulatory chapels the most interesting are the following: The first chapel in the right aisle is the Capilla Nueva with the *Madre Dolorosa de Camponuevo* by Pedro de Mena. The Capilla del Rosario contains a *Madonna of the Rosary* by Alonso Cano. The Puerta del Sol follows with paintings by Palma Vecchio; next is the Capilla de Nuestra Señora de los Reyes, containing the most significant works of art in the cathedral: the kneeling statues of the Catholic Monarchs by Pedro de Mena (1681), as well as the statuette of the Virgin which the couple are said to have carried with them on their crusades. In the left aisle the Capilla del Cristo de la Buena Muerte with sculptures by Pedro de Mena merits attention. The cathedral museum exhibits religious objets d'art in the chapter house.

Opposite the cathedral the 18th-century **Palacio Episcopal** (bishop's palace) now serves as an exhibition hall (opening hours: Tue–Sun 10am–2pm, 6–9pm).

One of the most important Renaissance churches in Andalucia

Sagrario This small chapel on the north side of the cathedral catches the eye with its very beautiful Isabelline portal. It was the episcopal church until the consecration of the cathedral.

✳
Museo Picasso
North of the cathedral a new **attraction for all Picasso enthusiasts** opened in autumn 2003: the Picasso Museum in the Renaissance palace Palacio de los Condes de Buenavista at C. San Agustín no. 8 (www.mpicassom.org). An endowment of 138 of Picasso's works by his daughter-in-law is the basis of the collection. Great works are lacking, as is a conceptual thread. Oil paintings, drawings, sculptures,

and ceramics from all the artist's creative periods are exhibited, insofar as they are represented in the family collection. However, the museum affords an intimate look into **Picasso's personal and family environment** (opening hours: Tue–Sun 10am–9pm, Fri, Sat to 9pm).

Further north on Plaza de la Merced lies the next Picasso site, house no. 15, where Pablo Picasso was born. Both the study centre of the Fundación Picasso and – in the family's erstwhile residence – a museum displaying ceramics and graphics by the artist, are held here (opening hours: Mon–Sat 10am–8pm, Sun 11am–2pm).

Museo Casa Natal de Picasso

> **! Baedeker TIP**
>
> **El Hammam**
> Luxurious Turkish baths in the former Jewish quarter of Málaga, not far from the Museo Picasso. Massages are offered (reservations recommended, tel. 952 21 23 27, www.elhammam.com).

On the spot where the Catholic Monarchs made camp in 1487 the **Nuestra Señora de la Victoria** church was erected. Inside within a camarin it holds the Virgen de la Victoria (15th century), a statue of the city's patron saint, a gift to the Catholic Monarchs from Emperor Maximilian I. Two sculptures by Pedro de Mena and the crypt of the counts of Buenavista merit attention.

The Museo de Arte y Tradiciones Populares is located in the 17th-century inn Mesón de Victoria, right in the west of the old town on the Río Guadalmedina. Amongst other things, coaches, wine presses, a bakery, furniture, and a collection of small figurines in 18th- and 19th-century garb can be seen here in a higgledy-piggledy arrangement (opening hours: mid June–Sept Tue–Fri 10am–1.30pm, 5–8pm; Oct–mid June Tue–Fri 10am–1.30pm, 4–7pm; Aug only 9.30am–2pm; Sat always mornings only).

Museo de Arte y Tradiciones Populares

✳ Alcazaba

Sightseers climb to the alcazaba, the castle of the Moorish rulers enthroned above the harbour and the old town, from the C. Alcazabilla, which proceeds below the western flank, via a steep stair passing through gardens. This route passes the remains of a Roman theatre situated on the slope, built in the time of Emperor Augustus and discovered in 1951.

Construction of the fortress began on Roman remains in the 11th century, with considerable enlargement to a size approaching that of the Alhambra of Granada under the Nasrids in the 14th century. After the downfall of the Moors the castle fell into disrepair, with earnest reconstruction only being undertaken from 1931 on, so that it is now possible once more to get an impression of its former glory. However, it is the **wonderful gardens** in the courtyards that consti-

Opening hours:
Summer
daily except Mo
9.30am–8pm,
Winter
8.30am–7pm

In the garden of the Alcazaba

tute the alcazaba's charm. Two curtain walls circle the castle hill. The inner fortress is entered by the Arco de Cristo, opening onto the weapons court. To the right and behind another gate lies the Cuartos de Granada, which was modelled on a simplified form of the architecture of the Alhambra during reconstruction. Beyond that lie the reconstructed palace rooms of the Nasrids and the residences of the royal household, with patios, baths, and cisterns. At the highest point rises the massive Torre del Homenaje. The Moorish collections of the Museo Arqueológico are to be presented in the castle once again in future.

Castillo de Gibralfaro

🕐 Opening hours: Summer daily 9am–8pm, winter to 5.50pm

✳ View ▶

From the alcazaba there is a view across to Gibralfaro (from the Arabic Yabal-Faruk meaning »lighthouse hill«). The Phoenicians probably already built a lighthouse on this spot. In the 14th century Jûsuf I of Granada constructed a fortress with six towers, connecting it to the alcazaba via a covered wall walkway, but this is no longer walkable. Other than the curtain wall little is preserved; an exhibition in the restored powder magazine outlines the castle history since 1487. It is reached either on foot (a lengthy trek via Camino Nuevo northeast of the Plaza de la Merced), by car, or by bus no. 35 from Paseo del Parque. A magnificent view of the city, harbour, and sea, as well as a break at the parador are the reward.

Around Málaga

Sports and leisure

Málaga has a large yacht harbour; the beaches Baños del Carmen, El Palo, Acacias, Pedregalejo, El Chanquete, and San Andrés lie with the city limits. Golf (several courses), tennis, riding and aqua parks provide a wealth of recreational opportunities.

✳ **Jardín Botánico La Concepción**

🕐

Take the motorway towards Granada, then the exit to Finca de la Concepción to a lovely botanical garden about 10km/6mi north of Málaga that was **established by the Englishwoman Amalia Loring** in the 19th century and has belonged to the city of Málaga since 1990. A fabulous variety of exotic plants, more than 3,000 different species, can be discovered on five different nature trails (opening hours: daily except Mon from 10am, closing times vary according to season; English speaking guides available).

Going east through sugar-cane plantations the coast road reaches Rincón de la Victoria after 10km/6mi, a beach resort popular among the inhabitants of Málaga. Above it is a **large cave** containing Neolithic paintings which was a hideaway for Christians and Moors. The name Cueva del Tesoro stems from the popular belief that the Moorish monarchs buried treasure here.

Rincón de la Victoria

Just 14km/8.5mi north of Málaga lies a national park 4762 ha/11,767 acres in size; take the N-331 towards Casabermeja to get there. It has Mediterranean vegetation and nesting places for birds of prey.

Montes de Málaga

✶ Marbella

F 8

Province: Málaga
Population: 98,300

Altitude: 14m/46ft

Marbella remains the glamorous centre of the ►Costa del Sol, surpassing all places on this coast in terms of the number of restaurants, shops and hotels of the upscale and highest category. An active party and social life has placed Marbella in all the world's glossy magazines.

The galas of celebrities are as renowned as ever – only the average age has increased somewhat – yet in addition Marbella has also been transformed into a cultured, albeit still expensive holiday resort, and is a fairly welcome change from places such as ►Fuengirola and ►Torremolinos. To be sure, the promenades here are also lined with new buildings with all kinds of bars, restaurants, and boutiques, and the main road through the town is used by some sports car drivers as a place for showing off, yet beyond that it is pleasant to stroll through the lovely old town. Huge hotel complexes hardly disturb the view, for above all Marbella is a place of villa owners – correspondingly, the surroundings consist of a fairly attractive array of bungalow estates.

Glamorous centre of the Costa del Sol

Marbella prides itself in its exclusive restaurants, night clubs, discos such as Oh! Marbella, bars, boutiques, the casino in Puerto Banús, and other places of public entertainment, the prices of which correspond directly to the number of luxury cars parked outside. Yet the place also holds all manner of diversions for the less well-off: long beaches with a variety of water sports; in addition to eleven golf courses, a large number of tennis courts, stables, three yacht harbours, and sailing clubs. The Playa de Fontanilla and Playa Nagüeles are considered the best beaches with regards to quality and services, and are accordingly well frequented.

Sports and leisure

▶ VISITING MARBELLA

INFORMATION (OFICINA DE TURISMO)

Plaza de los Naranjos, s/n,
E-29600 Marbella
Tel. 952 82 35 50
www.marbella2000.com

Glorieta de la Fontanilla, s/n
Paseo Marítimo
Tel. 952 77 14 42

WHERE TO EAT

▶ Expensive

La Hacienda
Hacienda las Chapas, N-340, km 193,
Las Chapas turnoff
Tel. 952 83 12 67
Much praised for its modern Andalusian cuisine; very nice terrace.

▶ Moderate

La Meridiana
Camino de la Cruz, s/n, 3.5km/2mi
direction Puerto Banús
Tel. 952 77 61 90
With its Mediterranean cuisine La
Meridiana numbers among the best
restaurants in Spain. Next door is the
classy nightclub La Notte.

Cuarto Hondo
In Benahavis, Plaza del Castillo, 1
Tel. 952 85 54 30
Fish and meat in the Moorish castle.

Refugio de Juanar
Near Ojén, Sierra Blanca, s/n
Tel. 952 88 10 00
Situated in the middle of hunting
grounds, 10km/6mi outside Ojén.
Pheasant with rosemary is highly
recommended.

▶ Inexpensive

① *Altamirano*
Plaza Altamirano

Tel. 952 82 49 32
Very good fish dishes and tapas in the
old town.

② *Bodega La Venecia*
Avda. de Miguel Cano, 15
Tapas and lots of young people.

③ *Restaurante Santiago*
Paseo Marítimo, 5
Tel. 952 77 00 78
The seafood here is among the best on
Paseo Marítimo.

WHERE TO STAY

▶ Luxury

③ *Marbella Club Hotel*
Blvd. Príncipe Alfonso de Hohenlohe
Tel. 952 82 22 11
Fax 952 82 98 84
www.es.marbellaclub.com, 132 rooms
Small luxury bungalows for lots of
money, spa and golf too.

▶ Mid-range

② *El Fuerte*
Avda. del Fuerte
Tel. 952 86 15 00
Fax 952 82 44 11, 263 rooms
This high-class house by the sea – and
yet close to the old town centre –
offers nice rooms, a spa and sports.

▶ Budget

① *El Castillo*
Plaza de San Bernabé
Tel. 952 77 17 39, 27 rooms
This very well-priced hotel occupies
an old building in the town centre.
Not far from the Plaza de los
Naranjos.

EVENT

Feria de San Bernabé
Around 7 June: the town's major
festival.

Marbella is the South European hot spot of the jet set – they never indulge themselves otherwise.

The Phoenicians founded a settlement on the coast here called Sal-
duba (salt town). In 1485, after the Catholic Monarchs had driven
out the Moors, Queen Isabella, upon seeing the coast, is said to have
cried out: »¡Qué mar bella!« – »What a beautiful sea!« – and the
name of the city was born. Marbella's entry into the world of tourism occurred in 1953, when **Prince Alfonso of Hohenlohe** founded
the Marbella Club, centre of high society even today. This is where
members of European nobility, industrialists, playboys, and all who
wanted to be part of it met, and they turned the small fishing village
into a place of incessant parties and luxury. Yet only at the beginning
of the 1970s did the truly rich come: **Arab potentates**, the King of
Saudi Arabia among them, selected Marbella for their summer re-
treats and had palaces built in which admittedly they led an existence
relatively secluded from the rest of the hustle and bustle, yet spent a
lot of money in Marbella's shops. Then **mass tourism** discovered
Marbella, until in the mid 1980s a grave crisis loomed as many in-
vestors withdrew. When the sheikhs also stayed away during the Gulf
War in 1991, the **scandalous figure of Jesús Gil y Gil**, an extremely
rich contractor and president of the Atlético de Madrid football club,
appointed himself saviour by gaining election as mayor – avowedly
because his socialist predecessor did not approve his real estate spec-
ulation. Gil y Gil now permitted this to both his friends and himself,
governed Marbella like a feudal lord, and brought in new money,
not caring whether it came from Russian Mafiosi or shady arms dealers. The Arabians also returned. In 2002 however, **Spain's supreme**

court deposed Gil from office, because he was indicted for embezzling funds from the city treasury. Shady doings at Atlético earned him 3½ years in prison at the beginning of 2003; he resigned as the club's president. After his death in 2004, a woman from his political party became mayor and continued Gil's methods until the swamp of corruption was so big – the damages were estimated at more then 2 billion Euros – that the Spanish government dissolved the city council in April 2006. But the credit for transforming Marbella into a top-class holiday resort has to go to Gil.

What to See in Marbella

City centre

Compared with the rest of Marbella the town centre is somewhat calmer with its white houses adorned with flowers, and the remains of the medieval wall. People meet at the Plaza de los Naranjos lined with orange trees, bars, and restaurants, by the fountain that has been flowing since 1704; the town hall is here, too, its upper storey painted with 16th-century frescoes. The **Museo del Grabado** explains the **art of engraving**, and displays pertinent works by Picasso, Miró,

Marbella Plan

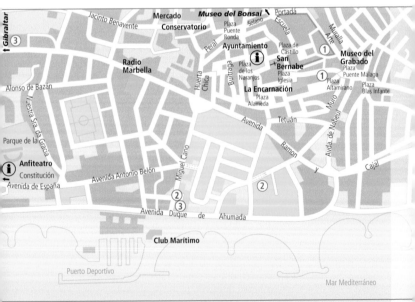

Where to eat
① Altamirano
② Bodega La Venecia
③ Restaurante Santiago

Where to stay
① El Castillo
② El Fuerte
③ Marbella Club Hotel

and Tapiés (opening hours: Tue–Sat 10am–2pm and 5.30–8.30pm); take a look at the Baroque retable in the Nuestra Señora de la Encarnación church not far from there. Above the city the remnants of a Moorish fort, including walls, bailey, and keep, still stand.

An impressive collection of bonsai plants can be admired at the Parque de Arroyo de la Represa (opening hours: daily 10am–1.30pm, 5–7.30pm).

Museo Bonsai

On the western edge of town in the direction of San Pedro and to the left above the coast road shines the mosque of Marbella, which Prince Salman, governor of the Saudi Arabian capital Riad, caused to be built as **the first Muslim place of worship in Spain since the 15th century**. Naturally stables and a helipad are included. Incidentally, King Fahd and family reside in a palace modelled on the White House.

Mezquita del Rey Abd-el Aziz

Opening hours: Daily except Fri 7pm–9pm

On the northwestern outskirts an oil mill in C. José Luis Morales y Marín was converted into an exhibition hall full of character, mainly showing **modern art** (opening hours: Tue–Sat 10am till 2pm, 5.30–8.30pm).

Cortijo de Miraflores

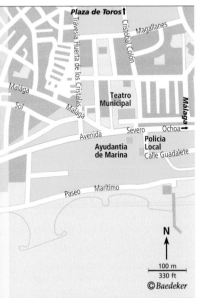

Around Marbella

Amateur sailors with a deep enough pocket can anchor at the luxury yacht marina Puerto Banús. Those without a boat may still marvel at **luxury yachts with a Rolls or Ferrari** to match, and **watch celebrities**, who like to dine at one of the luxury restaurants on the promenade before they go to party at a disco or casino.

★ **Puerto Banús**

In Marbella's backcountry, the Sierra Blanca, only a few miles distance from the hustle and bustle of high society, nature reigns serenely. There are worthwhile trips to Ojén with its 16th-century church, then on to Monda, where a lovely town centre encloses the Baroque

Sierra Blanca

ROYAL JOBS

Driving into Marbella on the N-340, just before reaching the inordinately large archway, a street sign lettered in Arabic is visible pointing to the right. Unusual? Not in Marbella because it is showing the way to the mosque of the Saudi ruler Fahd.

And so, 500 years after being driven out, the Arabs have returned to Andalusia. And they are highly welcome, spending as much money as they do. So of course there is no problem in building a separate highway exit just for the mosque. **King Fahd of Saudi Arabia** has been travelling to the Costa del Sol for many years now during the great heat of August. And because sleeping in hotel beds can be a real inconvenience, he had a palace built straight away.

Money is no object

The Saudi ruler is certainly the best-known Arab here, but other, much less illustrious guests from the Orient are coming increasingly often to Marbella. Money is no object; luxury villas are snapped up, hotel suites rented en bloc, restaurants completely taken over for private parties and boutiques are bought out completely by giggling princesses. And so money stays in Marbella. When King Fahd comes, he brings a few employees along – about a **jumbo jet** full. They all need support, so lots of seasonal jobs are to be had as gardeners or chauffeurs. That is why long queues form every morning in front of the main entrance to the royal residence. Jobs as drivers are popular because, after all, in the first week the palace rents 25 luxury cars a day (!). But a lot of personnel is also needed in the kitchen, what with €20,000-worth of food being delivered daily.

The green card

The lucky ones who manage to get a job receive a green accreditation card – in every sense of the word an entrance ticket into the world of the Orient. It is carried with pride like a medal and envied by those who were not selected, because the pay is around €90 a day, but »you hardly have to lift a finger«, as Abdil, a young Moroccan said with a grin. No wonder that the Marbellans hope each summer that the king might just extend his holidays a little bit.

Plaza de Naranjos is the heart of the old town

Iglesia de Santiago, whereas the remnants of the Moorish castle have been integrated into a hotel – which in turn provides beautiful and not-too-expensive accommodation.

San Pedro Alcántara

The commune of Marbella includes San Pedro Alcántara adjoining it to the west. It is outshone by its sophisticated neighbour, particularly as it lies about half a mile inland. The advantage is that the central Plaza de la Iglesia is reasonably quiet, and the disadvantage is that it takes a little longer to reach the sea front. Nevertheless, tourism manifests itself in a multitude of holiday apartments and bungalows. Marqués del Duero founded San Pedro as a country settlement in 1860; the sugar refinery El Trapiche de Gaudaiza dates from this time. Additionally there are three noteworthy antiquities.

A new town

A eucalyptus grove by the beach contains the preserved foundations of the early Christian basilica Vega del Mar. It was built in the 4th century, destroyed by a flood shortly after completion, and then re-built. Following a renewed collapse in 526, it served the Visigoths as a burial ground. Two baptismal fonts can be seen, one forming a cross, as well as two apses.

Basílica Vega del Mar

West of the basilica, at the mouth of the Río Guadalmina, lie the re-mains of a Roman bath from the 3rd century BC, consisting of a pool with seven rooms around it.

Roman baths

Going 4km/2.5mi back towards Marbella, remains of the Roman settlement Silniana were discovered near Río Verde: a rotunda with five arches, which served as a reservoir, and a villa with exquisite mo-saic floors depicting all kinds of **ancient kitchen utensils**.

Roman ruins

★ ★ Medina Azahara

F 6

Province: Córdoba   **Altitude:** 649m/2129ft

After Abd ar-Rahman III had consolidated his power as caliph of Córdoba, he began construction of a residence outside the city in keeping with his status. For this he chose a slope of the Sierra de Córdoba above the plain of Guadalquivir, and named it Madinat al-Zahrá (the flower), presumably in honour of his favourite.

Palace city of the caliphs of Córdoba

Even though most of the palace city is now destroyed, the remaining buildings, surrounded by cypresses, palms, holm oaks and orange trees, do give an overwhelming impression of the splendour that once was. Now called Medina Azahara, the place is best reached on the A-431 from ▶ Córdoba, where an access road turns off to the right after 8km/5mi. The entrance to the area is at the highest point of the former city; a signposted circuit leads from here to the most important excavated structures.

History

Construction began in November 936 under the direction of Abd ar-Rahman's son Al-Hakam and took almost 25 years. Over 10,000 workmen and craftsmen were engaged in building a city from limestone, bricks and most precious materials, including red, blue, and white marble, ebony, ivory and gold. At its peak, the city accommodated 30,000 people. It sprawled over an area of 1500 m by 750m (1640yd by 820yd) and except for its northern side, was surrounded by a double wall. Two gates provided admittance, the Mountain Gate in the north, and the Gate of the Three Domes (Bab al-Cubbá) in the south, which is crowned by the ancient sculpture of a woman believed by many to be an image of Zahrá. Medina Azahara was the setting for magnificent celebrations and receptions for ambassadors. Yet the glory did not even last 75 years – the internal strife that destroyed the Caliphate of Córdoba did not spare Medina Azahara, either. In 1010 the Berbers, who saw extravagance and sumptuousness as blasphemy, invaded the city and destroyed it. The Almohads and Almoravids used the debris as a quarry, and Medina Azahara sank into oblivion. Excavations only started at the beginning of the 20th century, and have not been completed to this day.

Circuit

The city was subdivided into three districts: the highest level was taken up by the palace district with the caliph's residence, the houses for the highest dignitaries, the hall of ambassadors, the military buildings and gardens. It was separated from the other parts of the city by a wall. Gardens and a menagerie were laid out in the second

The best preserved part of the Medina Azahara is the chamber of Abd ar-Rahman III.

level; dwelling houses for the servants of the royal household, shops and workshops were located on the lowest level.

The **entrance building is also a museum** that provides information on the history of Medina Azahara and exhibits finds such as ceramics, column capitals, and glass. To its right lie the inaccessible remains of the caliphs' palace proper and the house of the grand vizier. The circuit leads to the left and downhill from the entrance to the northern gate, and then continues on ramps to the Dar al-Yûnd on the right, which, with several inner courtyards, served as **military quarters**.

It then leads to the Dar al-Wuzara, the **house of the viziers**, where a spacious basilica forms its centre, in which the vizier held audience. Four massive arches are visible below and to the left of this building. They formed the gate to the **parade ground**, on which drills and parades took place. From the parade ground, there is a fine view of the **foundations of the mosque** below, which in 941 was the first building to be completed, including forecourt, a fountain for ritual ablutions, and a five-aisle prayer room. The orientation towards Mecca is clearly visible.

In the middle of the complex lies the hall of Abd ar-Rahman III, also called **hall of ambassadors**, for the caliph received the ambassadors of foreign princes here. It is the best restored and most magnificent building of the ruins. At first an antechamber opens behind a front of five horseshoe arches resting on red and blue marble columns

🕐
Opening hours:
May–mid Sept
Tue–Sat
10am–8.30pm,
Sun 10am–2pm;
mid-Sept–April
Tue–Sat
10am–6.30pm,
Sun 10am–2pm

★ ★
Hall of Abd ar-Rahman III

with ornate capitals. A three-aisle main room adjoins, likewise partitioned by horseshoe arches borne by red and blue columns. Beyond the two side aisles, partitioned off by walls, lay the bedrooms and relaxation rooms, so that the building altogether consists of five aisles. The diversity of forms of the walls carved with the most delicate stonework is stunning: floral themes such as the tree of life alternate with depictions of birds, and Kufic characters, which praise the caliph, give the names of the sculptors and the construction time of the palace (from 952 to 957).

Gardens In the days of the caliph the gardens, filled with exotic plants and irrigated by an ingenious system of channels, extended below the ramp in front of the hall of ambassadors. Exactly opposite the hall the remains of the caliph's pavilion can be seen, surrounded by four water basins. The area beyond the gardens is inaccessible.

Around Medina Azahara

San Jerónimo Only a little further up from the palace city lie the ruins of San Jerónimo monastery. It was built in 1408 and frequently hosted Isabella the Catholic, who had the banners stored here that were captured during the conquest of Granada in 1492. The grounds are private property.

Las Ermitas ►Córdoba, surrounding area

Almodóvar ►Córdoba, surrounding area

Medina Sidonia

Province: Cádiz
Population: 11,000

Altitude: 300m/984ft

Seat of the eponymous house of dukes, Medina Sidonia's white cubic houses gleam from a knoll in the middle of a region famed for breeding fighting bulls. The dukes are among to the wealthiest landowners of Andalusia – they have exchanged their political power for economic power that is no less great.

Old aristocratic estate The beginnings of Medina Sidonia go back a long way: the name refers to the Phoenician Sidon, so it is presumed that Phoenician sailors founded a settlement here.
Following the capture of Tarifa in 1292, Alfonso X, who had driven the Moors from the city in 1264, placed it in the hands of Guzmán el Bueno, whose family was elevated to the rank of duke in 1430 and became one of Spain's most powerful. Alonso de Guzmán, Duke of

Medina Sidonia, was commander of the Spanish Armada which sunk in the English Channel in 1588. He survived the fiasco, and was made Capitán General del Mar Oceanao in 1595. He would probably repudiate the current bearer of the title: she lives in ►Sanlúcar de Barrameda and is known throughout Andalusia as **la duquesa roja (the red duchess)**, for she has rendered herself conspicuous as a vehement fighter for social justice, and has once gone to prison for her convictions.

> ## ! Baedeker TIP
>
> ### Temptations
>
> The Moors brought confectionery with them to Andalusia. Medina Sidonia's confectioneries developed particular proficiency, and the city is a centre of this sweet craft even today. The alfajores made from almonds, hazelnuts, honey and cinnamon are famous – they are especially delicious at the confectionery Sobrina de las Trejas at Plaza de España no. 7. The barefoot Augustinian nuns from Convento de Jesús, María y José convent at the Plaza de las Descalzas are also skilled at baking.

What to See in Medina Sidonia

Town gates

Three medieval town gates are preserved: Arco de Belén, Arco del Sol, and, forming the gateway to the old town, Arco de la Pastora, constructed as a double horseshoe arch during the Moorish era.

Torre de Doña Blanca

Narrow alleys leading uphill reach the fortress district. The most important remnant of the castle is the Torre de Doña Blanca, where **Pedro the Cruel** imprisoned his consort Blanca de Borbón, preferring to amuse himself with María de Padilla. Another tragedy occurred in the castle: Pedro the Cruel had Leonór de Guzmán, the lover of Alfonso XI, murdered here. He himself was slain by Leonór's son Enrique in 1369.

▶ VISITING MEDINA SIDONIA

INFORMATION (OFICINA DE TURISMO)

Plaza de la Iglesia Mayor, s/n,
E-11170 Medina Sidonia
Tel. / Fax 956 41 24 04
www.medinasidonia.com

WHERE TO EAT

► Inexpensive
Cádiz
Plaza España, 13
Tel. 956 41 02 50
The locals too meet here at the main square for regional cooking.

Mesón Machín
Plaza Iglesia, 9
Good and low-priced dishes and tapas opposite Santa María church, panoramic view of the city from the terrace.

WHERE TO STAY

► Budget
Los Balcones
C. La Loba, 26
Tel. 956 42 30 33
www.losbalcones.turincon.com
Small and pretty town hotel.

Medina Sidonia at twilight

Santa María la Coronada ✳ In the late 15th century the parish church Santa María la Coronada was built on the castle hill. The **Inquisition** had its seat here, as carvings– sword, palm tree, Dominican cross – on a bench behind the choir stalls show. A portrait by Ribera, and the giant retable of the Virgin by Vazquez the older and Turín are also worth seeing.

Roman excavations The excavated **sewer system** allows a spectacular look at everyday Roman life. It dates from the 1st century BC and is a masterpiece of Roman engineering, with sewers about 30m/33yd long and 2m/6ft 6 in high (C. Espíritu Santo 3; opening hours: summer daily 10am–2pm, 6–8pm; winter daily 10am–2pm, 4–6pm.)

Ermita de los Santos Mártires The Ermita de los Santos Mártires on the edge of town dates from the first half of the 7th century, and is a **rare example of Visigothic architecture** in Andalusia. Processions in honour of the Virgen de Loreto take place here annually in the last week of September.

Around Medina Sidonia

Alcalá de los Gazules In Alcalá de los Gazules, another white village 23km/14mi to the east, the remains of an Arab castle and two gates of the town wall can be seen. Alcalá is an ideal starting point for exploring the wildlife park ►Los Alcornocales.

Cuevas del Tajo y de las Figuras Go southeast of Medina Sidonia via Benalup de Sidonia to reach the caves of El Tajo and Las Figuras, in which prehistoric paintings, tools, and arrowheads were discovered.

Melilla

Outlying

Spanish sovereign territory in Africa
Population: 65,000

Province: Málaga
Altitude: sea level

The seaport and garrison town of Melilla, termed Mlilya or Ras el Querk in Arabian (Berber: Tamlilt), a 12,3 sq km/4.7 sq mi Spanish enclave (Plaza de Soberanía) and free trade area, lies on the Moroccan Mediterranean coast in a bay of the Beni Sicar peninsula, 25km/16mi south of Cabo Tres Forcas (Cap des Trois Fourches).

The majority of Melilla's citizens are of Spanish nationality. The Andalusian character of the town, which stretches in a semicircle around the harbour and the coast, corresponds to this. It has a typically Spanish atmosphere with broad, straight streets crossing at right-angles, spacious squares and parks. The old centre, encircled by battlements and situated 30m/100ft up on a small headland, has remained almost unchanged since the 16th century. Although Melilla had a purely Spanish character until recently, it is noticeable that legal and illegal Moroccan immigrants are settling in the periphery and suburbs. They now constitute about 10% of the population.

Enclave in North Africa

Economically, the Spanish enclave is almost entirely dependent upon the mother country. The harbour was established at the time of the Spanish protectorate for the export of iron and lead ores from the eastern foothills of the Rif mountains above Melilla. At present, however, sardine fishing is more significant; a large part of the catch is processed on the spot in canning plants. Besides Christians and Muslims, an active Jewish community lives in Melilla, and there is even a Hindu temple.

 VISITING MELILLA

GETTING THERE

Planes leave from Almería and Málaga; Trasmediterránea ferries go from Almeria and Malaga 6 or 7 times a week (journey time 6–7hrs or 7–8 hrs respectively)

INFORMATION (OFICINA DE TURISMO)

Palacio de Exposiciones, C. Pintor Fortuny, 21, E-52004 Melilla
Tel. 952 67 54 44

Fax 952 67 96 16
www.melilla500.com

WHERE TO STAY

► **Mid-range**
Parador de Melilla
Avda. Cándido Lobera, s / n
Tel. 952 68 49 40
Fax 952 68 34 86
www.parador.es, 40 rooms
Modern place above the city with a view of the ramparts and harbour.

History Melilla developed from the Phoenician Rusadir, the oldest Phoenician settlement in Morocco other than Lixius. It suffered the same fate as all Phoenician settlements, first becoming Carthaginian, then Roman, Vandal, Byzantine, and finally Arab. The Arabs completely destroyed it during their second campaign of conquest in 705, yet rebuilt it in the 10th century, and from the 13th century made it one of the most important ports of the North African coast under the Merinids. The Spanish captured Melilla in 1497. Although it was heavily fought over in the following period, the last time being against Abd-el Krim in 1921, it remained in Spanish hands. Following its elevation to a duty-free area in 1887, Melilla finally reached its second economical peak during the protectorate period between 1914 and 1956.

Melilla's importance decreased again when the hinterland was lost due to Morocco's independence, and customers for duty-free goods from Algeria stayed away after this country's independence in 1962. The decline in population from 100,000 to about 65,000 clearly shows this. For the 500th anniversary of capture by the Spanish, celebrated in 1997, Melilla decked itself out and treated itself to a new marina.

What to See in Melilla

Melilla Vieja (old town) The Plaza de España lends itself as a starting point for a stroll around the town. To its west lies the new town (Ciudad Moderna or Nueva) and to its northeast is the old town, situated on a small, somewhat elevated peninsula with precipitous rocks above the sea. It is also called Pueblo, and is surrounded by fortification walls and bastions from the 16th century; it is entered via the Tunel de San Fernando, which soon leads to the central square Plaza de Armas, where stands the Capilla de Santiago, **the only Gothic chapel in Africa**. The town wall commands a view of the city and the coast.

In the eastern part of the old town are the **Iglesia de la Concepción** (16th century), containing the Madonna Virgen de Victoria (17th century), the town's patron saint, and the spectacular and especially venerated statue of Christ, Cristo del Socorro, dating from the 16th century. North of the church lies the town museum (**Museo Municipal**), which exhibits finds from the Neolithic period, pottery, coins, and iron items from Roman and Punic times, as well as weapons, flags, and plans from recent town history.

Ciudad Moderna (new town) A sight one would hardly expect to see in Africa: **rows of art nouveau buildings**, e.g. the telegraph office (C. Candido Lobera) or the Casa de los Cristales (C. General Prim). Developed from 1898 on, the new town was a **playground of Modernism**, for its planning was determined by Gaudí's pupil Enrique Nieto for almost 50 years. Joining the Plaza de España from the northwest, Avenida de Juan Carlos I Rey is the new town's main shopping street; shopping is also possible in C. del Ejercito Español / C. Lopez Moreno running parallel and to the north, as well as in some side roads. Parque Hernández lies to the west of the Plaza de España.

At the town's southern exit Playa de San Lorenzo and Playa de los Cárabos are good beaches for swimming. ◄ Beaches

25km/16mi north of Melilla at the end of the peninsula Cabo Tres Forcas,, the Moroccan mainland plummets **400m/1300ft to the sea below**. The view from the lighthouse is magnificent. A short trip to the lovely sandy beach Playa Charranes on the northwest coast of the Beni Sicar (Gelaia) peninsula is recommendable.

✳
Cabo Tres Forcas

As the whole area belongs to Morocco, the border needs to be crossed on this tour (remember to take your passport!) – usually a very time-consuming affair, particularly as the road is difficult.

Mojácar

M 7

Province: Almería
Population: 4500

Altitude: 172m/564ft

Forty years ago Mojácar, in the north of province Almería, dozed in peaceful solitude. Then it was discovered by foreign visitors, initially by artists and people looking to escape, and tourist development took its course.

A new district was constructed with the tourist development: Mojácar Playa, the discos, bars and hotels of which spread along the beach

Spectacular location

White walls and red blossoms in Mojácar

VISITING MOJÁCAR

INFORMATION (OFICINA DE TURISMO)

Plaza Nueva, s/n,
E-04638 Mojácar
Tel. and fax 950 47 51 62
www.mojacarviva.com

WHERE TO EAT

▶ Moderate
Mamabel's
Embajadores, 5
Tel. 950 47 24 48
www.mamabels.com
This lovely hotel boasts an equally lovely restaurant. Evenings on the terrace are very pleasant; Specialties: paella and couscous.

WHERE TO STAY

▶ Mid-range
Parador de Mojácar
Tel. 950 47 82 50
Fax 950 47 81 83
E-mail: mojacar@parador.es
www.parador.es,
87 rooms

The modern parador is located in a large park on the coast, several yards from the beach. The cuisine is generally acclaimed.

▶ Budget
Casa Justa
C. Morote, 5
Tel. 950 47 83 72
Informal guesthouse with roof terrace.

Mamabel's
Embajadores, 5
Tel. 950 47 24 48
www.mamabels.com, 9 rooms
First-rate place to stay in the old town high above the coast, some rooms with sea view.

EVENT

Moros y Cristianos
In early June, Mojácar colourfully calls to memory the battles between Moors and Christians which once raged about the town.

to both sides of the parador, whilst dispensing with ugly piles of concrete. This development has also left its mark on the old town seated about a mile inland, especially noticeable during the high season when the British in particular, but also many Germans, virtually occupy the place. Many have meanwhile settled down as permanent residents. Yet Mojácar's spectacular location on a ridge is still captivating, its gleaming white houses seemingly piled one on top of the other. The nearby beach is one of the most beautiful on this coast.

History   Mojácar lies in an area settled since the second millennium before Christ. It owes its present-day characteristic appearance to the Moors, who called the town Murgisacra. After Morisco Mojácar had proven loyal to the crown following the conquest of Granada, the Catholic Monarchs bestowed upon it religious freedom, so that Muslims, Jews and Christians lived peacefully together into the 18th century.

What to See in Mojácar

Other than the 15th-century church Santa María and the Mirador del Castillo, the remains of the Moorish alcazaba, which provide a fantastic view of the coast and hinterland, Mojácar does not possess any noteworthy sights. The platform at the Plaza Nueva offers nice views as well. Mojácar's charm lies in the clean and decked-out romance of its narrow lanes, which, with many flower arrangements, aim to convey to tourists the **atmosphere of a village of Moorish character** – with some success, provided one overlooks the host of bars, souvenir shops, restaurants and tourists taking a painting course. The Indalo, the town's symbol modelled on the archetype of a prehistoric cave painting found in the Cueva de los Letreros near► Vélez Blanco, is encountered everywhere in many forms, and has become the tourist emblem of the Costa de Almería.

✶✶ Views

Around Mojácar

Going 24km/15mi north of Mojácar via Garrucha – now a lido, yet also still a fishing village, and thus known for its fish restaurants – and the small country town of Vera, Cuevas de Almanzora is reached. It owes its name to prehistoric caves found outlying in a high escarpment (route is signposted). However, in town the fortress-like 16th-century Palacio del Marqués de los Velez, containing an archaeological museum, a museum for contemporary art, and an open air theatre, is perhaps more interesting.

Cuevas de Almanzora

South of Mojácar the road at first follows the coast, then turns off to Agua de Enmedio heading inland, circumnavigating the promontory in sharp curves. Many spectacular vistas open up on the way, until on the northern edge of the wildlife park ►Cabo de Gata the road reaches Carboneras, a relatively quiet and not too expensive beach resort – maybe because the huge power station behind the beach puts visitors off. 8km/5mi further is the much more lovely Agua Amarga in the Cabo de Gata (►p.197) wildlife park.

Carboneras

Montilla

F 6

Province: Córdoba
Population: 22,800

Altitude: 379m/1243ft

South of ►Córdoba lies Montilla, which gave its name to the wine produced in the DO region Montilla-Moriles. The wines here resemble those from ►Jerez de la Frontera so closely that a whole brand of sherry is called Amontillado.

⏵ MONTILLA

INFORMATION
(OFICINA DE TURISMO)

San Luis, 8
E-14550 Montilla
Tel. 957 65 24 62
www.montillaonline.com

WHERE TO EAT

▶ **Moderate**
Meson Las Camachas
Avda. Europa, 3, tel. 957 65 00 04
Meat and fish – fried
and grilled.

EVENT

Fiesta de la Vendimia
Grape harvest festival in the beginning
of September.

Montilla wine is nothing short of sherry; the main difference is the variety of grape (Montilla: Ximénez; Sherry: Palomino), which is harvested a little earlier – Montilla gives the **starting signal for the grape harvest throughout Spain**. The wine is filled into tinajas, pear-shaped earthenware jugs holding up to 5000 litres/1320 US gal. (▶ Baedeker Special p.308). Also known for its olive products, the region is one of the hottest in Spain with summer temperatures often exceeding 40°C/104°F.

Not far from the present-day town the battle of Munda Baetica took place between the civil war factions of Pompey and Caesar in 45 BC. Gonzalo Fernández de Córdoba, named El Gran Capitán, the famed general of the Catholic Monarchs, was born in Montilla.

What to See in Montilla

Alvear
Alvear is the largest **bodega** on the square, and having been **established in 1729** is one of the oldest in Spain: 20,000 barrels and tinajas are stored between the pillars of the Solera hall (information tel. 957 65 01 00).

Casa Museo del Inca Garcilaso
Inside the palace now occupied by the municipality a small museum commemorates Garcilaso de la Vega, the Inca Garcilaso (1539–1616), son of a Spanish nobleman and a cousin of the last sovereign of the Incas, Atahualpa. He made a name for himself as chronicler of Andean empire with his work *Comentares Reales de los Incas*.

Castillo
The castle built by Moors on Roman foundations once possessed 30 towers, yet lies in ruin today – the Catholic Monarchs had it razed to punish its defiant lord Pedro Fernández de Córdoba.

Churches and convents
Of Montilla's sacred buildings, the Mudéjar convent Santa Clara, built in the 16th century by Hernán Ruiz el Viejo in late Gothic style and furnished with an artesonado ceiling, the Convento de Santa Ana with sculptures by Pedro Roldán on the high altar, and the Iglesia de Santiago, which houses the small town museum, are worth a visit.

Round trip through Wine and Olive Country

Aguilar de la Frontera, a Visigothic seat of a bishop until conquered by the Moors, huddles on a hill 13km/8mi south of Montilla. It is a town characteristic of Andalusia, where visitors walking around its small lanes and streets discover beautiful mansions time and again. The **classical Plaza de San José** has an extraordinary design: a three-storey row of houses completely encloses the octagonal square, onto which four gateways open. Two other buildings worth seeing are the Baroque Torre de Reloj, which soars among the ruins of the Moorish castle, and the Churrigueresque church interior of the convent of the barefoot Carmelite nuns, completed in the 18th century. Opulent Baroque ornamentation in side chapels and the apse are the features of Nuestra Señora del Soterrano, the town's main church.

Aguilar de la Frontera

★

◄ Plaza de San José

Lucena, another 19km/12mi southeast, is the economic centre of Montilla-Moriles. This is where the tinajas are manufactured. Only once in Spanish history did the town make the news: in 1483 the Count of Cabra kept the Moorish King of Granada, Boabdil, imprisoned here. He was only released once he had paid a ransom and had declared himself to be neutral. Only the tower of Castillo del Moral where King Boabdil was kept is still in good condition.

Adjoining this is the Plaza Nueva with the church San Mateo, constructed in the 15th and 16th centuries. Its Capilla del Sagrario is a **treasure of Andalusian Rococo art**. A retable by Rivas showing scenes from the life of Jesus is also striking.

Cross Plaza del Coso to the convent Santo Domingo, the 19th-century façade of which conceals a Mannerist cloister; the abbey church dates from the first half of the 17th century. Visit the chapel in the whitewashed Hospital de San Juan de Dios with its flamboyant Churrigueresque altar. The magnificent Baroque portal contrasts with the stark exterior. Dating from the first half of the 16th century, the late Gothic Iglesia de Santiago, mixed with Mudéjar elements, possesses a monumental belfry and a painting by Pedro Roldán. A two-storey covered cloister adjoins the abbey church Madre de Dios, furnished by the local artist Francisco de Lucena in the 17th and 18th century. On a ridge a little to the south outside of Lucena, right amid a ruggedly romantic nature reserve, lies the hermitage **Nuestra Señora de Araceli**.

Aniseed liqueur is distilled according to a traditional recipe at **Rute**, 21km/13mi to the southeast. Visitors can find out how it is made at the **aniseed museum**. A scenic route then continues from Rute to **Iznájar**, an attractive village on the edge of the reservoir of the same name, around which there are pleasant paths.

Lucena

★

◄ San Mateo

◄ Churches and convents

Cabra, 12km/7.5mi north of Lucena, is the next stop; called Igabrum by the Romans, and later Egabrum by the Visigoths, it became a bishop's seat as early as the 4th century. Outside the town centre a

Cabra

Zuhereros towers like a gigantic eagle's nest on a mountain peak.

little way uphill the Iglesia de la Asunción dating from the 17th and 18th centuries rests on the foundations of a former mosque. Next to it stand the preserved remains of the Moorish alcazaba.

A small road branches off the road to ►Priego de Córdoba, 6km beyond Cabra, leading to the 16th-century **Ermita de la Virgen de la Sierra**, where, in the middle of the beautiful Parque Natural de la Sierra Subbética, the patron saint of Cabra is venerated. At a height of over 1200m/3937ft there is a **stunning view**.

✴ Zuheros

At Doña Mencia a small road branches off the scenic route that runs 25km/16mi northeast to Baena and leads to the charming village of Zuheros, where white houses hang above a vast canyon and cluster around the ruins of a Moorish castle. At the viewing platform the archaeological museum exhibits finds from the **Cueva de los Murciélagos**: this bat cave lies in the mountains 4km/2.5mi away from Zuheros (signposted). The one-hour tour reveals magnificent **dripstone formations and murals** dating from the Neolithic period.

✴ Baena

The countryside around Baena has changed: olive trees have taken the place of vines. Perched picturesquely on a hilltop, the small town of Baena, centre of this **DO olive region**, is known not only for its production of very high-quality olive oil, but also for its **tambourine players** who accompany the Easter processions during Holy Week in fantastic uniforms. The **upper town** (barrio alto), in which several Renaissance palaces are preserved, is still partially surrounded by a curtain wall. Santa María, the late Gothic main church of the town, features a remarkable Plateresque grille in front of its main chapel and displays its treasures, above all goldsmith work, in the vestry.

The belfry developed from the minaret of the Moorish mosque. Inside the church of the convent Madre de Dios founded in 1510, the large statue of Mary (15th century), Virgen de la Antigua, catches the eye, as she is holding a pear in her hand. Over 60 paintings on the walls show scenes from the life of Jesus; the ceiling of the main chapel is lined with azulejos. The **lower town** is called El Llano. On the Plaza de España stands the pilgrimage church consecrated to the Madonna of Guadalupe, an oil painting painted directly onto the wall, and splendid artesonado ceilings can be admired inside.

> ! **Baedeker** TIP
>
> **Sample**
>
> It goes without saying that the olive oil in Baena should be sampled. The right place to do this is the oil mill of the Nuñez de Prado family on Avenida Cervantes, which has been in existence since the 18th century. Here visitors can learn about the manufacture of cold pressed oil at any time, and then may also purchase the wonderful yellow liquid (opening hours: summer Mon–Fri 9am–1pm, 4–6pm, Sat 9am–1pm; tel. 957 67 01 41).

The next section of the route is a return from olive country to wine country. The second half of the 19km/12mi-long journey from Baena to northwestern **Castro del Río** follows the Río Guadajoz, where many traces of settlement dating from the Neolithic, Iberian, Carthaginian, Roman and Moorish periods were found in the surrounding area. The town of Castro del Río itself grew around a Roman bridge crossing the river; the remnants of the town wall and the foundations of the Moorish castle also date from this period. The Plateresque portal of the church La Asunción, which dates back to the 13th century, is particularly worth seeing. The cell in the town hall that **Miguel de Cervantes** occupied for three months in 1592 is shown with pride. As tax collector he had committed the gross error of demanding taxes from a clergyman, even though the clergy enjoyed tax exemption. Legend has it that Cervantes began writing *Don Quixote here.*

Via the pretty wine-growing village Espejo, dominated by the castle of the dukes of Osuna, the route reaches the starting point at Montilla again.

◄ Espejo

Nerja

H 8

Province: Málaga   **Altitude:** 21m/68ft
Population: 15,300

Nerja, situated where the Río Chillar flows into the Mediterranean, was known under the Moors as Narixa (abundant spring), and experienced its greatest prosperity during this period.

*Balcón de Europa – during the Moorish era it was a fortress tower,
today an observation terrace with a fabulous view.*

Beach resort with famous caves Today it is a well-frequented beach resort which, although new suburbs and amusement zones show that it has not been spared by the tourist boom, nevertheless is one of the quieter places on the Costa del Sol. Nerja has famous dripstone caves, in which the annual summer festival takes place with music and ballet between the second half of July and the first half of August.

What to See in and around Nerja

Nerja The dome of the Ermita de las Angustias in the old part of Nerja (16th century) was decorated with frescoes by Alonso Cano.

✴ Balcón de Europa ▶ Across from the town hall, where once a castle stood, the Balcón de Europa juts out over the sea. High above the waves this **viewing platform** commands a magnificent view of the varied coast and hinterland mountains. Nerja's beaches extend on both sides of the balcony. The best of them are Playa de la Burriana right in the east, and Playa de la Torrecilla right in the west.

✴✴ Cuevas de Nerja Discovered by children in 1959, the Cuevas de Nerja are found a few miles northeast above the village of Maro. They form a system of dripstone caves **over 4km/2.5mi long**, of which a section about 1400m/1531yd long can be visited. The caves have bizarre stalactite and stalagmite formations – the gigantic dripstone in the Sala del

▶ VISITING NERJA

INFORMATION
(OFICINA DE TURISMO)
Puerta del Mar, 2, E-29780 Nerja
Tel. 952 52 15 31
Fax 952 52 62 87
www.nerja.org

WHERE TO EAT
▶ Moderate
La Marea
Plaza Cantarero, 9
Tel. 952 52 57 78
The name and the blue interior
decoration announce what is served
here: fish and seafood.

▶ Inexpensive
Bar-Restaurante El Pulguilla
Bolivia, 1
Tel. 952 52 13 84
Tapas bar and restaurant.

El Refugio
Diputación, 12
Tel. 952 52 41 39
Prime address for paella, fish, and
seafood, served either in the
country-style restaurant or on the
street terrace.

WHERE TO STAY
▶ Mid-range
Parador de Nerja
Almuñécar, 8
Tel. 952 52 00 50
Fax 952 52 19 97
E-mail: nerja@parador.es
www.parador.es, 73 rooms
Modern building with nice garden;
above the coast, with access to the
beach.

▶ Budget
Paraíso del Mar
Prolongación Carabeo, 22
Tel. 952 52 16 21

Fax 952 52 23 09,
10 rooms
Two Andalusian-style houses in a
fantastic location on a cliff above the
sea. Add to that a touchingly caring
host – and a restful stay is assured.

EVENT
Festival de las Cuevas
End of July / beginning of August:
music and ballet festival in the caves
(tel. 952 52 95 20).

The limestone caves of Nerja are bizarre.

Opening hours:
Daily 10am–2pm,
4–6.30pm,
Aug–Jul
10am–6.30pm

Cataclismo is stunning – yet also wonderful effects produced by means of artificial lighting. People of the Mesolithic period left rock paintings and artefacts. Remains of skulls, pottery, tools, and other objects are on display in the small archaeological museum at the entrance.

Acueducto del águila

The four-tiered aqueduct crossing the gorge of La Coladilla at Maro near the N-340 was built not by the Romans, but by the local architect Francisco Cantarero in the 19th century.

La Axarquía

The part of the coast and hinterland of the Costa del Sol between Nerja and ▶Málaga is called La Axarquía. As it is protected from the cold north wind by the mountains of the Sierra Alhama, Sierra Tejeda, and Sierra Almijara, La Axarquía is known for its distinctly mild climate. The Moors made use of this, and grew vines and fruit, bred silkworms, and also withdrew here to the seclusion of the mountains following the fall of Granada. It is quiet in the villages of Axarquía even today.

✷ Frigiliana ▶

In Frigiliana, 5km/3mi north of Nerja, Málaga wine is pressed. The village, awarded a prize for its improvement activities, is exceptionally lovely, its centre dating back to Moorish times, and offers a magnificent view of Nerja and the sea. Its lanes are too narrow for cars. Frigiliana was a Moriscan stronghold: ceramic plaques on the houses recount a – quelled – revolt of the Moriscos against the Christians in 1569, the Batalla del Peñon.

> **! Baedeker TIP**
>
> **Delicacies from Frigiliana**
>
> Sweet Málaga wine is not the only thing to purchase in Frigiliana. Many shops also sell olive oil from the village, and – a rarity – honey made from sugarcane (miel de caña).

A short round trip through Axarquía leads from Nerja to the west through the holiday resort Torrox-Costa, and from there to Torrox, which is charmingly located in the mountains 4km/2.5mi further north. The Moors founded it in

Round trip through Axarquía

the 12th century. After Torrox the trip continues on a winding and scenic route to Cómpeta, 15km/9mi distant, where whitewashed houses nestle amid a wine-growing region on the mountainside. Visitors to the **Museo del Vino** can sample the dessert wine produced here from the Moscatel grape. The route then returns to the coast via Archez, Corumbela, and Vélez-Málaga, a pretty little town up high, its appearance characterized by white cubic houses and the Moorish alcazaba.

On the way back the route passes between Caleta de Vélez and Algarrobo, the **Necrópolis Fenicias de Trayamar**, where Punic and Phoenician tombs dating partly from the 8th century BC were discovered. The most significant finds are exhibited in the Alcazaba Museum in ▶Málaga. Return to Nerja via Caleta de Vélez, a fishing town right on the coast, and enjoy the beautiful drive along the Mediterranean.

* Niebla

Province: Huelva **Altitude:** 39m/127ft
Population: 3800

The small town of Niebla in the wine-growing region Condado de Huelva is one of the few Spanish places that still has a medieval curtain wall completely surrounding its centre – an imposing sight when coming from the east.

The first sign of the town's long history is the bridge over the Río Tinto, built by the Romans. Their settlement of Ilipula was renamed Elebla and made a bishop's seat by the Visigoths. The Moors called the town Lebla and erected its massive town fortifications; belonging at first to the Caliphate of Córdoba, it became the capital of a petty Moorish kingdom, a taifa, after the collapse of the caliphate. Alfonso X was able to overcome the ramparts after half a year's siege in 1257.

Ancient walls and wine

What to See in Niebla

3km/2mi of enormous battlements gird the small town. Iberians, Visigoths, Romans and particularly the Moors built the **walls and their total of 46 towers**. Five gates lead inside: Puerta del Agua to the south, both Puerta de Sevilla with Roman and Moorish traces

✳ Murallas

Niebla is surrounded by a medieval city wall – because of its red sheen it was called »The Red« in Arabic.

NIEBLA

INFORMATION
(OFICINA DE TURISMO)
Plaza Santa María, s/n
E-21840 Niebla
Tel. 959 36 22 70
Fax 959 36 38 31
www.castillodeniebla.com

WHERE TO EAT

▶ **Inexpensive**
El Galeria
Adelfa, 4
Tel. 959 36 33 08
Delicacies from the sea.

and Puerta del Agujero to the north, Puerta de Socorro with a horseshoe arch to the northwest, and finally Puerta de Buey, on which the art of Moorish craftsmen is most notably visible, to the southeast.

Right next to Puerta de Sevilla is the **castle of Guzmanes**, constructed in the 15th century, and destroyed by the French in 1813, yet meanwhile restored. Some rooms such as the kitchen and the dungeon have been renovated or contain exhibitions, e.g. on falconry, as **hunting falcons from Niebla** were treasured in Europe and the Orient (opening hours: daily 10am–6pm, June–Sept to 10pm).

San Martin
Behind Puerta del Soccorro, the church San Martin is a **curiosity** beyond compare: in the 1920s, unused at the time, the nave had to make way for a road, yet both apse and belfry with the main portal remained standing either side of the road. The church can be traced back to a mosque that Alfonso X gave to Niebla's Jewish community as a synagogue, which was then converted to a Mudéjar, and later Gothic church in the 14th century.

La Ciudad del Vino
Bollulos Par del Condado, 15km/9mi east of Niebla where the A-93 and A-483 intersect, is called »city of wine«. Try the tangy white wines or the heavy dessert wines of the Condado de Huelva region here, preferably at one of the bodegóns, where there is food and the wines are for sale.

Santa Maria de la Granada
On the site of a Visigothic predecessor, the church Santa María de la Granada stands at the central square. Two of its portals date from the 10th and 11th centuries, when Christians were allowed to use it under Moorish rule. The conversion to a mosque did not occur until the 13th century; the horseshoe ambulatories at the entrance derive from this period. In the 15th century the building was made into a church, whereby the minaret was retained as a belfry. Inside the mihrâb and the bishop's throne are preserved.

Dolmen de Soto
The The A-472 leads to the Dolmen de Soto, about 8km/5mi to the west. It is a Neolithic tomb with a passage leading 20m/21yd to a burial chamber containing rock drawings (opening hours: summer Tue–Sat 9am–1pm and 4–6.30pm, Sun 10am–2pm).

✴ Osuna

E 7

Province: Sevilla
Population: 17,300

Altitude: 326m/1069ft

Right on the southern edge of the hot plain of the Guadalquivir the houses of Osuna climb a slope. The town was seat of the dukes of Osuna, who beautified the town with marvellous Baroque palaces and churches, which makes a walk through the old quarter an experience.

Under the Romans Osuna was called Urso, and supported Pompey against Julius Caesar for a long time, until Caesar overthrew it. The Moors, who called the town Oxuna, lost it to the Castilian king in 1239, who transferred it to the Order of Calatrava; the order ceded it to the lords of Girón. In 1548 Juan Téllez de Girón founded the university at which only students who professed the dogma of the Immaculate Conception might enrol. This college, praised by Miguel de Cervantes, made Osuna into a spiritual centre of 16th- and 17-century Spain. Philip II bestowed upon Pedro Téllez de Girón the title of Duke of Osuna in

Baroque ducal town

 Baedeker TIP

In the casino

An ideal place for relaxing with a cup of coffee and watching the goings-on on the Plaza Mayor is the terrace of the casino, built in the 1920s. The interior is decorated with magnificently tiled walls and ceilings in a mix of art nouveau and Mudéjar styles (a must!).

 VISITING OSUNA

INFORMATION (OFICINA DE TURISMO)

Plaza Mayor, s/n,
E-41640 Osuna
Tel. / fax 954 81 57 32
www.ayto-osuna.es

WHERE TO EAT
▶ Moderate
Restaurante Doña Guadalupe
Plaza Guadalupe, 6
Tel. 954 81 05 58
Vegetables, meat, and fresh fish are also served outside on a lovely small square. The Doña Guadalupe rates as one of the town's best restaurants.

▶ Inexpensive
Casa Curro
Plaza Salitre, 5
Tel. 955 82 07 58
The tastiest tapas in Osuna.

Mesón del Duque
Plaza de la Duquesa
Tel. 954 81 28 45
Traditional Andalusian dishes.

WHERE TO STAY
▶ Budget
Hostal Caballo Blanco
Granada, 1
Tel. 954 81 01 84
Friendly hotel in a quiet location.

1562; in the 17th and 18th centuries this noble family was one of Spain's most powerful.

What to See in Osuna

Four beautiful aristocratic palaces of Osuna dating primarily from the 17th century are of note: in C. San Pedro the Palacio del Marqués de la Gomera, with a grand Baroque façade dominated by a balcony onto which an extravagant door framed by spiralled columns opens; in the same street and no less beautiful is the Palacio del Cabildo Colegial, which has a façade adorned with white decorative tiles and displays a replica of Giralda of Seville above the portal; lastly the Palacio de los Cepedas (now a court; C. de la Huerta) and the Palacio de Govantes y Herdara in C. Sevilla.

✳ **Aristocratic palaces**

The abbey church, located higher up, was built with three Plateresque portals from 1535 to 1539. Four paintings by Ribera (Saints Jerome, Peter, Sebastian, Bartholomew) hang in the Capilla Mayor, and were brought to Osuna during the third Duke of Osuna's time as Viceroy of Naples, where Ribera worked primarily; another Ribera painting shows the crucified Christ. Further treasures include a Madonna by Alonso Cano, a retable by Sebastián Fernández, the Catalan Madonna with the pomegranate and a Flemish triptych (both 16th century), and lastly Cristo de la Misericordia by Juan de Mesa, a sculpture from the church Santo Domingo. Enter by the Plateresque Patio del Capellán, surrounded by a two-storey arcade, to reach the mausoleum of the Dukes of Osuna (Santo Sepulcro or Panteón). Juan Téllez de Girón had it built in 1545; its magnificent stucco, paintings, sculptures, and the small but superb choir stalls gave it the **byname Escorial of Osuna** (opening hours: May–Sept Tue–Sun 10am–1.30pm and 4–7pm, Oct–Apr Tue–Sun 10am–1.30pm and 3.30–6.30pm).

✳ **La Colegiata**

◄ **Santo Sepulcro**

⏲

The Convento de la Encarnación across from the church was founded as a hospital in 1549. Take a look at the cloister lined with coloured azulejos and visit the Museo de Arte Sacro, with four rooms dedicated to sacred art (same opening hours as La Colegiata).

Convento de la Encarnación

Cervantes mentions the university opposite the eastern façade of the Colegiata in *Don Quixote*. The former university (until 1824) encloses a Plateresque inner courtyard with gallery.

Antigua Universidad

Between La Colegiata and the Plaza Mayor stands the Torre del Agua, an Almohad tower dating from the 12th century and the oldest building of the town, which houses the archaeological museum.

Museo Arqueológico

← *The Palacio del Cabildo Colegial is decorated with a copy of the Giralda of Seville.*

🕐 Copies of Roman bronze work are of note here (opening hours: May–Sept daily 11.30am–1.30pm, 5–7pm; Oct–April Tue–Sun 11.30am–1.30pm, 4.30–6.30pm).

Around Osuna

Estepa

Estepa, situated 24km/15mi east of Osuna at the foot of the eponymous Sierra, was Carthaginian Astapa, where in 207 BC the inhabitants burned themselves to death rather than surrender to Scipio Africanus. The mighty Torre del Homenaje is the most striking remnant of the castillo; the terrace of the Gothic church Santa María de la Asunción next to the castle features a beautiful panoramic view. The parish church Iglesia del Carmen possesses an elaborately ornamented main entrance with black azulejos. Thanks to the jasper-encrusted Camarín de la Vera Cruz, created by Nicolás Bautista Morales in 1745, the church Nuestra Señora de los Remedios is among the most significant Baroque churches of Andalusia.

★
Camarín de la Vera Cruz ▶

★ Priego de Córdoba

G 7

Province: Córdoba
Population: 22,100

Altitude: 652m/2139

The small town of Priego de Córdoba lies at the edge of the Sierra Subbética wildlife park in marvellous mountain scenery. Moreover Priego still retains a town centre with characteristic Andalusian charm.

Baroque pearl of the province

Just like in the old days the small town is still a centre of textile manufacture and olive oil production, though less important than in the 17th and 18th centuries. During that time Priego experienced a period of prosperity from silk production, which enabled **sumptuous Baroque churches** to be constructed.

What to See in Priego de Córdoba

Castillo

A square, three-storey keep with twin windows juts out above the castle, which was built in the 13th and 14th centuries and towers virtually at the entrance to the Moorish quarter.

★★
Nuestra Señora de la Asunción

Nuestra Señora de la Asunción, a church begun opposite the castle in 1525, was rebuilt in Baroque style in the 18th century. Numerous altars decorate the aisles; the life of Christ and the Assumption of the Virgin are the themes of the high altar. The undisputed highlight, the Sagrario, is entered from the left aisle. This octagonal chapel, surrounded by balustrades, was adorned between 1772 and 1784 by

Francisco Javier Pedrejas with biblical scenes rendered in exuberant stucco. Sculptures of the apostles are placed before the columns, the fathers of the church in the middle.

The layout of the old town quarter Barrio de la Villa behind Nuestra Señora de la Asunción is unmistakeably Moorish. Its lanes, flower-bedecked façades and tiny squares are a pleasant place for a walk. The viewing point El Adarve, high above the valley, is reached by going this way. It commands a wonderful panorama of the surrounding area.

✶ Barrio de la Villa

✶ ◀ El Adarve

Inside the Iglesia de San Pedro at the eponymous plaza near the castle, adorned with spiral columns and gold leaf, the high altar displays the patron saint of the church. The chapel behind it holds an Immaculada, ascribed to the group of artists around Alonso Cano.

Iglesia de San Pedro

Below Iglesia de San Pedro lies the former 16th-century abattoir and the town market. A Mannerist portal opens onto the central patio with columned arcades, corner towers, and a stone spiral staircase that leads to the previous abattoir, which now contains an exhibition room.

Carnicerías Reales

Above the Placa de la Constitucion with the town hall, C. Río leads to the Iglesia de las Angustias, where the Rococo-style interior was completed in 1773 by Juan de Dios Santaella. The major works here are the Baroque Pietà on the high altar and statues by José Risueño portraying the Holy Family.

Iglesia de las Angustias

▶ VISITING PRIEGO DE CÓRDOBA

INFORMATION (OFICINA DE TURISMO)

C. Río, 33, E-14800 Priego de Córdoba
Tel. and fax 957 70 06 25
www.aytopriegodecordoba.es

WHERE TO EAT

▶ Inexpensive
Hostal Rafi
Isabel la Católica, 4
Tel. 957 54 70 27
www.hostalrafi.com
The restaurant of the guest house enjoys a good reputation for local Andalusian cuisine.

WHERE TO STAY

▶ Budget
Hostal Rafi
Isabel la Católica, 4
Tel. 957 54 70 27
Fax 957 54 07 49, 26 rooms
Tastefully furnished family-run guest house.

Villa Turistica de Priego
In Aldea Zagrilla
Tel. 957 70 35 03
Fax 957 70 35 73
52 apartments
Holiday park in Andalusian country style in natural surroundings, 7km/4.5mi outside Priego.

Casa Niceto Alcalá-Zamora
⏲

Follow the street downhill to reach the birthplace, furnished true to the original, of Niceto Alcalá-Zamora (1877–1949), who was **President of the Second Spanish Republic** from 1931 to 1939. The town's tourist office is located on the ground floor (opening hours: Tue–Sun 10am–1.30pm, 5–7.30pm, Sun 10am–1.30pm).

✳
Fuente del Rey

C. Río runs past the Iglesia del Carmen to the monumental fountain Fuente del Rey, erected in the 19th century. Water pours into the main basin from **139 marble openings**, in its centre Neptune on a chariot slicing through the waves. The first fountain here was Fuente de Salud, erected a little higher up in the 16th century.

Further churches

In the eastern part of the town centre there are two more interesting churches: the 16th-century Iglesia de la Aurora, its glorious façade a typical example of this region's Baroque style, and not far from there the Iglesia de San Francisco, containing an enormous number of Baroque side altars, its high altar portraying Christ at the Column.

Museo Histórico
⏲

In Carrera de las Monjas in the western part of town the town museum mainly exhibits archaeological finds from the surrounding area. Here, too, are the Museo de Paisaje with contemporary landscape art and a museum commemorating the local painter Adolfo Lozano Sidro, who lived in this house for many years (opening hours: Tue–Sat 10am–1.30pm, 6–8.30pm, Sun 10am–1.30pm).

Around Priego de Córdoba

Carcabuey

7km/4.5mi west of Priego at the foot of a massive ruined castle amidst a beautiful landscape of mountains and hills lies the small village of Carcabuey. The imposing Iglesia de la Asunción dating from the early 17th century is easy to find here.

Alcalá la Real

From afar the mighty castle of Alcalá la Real, located 24km/15mi to the east, is already visible. Built from the 13th to the 15th century, the Castillo de la Mota still betokens the strength of Moorish Al-Kalaat be Zayde, which gave protection to many refugees from those areas which remained Moorish after the Christian conquest. The tower of the castle chapel provides a panoramic view of the surrounding olive groves. In the town itself are remains of the town fortifications, the church Santa María, in which the sculptor Martínez Montañés was baptized, a Plateresque fountain, and the classical town hall at the main square.

✳
Montefrío

Montefrío is situated 44km/27mi southeast in spectacular scenery **between two mountain spurs each crowned by a church**. Whereas the Iglesia de la Villa, designed by Diego de Siloé, stands on the ruins of the Moorish alcazaba, the Baroque Iglesia de San Antonio once belonged to a Franciscan monastery. In the town centre the classical

Montefrío, watched over by the Castillo de la Villa, is set in a unique hilly landscape.

rotunda of Iglesia de la Encarnación, vaulted by a grand dome, catches the eye.

8km/5mi further east towards Illora lies an extensive Neolithic site, **Peña de los Gitanos**, where megalithic tombs and cave paintings were discovered.

★ El Puerto de Santa María

C 8

Province: Cádiz
Population: 73,700

Altitude: 6m/19ft

18km/11mi north of ►Cádiz, where the Río Guadalete empties into the Atlantic, wine from the traditional sherry triangle Jerez de la Frontera – Sanlúcar de Barrameda – El Puerto is shipped from the harbour of El Puerto de Santa María. Yet sherry, and especially brandy, is also produced in the town itself at such traditional bodegas as Osborne and Terry.

Andalusia's sherry harbour The bodega Osborne has even given Spain a national symbol: the **oversized advertising bull**, standing conspicuously by main roads throughout the country. Thanks to the protests after some Madrid bureaucrats wanted to do away with the bull on the grounds that it was a blight on the countryside, it is now even protected as a national treasure. In summer Sevillians come to bathe at the beaches between here and ►Sanlúcar de Barrameda; for them El Puerto's old town with its 18th-century noble palaces and numerous tapas bars is just the right place for a change, which they also get at the casino.

> ! **Baedeker TIP**
>
> **Mariscos from Cartuchos**
> El Puerto is renowned for its excellent seafood. Many tapas bars are strung out along the Ribera del Marisco, and Romerijo 1 and 2, where freshly grilled, deep-fried, or boiled seafood (mariscos) is sold by weight and packed in paper bags (cartuchos) to take away, are among the best. The terrace outside is a good place to enjoy the seafood.

History El Puerto de Santa María was founded by the Greeks, and was called Portus Menesthei in the days when it was a Roman seaport. Alfonso X ousted the Moors in 1264. He arranged for the reconstruction of the port, which held great significance for the voyages to the new colonies. Columbus started on his second journey from here; men such as Juan de la Cosa, a helmsman of Columbus and first cartographer of the New World, and Amerigo Vespucci stayed here.

What to See in El Puerto de Santa María

Fuente de las Galeras At the place where the ferry Adriano III moors, sailors were supplied with water from the 18th-century fountain Fuente de las Galeras. Also called Vaporcito (»little steamship«, from a time in the 1950s when steamships did indeed ply these waters),, the ship is a novel way to travel from Cádiz to El Puerto – the trip takes 45 minutes across the Bahía – and the return is even more impressive, for a panoramic view of Cádiz can be seen from the sea here.

A little to the north at the Plaza del Castillo stands the crenellated Castillo de San Marcos, which the Moors built in the 13th century and was later the seat of the dukes of Medinaceli. Christopher Columbus and Juan de la Cosa took quarters here. Six towers and the curtain wall are still well preserved. The castle chapel was once part of the mosque, as remnants of the mihrâb, Kufic characters, and horseshoe arches attest. The shape of the former minaret is clearly visible in the octagonal main tower.

★
Castillo de San Marcos

🕐
Opening hours:
Mon, Wed, Fri
noon–2pm

▶ VISITING EL PUERTO DE SANTA MARÍA

INFORMATION (OFICINA DE TURISMO)

C. Luna, 22,
E-11500 El Puerto de Santa María
Tel. 956 54 24 13
Fax 956 54 22 46
www.elpuertosm.es

WHERE TO EAT

▶ Moderate

Los Portales
Ribera del Río, 13
Tel. 956 54 21 16
www.losportales.com
The best restaurant on the »Ribera del Marisco« offers excellent cuisine from the coast of Cádiz, i.e. fresh seafood.

Mesón del Asador
Misericordia, 2
Tel. 956 54 03 27
For everyone who doesn't feel like fish and seafood: meat galore, which guests can even grill at the table themselves.

WHERE TO STAY

▶ Mid-range

Monasterio de San Miguel
Larga, 27
Tel. 956 54 04 40
Fax 956 54 26 04, 150 rooms
Finest hotel in the town in a magnificent Baroque monastery at the centre.

▶ Budget

Los Cántaros
Curva, 6
Tel. 956 54 02 40
www.hotelloscantaros.com
39 rooms
A conversion done with loving care of the former women's prison at Plaza del Cárcel, one of El Puerto's nightlife hotspots – thus not always quiet.

EVENTS

Virgen del Carmen
Festival of Seafarers on 16 July

Virgen de los Milagros
Grape-harvest festival on 8 September

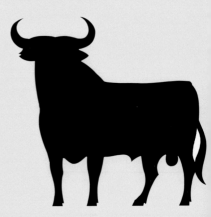

The bodega, whose logo is the Osborne bull, produces top quality sherry and brandy.

Fundación Rafael Alberti C. Santo Domingo leads northwest away from the castle to the birthplace of the **poet Rafael Alberti** (1902–1999), which has now been converted into a small museum (information on tours under tel. 956 85 07 11).

Iglesia Mayor Prioral It is not far from Alberti's birthplace to the Plaza de España, where the Gothic Iglesia Mayor Prioral Nuestra Señora de los Milagros stands. Its 13th-century façade has remained; the Plateresque south portal Puerta del Sol, which portrays the Virgin amongst saints between pairs of columns in a tympanum, is exceptionally beautiful. The church received its name from a Madonna dating from the 13th century that stands in the Capilla Mayor under a domed canopy. The Virgin Mary, the patron saint of the town, is said to have appeared to Alfonso X during the conquest.

Museo Municipal Opposite the church the town museum presents local history in the Casa Palacio Marquesa de la Candia (opening hours: Tue–Fri 10am–2pm, Sat and Sun 10.45am–2pm).

Plaza Isaac Peral East of the Iglesia Mayor lies Plaza Isaac Peral. It is the city's official centre, for the old town hall, Palacio Imblusqueta, stands here. On the way there look out for Casa de los Leones, which contains an exhibition devoted to Baroque art in El Puerto (opening hours: daily 10am–2pm and 6–8pm).

Naturally the bodegas of El Puerto can be toured. **Bodega Terry** is possibly the most beautiful. Visitors can not only sample **wine** and **brandy**, but also admire thoroughbred **Andalusian horses** and **magnificent carriages** (advance booking tel. 956 85 77 00). The best-known bodega is of course **Osborne**; sherry is produced in the winery at the town centre, brandy outside next to the N-IV (information: tel. 956 86 91 00 and 956 86 90 59 respectively; opening hours: Mon–Fri 10.30am–1pm, Sat 10.30am–12pm).

✴ Bodegas

⊙

Built in 1880 the bullring somewhat north of Osborne is **Spain's third-largest** after those in Madrid and Seville: it seats 15,000 aficionados (tours: Tue–Sun 11am–1.30pm and 6–7.30pm).

✴ Plaza de Toros

In the early 1990s the yacht harbour Puerto Sherry was developed beyond the trading port. 790 berths make it one of the largest in Andalusia. The attractive town beach Playa Santa Catalina adjoins it.

Puerto Sherry

Around El Puerto de Santa María

Those wishing to get from El Puerto to Rota, only a few miles westwards, have a long drive nevertheless, for the road curves around the huge area of the US naval and air-force base. It is worth the effort, for Rota is a very pleasant, uncrowded resort with long beaches lined with pines to the north, a pretty promenade, and a small marina. Advertising itself as a 21st-century holiday village, i.e. aiming to provide **environmentally friendly holiday accommodation**, **Costa Ballena** is being constructed on the coast to the north around an 18-hole golf course.

✴ Rota

El Rocío

Province: Huelva
Population: 784

Altitude: 36m/118ft

El Rocío on the northern edge of Coto de Doñana national park is Andalusia's most famous place of pilgrimage. The Romería del Rocío attracts tens of thousands at Pentecost every year (▶Baedeker Special p.362).

The Madonna venerated at the Romería del Rocío, carved out of wood in the 13th century, and decked with jewellery and a brocade cloak from the 18th century, is kept in the 1960s pilgrimage church. Brotherhood buildings surround the church; when a rider or horse and cart come around a corner, the town almost seems to be a scene from a Western. At its eastern and southeastern edges El Rocío also offers excellent opportunities for birdwatching in Coto de Doñana

Andalusia's most famous place of pilgrimage

THREE DAYS OF COMMOTION AND DEVOTION

On 362 days of the year, El Rocío is a dusty village of 800 souls with a curiously large plaza and a striking white church. But from Whit Saturday until Whit Monday, the most boisterous pilgrimage in Andalusia takes place here: the Romería del Rocío. It is so boisterous that even the Church observes the goings-on with a certain reserve.

Our Lady of the Morning Dew (Nuestra Señora del Rocío) is the object of veneration. She is also called La Paloma Blanca (White Dove) and Clavel de las Marismas (Carnation of Marismas). The morning dew is understood to be a **fertility symbol**. According to legend, a black Madonna figure was worshipped in this village in early Christian times. It had to be hidden after the invasion of the Moors and was forgotten over the centuries. In the 13th century, a hunter claimed to have found her again in a hollow tree in a wood called La Rocina. **King Alfonso X the Wise** had a chapel erected in 1725 that thereafter became a destination for pilgrims from all over Andalusia. The cult gained followers in the rest of Spain and since the 17th century brotherhoods (cofradías or hermand-

ades) have formed that make pilgrimages to the Madonna figure still to this day.

A merry atmosphere

On Whit Saturday, the pilgrims stream from all parts of the country to El Rocío in their hundreds of thousands. Most of them come by car, but the close to 80 traditionally-minded brotherhoods take several days to march, ride or drive there – with special permits – through the Sankácar de Barrameda National Park. The caballeros ride in their Sunday best, the señoras and señoritas in colourful flamenco dresses behind them on the horse's croup. They accompany the two-wheeled, festooned procession carts (carretas), pulled by donkeys or oxen. The pilgrims camp at night, partying and singing (and drinking) around the campfire on which they prepare their meals. Upon arrival, the brotherhood of Rocío greets its guests and a three-day folk festival begins, celebrated day and night with music, dance, sumptuous food and a lot of alcohol. Each brotherhood celebrates in a bar. The climax on Whit Saturday consists of mass and the procession in which the figure of the Virgin is carried around in a tumultuous parade by the brotherhood of Almonte – and only by them – to the accompaniment of the racket of firecrackers and musical instruments. The following day the pilgrims leave – leaving behind a mountain of trash, particularly all along their path through the national park.

(e.g. Observatorio del Madre de Rocío with an information centre); watchers can also go by car on the dirt road via Villamanrique de la Condesa to the observation point Cerrado Garrido (30km/20mi; the shorter route of 15km/9mi should be attempted with four wheel drive only!).

Matalascañas   Matalascañas lies 16km/10mi southeast of El Rocío. The artificial village, containing five large hotel complexes, offers every type of seaside recreational activity. The place is not attractive, but the beach is terrific.

▶ VISITING EL ROCÍO

INFORMATION (OFICINA DE TURISMO)
Avda. de la Canaliega, s/n
E-21750 El Rocío
Tel. and fax 959 44 38 08
www.rocio.com

WHERE TO EAT AND STAY
► Expensive
Aires de Doñana
Avenida Canaliega, 1
Situated on the edge of the national park, with a great view and good fish dishes.

► Budget
Puente del Rey
Avenida del Canaliega, s/n
Tel. 959 44 25 75
Fax 959 44 20 70

On the main road; large and elegant.

Toruño
Plaza del Acebuchal, 22
Tel. 959 44 23 23
Fax 959 44 23 38
Right on the edge of Coto de Doñana national park; some rooms are excellent for watching birds, quiet rooms, and restaurant with regional cuisine.

EVENT
Romería del Rocío
Tens of thousands of pilgrims regularly turn the tiny village into Andalusia's festival centre at Pentecost.

Ronder Ronda

Province: Málaga   **Altitude:** 723m/2372ft
Population: 33,800

Ronda is considered to be the cradle of modern bullfighting. It became a place of pilgrimage for bullfighting aficionados, amongst them celebrities such as Ernest Hemingway and Orson Welles. This in itself would not make Ronda an absolute must on a tour of Andalusia, but in addition the town has a fantastic setting.

The **Romero bullfighter dynasty** lived in Ronda. Francisco, José, Juan, and Pedro Romero were amongst the most renowned toreros of their time, and it was Pedro (1754–1839), who developed the rules of the Ronda school, and who still entered the arena aged 80. The Ronda school teaches bullfighting using the Capa, Muleta, and Espada, with which the torero or matador confronts the bull on foot and not on horseback, while not showing the least fear, and fearing shame more than the bull's attacks. Ronda is also reflected in literature: the archetype of **Prosper Merimée's Carmen**, epitome of the fiery-eyed temptress and immortalized in **Bizet's opera**, is said to have turned men's heads in the smugglers' hideout Ronda. Even authors less interested in bullfighting tarried in the town: **James Joyce** completed *Ulysses here;* **the sojourn of Rainer Maria Rilke** in Ronda has become breathtakingly on the brink of a rocky plateau that plunges down in rocky walls to the west, and is divided into two parts by the gorge of the Río Guadalevín (El Tajo), 40–90m/130–300ft wide and up to 160m/520ft deep. Ronda has spread over these two heights – the wonderful Moorish old town (La Ciudad) to the south, joined by three bridges with the new town (El Mercadillo) to the north.

Cradle of bullfighting in a breathtaking location

Ronda is one of the oldest towns in Spain. Iberians founded a settlement on the seemingly impregnable heights. They were succeeded by the Carthaginians, who were expelled by the Romans, who then founded their colony of Arunda. The dominion of the Moors lasted over 770 years; in the 11th century the town was seat of a taifa emir and called Madinat Runda. Not until 1485, after a week-long siege, did Ronda fall through treachery to the Catholic Monarchs, who subsequently founded the new town. In 1808 Ronda suffered heavy destruction during Napoleon's campaign. In the years following it grew into a stronghold of smugglers and highwaymen, who controlled the greater part of the illegal goods flowing from Gibraltar to the north. The activities of these malefactors, who found plenty of backing among local people, became so rampant that **in 1844 the Guardia Civil was founded especially to combat them.**

History

► VISITING RONDA

INFORMATION (OFICINA DE TURISMO)

Paseo de Blas Infante, E-29400 Ronda
Tel. 952 18 71 19
Fax 952 18 71 47
www.turismoderonda.es
www.ronda.net

WHERE TO EAT

► Expensive

④ *Tragabuches*
José Aparicio, 1
Tel. 952 19 02 91
www.tragabuches.com
The shooting star of the Ronda restaurant scene: imaginatively varied Andalusian cuisine.

Tragabuches (Gobblemouth) was a bullfighter and bandit.

Molino del Santo
Ronda Estación
Tel. 952 16 71 51
Small high-class country inn with creative local fare.

► Moderate

① *Don Miguel*
Plaza de España, 3 y 5
Tel. 952 87 10 90
www.dmiguel.com
The tables here are on the terrace, below Puente Nuevo and directly over the gorge – Andalusian cuisine served with a breathtaking view into the abyss.

③ *Pedro Romero*
Virgen de la Paz, 18
Tel. 952 87 11 10
Delicious local cooking in a restaurant obviously decorated by a bullfighting aficionado, incl. items from Rabo de Toro.

► Inexpensive

② *Patatín Patatán*
Borrego, 7
Popular, imaginatively decorated tapas bar.

WHERE TO STAY

► Mid-range

② *En Frente Arte*
Real, 40
Tel. 952 87 43 12
Fax 952 87 72 17
www.enfrentearte.com
Rooms decorated with antiques; pool and sauna.

③ *Parador de Ronda*
Plaza de España, s / n
Tel. 952 87 75 00
Fax 952 87 81 88
E-mail: ronda@parador.es

www.parador.es, 78 rooms
Modern hotel behind a historic
façade, centrally located directly above
the Tajo gorge and in the vicinity of
the bullring.

⑤ *San Gabriel*
C. José M. Holgado, 19
Tel. 952 19 03 92
www.sangabriel.com
Nicely furnished hotel in the old part
of town.

► **Budget**
① *La Alavero de los Baños*
Hoyo san Miguel
Tel. / fax 952 87 91 43
www.Andalusia.com/alavera
E-mail: alavera@telefonica.net, 10
rooms
A new, cosy Andalusian country
house in an unusual place; not high
up above the gorge, but down below
near the Moorish baths, which also
inspired the interior decorating. Fantastic evenings on the terrace are
guaranteed.

Virgen de los Reyes
Lorenzo Borrego, 13
Tel. 952 87 11 40, 52 rooms
Respectable, well-managed, reason-
ably priced accommodations in the
new town.

PLAZA DE TOROS
C. Virgen de la Paz
Tel. 952 87 41 32
Opening hours: daily 10am–6pm
The roots of bullfighting are to be
found here. It is Spain's oldest arena.
The Corrida Goyescas in September
with costumes from the time of Goya
is a truly special event.

Baedeker recommendation

► **Mid-range**
④ *Reina Victoria*
Jerez, 25
Tel. 952 87 12 40
Fax 952 87 10 75, 89 rooms

The irresistible charm of the early 20th
century emanates from every corner. Rainer
Maria Rilke spent the winter of 1912/1913
in room 208 (today the memorial room);
fantastic terrace directly above the precipice
– magnificent view. It isn't necessary to stay
the night in Reina Victoria to enjoy the view
that Rilke had; the restaurant and bar
terraces offer it too – unforgettable on a
summer evening.

EVENTS
Fiestas de Pedro Romero
The era of the Romero brothers
comes to life annually around 12
September when Ronda celebrates the
festival named for Pedro Romero.
Bullfighting isn't for everyone, but the
grand parade, flamenco and the
awarding of prizes for the carriages
can be enjoyed by all.

✷ ✷ El Tajo

The first thing every visitor to Ronda wants to do is have a look down into Río Guadalevín gorge. It was created by a tectonic fissure through which the river carves it course over several cascades. The name Tajo has nothing to do with the central Iberian river of the same name, it means to cut or slice or a drastic slash, and the gorge actually does seem to have been hacked out of the rock with an axe.

✷ ✷
Puente Nuevo

Of the total of the three bridges, Puente Nuevo offers the most beautiful and impressive view. The bridge has three arches, is 70m/230ft long, and over 150m/490ft high and was built between 1751 und 1793 by José Martín de Aldehuela, who died from a fall from this same bridge – supposedly he committed suicide because he believed he would never be able to construct anything so perfect again. The view looking down from the bridge, with swallows and crows

Ronda Plan

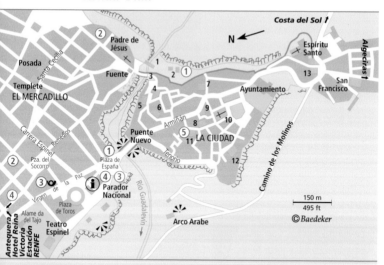

© Baedeker

1 Puente Árabe	10 Santa María la Mayor	**Where to stay**
2 Baños Árabes	11 Casa del Marqués	① La Alavera de los Baños
3 Puente Romano	de Moctezuma	② En Frente Arte
4 Casa del Marqués	12 Palacio de Mondragón	③ Parador de Ronda
de Salvatierra	13 Puerta de Almocábar	④ Reina Victoria
5 Casa del Rey Moro		⑤ San Gabriel
6 Museo Lara	**Where to eat**	
7 Museo Histórico Popular	① Don Miguel	
del Bandolero	② Patatín Patatán	
8 Museo Peinado	③ Pedro Romero	
9 Minarett	④ Tragabuches	

High above El Tajo gorge sits the former smugglers nest Ronda, where bullfighting has its roots.

swooshing underneath it, is truly breathtaking. Above the middle arch, a door and a gallery can be seen that used to be the entrance to the **former prison**, which now houses an exhibition explaining the history of the structure (opening hours: Mon–Fri 10am–6pm, Sat, Sun until 3pm).

The daring construction can really only be appreciated from below, however. There are three ways down from the old town. The shortest leads from Plaza del Campanillo a little right of the Casa de Mondragón down the slope of the town's rock-face in steep bends and after some distance meets the main road, Camino de los Molinos. The longer version begins on the southern end of the old town to the right of Puerta de Almocóbar and leads to the dilapidated mills on the riverbank. A very steep path branches off to the right where both routes meet leading to the Moorish gate Arco árabe (Arco del Cristo), the remains of the city fortifications. Here are the best views of the waterfalls, the Puente Nuevo and the houses perched on the rock face. The descent to the **lower bridges** and the Arab baths is less strenuous. Turning left on the old town side eventually leads to Puerta de Felipe V, a city gate built in 1742, from which the well-preserved city wall is visible all the way to the Espíritu Santo church. Behind that, the Puente Viejo (Puente de la Mina; 1616) spans the river with a 30m/98ft-high horseshoe arch. From the bridge there is a view down onto Puente de San Miguel, which was quite possibly originally constructed by the Romans. Around 1300, the Moorish rulers had a large bath built. It was divided into three rooms by horseshoe arches (opening hours: Mon–Fri 10am–6pm, Sat, Sun 10am–3pm).

Down into the gorge

★
◀ Baños árabes

THE CORRIDA –
LAST BASTION OF MACHISMO

What is for many Europeans and meanwhile even for Spaniards nothing more than a bloody spectacle, is for aficionados, the bullfighting connoisseurs and enthusiasts, great art. They speak of »arte de lidiar«, the art of enchanting the bull, standing up to it in battle and not just physically defeating it.

Giving up bullfighting, however, would mean for the Spanish the loss of a part of a deeply rooted culture, yes, even a part of their own identity. For many, the corrida de toros is one of the last approximations to the **primordial battle** between man and beast. A battle in which there can be more than just one loser and in which the animal is accorded more dignity than in many other expressions of culture in our time.

The classic bullfighting region is Andalusia, even though matadors face bulls in rings in all major cities in Spain, in some countries in Latin America and even in southern France. Madrid may have the largest **Plaza de Toros**, but Ronda in Andalusia has the oldest.

So it is no wonder that the most celebrated toreros of all time were mostly Andalusians: Manolete, Lagartijo, Joselito, Paquirri and El Cordobés, some of whom lost their lives in the arena.

The **»toros bravos«**, half-wild beasts bursting with strength, have been raised for generations predominantly by Andalusian dynasties of breeders.

Fitting before the fight

Practising the grand paso

Their great latifundia lie in the provinces of Seville, Huelva and Cádiz, and are still the absolute epitome of old señorito splendour.

Origins

The historical traces of the battle between man and bull are ancient, lost in prehistoric times in a variety of cultures.

Until the rules valid today crystallized in the course of the 18th century, there were many forms of the fight. During and after the **Reconquista**, it was primarily the upper class that took on the bull at court fiestas and during shows of combat on horseback. During the course of the 18th century, the Bourbons began to tolerate martial sports at court less and less – so it became the servants of the aristocrats who fought the bulls on foot before an audience, thus founding the present-day form of bullfighting.

At the same time, the systematic breeding of »toros bravos« began in the vicinity of the village of Utrera, and today the pedigrees of some of the most famous animals reach back to that time.

Goya captured the historic moment in the 18th century when the equestrian bullfighters were pushed into the background and replaced by the torero a pie, the bullfighter on foot, in his cycle of etchings »Tauromaquia«.

Drama in three acts

Generally, bullfighting takes place during feria or other local fiestas. Then, from Easter until the end of autumn the aficionados gather in their thousands late in the afternoon

in the circular Plaza de Toros. Those who can, avoid the almost unbearable heat of the »sol seats« situated on the sunny side and procure a much more expensive ticket for the shady »sombra side«.

There are almost always **three toreros or matadors**, who have six animals to kill each afternoon with their cuadrilla, the assistants.

The ceremony begins with the vibrantly colourful entrance of all participants to the sounds of a stirring paso doble. The uniforms (so-called **suits of light**), embroidered all over with sequins and spangles, are a relic from the aristocratic era of bullfighting.

Before the bull can be killed, it must first be goaded and weakened by the **cuadrilla**. It is brought to a state of excitement by the flashy-coloured, wide capa so that its energy is shown to the public and the torero can assess its strengths and weaknesses. After this first contact between matador and toro, the **picadors** appear on horseback. While the bull attacks his protectively padded horse, the picador tries to weaken it by jabbing it in the neck with a lance. Next appear the **banderillas**. With quick, prancing steps, they run up to the animal head on and at the last moment stick in it a pair of banderillas, sharp barbed sticks decorated with tinsel. Only after three banderillas have been placed does the matador again appear and begin the climax and end of the fight. The skill of the man must master the brute force of the 500 kilo/1,100 pound animal.

The torero must captivate the bull with his scarlet cape, the muleta, and lead it past his body. In Andalusia it is said, »a bull can only be deceived once – the second time it seeks the body«. Each of the dancing movements (»paso«) has its own name in bullfighting terminology.

Only when the will of the bull has been broken and the torero dares to turn his back to the bull to receive acclaim from the audience may the **death-thrust** be dealt. The bull must sink its head so that the sword, called an estoque, can pierce a certain area of its neck and hit the heart. Matadors who miss this spot are mercilessly booed and ridiculed by the public.

Archaic survival

In his book *Death in the Afternoon*, **Ernest Hemingway**, himself an aficionado, described like no other the torero's fear of and respect for the bull, the playful ease as well as the deep sadness of this ritual act of killing in the ring.

Courage, contempt of death and physical strength, as well as aesthetics and, in some movements, eroticism, are combined in a single figure, the torero, in the hot afternoon hours of a corrida.

He is the very personification of the proverbial Andalusian machismo, which, however, essentially already belongs to the past.

The matadora

It makes no difference that even a woman – **Cristina Sánchez** – has succeeded in becoming a recognized matadora. But in the end, she fell victim to machismo because despite her performances in the most important rings in Spain, the male toreros no longer wanted to appear with her. After her last fight on 12 October 1999 in Las Ventas in Madrid, she withdrew at the age of 27.

✳ La Ciudad (Old Town)

Museo Lara
🕐 Opening hours: Daily 11am–7pm

Palacio de los Condes de las Islas Batanas is only a short way to the left from Puente Nuevo along C. Armiñan. Here the Museo Lara is housed, **Spain's largest private collection**. It offers a huge range of exhibits, including weapons, folk art, archaeological items and particularly beautiful clocks.

✳ Museo del Bandolero
🕐

Almost at the end of the street there are two museums, the Museo de Caza (hunting museum) and the much more interesting Museo del Bandolero, which very vividly portrays banditry in and around Ronda and the **careers of famous bandits** through weapons, wanted posters and dolls. One of the most famous was Diego Mateos, known as *el bandido generoso,* who was hanged and then quartered in 1781 (opening hours: 10.30am–6.30pm).

Plaza de la Duquesa de Parcent

C. Armiñan leads into Plaza de la Duquesa de Parcent, where the church of **Santa María la Mayor** (16th century) stands. It was originally a mosque and still has four Moorish domes. The bell tower stands on the foundation walls of the former minaret. The three-storey portico is unusual. The interior holds Renaissance pews, as well as the remains of the Moorish mihrâb left in the entrance area. The very beautiful arcade of the town hall in which the Infante Juan lived after the conquest of Ronda occupies the east side of the plaza.

Barrio de San Francisco

A side-trip can be made from the plaza to the southernmost tip of Ronda, the barrio de San Francisco. Parts of the town's fortifications have survived the passing of time here, above all the Moorish Puerta de Almocábar, which for centuries was the main entrance to the town and was enlarged by an additional gate under Charles V. The remains of the wall of the Alcazaba destroyed in 1808 run from both gates. The Catholic Monarchs had the fortress-like church of Espíritu Santo built after they had taken Ronda.

✳ Palacio de Mondragón

Back at Plaza de la Duquesa de Parcent, the alley left of Santa María leads around it to the 16th-century Palacio de Mondragón, which was built over the precipice. It has a beautiful Renaissance portal with a typical Moorish gemel window above, two very beautiful Mudéjar inner courts and a terrace from where a magnificent view can be enjoyed. The palace, in which among others the Catholic Monarchs resided, today houses the Museo Municipal for the region's history, folklore and natural history (opening hours: Mon–Fri 10am–6pm, Sat, Sun until 3pm).

Casa del Marqués de Moctezuma

The way back to the main road leads past two more houses of the nobility. First, the Renaissance palace Casa del Marqués de Moctezuma, which, despite its name, has no connection with the Aztec ruler and is where Joseph Bonaparte had his quarters in 1810 – today it is

Bullfighter Cayetano Ordóñez in front of the bullring of Ronda

a museum for the Ronda-born painter Joaquín Peinado (1898–1975); diagonally opposite is the **Casa del Gigante** dating from the 14th century, Ronda's most original Arab palace with all the appropriate decorative elements and a beautiful patio.

On the main road back toward Puente Nuevo, Cuesta Santo Domingo branches off to the right before the bridge. Here stands Casa del Rey Moro, which has a terrace garden and an observation tower. Its name is deceptive because the present building was constructed in the 18th century. An Arab palace most likely stood here prior to that, however, and there remains a stone stairway dating back to that time with 365 steps leading from the river up to the house on which Christian slaves had to heave water upwards in bucket chains.

✳
Casa del Rey Moro

◷
Opening hours:
Daily 10am–7pm

A little way down the alley, Palacio del Marqués de Salvatierra can easily be recognized by the unusual decoration on its balcony above the portal. The gable is supported by two naked Indian figures, a reminder of the Spanish conquests in Central and South America. The lower bridges are further on past the palace. The chapel of Templete Virgen de los Dolores from 1734 can be found in the east part of the old town. This was Ronda's place of execution, as shown by the mythical creature with a noose around its neck.

✳
Palacio del Marqués de Salvatierra

Mercadillo (new town)

Plaza de España opens up on the other side of Puente Nuevo, dominated by the parador – no historic building this, but a totally new structure. The new town is where everyone goes to shop or for a night out. The main shopping street is the pedestrian zoned Carrera de Espinel, which leads into the C. Virgen de la Paz.

Across from the junction is the attraction for bullfighting enthusiasts, Plaza de Toros. Built in 1785, it is **Spain's oldest bullfighting arena** and the place where the Romeros performed. Even visitors who have no liking for this spectacle should tour the arena: it is architecturally interesting due to its two-storey spectator ring, 66m/217ft in diameter. The **bullfighting museum** set up in the rooms of the arena contains a lot of different memorabilia of famous bullfighters, above all the Romeros and the Ordoñez, as well as photos of prominent visitors like Hemingway and Orson Welles.

🕐 Opening hours:
Mon–Sun
summer
10am–8pm;
winter
10am–6pm

✶ ✶
Observation walkways

The observation walkways enclosed by railings jutting out over the cliffs that run behind the arena offer a spectacular view of the river canyon carved out almost 200m/650ft deep below and beyond the Vega to the ▶Sierra de Grazalema mountain range. In Alameda del Tajo park there is a memorial to Pedro Romero.

Hotel Reina Victoria

A little way past the La Merced Church is the Reina Victoria Hotel where Rainer Maria Rilke stayed in room 208 from 1912 to 1913. It is now a small museum and can be viewed upon request. Since 1966 there a bronze statue has commemorated the writer in the garden. The hotel is almost legendary as a fashionable place to stay, especially among British guests.

Around Ronda

✶
Serranía de Ronda

The barren rocky mountains of the Serranía de Ronda stretch to the south-east of Ronda. Iberian ibex and royal eagles still live in Sierra de las Nieves , an area placed under nature conservation that is only accessible over a poor road. The pinsapotanne, an ancient type of conifer, is native here. Take an excursion and discover picturesque villages like Yunquera or Tolox.

✶
Cueva de la Pileta

🕐 Opening hours:
Daily 10am–1pm,
4pm–5pm
reservations
tel. 952 16 73 43

After driving 12km/7.5mi in the direction of ▶Arcos de la Frontera on the A-473 through attractive landscape, there is a turn-off to the left near La Quinta that leads past Montejaque to Benaoján (11km/7mi); from there it is another 4km/2.5mi on a small, narrow mountain road to Cueva de la Pileta, a limestone cave with stalactites and stalagmites. When this cave was discovered in 1911 it was found to contain, along with bones and tools, realistic **Stone Age paintings of animals** similar to those found in Altamira, Cantabria, but older. The oldest drawing, a depiction of a horse, is about 25,000 years old ▶photo. p.35). Visitors should be prepared for waiting times, as only groups are allowed to enter, usually about one per hour of up to 25 persons. The tour through the cave, which has a constant temperature of 15°C/59°F and 100% humidity, is in an adventure. All visitors receive petroleum lamps in order to light their own way. Further caves in the vicinity are Cueva del Hundidero, where Río Guadiaro River disappears, and Cueva del Gato, where it reappears.

The castle and church of La Encarnación dominate Olvera.

Ronda la Vieja (12km/7.5mi north-east of town) dates back to Roman Acinipo, from which remains of the theatre still exist.

Ronda la Vieja

Take time to look at Olvera when on the way to ►Arcos de la Frontera. It is a white village in a beautiful setting dominated by the 16th-century La Encarnación church and the castle rock with the 12th-century castillo as a counterpoint.

★
Olvera

It is another 15km/9mi south-west from Olvera to Setenil, a little town in a fantastic setting in a valley that has been carved out by a river. It is dominated by a Gothic church. Far more interesting, however, are the numerous homes built into the rocks.

★
Setenil

►p.415

Sierra de
Grazalema

★ Sanlúcar de Barrameda

C 8

Province: Cádiz   **Altitude :** 0–30m/100ft
Population: 61,100

Sanlúcar is the home of the bone-dry Manzanilla wine that comes exclusively from the local bodegas and can hold its own against its much better-known rival from Jerez de la Frontera, sherry. But Sanlúcar is also famous nation-wide for its seafood specialties – which, in turn, go wonderfully with Manzanilla.

History Taken from the Moors in 1246, Sanlúcar de Barrameda was the seat of the dukes of Medina Sidonia and the port for Seville. It is from here that **Christopher Columbus** embarked on his third voyage to America in May 1498. **Hernán Cortes** also sailed from here to the New World and finally, coming from Seville, **Fernão de Magalhães** (Magellan) set off in 1519 from Sanlúcar on the first circumnavigation of the globe.

What to See in Sanlúcar de Barrameda

Orientation Sanlúcar consists of three parts. The barrio alto, the historic old town, lies on the heights, while the Bajo de Guía, the fishing and restaurant quarter, is below on the waterfront. The barrio bajo (lower town), with Calle Ancha and Calle de San Juan meeting at Plaza del Cabildo, forms a hinge between the two.

This is where the tourists and locals flock to the bars in the evenings. There is a market every morning on the adjoining Plaza de San Roque.

From Plaza de San Roque – passing on the left-hand side the small church of the Holy Trinity with its magnificent 15th-century artesonado ceiling – climb up C. Bretones to the old town hill, passing by the so-called **Covachas**, part of the late Gothic façade of the palace of the dukes of Medina Sidonia, consisting of ten arches adorned with mythical creatures.

> ### ! Baedeker TIP
>
> **Manzanilla wine-tasting**
>
> Manzanilla can be sampled at Bodega Antonio Barbadillo with its Manzanilla museum next to the castle (Luís de Eguilaz, 11; tours Mon–Sat noon and 1pm, tel. 956 38 55 00) and at Pedro Romero (C. Trasbolsa, 60; tours Mon–Sat at noon).

✳ Nuestra Señora de la O On the top to the right of C. Caballeros is the Palacio de Orléans y Borbón, now the town hall, which was constructed in the middle of the 19th century for Antonio de Orléans and his wife. Heading left to the Church of Nuestra Señora de la O founded by Isabel de Cerda in 1360. It appears nondescript on the outside, except for its magnificent Mudéjar portal, but this is a hint of the richness of the decoration inside. The tile-covered interior is richly decorated with plaster work and has a splendid panelled Renaissance ceiling. The Capilla Mayor, in which the high altar by Esquivel (18th century) stands, is no less beautifully painted. The Capilla del Sagrario to the left with its open-work dome also has magnificent paintings.

Palacio de los Duques de Medina Sidonia ⏲ The Palacio de los Duques de Medina Sidonia adjacent to the church is occupied today by the **Red Duchess** of ▶Medina Sidonia, Dña. Luisa Isabel Álvarez de Toledo y Maura, Duchess of Medina-Sidonia. It was begun in the 16th and extended in the 17th century (open to the public: Sun 10.30am–1.30pm, tel. 956 36 01 61).

⏵ VISITING SANLÚCAR DE BARRAMEDA

INFORMATION (OFICINA DE TURISMO)

Calzada del Ejército, s/n, E-11540
Sanlúcar de Barrameda
Tel. 956 36 61 10
Fax 956 36 61 32
www.aytosanlucar.org

WHERE TO EAT

► Expensive
Mirador de Doñana
Bajo de Guía
Tel. 956 36 42 05
One of the best addresses in the town.
Fish and seafood are served on the
terrace with a wonderful view of the
Guadalquivir and the national park
on the opposite bank.

► Inexpensive
Casa Balbino
Plaza del Cabildo, 11
Tel. 956 36 05 13
The fantastic selection of tapas here
will win you over (the tortillas with
crabs are delicious) and the many
varieties of Manzanilla – a must in
Sanlúcar.

Casa Juan
Bajo de Guía
Tel. 956 36 26 95
Low-cost option among the restau-
rants that line the Guadalquivir.

WHERE TO STAY

► Mid-range
Cruz del Mar
In Chipiona
Avda. de Sanlúcar, 1
Tel. 956 37 11 00
Fax 956 37 13 64
www.hotelcruzdelmar.com, 67 rooms
The no. 1 of the riverfront hotels in
the bathing resort, yet not overpriced.
Try to get a room in the annex; nice
inner courtyard with pool.

► Budget
Tartaneros
Tartaneros, 8
Tel. 956 38 53 78
Fax 956 38 59 94, 22 rooms
Charming art nouveau gem in the
town centre.

Posada del Palacio
Caballeros, 11
Tel. 956 36 48 40
Fax 956 36 50 60
www.posadadelpalacio.com, 11 rooms
Posada means inn, but the name is
deceptive; the hotel in the town centre
is situated in a 17th century nobleman's palace.

La Española
Isaac Peral, 4
Tel. 956 37 37 71
Fax 956 37 30 35, 21 rooms
Good, simple hotel directly on the
riverfront promenade.

EVENTS

Feria de la Manzanilla
End of May

Romería del Rocío
At Whitsun, the pilgrims cross the
Guadalquivir from here (see Baedeker
Special p.362).

Carreras de Caballo de Sanlúcar de Barrameda
This is a must-see – at least for anyone in Andalusia in August. These horse races held on the beaches of Sanlúcar are among the most spectacular events in Andalusia. The exact times are determined by the changing tides, so ask in the tourist office or check the internet at www.carrerasanlucar.com.

Exaltación al Río Guadalquivir
Boat procession in praise of the river.

»Thunder on the beach« during the horse races at Sanlúcar

Castillo de Santiago
Go past Bodegas Antonio Barbadillo to Castillo de Santiago (13th–15th century), the castle of the dukes of Medina Sidonia that towers above the old town. The castle commands a marvellous view of the old town and the Coto de Doñana National Park on the opposite bank of the Guadalquivir.

Barrio bajo
There are two further interesting churches in C. de Santo Domingo in barrio bajo: Santo Domingo with the tomb of Medina Sidonia (17th century) and San Francisco, whose façade was donated by the English king Henry VIII.

Bajo de Guía
The lower town of Sanlúcar de Barrameda, called Bajo de Guía, stretches along the mouth of the river. There is a row of fish restaurants here. They procure their wares from the **fish auction** that is held workdays around 5pm 4km/2.5mi up the river at the port of Bonanza – well worth a visit. Columbus and Magellan both set sail from there.

Bajo de Guía is also a good place for an excursion by boat into ►Coto de Doñana national park. First obtain information in the older visitor centre or in the newer Fábrica de Hielo (with a large exhibition on nature and history, films, and an observation terrace), and then cruise along the opposite bank with the Real Fernando.

This cruise lasts about four hours and includes two stops on land. Tickets in the Fábrica de Hielo (departures: June–Sept. daily 10am and 5pm; April, May and Oct. daily 10am and 4pm; Nov. daily 10am; tel. 956 36 38 13).

Ending the day on a relaxed note in one of the bars in Barrio bajo.

Around Sanlúcar de Barrameda

Wide and fine beaches for swimming stretch to the south-west all the way to the seaside resort of **Chipiona**, which is very popular with the Andalusians. Full of action on the weekends, rather tranquil during the week, Chipiona has been able to avoid the ugly concrete developments of the Costa del Sol until now, making do with lower blocks of flats, though they are constantly multiplying. Waves from the Atlantic roll in on the most beautiful beach, Playa de Regla, which stretches south of the lighthouse. Activities on the beach can be spoiled, however, by the constantly whistling wind and the fine sand. At the end of the beach, almost on the edge of the breakers, stands the church of Santuario Nuestra Señora de la Regla, which enshrines a miraculous image venerated by seamen. Plaza de España with the tile-adorned church of Nuestra Señora de la O in the heart of Chipiona turns out to be a cosy little place. There is even a castle. The inhabitants of Chipiona are very proud of their lighthouse; built in 1867. With a height of 69m/226ft, it is **Spain's tallest lighthouse**.

! *Baedeker* TIP

Moonlight horseback riding

An unforgettable holiday experience can be had on the edge of the Coto de Doñana national park – horseback riding by moonlight! Alargavista organizes it (Calle Ancha, 20, tel. 617 97 88 13, www.alargavista.com).

Seville

C/D 7

Province: Seville
Population: 701,100

Altitude: 8m/26ft

Seville is one of the hottest places on the European mainland. No wonder that the city wakes up only when elsewhere everybody is already in bed – the nights in Seville, making the rounds of the bars, one after the other, are an experience. Although there is by no means dancing and singing everywhere, as the cliché would have it, Seville is still undoubtedly the most Andalusian of all cities. This is still apparent in the old and traditional quarters.

Even if Seville cannot match the Moorish heritage of ► Córdoba or ► Granada, the synthesis of Muslim and Christian architecture was most convincing here, as can be seen and admired in the cathedrals and Alcázar built in Moorish style for the Christian king Pedro the Cruel.

Capital of Andalusia

Highlights *Seville*

Semana Santa
During Holy Week Seville is in a state of high excitement; lamentation followed by celebration. Nowhere in Spain is Semana Santa celebrated as magnificently.
► page 386

Cathedral
Nothing but superlatives – the largest church worldwide after St Peter's in Rome and St Paul's cathedral in London, the world's largest Gothic church with the world's largest altar, plus a marvellous view of the rooftops of Seville from the Giralda.
► page 394

Real Alcázar
The royal palace is a jewel of Mudéjar inner courts, rooms and Arabian gardens.
► page 397

Barrio de Santa Cruz
Picturesque barrio with small plazas and little white houses adorned with flowers.
► page 401

Museo de Bellas Artes
One of Spain's best art collections.
► page 403

Casa de Pilatos
Seville's most beautiful city palace next to the Alcázar
► page 404

Plaza de Toros de la Maestranza
Famous bullfighting ring with world-class corridas.
► page 406

Torre del Oro
Tower with battlements, built in the 13th century to protect the harbour; today it houses the oceanography museum.
► page 408

← *Plaza de España – structural quotes from Spanish architectural history*

▶ VISITING SEVILLE

INFORMATION (OFICINA DE TURISMO)

Costuero de la Reina,
Paseo de las Delicias, 9
E-41012 Seville
Tel. 954 23 44 65
Fax 954 27 30 78

Plaza del Triunfo 1-3
E-41004 Seville
Tel. 954 50 10 01
Fax 954 50 08 98

Avda. de la Constitución 21b
E-41014 Seville
Tel. 954 22 14 04
Fax 954 22 97 53

Additional offices at the airport, Santa Justa station and in the Royal Pavillon on Cartuja Island.
www.turismo.Seville.org,
www.Seville.org
www.Seville-es.com

WHERE TO EAT

▶ Expensive

④ *Casa Robles*
Alvarez Quintero, 58
Tel. 954 56 32 72
Sample top-quality Sevillian cuisine in one of the best restaurants in the city. If it is too expensive for a full meal, try the excellent tapas.

⑤ *Egaña Oriza*
San Fernando, 41
High-class ambience, finest Spanish cooking served in a former palace.

⑦ *La Albahaca*
Plaza Santa Cruz, 12
Tel. 954 22 07 14
Top-class restaurant in the middle of the barrio, very stylish furnishings.

▶ Moderate

② *Ancora*
Virgen de las Huertas, s/n
Tel. 954 27 38 49
Well-frequented fish restaurant in Triana barrio.

③ *Bar Giralda*
Mateos Gago, 1
Elegant bar with award-winning tapas.

⑨ *Taberna del Alabardero*
Zaragoza, 20
Tel. 954 50 27 21
www.tabernadelalabardero.com
Famous for having elevated Sevillian dishes into the Olympus of sophisticated cuisine – in an old city palace.

▶ Inexpensive

① *Albariza*
Betis, 6
Tel. 954 33 20 16
Authentic Sevillian cuisine: revueltos, tortillas and frituras al Andaluz.

⑥ *El Rinconcillo*
Gerona, 40–42
Bar with a long tradition: since 1670 – meet here at the bar and chat under a ceiling of smoked hams.

⑧ *Sol y Sombra*
Castilla, 151
The tapas bar is one of the best in the city.

WHERE TO STAY

▶ Luxury

① *Alfonso XIII*
San Fernando, 2
Tel. 954 91 70 00
Fax 954 91 70 99
www.alfonsoxiii.com, 146 rooms
Grand hotel of the luxury class, built

for the World Fair of 1929, flagship of the Andalusian hotel industry and very pricey. This is where the Spanish king and queen stay when they visit Seville; other crowned heads are also among the guests.

► Mid-range

③ *Las Casas de la Judería*
C.jón de Dos Hermanas, 7
Tel. 954 41 51 50
Fax 954 42 21 70, 95 rooms
Almost a district in its own right in the Barrio de Santa Cruz; this enchanting city hotel has stylish rooms and fountain courtyards. It is comprised of several of the Duque de Béjar's houses, connected to each other by patios and arcaded walkways.

► Budget

② *Europa*
Jimios, 5
Tel. 954 21 43 05, fax 954 21 00 16
www.hoteleuropaSeville.com
16 rooms
Stylish 18th-century house between Plaza Nueva and the cathedral.

④ *Patio de la Cartuja*
Lumbreras, 8
Tel. 954 90 02 00
Fax 954 90 20 56, 56 apartments.
A small pearl away from all the grand luxury at the north end of Alameda de Hércules; classy, comfortably and simply furnished, spacious apartments grouped around a central patio.

⑤ *San Gil*
Parras, 28
Tel. 954 90 68 11
Fax 954 90 69 39
Colourful mosaics decorate the interior and court; vista of the old city from the pool on the roof terrace.

⑥ *Simón*
García de Vinuesa, 19
Tel. 954 22 66 60
Fax 954 56 22 41
www.hotelsimonSeville.com, 29 rooms
Traditional, house with an intimate atmosphere not far from the cathedral.

⑦ *Los Seises*
Segovias, 6
Tel. 954 22 94 95
Fax 954 22 43 34
www.hotellosseises.com, 43 rooms
Architectural gem from the 16th century with tasteful interior in close vicinity to the cathedral. The Giralda can be seen from the roof terrace.

SHOPPING

Seville's main shopping area lies between Plaza Nueva and Plaza San Francisco and to the north of Plaza del Duque de la Victoria. The major shopping drag of the city is Calle Sierpes, offering fashion (including the internationally known fashion designer duo Vittorio y Lucchino), Spanish textiles (including scarves and shawls at Molina, Sierpes 11, or lace at Artesanía Textil in no. 70, Sevillarte including fans and arts and crafts), jewellery and also cakes and pastries. There are flea markets on Sundays on Alameda de Hércules and every Thursday not far from there in C. Feria. A visit to the Triana barrio is worthwhile for anyone looking for pottery; take a look in C. San Jorge

Posh – Vittorio y Lucchino

(try Ceramica Santa Ana in no. 31) and around Plaza Callao.

Agua de Seville
C. Rodrigo Caro, 3
Chic – perfume with the scent of orange blossom and other fine fragrances.

Daniela
C. San Eloy, 25
If you have a fancy for beautiful shoes, this is the place!

PLAZA DE TOROS DE LA MAESTRANZA
Paseo de Cristóbal Colón, 12
Advanced ticket sale, tel. 954 50 13 82
Fax 954 50 15 59
Experience world-class corridas with famous matadors in June and July. Bullfighting season ends here on 12 October with the Feria de San Miguel.

EVENTS
Semana Santa
Of all the Semana Santa (Holy Week) celebrations, those in Seville are the most impressive. The processions of the brotherhoods (cofradias or hermandades) begin on Palm Sunday in the individual barrios. Lavishly adorned religious shrines (pasos) are carried through the streets. This demands a great deal of hard work from the bearers (costaleros) – the pasos weigh several hundred kilos and the lanes are narrow. The penitents (Nazarenos or Penitentes) cloaked in robes and conical hoods are also part of every procession. The main procession with all 58 brotherhoods united takes place from the night before Good Friday through to Good Friday morning and ends in the cathedral.

Feria de Abril
The Feria de Abril (begins in the second week after Easter) is Seville's major six-day secular festival. Families, friends and organizations put up tents and pavilions on the vast festival grounds in Los Remedios quarter and privately celebrate with singing and dancing into the small hours of the morning. The magnificent parades of horse riders and carriages held daily are, on the other hand, public, and naturally so are also the daily bullfights in the Arena La Maestranza.

This wealth of superb artistic and cultural monuments from all eras of the city's lively history certainly justifies the old saying »Quien no ha visto Sevilla, no ha visto maravilla« – »He who has not seen Seville, has not seen a miracle«. Seville is the birthplace of the painters **Diego Velázquez** (1599–1660) and **Bartolomé Esteban Murillo** (1617–1682). Plaques commemorate scenes from Cervantes' works. **Seville is well-known as a backdrop for operas:** Mozart's *Don Juan* and *The Marriage of Figaro* as well as Bizet's *Carmen* were set here, and several streets vie for recognition as the site of the shop in Rossini's *The Barber of Seville.* Here is where the Río Guadalquivir reaches the Andalusian lowlands and flows through this, the capital of Andalusia and Spain's fourth-largest city. Although almost 100km/60mi from the sea, the tide is still noticeable here, allowing large sea-going vessels to enter the harbour outside the city; for Seville has another side: an industrial city that produces foodstuffs, textiles and metal products. Yet another aspect is that of a city with over a million people surrounded by a belt of, to some extent, extremely poor areas – the unemployment rate is high, bringing petty crime in its wake, as well. The hosting of the world fair EXPO '92 failed to change very much in this regard. The infrastructure was considerably improved – Seville is now connected to Madrid by a continuous motorway and by the high-speed railway AVE that arrives at the new Santa Justa station – and the cityscape has changed, for one thing through the exhibition grounds, for another through new bridges, one of which, the elegant **La Barqueta**, has become the **new symbol of the city**. However, the hoped-for sustained economic upswing failed to materialize. The closing of the EXPO left 22,000 persons unemployed. Subsequent jobs never appeared, mainly because the envisioned technological park was not a success. All that remains is the Isla Mágica amusement park on the old Expo grounds that opened in 1997.

> ! **Baedeker** TIP
>
> **Not too late!**
> Anyone who wants to be in Seville for the Semana Santa or the Feria de Abril should book well in advance. And don't besurprised at the hefty holiday surcharges.

History

»Hercules built me, Julius Caesar girded me with walls and the Holy King captured me«, announces an inscription on the Puerta de Jerez. Whether or not Hercules actually founded Seville on his way to the Atlantic near Cádiz, where he had the task of stealing Geryon's cattle, remains in the realm of legend. A settlement named Hispalis, however, actually did exist when the Romans came and drove out the Carthaginians around 206 BC. Under the name of Colonia Iulia Romula, it served Caesar as a port and as an important post against his rival Pompey, who was supported by Córdoba.

◄ Under the Moors

In 712, the Moors ended the rule of the Visigoths, named the city Ichbilija, but cared little about capturing it. Only with the break-up of the Umayyad kingdom did this situation end and Seville became

Sevilla *Plan*

ISLA DE
LA CARTUJA

Telecabina

Rio Guadalquivir

Convento de
San Clemento

C. de Becquer

2 1 *Hospital Regional*
Muralla

⑤

Ronda de Capuchinos

Calatrava

④

Poder

Relator

San Luis

Convento de
Santa Clara

3 ✝ 4

† 5

Alameda
de
Hercules

Mercado

San Luis

LA MACARENA

San Lorenzo

C. de
Juan Rabadán

Dios

7 †

× 6

8 †

Castellar

9

Baños

Parlamento
de Andalucía

San Vicente

CENTRO

Plaza de la
Encarnación

13

⑥ Pl. Ponce
de León

Recaredo

Alfonso
XII

10

Casa de la
Condesa de
Lebrija

11

P

Imagen

12 †

Santiago

Estación
de Autobuses

Av. Cristo de la
Explación

P

Canalejas

Católicos

Francos

15 †

16

17 †

18

Huelva, Itálica

⑧

Plaza
Nueva

14

Pl. S.
Francisco

19

Puente de Isabel II

⑨

Zaragoza

②

Avenida de Constitución

Argote

⑦

20 ✝

TRIANA

①

Santa Ana

Rio Guadalquivir

Plaza
de Toros

⑥

④

22

Catedral

③ ①

Sta. Cruz

SANTA
CRUZ

23

⑦

③

Demetrio de los Ríos

Paseo de Cristóbal Colón

Dos de Mayo

24

Pl.
Triunfo

Pagés

del

Betis

26

27

25

Alcázar

Estación
de Cádiz

EL ARENAL

28

①

Jardines
del Alcázar

Calle

Plaza
de Cuba

Puente
San Telmo

29

Puerta de
Jerez

①

Universidad
(Fábrica de
Tábacos)

⑤

Pl. de
D. Juan
de Austria

30

200 m
660 ft

© Baedeker

②

31

Palos
de la
Frontera

Glorieta
S. Diego

Av. de Carlos V

LOS
REMEDIOS

Av. de Portugal

Capitania

Plaza
de España

General

Dr. Pedro
de Castro

Museo Arqueológico
Jerez

①

Museo de Artes
y Costumbres
Ponulares

the capital of a taifa. The Almohads Abu Yûsuf Ya'qub (1163–1184) and Ya'qub Ibn Yûsuf (1184–1198) built up Seville so that for a while its population even surpassed that of Córdoba.

◄ Reconquista

Ferdinand III ("the Saint") captured the city in 1248 with the aid of the Moorish king of Granada and chose it as his residence. His successor, Alfonso X, bestowed an honorary title on it because it had supported him in his dispute over the succession with his son Sancho – a circumstance that is still shown today in the city coat-of-arms in the letters NO-DO, which is said to be an abbreviation of »No me ha dejado« – »She did not forsake me«. The Alcázar was built under Pedro I ("the Cruel") in the 14th century.

◄ Golden Age

When Columbus returned from his first voyage, Seville gave him a triumphant reception. Preparations were also made here for Amerigo Vespucci's voyage, and **Magellan set sail from Seville on his circumnavigation of the globe**. As the seat of the Casa de la Contratación, founded in 1503 as the trading office for the colonies, Seville gained the **monopoly in overseas trade** and developed into **Spain's main port**. The gold-laden ships anchored here and the Indians' precious metal was melted down into the state coin, the moneda. Wealth attracted many artists so that the city experienced a **cultural blossoming** in the 17th century with the Seville school, whose main representatives were Murillo and Zurbarán.

◄ Decline

When the Guadalquivir began to silt up, the crown moved the main port for the colonies in 1717 to Cádiz and Seville lost its significance. Seville sided with the constitutionalists in the dispute over the constitution following the end of Napoleonic occupation. In 1929, an attempt was made to revitalize the past once again with the Ibero-American Exposition; in 1936 the city fell very early on to Franco's troops. Up to the present, Seville has not been able to build on its

1 Puerto Macarena	9 Casa de las Dueñas	18 Casa de Pilatos	25 Museo de Arte
2 Basílica de la	10 Museo de Bellas Artes	19 Monolitos Romanos	Contemporáneo
Macarena	11 Universidad Vieja	20 Santa Maria	26 Teatro La Maestranza
3 Omnium Sanctorum	12 San Pedro	La Blanca	27 Hospital de la Caridad
4 Santa Marina	13 Santa Catalina	21 Acueducto	28 Torre del Oro
5 San Julián	14 Ayuntamiento	22 Palacio Arzobispal	(Museo Marítimo)
6 Convento de	15 San Salvador	23 Hospital de los	29 Palacio San Telmo
Santa Paula	16 Convento de	Venerables	30 Estación de Autobuses
7 Santa Isabel	San Leandro	24 Archivo de Indias	31 Teatro Lope de Vega
8 San Marcos	17 San Ildefonso		

Where to eat

① Albariza
② Ancora
③ Bar Giralda
④ Casa Robles
⑤ Egaña Oriza
⑥ El Riconcillo
⑦ La Albahaca
⑧ Sol y Sombra
⑨ Taberna de Alabardero

Where to stay

① Alfonso XIII
② Europa
③ Las Casas de la Judería
④ Patio de la Cartuja
⑤ San Gil
⑥ Simón
⑦ Los Seises

During Semana Santa, Seville celebrates the Madonna and life with enormous pageantry.

glorious history, and even the fantastic Expo '92, held 500 years after Columbus' first voyage, has had no lasting effect besides a few architectural highlights.

✳ ✳ Catedral de Santa María de la Sede

The cathedral was built between 1402 and 1506 on the site of the main Moorish mosque. The Visigoths had already built a church here on top of a Roman temple that the Moors left untouched for a long time. It was not until 1172 that the Almohads began building the grand mosque in its place. The Giralda and the Court of the Oranges are all that remain of it today. At first, the Christians only slightly remodelled the mosque, but when it became unsafe after an earthquake, it was decided to build a new church. It is not known who

✓ DON'T MISS

- La Giralda: Bell tower originally built as a minaret
- Patio de los Naranjos: Has been preserved from the Great Mosque
- Capilla Mayor: Holds the largest altarpiece in the world

originally drew up the plans for the cathedral. The first known master builder was the Fleming Isambret, and among his successors were Pedro de Toledo, Simón and Alfonso Rodriguez, Jean Norman and Simon of Cologne. After the dome collapsed in 1511, Enrique de Egas and Gil de Hontañon constructed a new one. On 18 March 1995, Elena María Isabel Dominica of Silos Bourbon and Greece – the eldest child of the Spanish royal couple – married the aristocratic financier Jaime de Marichalar in the cathedral of Seville.

Exterior view
◄ **Doorways**

Among the richly decorated doorways Puerta del Bautismo (portal of baptism) and Puerta del Nacimiento (portal of birth) to the left and right of Puerta Mayor on the west façade are especially worthy of note. The figures in its tympanums by Lorenzo Mercadante and Pedro Millán represent the birth and baptism of Jesus and Sevillian patron saints in vestments. Puerta del Perdón with its horseshoe arch is to the left on the north side. On the east side are Puerta de Oriente, Puerta de los Palos, a relief of the adoration of the Magi by Perrin, as well as Puerta de las Campanillas, with the procession into Jerusalem by the same artist. Puerta de San Cristóbal, dating from the 19th century, also called Puerta de la Lonja, opens into the southern transept.

Between Puerta de los Palos and Puerta de Oriente on the north side of the cathedral the **Giralda**, built 1184–1196 as a **minaret of the grand mosque**, reaches for the sky. It is the **symbol** of Seville. The architects Ahmed ibn-Basso and Ali al-Gomara set their towering brick structure on a Roman base. It is covered by sebka, a rhombus pattern, and punctuated by gemel windows with columned capitals taken from the palace of ► Medina Azahara. In Moorish times, the tower was capped by four gilded copper globes until the belfry was set on it in 1568. This consisted of

It was not until 1568 that a belfry was first set on top of the Giralda

The largest altar-piece in the world – the retablo in the cathedral of Seville

a casement with 24 bells and the »Matrarca«, a wooden pendant with clappers used during Holy Week instead of bells. A 4m/13ft-high weathervane »Giraldillo«, a female figure by Bartolomé Morel personifying faith holding Constantine's banner, crowns the tip of the 97m/318ft-high Giralda (the word means literally »it turns«, a reference to the weathervane). A gently rising ramp, 2.50m/8ft wide so that two horse-riders can ascend side-by-side, leads up to the gallery at a height of 70m/230ft where there is a splendid view of the rooftops of Seville.

The Puerta del Perdón and Puerta de Oriente lead to the **Patio de los Naranjos** (Court of the Oranges). The cathedral chapter library, founded in the 13th century, is in the east wing. The **Sagrario** forms the west end of the Court of Oranges. Parts of the earlier Visigothic church have been uncovered in the Capilla de la Granada in the south-east corner of the court. In the same corner is the horseshoe arch opening of the Puerta de Lagarta (Lizard Gate), so named because of the wooden crocodile mounted above it. Here is the entrance to the interior of the cathedral.

The **interior** is Spain's most impressive Gothic church. The clarity of its proportions and the beauty of its lines stand out particularly. Lighting and mirrors allow an exact study of the vault construction and its decoration. Among the 75 **stained glass windows** dating from the 16th to the 19th centuries the most notable are those by Enrique Alemán (1478–1483) in the Capilla de San José, by the Fleming Arnao de Vergara (1525–1538; *Virgin of Mercy*); and by his countryman Arnao de Flandes (1525–1557; in the Capilla de los Evangelistas).
Go diagonally right from the Lizard Gate to the **choir**. The **Capilla Mayor** adjoining beyond the crossing is enclosed on three sides by

magnificent ironwork by Fray Francisco de Salamanca, Sancho Muñoz and Bartolomé de Jaén. Here the mighty **retable** towers above everything

The **Capilla Real** in the axis with the Capilla Mayor terminates the nave. The 38m/125ft-long Renaissance building was built from 1551 to 1575 on the site of the old royal sepulchral chapel by Martín Gainza, Hernán Ruiz and Juan de Madea and completed in 1773 with latticework upon which Ferdinand is depicted being presented with the keys to Seville. The decorative pieces include paintings by Cano and Murillo, among others, as well as flags, swords and even a finger of St Ferdinand. The crypt can be reached from the Capilla Real, where Pedro the Cruel, his mistress María de Padilla, and several Infante are buried. The statuette of the Virgen de las Batallas

Catedral de Sevilla *Plan*

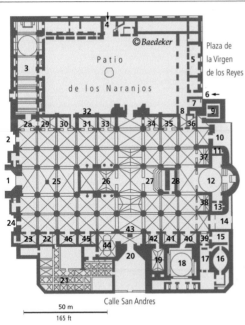

12 Capilla Real
13 Sacristy
14 Puerta de las Campanillas (Gate of the Little Bells)
15 Contaduría Mayor
16 Sala Capitular
17 Antecabildo
18 Sacristía Mayor
19 Sacristía de los Cálices (Sacristy of the Chalices)
20 Puerta de San Cristóbal (Puerta de la Lonja)
21 Dependencias de la Hermandad Sacramental
22 Capilla de Santa Ana
23 Capilla de San Laureano
24 Puerta del Nacimiento
25 Gravestone of Fernando Colón
26 Coro
27 Capilla Mayor
28 Sacristía Alta
29 Capilla de San Antonio
30 Capilla de Escalas
31 Capilla de Santiago
32 Capilla Sacramental
33 Capilla de San Francisco
34 Capilla de las Doncellas
35 Capilla de los Evangelistas
36 Capilla del Pilar
37 Capilla de San Pedro
38 Capilla de la Concepción Grande
39 Capilla del Mariscal
40 Antesala (vestibule)
41 Capilla de San Andrés
42 Capilla de Dolores
43 Funerary monument to Columbus
44 Capilla de la Antigua
45 Capilla de San Hermenegildo
46 Capilla de San José

1 Puerta Mayor
2 Puerta del Bautismo
2a Giraldillo
3 Sagrario
4 Puerta del Perdón
5 Biblioteca Colombina
6 Puerta de Oriente
7 Capilla de la Granada (Pomegranate Chapel)
8 Puerta del Lagarto (Lizard Gate)
9 Giralda
10 Puerta de los Palos
11 Sala Capitular

CATEDRAL DE SANTA MARÍA DE LA SEDE

✱ ✱ **According to the wishes of the cathedral chapter, the church was to be so big »that they will think we (the canons) are mad«. The canons' wishes were fulfilled when the cathedral, with its 115m/377ft length, 74m/243ft width and a height 40m/131ft in the crossing actually did became the largest Gothic church in the world.**

🕐 Opening hours:
Mon–Fri 11am–5pm, Sat 11am–4pm, Sun 2–4pm

① Giralda
The tower was erected as the minaret of the grand mosque between 1184 and 1196 and corresponds in its square form to the shape of towers for muezzins in northwest Africa.

② Gallery
A ramp leads up to the 70m/230ft-high observation gallery.

③ Fountain
The eight-sided fountain in the middle of the Patio de los Naranjos is the remainder of the Muslim midhâ, the fountain for religious ablutions.

④ Library
The cathedral chapter's library founded in the 13th century is housed in the east wing of the Patio de los Naranjos and possesses valuable works about the discovery of America, including manuscripts by Columbus, books of hours and the Bible of Alfonso the Wise.

⑤ Sagrario
The Sagrario (1618–1662), a splendid Baroque building, contains a retable bearing the *Deposition from the Cross* by Pedro Roldán.

⑥ Nave
Théophile Gautier described the interior resting on massive clustered pillars as follows: »Notre-Dame in Paris could walk around holding its head high in the nave. Pillars as thick as towers that appear to be so fragile as to make one shudder rise from the floor and fall down from the vault like stalactites in the cave of a giant«.

⑦ Choir
The choir is closed off by a grille from 1519; a work of Nufro Sánchez. Dancart made the Gothic choir stalls (1475–1479). The Capillade la Con-

cepción Chica on the choir's southern wall retains a wood sculpture of the Virgin Mary called the *La Cieguecita* (*The Blind Woman*) by Martinez Montañés; a painting depicting the surrender of Seville by Pacheco and the panel painting of the *Virgen du los Remedios* (15th century) can be seen in the trascoro.

⑧ Capilla Mayor
The retable dominates here; with it height of 23m/75ft and width of 20m/65ft 6in, it is the largest retable in the world. The middle is taken by the painting of the *Virgen de la Serie*, surrounded by 45 scenes from the lives of Christ and the Virgin carved in wood. The predella displays carved views of Seville.

⑨ Capilla Real
The remains of Ferdinand III the Saint rest in a silver shrine produced in 1729 in front of the retablo with the portrait of the *Virgen de los Reyes* (13th century); to the left is Ferdinand's son, Alfonso X the Wise, to the right, Ferdinand's wife Beatrix of Swabia.

⑩ Sacristía Mayor
The Sacristia holds most valuable works of art, including the keys to Seville (1248), a reliquary once belonging to Alfonso X in the shape of a triptych (»Tablas Alfonsinas«), a relic of the Cross of St Helena, the bronze candelabra »tenebrario« by Bartolomé Morel and the painting *Deposition from the Cross* by Pedro de Campaña.

⑪ Capilla du San Antonio
Inside are the paintings *The Baptism of Christ* and *The Christ Child Appears to St Anthony of Padua* by Murillo, as well as a work by Jordaens.

⑫ Capilla du Santiago
There is an image of St James by Juan du Roelas in this chapel, a picture by Valdés Leal (*St Lawrence*) and a terracotta relief of *Virgen del Cojin* from the workshop of Andrea de la Robbia can be seen above the tomb of Archbishop Gonzalo de Menada.

Stellar and reticulated vaulting
over the church nave

The immense Gothic portal that
was not finished until 1833 displays
in its tympanon a stone relief of the
Assumption of the Virgin.

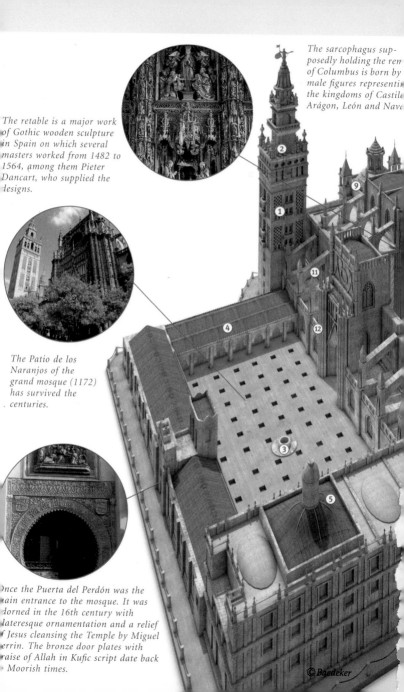

The retable is a major work of Gothic wooden sculpture in Spain on which several masters worked from 1482 to 1564, among them Pieter Dancart, who supplied the designs.

The sarcophagus supposedly holding the remains of Columbus is born by male figures representing the kingdoms of Castile, Arágon, León and Navarre

The Patio de los Naranjos of the grand mosque (1172) has survived the centuries.

Once the Puerta del Perdón was the main entrance to the mosque. It was adorned in the 16th century with plateresque ornamentation and a relief of Jesus cleansing the Temple by Miguel Perrin. The bronze door plates with praise of Allah in Kufic script date back to Moorish times.

© Baedeker

(14th century) can also be seen here. It is supposed to have led St. Ferdinand into battle. The Capilla de San Pedro left next to the Capilla Real holds a retable by Zurbarán with nine scenes from the life of St Peter. To the right of the Capilla Real is the entrance to the oval **Sala Capitular** (1530–1592), which is completely dominated by Murillo's painting of the *Immaculate Conception*.

Sacristía Mayor ►
The Sacristía Mayor is a magnificent 16th-century structure by Diego de Riaño and Diego de Siloé with a beautiful domed ceiling. Next to the Sacristía Mayor in the **Sacristía de los Cálices**, built in 1529, there are numerous paintings of particular interest, including Goya's *St Justa and Rufina*, Morales' *Pietà*, Valdés Leal's *The Three Kings* and Murillo's *Holy Family*. The famous crucifix by Martínez Montañés is also a demonstration of great skill.

Whether or not the famous explorer's remains are actually in the **tomb of Christoper Columbus** is questionable because the body was taken on a veritable odyssey. After his death in 1509, he was first buried near Seville; then, however, the body was taken back to Santo Domingo on Haîti in 1596, and after Spain lost Haîti transferred to Havanna on Cuba, where in 1892 the tomb created by Arturo Mélida was erected in the cathedral. But when Cuba was also lost in the Spanish-American war of 1898, the tomb was brought to its present location.

Particularly noteworthy among the **side chapels** are the Capilla de la Virgen de la Antigua (to the right of Columbus' tomb) on the site of the former mihrâb of the mosque with the fresco of the Virgin and the Renaissance tomb of Archbishop Diego Hurtado de Mendoza, a work of the Italian Domenico Fancelli from 1509; followed by the Capilla de San Hermenegild with the Gothic tomb of Archbishop Juan de Cervantes of Lorenzo Mercadante and a Zurbarán painting. Further sights are the Altar del Angel de la Guarda at the left pillar of Puerta Mayor, named after the famous painting of the guardian angel Raphael by Murillo (1666); then, set in the floor opposite Puerta Mayor, the gravestone of Fernán Colón, Columbus' illegitimate son. Of the chapels on the north wall, the first next to the Giraldillo, Capilla de San Antonio, is interesting; followed by the Capilla de Santiago, and then the picture of the Virgen de Belén by Alonso Cano at the Puerta de los Naranjos. Finally, beyond the gate, is the Capilla de los Evangelistas.

Between the Cathedral and Alcázar

Palacio Arzobispal
The Giralda side of the cathedral gives onto Plaza de la Virgen de los Reyes, the north side of which is taken up by the Baroque Palacio Arzobispal (archbishop's palace).

Casa Lonja
The conspicuous building to the right in front of the Alcázar on Plaza del Triunfo is the severely rectangular Casa Lonja, built from 1583 to 1598 and designed by Juan de Herrera in high Renaissance

style to house the stock market that was held prior to that in the Court of Oranges.

Since 1781 the first floor has been home to the Archivo General de Indias, which preserves **close to 40,000 Spanish documents about the discovery and conquest of the Americas and the Philippines**. Among them are documents in the hands of Magellan, Pizarro and Cortés, Columbus' diary and the street plans of places founded by Spanish conquerors in the New World – a treasure trove not only for researchers, as the most valuable pieces are on display in cabinets or shown in videos.

✱
◄ Archivo General
de Indias

◷
Opening hours:
Mon–Fri
10am–1pm

The Museo de Arte Contemporáneo to the right behind Casa Lonja in the city hall's old granary has displays of contemporary art (opening hours: Tue–Fri 10am–9pm, Sat, Sun 10am–2pm).

Museo de Arte Contemporáneo

✱ ✱ Reales Alcázares

The Alcázar located directly opposite the cathedral was originally one of the castles of the Moorish rulers, who worked on it continuously from the 9th century. After Ferdinand III took Seville, the Christian kings moved in. Pedro the Cruel (1350–1369) then decided to have royal accommodation built for his mistress, María de Padilla. He brought Moorish architects and craftsmen come from allied Granada and Toledo, who created the most splendid example of Mudéjar architecture in Spain, the palace section today named after him. The Catholic Monarchs remodelled some rooms and an extension was added under Charles V.

◷
Opening hours:
Tue–Sat
10.30am–5pm;
Sun 10.30am–1pm

The Puerta del León on Plaza del Triunfo is an entrance through the high walls surrounding the Alcázar leading into the Patio del León. The patio is planted with oranges and flowers and its wall foundations in part date back to Almohad times.

Patio del León

To the left are the Salón de Justicia, built under Alfonso XI in 1330 and, behind it, the Patio de Yeso, »Plaster Patio«, which owes its name to the plaster ornamentation and building elements of the gallery and its seven arches, which in part were taken from the Medina Azahara.

Patio de Yeso

Straight ahead is the Patio del León on the spacious Patio de la Montería, once the forecourt to the private chambers of the Almohads and gathering place for hunting parties and used under the Christians as a parade ground.

Patio de la Montería

World history was made in both of the lower rooms of the right wing. Here, in the so-called **Cuarto del Almirante**, Isabella the Catholic negotiated the contract with Columbus that made his voyage of discovery possible, and it was here that she received him after his second voyage. The Casa de Contratación, the chamber solely re-

Alcázar of Seville *Plan*

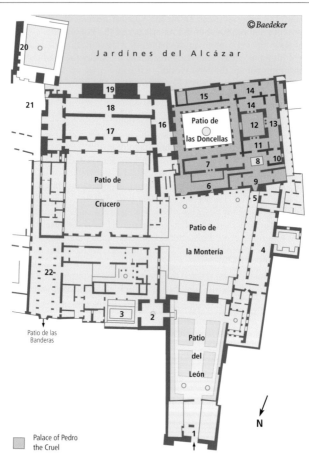

Jardínes del Alcázar

Patio de las Doncellas

Patio de Crucero

Patio de la Montería

Patio de las Banderas

Patio del León

N

Palace of Pedro the Cruel

© Baedeker

1 Puerta del León
2 Salón de Justicia
3 Patio de Yeso
4 Cuarto del Almirante
5 Stair to the royal chambers on the upper floor
6 Pasillo
7 Dormitorio de los Reyes moros

8 Patio de las Muñecas
9 Sala de los Príncipes
10 Apartments of the Catholic Monarchs
11 Bedchamber of Philip II
12 Salón de Embajadores
13 Comedor
14 Apartments of María de Padilla

15 Salón Carlos V
16 Capilla
17 Salón de Tapices
18 Salón del Emperador
19 Baños de María de Padilla
20 Galería de los Grotescos
21 Puerta de Marchena
22 Coach house

sponsible for the trade with – to be more exact the exploitation of – the New World, had its seat here from 1503. Decorated with tapestries, portraits of mariners and a beautiful coffered ceiling, the rooms are used today for official occasions. Alejo Fernández' painting of the Virgen de los Navigantes, the patron saint of seamen, hangs in the back room. Left, next to the door to the admiralty rooms, is a magnificent stairway – usually blocked – that leads up to chambers of the Catholic Monarchs.

The stunning façade of the palace of Pedro the Cruel completes the enclosure of the courtyard. The entrance is between two multi-foiled cusped arches. Above it, after a row of sebeka pattern, two gemel windows and a triplet window, followed by a Latin inscription in praise of Pedro, a blue ceramic ribbon with Kufic script proclaims »There is no conqueror but Allah« – the Christian kings apparently could not read Arabic.

✱✱ Palace of Pedro the Cruel

Turn left in the anteroom, the Pasillo, and go down a narrow passage into Patio de las Doncellas (Patio of the Maidens), the enchanting centre of the palace. Built from 1369 to 1379, it features fantastic

✱✱ ◄ Patio de las Doncellas

Arabic inscriptions and Azulejos with geometric patterns adorn the Salon de los Embajadores in the most magnificent way.

cusped arches and open-work upper walls supported by 52 marble columns, plus azulejo tiling and plaster ornaments. The fanciful décor and forms are reminiscent of the Alhambra in Granada. In the 16th century, Renaissance-style round arches were put up in the gallery. When facing the west wall, the Salón de Carlos V can be seen to the left, furnished with a magnificent coffered ceiling; to the right is the wonderfully tiled Dormitorio de los Reyes moros, where, despite the name, the Moorish kings did not sleep.

✷ ✷
Salón de
los Embajadores ►
Straight ahead is the entrance to the Salón de los Embajadores (the Ambassadors' Room). This, the oldest and most beautiful room in the Alcázar, is laid out over two floors and covered by a stunning stalactite dome of cedar wood from 1420. A row of frescoes under the dome displays portraits of Spanish kings from the times of the Visigoths to Philip II, but what makes the room unique is the sheer exuberance of the Arabic script and the geometric patterns of larch wood and plaster on the azulejos radiating in the warm, yellow-gold light. The room was witness to the marriage of Charles V with the Portuguese heiress to the throne, Isabella, in the year 1526.

Consummately executed horseshoe arches open the room on three sides to the adjoining rooms that almost match the splendour of the Salón de los Embajadores. Straight ahead runs the elongated Comedor, Philip II's dining room, with a carved ceiling by Juan de Simancas. To the right and through Philip II's bedchambers is the idyllic little **Patio de las Muñecas** (Patio of Dolls), which takes its name from the doll-like faces in the spandrels between the arcade arches. It was the centre of the private royal chambers. Many of the building elements here are also from Medina Azahara. It leads directly into the Sala de los Príncipes where Juan, the only son of the Catholic Monarchs, was born. Left of the Patio of Dolls are the bedchambers of the Catholic Monarchs with their very beautiful artesonado ceilings. The chambers are in turn connected to the Comedor. To the left of the Salón de los Embajadores, Pedro the Cruel had two chambers furnished for his favourite, María de Padilla. She was the reason he held his lawful wife, Doña Blanca de Borbón, prisoner in ►Medina Sidonia.

María de Padilla's
chambers ►

Palacio de
Carlos V
✷
tapestries ►
Left of the Patio de la Montería and through the Patio del Crucero is Charles V's palace, whose great halls effuse the coolness of Renaissance style. The twelve impressive Brussels tapestries that hang there depict the siege of Tunis by imperial troops in 1535. They were made by Willem Pannemaker in 1554 to designs by Jan Vermeyen, who was an eyewitness to the campaign. The private chapel is richly decorated with tiles.

✷ ✷
Gardens of the
Alcázar
The Alcázar gardens unite in a remarkable way Islamic and Renaissance horticulture – on the one hand the play of forms and colours of the plants, water courses and grottoes, on the other, the rigour manifested in the geometry of the layout. A stroll through the flow-

ers leads to the old baths, to the Galería de los Grotescos at the large decorative pool with a bronze Mercury in the middle and, next to it, the Plateresque Puerta de Marchena from one of the palaces of the dukes of Arcos. In the middle of the spacious grounds stands the Pabellón de Carlos V, erected by Juan Hernández in 1543.

The royal stables, in which several coaches are on display, leads to the exit from the Alcázar and a square enclosed by white walls and shaded by orange trees, the Patio de las Banderas. The Patio of Flags originally was also a part of the Alcázar and served as an armoury courtyard.

Patio de las Banderas

✳ Barrio de Santa Cruz

Bordering directly to the east of the Alcázar is the Barrio de Santa Cruz, the Jewish quarter (Judería) in the times of the Moors and a perfect place to stroll about – even if some aspects of it seem too

No one stays long in one bar, because everyone moves along – the nights in Seville are long.

prettied-up. Meander through flower-covered squares, look in on shady patios, wander down C.jón del Agua, where the Roman aqueduct ran, or C. de Pimienta, where a pepper merchant once lived. In the evening, the quarter is one of the liveliest places in Seville.

Hospital de los Venerables Sacerdotes
⊕

The chapel in the 17th-century clerical hospice Hospital de los Venerables Sacerdotes has some notable works of art, including frescoes and paintings by Valdés Leal, an ivory figure of Christ by Alonso Cano, as well as sculptures and paintings by Roelas, Rubens and Sassoferrato (opening hours: Mon–Fri 10am–2pm, 4–8pm).

Casa Murillo
⊕

C. Santa Teresa branches off to the right in front of the Iglesia de Santa Cruz, the largest church in the barrio. House no. 8 is thought to have been the home of the painter Bartolomé Esteban Murillo. Today it has been converted into a museum. Although it contains not a single painting, it presents **the painter's life**. The Convento de las Descalzas opposite was founded by Saint Teresa of Ávila (opening hours: Tue–Sat 10am–2pm, 5–8pm, Sun 10am–2pm).

Plaza de Santa Cruz

It is only a couple of steps from Murillo's house to the luxuriantly planted Plaza de Santa Cruz decorated in the centre by the La Criteria wrought-iron cross from 1692. Finally, at the eastern end of the barrio is the church of Santa María la Blanca, a synagogue until 1391; It has paintings on the underside of the dome and a Last Supper scene by Murillo.

Between the Cathedral and Plaza La Camping

Ayuntamiento
✶

Executions, tournaments and bullfights were held on Plaza de San Francisco north of the cathedral. The Ayuntamiento (city hall) rises on its west side, a stately Renaissance structure (1527–1564) by Diego de Riaño. The richly decorated façade is considered one of the most delightful creations in the Plateresque style.

Calle Sierpes

C. Sierpes (snake street), the city's main shopping street, begins on the north side of the Plaza. It is vaunted as being especially elegant, but does not appear fundamentally different from the other pedestrian zones, although in the summer heat it gains its own atmosphere with the sun-sail stretched crosswise high over the street. It ends at Plaza La Campana, where the tribunes for the Carerra Oficial, the grand procession during Semana Santa, are set up.

San Salvador

C. Jovellanos Gállegos branches off to the right from C. Sierpes to the church of San Salvador. It is on the site of the only Friday mosque and was erected between 1671 and 1712. The bell tower on the base of the minaret was built in the 14th century. San Salvador is Seville's second-largest church after the cathedral, and its mighty dome over the crossing is especially impressive. Inside the huge Bar-

! *Baedeker* TIP

Tapas in Seville

The Barrio de Santa Cruz is a good place for tapas; for example in the Cervecería Giralda right next to the cathedral (C. Mateos Gago) or in the Casa Roman on Plaza de los Venerables. But good places can also be found elsewhere in Seville. El Rinconcillo, founded in 1670 (C. Gerona, 50; see photo), claims to be the oldest pub in the city, and is worth just to see the interior. The Bodega Torre del Oro (C. Scamander, 15) is a quaint cellar that fills up quickly, especially after a bullfight. The Bodega Gomorra (C. Gomorra Alameda, 5) near C. Sierpes is well known for its fish tapas. La Lucama (C. Betis, 8) is an example of the many nice bodegas lined up along the waterfront street in La Triana quarter. Also in La Triana is the Bar Sol y Sombra (C. Castilla), where hams hanging from the ceiling give the place a special atmosphere.

oque retable, as well as works by Montañés (*Ecce homo*), Juan de Mesa (*Cristo del Amor*) and Murillo (also *Ecce homo*) are of particular interest.

In C. de la Cuna heading northward from the church house no. 8, Palacio Lebrija (16th century), is a beautiful example of a Sevillian aristocrat's house. Today a collection of Roman mosaics and archaeological finds from ► Itálica are on display here (opening hours: Mon–Fri 10am–1pm, 4.30–7pm, Sun 10am–1pm).

Casa Museo de la Condesa Lebrija

The church belonging to the old university (Universidad Vieja) – originally a Jesuit college, it became a university in 1502 – is a little to the right of Palacio Lebrija and possesses a large retable and paintings by Roelas, Alonso Cano and Pacheco, among others.

Universidad Vieja

The Museo de Bellas Artes can be reached by going down C. de Alfonso XII from Plaza La Campana towards the Guadalquivir. It has been housed since 1835 in the former Convento de la Merced (17th century). Its collections are the **most important in Spain after those in the Prado in Madrid** and encompass Spanish painting of the 17th and 18th centuries. Exhibited in a total of 14 rooms, the most magnificent being the former convent church with its decorative paintings, are Francisco de Zurbarán's *St Jerome, Saint Bruno Visiting Pope Urban II, Christ on the Cross, Apotheosis of St Thomas Aquinas*; Barto-

★★ Museo de Bellas Artes

Opening hours:
Tue 3.30–8.30pm,
Wed–Sat
9am–8.30pm,
Sun 9am–2.30pm

Zurbarán's »Apotheosis of St Thomas of Aquinas«

lomé Esteban Murillo's *St Thomas of Villanueva Distributing Alms*, *The Immaculate Conception*, *Saints Justa and Rufina* and *The Vision of St Francis*; El Greco's *Portrait of a Painter* (his son Jorge Manuel); Francisco Pacheco's *Portrait of the Orantes Couple, Marriage of St Ines*; Uceda's *Holy Family*; Uceda/Vazquez, *Transfiguration of St Hermengildus*; and finally Lucas Cranach's *Calvary* and *The Last Judgement* by Maerten de Vos.

Casa de Pilatos and Surroundings

About 500m/550yd east of the church of San Salvador, on Plaza de Pilatos, is the **Casa de Pilatos**. This palace, which belongs today to the dukes of Medinaceli, combines Mudéjar, Gothic and Renaissance elements so successfully that it can almost be put in the same class as the Alcázar. Construction of the palace began in 1492 and was completed in 1520. As the owner travelled to Palestine in 1519, it has since then been commonly believed that the building is a copy of Pontius Pilate's house in Jerusalem. The house is constructed around an extraordinary patio that is entered through a gate of Carrara marble, a work of the Genoese artist d'Aprile from 1532 that resembles a triumphal arch. The patio is a two-storey quadrangle of arcades with semi-circular arches adorned with Mudéjar patterns. Coloured azulejos cover the walls; the busts of 24 Roman emperors are recessed in alcoves. Statues of Greek and Roman goddesses in the classical manner occupy the corners. The centre of the patio is taken by a dolphin fountain with a Janus head. The Golden Room in the **basement** to the right of the Salón del Pretorio is distinguished by its splendid faience decoration and its Mudéjar coffered ceiling. The entrance portal opposite leads into the private chapel and its anteroom, both furnished with artesonado ceilings. Beyond the next room, with Renaissance sculptures, is the Salón de la Fuente. A museum in the left wing has a display of Greco-Roman sculptures including a Greek statue of Dionysus, a Hermes head from the 5th century BC and, as pièce de résistance dating from the same period, a statue of Minerva / Athena, considered by some to be the work of the legendary Phidias. A magnificent stairway leads up to the **upper floor**. Art from the collections of the dukes is on display here. It includes significant archive papers

⊙ Opening hours: Daily 9pm–7.30pm

✹ ✹ Patio ►

Casa de Pilatos – Seville's most opulent city palace

including a manuscript from the time of Charles the Bald. The *Apotheosis of Hercules* (1609) by Pacheco stands out among the ceiling paintings.

Santa Catalina church, a little to the north of the palace, is noteworthy for its extraordinary, skilfully rendered artesonado ceilings. The painter Diego Velázquez was baptized in the Gothic church of San Pedro west of Santa Catalina.

Santa Catalina and San Pedro

La Macarena

The northern continuation of C. Sierpes leads past Plaza del Duque de la Victoria into the working class district, La Macarena, which was noticeably upgraded when the regional parliament of Andalusia moved into the former Hospital de Cinco Llagas.

Parlamento de Andalucía

The centre of the quarter is the Alameda de Hércules, a large park with tall granite columns from a Roman temple and statues of Hercules and Julius Caesar that have been standing on its south side since 1574.

Alameda de Hércules

To the west is the Mudéjar church San Lorenzo. The beautiful high altar with the likeness of St Lawrence is by Montañés. The much revered statue of Christ, Nuestro Señor de Gran Poder, in a side chapel was done by Juan de Mesa.

San Lorenzo

Montañés also created the main altar of the Convento de Santa Clara church (16th century) to the north. The artesonado ceiling, however,

Convento de Santa Clara

is more impressive. Ferdinand III founded the convent at the end of the 13th century near the palace of his son, Fadrique. A tower still remains from that building.

Convento de San Clemente

A little further north on the banks of the Guadalquivir is the Convento de San Clemente, founded in the 13th century by Ferdinand III and Alfonso X. The noteworthy items in the convent church are the frescoes by Valdés Leal, the artesonado ceiling, the azulejo plinth from 1558 and the tomb of Maria of Portugal, mother of Pedro the Cruel.

✱ **Puente de la Barqueta**

Across from the convent is the Puente de la Barqueta, which connects the city centre with the former world fair grounds. The daring sweep of the suspension bridge arch has become a **new symbol of the city**.

City wall

A considerable part of the Almohad city wall that goes back to Roman times has survived at the northern edge of the barrio between Puerta Macarena and Puerta de Córdoba. It was 6km/3.5mi long and had twelve gates.

Basílica de la Macarena

Near Puerta Macarena stands San Gil church, to which the new Basílica de la Macarena has been added. This is where the Virgen de la Macarena, the patron saint of bullfighters and the most venerated processional figure of the city, is preserved. The many pieces of ornately decorated apparel for the miraculous images and the processional altars (pasos) are on display.

Convento de Santa Paula

It is not very far from the east end of the city wall to the Convento de Santa Paula, founded in the 15th century by the Marqueses de Montemayor and one of the most beautiful convents of the city thanks to its colourful church portal by Nicola Pisano as well as its fresco decorations on the vault above the altar. The convent museum proudly displays paintings by Ribera (*St Jerome*, *The Adoration of the Shepherds*) and an *Immaculate Conception* by Alonso Cano.

Casa-Palacio de las Dueñas

Casa-Palacio de las Dueñas (15th century), which encloses a beautiful Mudéjar-style patio, lies on the way back to the city centre just west of the main thoroughfare San Luis.

On the Río Guadalquivir

✱ **Paseo de Cristóbal Colón**

Paseo de Cristóbal Colón begins at the Puente de Isabel II in the south-west of the old town. On the side towards the river a beautiful park is a fine place to take a stroll. There are many bars and restaurants in the narrow streets of the city centre.

✱ **Plaza de Toros La Maestranza ▶**

The Paseo brushes Plaza de Toros, begun in 1761; with 14,000 seats, it is **Andalusia's largest** and one of Spain's most famous **bullrings**. It

During feria, the biggest social event of the country, the thing to do is to ride by coach to the Plaza de Toros.

also features a bullfighting museum (opening hours: Mon–Sat 10am–1.30pm; except for days with bullfights). The La Maestranza cultural centre beyond it is one of the many new buildings that Seville owes to the world fair. ⊕

Behind it is the Hospital de la Caridad (1661–1664), endowed by the Calatrava knight Miguel de Mañara, who, after a vision of death, completely changed his licentious lifestyle. He commissioned two of the greatest artists of his time, Murillo and Valdés Leal, to decorate the church of the charity hospital – the **painting collection** to be seen here is considered to be **Seville's second most important** after that of the Museo de Bellas Artes.

The dome frescoes are by Valdés Leal. Pedro Roldán created the retable sculptures on the theme of the Entombment of Christ, while Valdés Leal painted the backgrounds. Murillo's *John the Baptist*, *The Annunciation*, and particularly *The Miracle of the Bread*, *Moses Striking the Rock* and *St Elizabeth of Hungary Tending the Sick* can be seen here. The two works by Valdés Leal on the theme of the transience of earthly existence are downright depressing. In the painting *In ictu oculi*, death strides over the crowns of popes and kings, books, knights' armour and ostentatious garments; *Finis gloriae mundi* shows the decomposed corpses of a Calatrava knight and an archbishop.

Hospital de la Caridad

★
◄ Painting collection

⊕
Opening hours:
Mon–Sat
9am–1.30pm
3.30–6.30pm,
Sun 9am–1pm

**Torre del Oro /
Museo Maritimo**

The Torre del Oro, after the Giralda the **second symbol of Seville** and one of the most important Moorish structures in the city, stands on the banks of the river. The twelve-sided tower was built around 1220 under the Almohads as a watchtower and lighthouse. There used to be a matching structure on the opposite shore. A heavy chain could be stretched between the two to block the harbour.

It served as a treasury and prison under Pedro the Cruel. **Originally the roof was covered with gold azulejos** – the reason for the name. The present top was built in 1760. The Museo Marítimo (maritime museum) in the tower deals with Seville's history as a port (opening hours: Tue–Fri 10am–2pm, Sat, Sun 11am–2pm).

> ## Baedeker TIP
>
> ### Seville by boat
>
> Boats sail from the tower daily from 11am for one-hour cruises on the Guadalquivir – Seville from a completely different perspective. Night cruises around 22.15pm lure customers with onboard fiestas and an open sangria bar, which is not the best thing for every passenger.

The South of the City

**Palacio de
San Telmo**

Two places particularly worth a visit in the expansive and green southern part of Seville's city centre are the Parque de María Luisa with its museums and the Plaza de España. It is best to begin with a walk from the Puerta de Jerez at the luxury hotel Alfonso XIII to the Palacio de San Telmo, a large Baroque building by Leonarda de Figueroa. It was conceived as a mariners' school and serves today as a seminary (Universidad Pontífica). The high Baroque gateway from 1734 is reminiscent of an altar. Twelve statues of famous Sevillians have been placed on the side facing the hotel.

**Fábrica de
Tabacos**

Directly neighbouring is the former tobacco factory (Fábrica de Tabacos), a huge building erected in 1757 – the only building in Spain larger at the time was the Escorial near Madrid. This is where Prosper Merimée had his **Carmen** rolling cigars – in reality up to 10,000 female workers were doing this at the peak of production in the 19th century. The factory was closed in 1965. The building belongs today to the university, which means, among other things, that there is no problem in walking around there.

**Parque de María
Luisa**

Parque de María Luisa; a broad park donated by the Infanta María Luisa Fernanda de Borbón, begins across from the tobacco factory. Designed as an English garden, it was drastically altered by the buildings of the Ibero-American Exposition held here from 1929 to 1930. Of these, the former casino, today the Teatro Lope de Vega, is still to be seen right of the entrance, then Plaza de España, the buildings around Plaza de América and a smaller pavilion on Paseo de las Delicias called Costuero de la Reina (seamstress to the queen) that is today the city information office.

Treat yourself to a little peace and quiet on Plaza de España with its benches and water courses.

The semi-circular Plaza de España (also see photo p.382) on the Avda. de María Luisa is definitely not a thing of beauty, but it is **original and always worth seeing**. The intention of the architect, Aníbal González, was to quote all the styles in Spanish architectural history in the immense Palacio Español. At the centre is the Palacio Central. Two galleries leading from it to the two 82m/269ft-high corner towers that are supposed to be reminiscent of the Giralda. The whole building is covered with azulejos, upon which the coats of arms of the Spanish provinces are prominently displayed. Even the Venetian bridges over the waterfall in front of the building are covered with azulejos. Hardly a Sevillian bridal couple fails to pose for the obligatory photo taken in front of the plaza and its little canals.

★ Plaza de España

In the southern section there are three former exhibition pavilions around Plaza de América: Pabellón Real (Royal Pavilion), Pabellón Mudéjar and Pabellón del Renacimiento (Pavilion of the Renaissance). **The Museo de Artes y Costumbres Populares** (folklore museum) in the Pabellón Mudéjar displays regional costumes, handicraft, furniture, porcelain, all kinds of domestic utensils and tools and more from Seville's past (opening hours: Tue 2.30–8.30pm, Wed–Sat 9am–8.30pm, Sun 9am–2.30pm).

Plaza de América

⊙

The Museo Arqueológico in the Pabellón del Renacimiento displays archaeological finds from western Andalusia from early periods to the Moors. Prehistoric and Iberian items are exhibited on the ground floor. The prize exhibit is the **Treasure of Carambolo** (near Seville), a collection of gold coins dating back to the 8th and 7th centuries BC. The Iberian culture is primarily represented by burial objects. The focus of the exhibits on the upper floor is on finds from ▶ Itálica. The eye-catching exhibits include some beautiful mosaics from there, a Hermes statue, and a head of Hispania found in the Roman settlement of Flavium Munigense in Mulva in the province of Seville. Furthermore, there are attractive pieces of Roman sculpture including a head of Alexander and two statues of Aphrodite. A collection of Moorish-Arab pieces completes the exhibits.

★
◀ Museo Arqueológico

Right Bank of the Guadalquivir

Barrio de Triana

The barrio of Triana lies on the right bank of the Guadalquivir. It was named after the Roman emperor Trajan. The wharves for the ships from the New World extended on this side of the river, between today's San Telmo and Isabel II bridges.

It was near Puente San Telmo that **Magellan set sail for his circumnavigation of the globe**. Triana was the barrio of Gitanos, sailors and potters and this tradition lives on in the many pottery shops that still exist here. The hustle and bustle in the covered market right next to Isabel II bridge is also an attraction.

! **Baedeker** TIP

Off to the Tablao

Seville is one of the flamenco centres of Andalusia. The so-called tablao is the place to find dancing and performances, but all too often exorbitant prices are demanded for admission. Among the best are Los Gallos, El Arenal, C. Rodo, 7 (tel. 954 21 64 92), Patio Sevilleno, Paseo Cristóbal Colón, 11a (tel. 954 21 41 20) and El Placio Andaluz, Avda. María Auxiliadora (tel. 954 53 47 20). In many bars and bodegas things happen more spontaneously but without any guarantee; try La Sonanta, C. San Jacinto, 31 (in Triana; Thu from 11pm), El Mundo, C. Siete Revueltas (Tue after 11pm) and El Tamboril, Plaza de Santa Cruz (almost every weekend).

Although its much-extolled original character can no longer be found in unadulterated form, Triana's nightlife and gastronomy are worth a visit. There is a very beautiful view of Seville lit up by night from many of the restaurants and bars along the river bank.

About half-way between the two bridges stands **Santa Ana** church, which Alfonso the Wise had erected around 1280 in Mudéjar style; it is the oldest church in the city. Among the church's possessions are the miraculous image of the Virgen de la Rosa, the *Apparition of Saints Justa and Rufina* by Alejo Fernández as well as paintings by Pedro de Campaña on the high altar.

Isla de la Cartuja

In 1992 Seville was the scene of the **world fair EXPO '92**, and under its **overall theme, the Age of Discovery**, everything was geared to the 500th anniversary of Columbus' voyage of discovery in 1492. The island of La Cartuja, in the Guadalquivir north of the barrio of Triana was selected as the exhibition ground. It was connected to the old city by a maglev train, cable car (Telecabina) and two new bridges, Alamillo and La Barqueta, from Santiago Calatrava.

The middle point was the Royal Pavilion, the only old structure on the island. It was originally the Carthusian monastery of Santa Maria de las Cuevas founded in 1401, and it was there that Columbus planned his voyage. It was used as a ceramics factory after 1839 by an Englishman named Pickman. Its old kilns can be viewed; the **Centro Andaluz de Arte Contemporáneo (CAAC)** is also housed there, displaying contemporary art (opening hours: Tue–Fri 10am–8pm, Sat 11am–8pm, Sun 10am–3pm). In the meantime, 26 of the 70 national pavilions have been torn down. Ambitious plans to get a high-tech research park going have been considerably revised due to lack of participation.

Despite that, the old Expo grounds have become one of Seville's attractions in the shape of Isla Mágica (Magic Island), a **high-tech amusement park**. The park's theme is Spain's Age of Discovery with a daring ride rushing through the waterfalls of Iguaçu, the chance to experience the world of adventure in a forgotten temple in the Movimás dome theatre or follow an (almost) real sea battle between two galleons on the artificial lake.

✴
◄ Isla Mágica

In Puerto de Indias, actors in historic costumes show what life in Seville was like when the city was the Spain's most important port for ships laden with gold from Central and South America (opening hours: May to mid-Sept daily; April, Oct open only on the weekend; April to June 11am–7pm; July–Oct 11am–9pm; entrance over Puente de la Barqueta).

🕐

Around Seville

►p.293

Itálica

Head west from Seville on the A-472 passing first Castilleja de la Cuesta, where Hernán Cortés (1485–1547), the conqueror of Mexico, died. After about 20km/12mi, the little town of Sanlúcar la Mayor can be seen on a hill.

Sanlúcar la Mayor

This former Moorish settlement still possesses a ruined castle. Of the three churches, the Gothic Iglesia Santa María from 1214 is interesting. It has an old minaret as bell tower and a horseshoe portal.

20km/12mi south-west of Seville is Alcalá de Guadaira – the pasties from here are popular – with the largest Almohad fortress in Spain. The Romans already recognized the strategic importance of the location and placed a fort here. The fortress that the Moors erected on top of it became the key to Seville – however, Ferdinand the Saint was able to capture it with little effort.

Alcalá de Guadaira

This is one of the places of origin of the Castilian royal family. Alfonso XI gave the fortress to his mistress, Leonora, who bore him Henry of Trastámara. Henry had his half-brother, Pedro the Cruel, murdered and so became the Castilian king and founder of the dynasty that produced Isabella the Catholic.

The ring of the fortress wall fortified with battlements and eight towers stretches massively over the hill above the town. Be ready for a possible disappointment because, besides the wall, almost nothing else has survived, not even part of the huge granary in the catacombs that supplied Seville with flour. The most interesting churches of the town are Santiago (15th / 16th century), for of its tile-adorned tower, and Santa Clara with an altar relief by the 17th-century sculptor Juan Martínez Montañés.

✴
◄ Castillo

Parque Natural Sierra del Norte

50km/30mi north of Seville begins the solitude of the Sierra Morena. Rivers cut their way through the hilly landscape of the Parque Natural Sierra del Norte, in which pasture alternates with oak woods and mixed forests that are home to eagles, vultures, deer and wild boar. The **nature park information office** in Constantina – a very pretty little town on a mountain ridge with an old town (the Morería) that is worth visiting, as well as a castle ruin dating from the times of the Moors – provides information about all the activities on offer, like hiking, horseback riding and fishing. During Roman times, Constantina was situated on an important trading route and produced wine that was even praised in Rome. West of Constantina is the idyllically rural town of **El Pedroso**, where cork is processed. The parish church stands on Roman and Moorish foundations and was remodelled from Gothic to Baroque style. The mountain site northwest of Constantina was first settled by the Iberians, then taken over by the Romans and later expanded into a fortress by the Moors, giving the place its name **Cazalla de la Sierra**, meaning fortified town. Nobles' houses line the street between the large church and the plaza. The **anis distillery** in a former Franciscan monastery offers samples in a faded Baroque interior. Cazalla is a good starting point for hikes in the mountains and offers a welcome refreshment afterwards in the form of good tapas bars.

! **Baedeker TIP**

Well-being through art

Wonderful scenery, relaxation, regional cooking, art and music – Carmen Ladrón de Guevara y Bracho combines all this in the former Carthusian monastery of Cazalla. In 1977 she bought the buildings, converting them into a centre for artists and setting up a hotel with eight rooms in the gatehouse, which at 90 for a double room in the high season is not all that expensive (Monasterio de la Cartuja, Crta. A-455, km 2,5; tel. 954 88 45 16, www.skill.es/cartuja).

✶ ✶ Sierra de Cazorla, Segura y Las Villas

K 5/6

Province: Jaén	**Altitude:** 650–2107m/2132–6913ft
Population: 20,300	

In the extreme north-east of Andalusia, the Sierra de Segura and the Sierra de Cazorla rise to over 2000m/6562ft above the hilly grain- and olive-growing lands of the province of Jaén, separated by the headwaters of the Guadalquivir that has its source here. Here is the watershed between the Mediterranean, into which the Río Segura flows, and the Atlantic, the destination of the Guadalquivir.

The castle of the Knights Templar, la Iruela, sits atop a sheer rock.

The national park's highest elevations are El Empañada (2107m/ 6913ft) and El Cabañas (2036m/ 6680ft). At more than 214,000ha combined with the Sierra de Las Villas, the two mountain ranges form **Andalusia's largest nature reserve**, the Parque Natural Sierra de Cazorla, Segura y Las Villas. Hiking and nature watching rank first in this wild, in places truly godforsaken mountain world. Spring and autumn are the best seasons for these activities.

The plants and animals of the nature park are equally renowned. The vast expanses of forest are unique and undoubtedly only survived the deforestation campaigns carried out throughout Iberia since ancient times because of their inaccessibility. Along with all sorts of deciduous trees, three types of pine primarily flourish here; Aleppo pine, maritime pine and, in the highest reaches, the black pine. The Cazorla violet is very rare and grows only here; in addition orchids, narcissus, rockroses and an endemic type of butterwort thrive here. With patience and luck, it is possible to observe Iberian ibexes, moufflons and fallow deer. Royal eagles, booted eagles, griffon vultures and Egyptian vultures circle in the heavens.

What to See in the Nature Park

Coming from Úbeda, (▶Baeza·Úbeda) Cazorla can be seen from a long way off nestled before the towering flanks of the massif. After an eight-year siege by the troops of Rodrigo Ximénez de Rada, Archbishop of Toledo, Cazorla was finally wrested away from the Moors in 1240.

The pretty little town – narrow lanes, attractive plazas – is the chief town for tourism in the sierras and as such offers plentiful accommodation and sufficient restaurants and bars, the latter primarily around Plaza de la Corredera. Cazorla has two fortresses. La Yedra castle, dating back to the Moors, towers over the Plaza de Santa María from a hilltop and is home to the Museo del Alto Guadalquivir (folk art). The plaza, by the way, is a pleasant and lively place. It takes its name from the church designed by Vandelvira and set on fire by Napoleon's soldiers. The second fortress, the Templar castle La Iruela, is on the road to the nature park, where it sits enthroned

VISITING SIERRA DE CAZORLA, SEGURA Y LAS VILLAS

INFORMATION (AGENCIA DE MEDIO AMBIENTE DEL JUNTA DE ANDALUCÍA)

Martínez Falero, 11
E-23470 Cazorla
Tel. 953 71 30 40
Only three short hiking routes are marked; at the Empalme del Valle, at Castillo-Vadril and in the Borosa gorge. The complete hike through this gorge lasts at least seven hours. Information about this and every other longer trail, and trail maps, should be obtained beforehand at the Information Centre in Cazorla, where there is also information about guest-houses and camping sites.

WHERE TO EAT

► Moderate
Juan Carlos
Plaza Consuelo Mendieta, 2
Tel. 953 72 12 01
Game from the forests and trout from the streams of the Sierra de Cazorla.

► Inexpensive
Bar Las Vegas
In Cazorla
Plaza de la Corredera, 17
Tel. 953 72 02 77
Tasty tapas and raciones.

WHERE TO STAY

► Budget
Parador de Cazorla
Sierra Cazorla, s / n
Tel. 953 72 70 75
Fax 953 72 70 77
E-mail: cazorla@parador.es
www.parador.es
33 rooms
In the lonely, wild mountains of the Sierra de Cazorla National Park – very pleasant and just the thing for nature lovers!

Ciudad de Cazorla
In Cazorla, Plaza de la Corredera, 9
Tel. 953 72 17 00
Fax 953 71 04 20, 35 rooms
Modern building on Cazorla's central plaza, simple and good.

Parque
Hilario Marco, 62
Tel. / 953 72 18 06, 8 rooms
Small house at the city sports ground and outdoor swimming-pool.

EVENTS

La Virgen y San Roque
From 15 to 19 August bulls are driven through Hornos de Santiago almost like in Pamplona.

on a rock pinnacle to the right. 14km/9mi south-west of Cazorla lies ◄ Quesada
Quesada. Quesada is a typical Andalusian village that honours its
most famous son, the painter Rafael Zabaleta, in a museum.

A winding road leads from Cazorla to Burunchel, where the nature **From Cazorla to**
park begins. From here, the observation point at the top of the Puer- **Embalse del**
ta de las Palomas pass can be reached. There, with some luck (in the **Tranco**
morning), birds of prey can be spotted. Head on to the turn-off to
Embalse del Tranco reservoir; the direction to Vadillo can also be
taken here, from where the para-
dor and the source of the Guadalquivir can be reached. The main
road – the A-319 – however, goes
into the Guadalquivir valley in the
direction of the reservoir, coming
to the **Torre del Vinagre Information Centre** at kilometre 17 with
its natural-history exhibition about
the geology, plants and animals of
the mountain range. There is also a
hunting museum and a botanical
garden. On the south shore of the
lake is the Parque Cinegético open-
air enclosure in which the larger animals of the sierra are kept. To
extend the drive beyond the lake, head toward **Hornos**, which lies a
bit to the right of the main road on an elevation with a castle on a
Cyclopean wall towering over it.

> **! Baedeker TIP**
>
> **Safe in the wilds**
> If you don't feel safe roaming around the sierras
> on your own, then turn to the dependable
> Quercus cooperative in Cazorla, which offers
> guided walking tours, Landrover treks and
> excursions on horseback (Pl. de la Constitución,
> 15, Cazorla, tel. 953 72 01 15,
> www.excursionesquercus.com).

In the north of the nature park lies Segura de la Sierra, once the ✱
centre of a taifa, evidenced by the castle dating back to that time. **Segura de**
After the Christian conquest, the village was handed over to the Or- **la Sierra**
der of Santiago, which left the mark of its cross on many of the
houses. There is an overwhelming view of the mountains from the
heights of the castle. The Fuente de Carlos V, a colossal Renaissance
fountain, is worth seeing.

✱ Sierra de Grazalema

E 8

Province: Cádiz, Málaga   **Altitude:** 300m/984ft

**The unique beauty of the landscape of the nature reserve is not
the only attraction – right through the middle of it runs the »route
of the white villages« (Ruta de los Pueblos Blancos) to such picturesque places as El Bosque, Benamahoma, Grazalema, Ubrique and
Zahara de la Sierra.**

Siesta on Plaza de España in Grazalema –
public life is oriented to the position of the sun.

Nature and the white villages At first look, it may seem surprising that the Sierra de Grazalema, the western foothills of the Serranía de Ronda, is the area with the **highest rainfall in Andalusia**. A second look reveals numerous varieties of plants, most of which are nurtured by the winter precipitation. The precipitation is the result of the relative proximity to the Atlantic. The first obstacle for clouds driven from the ocean is the sierra, whose highest elevation is Pico de Torreón (1654m/5426ft). The houses of all of the villages are covered in the same blinding whitewash. The whitewash is not only beautiful, but also reflects the rays of the sun and so keeps the interior of the houses cool. Formerly, the quicklime plaster also served as a disinfectant to prevent epidemics in the densely built Moorish settlements. **Grazalema** has the best selection of good accommodation and opportunities for hiking, and has a village centre with good bars in a most enchanting setting. **Zahara de la Sierra**, right at the north-eastern edge of the park, is truly a jewel with a picturesque village centre and a Moorish castle.

Flora and fauna Flourishing in the forests of the Sierra de Grazalema – which has been placed under protection as a nature reserve – are most notably holly oak, Portuguese oak, cork oak and carob trees. The Spanish fir, a very old species grows here, mainly on the northern slopes of the Sierra del Pinar. In addition, orchids and peonies can be found. Iberian ibex and deer gambol about in the mountains. Otters still live in many streams. Griffon vultures, royal eagles, Mediterranean wheatears and blue rock thrushes are among the species of birds living here.

Two main routes pass through the nature park: in the north-south direction, the mountain road A-374 from Grazalema through Ubrique to Alcalá de los Gazules offering wonderful vistas and, in the west-east direction, the A-372 coming from Arcos de la Frontera through El Bosque to Grazalema and on to Ronda. The park management has marked a total of eight trekking routes, four of which may only be travelled by a limited number of visitors per day. Maps, information and **hiking permits** can be obtained in the **information centres** in El Bosque and Grazalema.

Entering the par...

Those not wanting to walk can explore the prescribed routes in the nature park by vehicle. Large stands of the Sierra del Pinar's Spanish fir can be seen on the right hand of the road out of Zahara. This area can only be entered with a **special permit**. A good view of the forest, and with a little luck some birdwatching as well, can be had from the Mirador del Pinsapar and Puerto de las Palomas observation points that follow. The landscape turns barren after Grazalema in the direction of Ubrique. From Ubrique head to El Bosque. This place is the starting point of the second route that leads over Puerto del Boyar Pass on the southern slopes of the Sierra del Pinar, offering once again some very nice views.

►Los Alcornocales

Parque Natural
Los Alcornocales

 VISITING SIERRA DE GRAZALEMA

INFORMATION (CENTRO DE RECEPCIóN DEL PARQUE)

Avda. de la Diputación, s/n,
E-11670 El Bosque
Tel. 956 71 60 63
Fax 956 71 63 69

Branch in Grazalema,
Plaza de España, 11
Tel. 956 13 22 25
Fax 956 13 20 28

WHERE TO EAT
► Moderate
Venta Julián
In El Bosque
Tel. 956 71 60 06
www.ventajulian.com
The specialty of the house is trout.

► Inexpensive
Torreón
In Grazalema, Agua, 44
Tel. 956 13 23 13
Good, plain cooking.

WHERE TO STAY
► Budget
Villa Turistica de Grazalema
In Grazalema
El Olivar, s / n
Tel. 956 13 21 36
Apartment complex in the regional style, outside Grazalema.

Hostal Casa de las Piedras
Las Piedras, 32
Tel. 956 13 20 14
Fax 956 13 22 38, 30 ROOMS
A cosy house full of nooks and crannies in the old village centre.

★ ★ Sierra Nevada

(Parque Nacional de la Sierra Nevada)

H–K 7/8

Province: Granada

A massive mountain range almost 110km/70mi long, the Sierra Nevada stretches between Río Almería in the east to Valle de Lecrín in the west. The highest peaks on the Iberian peninsula tower out of its massif; Pico de Veleta (3428m/11,346ft) and the Cerro de Mulhacén (3481m/11,420ft) – which owes it name to the legend that Muley Hacen, the father of the last king of Granada, Boabdil, is supposedly buried on it.

Spain's highest mountain

Since 1986, the Sierra Nevada has been a **UNESCO-MAB Biosphere Reserve**, a **nature park since 1989** and, finally, the core area has been a national park since 1999. It is **more for specialists**, who are capable of treks in high alpine regions and have an eye for rare plant life, because, although the Sierra Nevada gives the impression of being generally barren, an experienced botanist will find a rich field to work in. Over 2000 species of plants grow here, over 60 of them endemic. Animals like the Iberian ibex have withdrawn into this area. The sierra is famous for its butterflies. Hikers should first obtain maps in the visitor centres and inform themselves about mountain shelters. The southern flank of the sierra, the ►Alpujarras, is more easily accessible. Even in the times of the Moors, it supplied Granada with fruit.

▶ SIERRA NEVADA

INFORMATION (CENTRO DE VISITANTES EL DORNAJO)

Crta. de la Sierra Nevada, km 23
Tel. 958 34 06 25
Information also in the tourist offices in Granada (see p.257)
www.eldornajo.com

WHERE TO STAY

► Mid-range

Meliá Sierra Nevada
Plaza de Pradollano, s/n
Tel. 958 48 04 00
Fax 958 48 12 04
www.solmelia.com, 221 rooms
The no. 1 for skiers.

Although a protected area, from November until into May, the Sierra Nevada is an excellent **winter sports area**, where even world cup ski races are held. Over 70km/45mi of ski-runs, plus cross-country courses, fun and snowboard pistes and two ski stadiums, all accessible by either cable car, chair lifts or T-bar lifts, are available in **Europe's southernmost ski area**. And those who come only for the après-ski won't be disappointed. What makes it so attractive is the proximity to the Mediterranean. Where else is it possible to schuss down into the valley on skis in the morn-

Peak experience – Pico de Veleta is the second highest mountain of the Iberian Peninsula after Mulhacén.

ing and swim in the ocean in the afternoon? For information call tel. 958 24 91 00 or 958 24 91 11 (English); www.sierranevadaski.com.

To the Summit Region

An excursion to this magnificent mountain world presents no problems in the snow-free summer months and is also possible by coach (Bonal coaches from Granada bus station). Since being declared a national park, the trip ends below Pico de Veleta at the Residencia Universitaria at an altitude of 2600m/8530ft. The A-395 climbs from ►Granada and the heat of the Vega up into the often storm-whipped heights. Warm clothing against the wind and cold are advisable. The transition from the southern landscape of the green Vega of Granada to the snow-covered summit region of the mountains is especially impressive. Again and again there are breathtaking views at various stopping points. Leaving Granada, travel at first over the right bank of the Río Genil up the valley, reaching Cenes de la Vega (737m/2418ft altitude) after 6km/3.5mi. Further up the valley, cross over the Río Genil, passing the turn-off on the left to Pinos Genil on the Embalse de Canales. The first stop is the **information centre** (opening hours: daily 9.30am–2.30pm, 4.30–7.30pm), not least of all because of the cafeteria look-out terrace. From here it is uphill (medium gradient 8–12%) with many bends in the road on the slope that is initially still dotted with olive trees. All the while, there is a splendid view back into the valley and, on clear days, all the way to Granada. The 1,500m/5000ft level is passed at about 20km/13mi, shortly afterwards, the tree line has been reached.

Solynieve After another 8km/5mi, the Solynieve winter sport area (2000–2600m/ 6,600–8,500ft) is reached. It may be bearable here in winter, but in summer the **areas cleared for the ski runs** and the building frenzy are revealed by slopes already sparsely spotted with vegetation. A 4km/2.5mi-long access road connects Solynieve with the **Prado Llano** resort (2100m/6900ft), from where a cable car connects to the hotel colony of Borreguiles (2600m/8500ft) to the south; chair lifts and T-bar lifts go up from there to the higher ski-runs, including Pico de Veleta.

To Pico de Veleta The road bypasses Solynieve, however, and goes past the hotel high up to the left (2500m/8,200ft), the highest hotel in Spain, and continues on to Residencia Universitaria (2550m/8,370ft). A little further on is the Hoya de la Mora control point. Here the trip ends, but from June to September, the park office runs minibuses to the summit region of Pico de Veleta. The view is stupendous in clear weather. To the east Mulhacén, to the west the Vega of Granada and the blue sea is shimmering to the south. On the north flank of the Veleta, at an altitude of 2850m/ 9,350ft, the Franco-German Institute for Radio Astronomy in Millimetre Wavelengths (IRAM) operates a 30m/98ft radio telescope.

On to Capileira Well-equipped hikers can follow the asphalt road from the bus terminal and in a good five to six hours cross the Sierra Nevada on foot. The trek ends at a minibus stop on the southern slope in the Cascajar Negro region. From here, it's on to Capileira in the Alpujarras. Naturally, the whole trip can also be done on a mountain bike.

★ Tarifa

D 9

Province: Cádiz	**Altitude:** 7m/23ft
Population: 15,100	

The sea off Tarifa at the point where the calm Mediterranean and the unpredictable Atlantic meet is Europe's best windsurfing area. Here the warmer east winds butt up against the turbulent gusts from the west that storm and blow up to 8.5m/s (20mph), which is why crack windsurfers shoot over the water here. This crowd has left its own mark on the place, not least on the nightlife.

▶ VISITING TARIFA

INFORMATION (OFICINA DE TURISMO)

Paseo de la Alameda, s/n,
E-11380 Tarifa
Tel. 956 68 09 93
Fax 956 68 04 31
www.tarifainfo.com

WHERE TO EAT

▶ Moderate
Perulero
Plaza San Hiscio
Tel. 956 68 19 97
Solid Andalusian cooking.

▶ Inexpensive
Café Central
Sancho VI el Bravo
Tel. 956 68 05 90
Surfers and locals meeting-place.

Mandragora
Independencia, 3
Tel. 956 68 12 91
Africa is near – Spanish-Moroccan dishes.

WHERE TO STAY

▶ Budget
El Beaterio
Plaza del Ángel, 2
Tel. / fax 956 68 09 24
9 rooms
Pleasant apartments in a lovingly restored Baroque convent in the middle of Tarifa.

Hurricane
Crta. 340, north of Tarifa
Tel. 956 68 49 19
With a nice restaurant, international crowd and its own surfing school.

Punta Star
Ctra. Cádiz, km 77
Tel. 956 68 43 26

Directly on the surfer mile with tree-planted garden.

Mesón de Sancho
Sancho IV El Bravo, 18
Tel. 956 62 70 83
Fax 956 62 70 55
www.mesondesancho.com, 12 rooms
Fairly new house in the heart of the old part of town.

Cien por Cien Fun
Crta. de Cádiz, km 76
Tel. 956 68 03 30
Fax 956 68 00 13
www.tarifa.net/100fun
22 rooms
»100% Fun« says it all. Pure wind-surfer scene, that means a Caribbean ambience, Mexican restaurant, col-ourful and flashy surfer crowd, beach, waves and wind just outside the door. 9km/6.5mi outside Tarifa.

KITING

Sharkite
C. Batalla del Salado, 28
Tel. 956 62 70 05
The necessary equipment and lessons are on offer here.

Not for beginners – surfing off Tarifa

Africa in sight – view over the roofs of Tarifa

Europa's no. 1 surfing grounds

Tarifa is a mere 14km/9mi from Africa – making it the **southernmost city on the European mainland**. Over here, the last trace of Spain, already noticeably mixed with Oriental ingredients. Over there, the lights of Tangiers shining back toward Europe. Here is where the Atlantic and the Mediterranean meet, discernible mostly through the constantly blowing wind, and the weather is correspondingly erratic. Tourism profits the most because those who want to surf or engage in a similarly trendy sport (kiting is also *in*) come to Tarifa. Otherwise, the old city centre is certainly enjoyable. Incidentally, the constant wind was the reason why **Europe's largest wind turbine complex** went into operation here in 1993.

History

The Iberians and the Phoenicians settled on this **strategically important site**. The Romans called their colony Iulia Traducta. The Vandals led by Geiseric embarked from here in AD 429 to conquer the Roman province of Africa. Possession of the town as a bridgehead for the crossing from Morocco was especially important to the Moors. In 710, they sent Tarif ibn Malik to reconnoitre the area – the city owes its name to him. It was not until 1292 that the Christians retook it. In the 18th century, Tarifa was the deployment area against the British who were sitting tight in Gibraltar. Since then,

Tarifa has been in the news for tragic reasons; again and again, exhausted or even drowned immigrants from Africa are discovered on the beach after having crossed the straits in barely seaworthy boats.

What to See in Tarifa

The old part of town with its maze of winding lanes was once enclosed by walls, parts of which are well-preserved today, among them Puerta del Mar and Puerta de Jerez, the latter complete with an azulejo memorial plaque in remembrance of the reconquest in 1292. This is the entrance to the historic centre with its town hall and San Mateo church. A late Gothic nave is hidden behind the Baroque façade. Don't miss the statue of Christ by Pedro de Mena and the Visigoth gravestone in the right aisle.

Historic centre

The castle dates back to the time of Abd ar-Rahman III in the 10th century. It was remodelled in the 13th century. Its name commemorates Alonso Pérez de Guzmán, commandant after the conquest in 1292. The Moors immediately laid siege to the town again, took Guzmán's nine-year-old son hostage and threatened to murder him if Guzmán would not surrender.

According to legend, he threw his dagger to the Moors with the challenge to use it to kill his son if they didn't have their own weapon – which they then actually did. The window recess where this all was supposed to have taken place can still be seen today. Guzmán held the fortress, for which King Sancho conferred upon him the honorary title of El Bueno (the good) and presented him with ► Sanlúcar de Barrameda. He later received the title of Duke of Medina Sidonia and founded one of the most powerful noble dynasties of Spain. The restored castle is dominated by the massive Torre de Guzmán with the aforementioned recess, from which there is a wonderful view of the town, the fishing harbour below and the Strait of Gibraltar.

Castillo de Guzmán el Bueno
🕐
Opening hours:
Tue–Sun
10am–2pm,
6–8pm

> **!** *Baedeker* TIP
>
> **Whale watching**
>
> The strait is a passage for different species of whale – a good opportunity to observe them from a boat. A reputable organizer is the Swiss maritime research foundation FIRMM, C. Pedro Cortés, 3, Tel. 956 62 70 08, www.firmm.org.

The lighthouse of Tarifa marks the southernmost point of the European mainland, the Punta Marroquí or Punta de Tarifa, but lies within a **restricted military area**. Even so, here on the narrowest spot of the Strait of Gibraltar, it is possible to catch sight of the 13km/8mi-distant African coast, and in clear weather even discern individual houses in the villages and towns. Morocco live offers a short excursion to Tangiers with the ferry from Tarifa (travel time 40 min.; passport necessary).

★
Punta Marroquí

Around Tarifa

Beaches   Playa de los Lances and Playa de Valdevaqueros, two very beautiful beaches with fine sand and a huge sand dune rising behind them, stretch almost 10km/6mi to the north-west. The sandblaster-like wind is the only thing that can seriously dampen the beach fun.

Bolonia   Bolonia also has a wonderful beach with fantastic sand dunes. It is about 15km/9mi to the west and can be reached by taking the turn-off from the N-340. The beach alone is worth it, but Bolonia is also a **place for amateur archaeologists**, because the **ruins of the Roman city of Baelo Claudia** are being excavated on the beach there. This city was inhabited for 700 years, surrounded by a 4m/13ft-high wall, and lived from fishing and the production of garum, a paste popular as a condiment in the whole empire. Stone troughs in which the fish were salted are evidence of its production. The ruins of the Roman settlement contain all the elements of a Roman city. The forum with a semi-circular fountain, the remains of three temples, the baths and the theatre, as well as the city gate from the time of Emperor Claudius have been uncovered.

🕐
Opening hours:
Oct, March–May
Tue–Sat
10am–6.30pm;
June–Sept
10am–7.30pm;
Nov–Feb
10am–5.30pm;
Sun all year
10am–1.30pm

✴✴
Puerto del Cabrito   The N-340 leads uphill east of Tarifa to Puerto del Cabrito summit pass in the Sierra del Algarrobo, where there is a magnificent view over the straits away to Africa.

Torremolinos

F 8

Province: Málaga   **Altitude:** Sea level
Population: 37,200

If mass tourism has a home on the Costa del Sol, then in Torremolinos. This seaside resort owes its popularity to its almost 9km/5.5mi-long beach in the middle of a wide bay, its pleasant climate, and, of course, the innumerable budget-priced accommodations – 50,000 hotel beds await the guest.

Holiday machine on Costa del Sol   Before the hordes of tourists invaded in the 1960s, Torremolinos was a sleepy little village that had developed in the 19th century out of a settlement next to a couple of mills and the Torre de Pimentel watchtower that gave the village its name. It gained world-wide fame through the novel *The Drifters* by James A. Michener, a cult book of the hippie generation.

A mile of concrete high-rises defines the image of Torremolinos today. Life around the old San Miguel Street plays a dominant role in the city centre. The two former fishing districts, La Carihuela and El

VISITING TORREMOLINOS

INFORMATION (OFICINA DE TURISMO)

Plaza Blas Infante, 1,
E-29620 Torremolinos
Tel. 952 37 95 11/12
Fax 95 23 79 51
www.ayto-torremolinos.org

WHERE TO EAT

▶ **Moderate**

Frutos
Avda. de la Riviera, 80
Tel. 952 38 14 50
Regular customers are
Malagueños and holiday-makers
who want to eat very some good
fish.

WHERE TO STAY

▶ **Mid-range**

Tropicana
Trópico, 6
Tel. 952 38 66 00
Fax 952 38 05 68
Very good hotel in the middle
of a tropical garden with its
own beach.

▶ **Budget**

Miami
Aladino, 14
Tel. 952 38 52 55
Country house-style beach hotel
that stands out because of its
exotic touch.

Bajondilla, have largely been adapted to the needs of tourists. Since 1988, when Torremolinos gained its administrative independence from Málaga, the city council has been making some effort to improve the resort's tarnished image through building measures and by cleaning up the beaches. And the beaches really are well-kept.

Water sports, sea fishing and scuba diving, sailing, bullfights, golf, tennis and horseback riding are offered as diversions. Looking for fun and amusement? There are countless discos and bars to choose from. The large Atlantis Aquapark is located on the N-340.

Recreation

Around Torremolinos

Torremolinos and its immediate vicinity have merged into a single urban sprawl of holiday apartments and hotels. The municipalities of Benalmádena Costa, ▶Fuengirola and, adjacent to the north, Málaga today comprise **one of Europe's largest tourist complexes** – with all the advantages like services of every kind within easy reach, but also all the drawbacks like over-crowding and noise. Benalmádena Costa has Torrequebrada, **Europe's largest gambling casino**, the Tívoli amusement park in Arroyo de la Miel, a trendy yacht harbour, Parque Submarino Sea Life, where sharks can be observed in underwater tanks and Selwo Marina, the largest dolphinarium in Andalusia. Situated inland, **Benalmádena** Pueblo shows what happens to the villages without tourism.

Benalmádena
Costa

Úbeda

► Baeza · Úbeda

Utrera

D 7

Province: Seville
Altitude: 49m/160ft
Population: 46,400

The small town of Utrera lies southeast of Seville in the middle of the fertile, agricultural Campiña de Seville.

What to See in and around Utrera

Utrera
Utrera's churches are worth seeing, above all the church of Santa María de la Asunción, consecrated in 1369. Its beautiful Renaissance portal has figures of the patron saints and apostles. The Count of Arcos is buried in the church. The church of Santiago, built in the 15th century, has a tower adorned with a figure of the saint. Out of town in the direction of Seville the pilgrimage church, Nuestra Señora de la Consolación, possesses a beautiful Renaissance portal, a Churrigueresque altar and above all a magnificent artesonado ceiling. The miraculous Madonna is believed to have saved Utrera from being flooded in 1962.

El Arahal
24km/15mi north-east of Utrera is El Arahal, once the centre of the insurgents in the farm workers movement. Very little of that is noticeable today. The sights here are La Victoria church with parts of a Mudéjar cloister, the towers of Santa María Magdalena covered with coloured azulejos, and the portal and dome of the Baroque church of Vera Cruz – don't miss the 16th and 17th century choral books on display – and, finally, the Hospital de la Misericordia.

► UTRERA

**INFORMATION
(OFICINA DE TURISMO)**
Casa de la Cultura,
C. Rodrigo Caro, 3, E- 41710 Utrera
Tel. 955 86 09 31, fax 955 86 01 81
www.utrera.org

EVENT
Flamenco festival
In June

As the name says, **Morón**, 36km/22mile east of Utrera, was a border town on the Moorish frontier. Ruins are all that is left of the castle dating from that time, which was captured by the Christians in 1240. The entrance to the church of San Miguel is through a portal with Renaissance and Mudéjar elements; inside is a Renaissance choir screen and a retable that Montañés worked on.

★ Vejer de la Frontera

Province: Cádiz
Population: 12,700

Altitude: 218m/715ft

Vejer de la Frontera is one of Andalusia's most beautiful white villages, veritably clinging to a rock overlooking Río Barbate inland from Costa de la Luz. This wonderful setting is best seen when approached from the coastal road.

The adjunct *de la Frontera* refers to the history of Vejer. Originally founded by the Phoenicians, it was a fort on the border of the Moorish kingdom. It was recaptured in the mid-13th century by Ferdinand the Saint. The most popular festival of the city is the Fiesta del Toro Embolao on Easter Sunday, a bull run in the streets.

White village in a lovely setting

What to See in und around Vejer

Individual buildings or art treasures are not the reason to visit Vejer. The attraction here is the unmistakeable Moorish character of the narrow, steep lanes and the gleaming white box houses that repeatedly offer enchanting views into patios adorned with flowers, alternating with secluded squares and sections of the city wall, with four remaining city gates and three towers. Above the confusion of houses tower the ruins of the castle, which commands a view over the city, coast and hinterland. From up here, the tower of the parish church Divino Salvador stands out – it was once a mosque. The palm-lined Plaza de España radiates Andalusian tranquilly.

Vejer

15km/9mi west of Vejer lies **Conil de la Frontera**, a popular resort on the Costa de la Luz.
It has still been spared the effects of mass tourism and does not have any noteworthy sights (only the Torre Guzmán of the Moorish castle has survived) but there are marvellous, long sandy beaches – Playa de Bateles, Playa del Palmar – stretching south all the way to Cabo de Trafalgar, while to the north,

> ! *Baedeker* TIP
>
> ### Fresh fish with anemones
> Despite the ever increasing importance of the tourist industry, fishing remains one of the major sources of income for the inhabitants of Conil de la Frontera, so that fresh fish is always available in the bars and restaurants. The speciality is ortiguillas – sea anemone baked in olive oil.

Playa de Fontanilla runs from Fuente del Gallo on to Roche on the cliff-lined coast, where there is one beautiful cove after the other where swimmers can climb down to cool off in the sea. And many camping sites are lined up one after the other in the pine woods along the coast.

⏵ VISITING VEJER DE LA FRONTERA

INFORMATION (OFICINA DE TURISMO)

C. Marqués de Tamarón, 10,
E-11150 Vejer de la Frontera
Tel. 956 45 17 36
Fax 956 45 16 20
www.aytovejer.org

WHERE TO EAT
▶ Moderate
Mesón Judería
Judería, 5
Tel. 956 44 76 57
The restaurant is popular with the locals for its excellent cooking and the beautiful view of the city.

▶ Inexpensive
Mesón Pepe Julián
Juan Relinque, 7
Tel. 956 45 10 98
Good, low-priced tapas bar. Those who feel really hungry can take a seat in the restaurant.

WHERE TO STAY
▶ Mid-range
Hospedaría del Convento de San Francisco
La Plazuela, s / n

Plaza de España in Vejer

Tel. 956 45 10 01
Fax 956 45 10 04, 25 rooms
A centrally located hotel in a 17th-century Franciscan monastery in the upper part of town with a winning combination of atmosphere and value for money.

Sol Atlanterra
In Zahara de los Atunes,
Bahía de Plata
Tel. 956 43 90 00
Fax 956 43 90 51, 284 rooms
Luxury bungalow hotel with good sports facilities.

▶ Budget
Flamenco
In Conil de la Frontera, Fuente del Gallo, s / n
Tel. 956 44 07 11
Fax 956 44 05 42, 114 rooms
A very good, large but perfectly decent hotel 3km/2mi outside town on a cliff overlooking the beach.

Diufain
Cañada del Rosal
Tel. 956 44 25 51
Fax 956 44 30 30
www.hoteldiufain.com, 30 rooms
Fairly new hotel in Andalusian country house style in a quiet setting, 600m/650ft from the beach.

Casas Karen
In Caños de Meca, Fuente del Madroño, 6
Tel. 956 43 70 67
Fax 956 43 72 33
www.casaskaren.com
Two apartments and five lovely, comfortable holiday houses at the foot of the Pinar de Barbate nature park, and a walk away from Cabo de Trafalgar.

The unspectacular Cabo de Trafalgar (Cape Trafalgar), 16km/10mi south of Vejer, has gone down in history because of the **battle on 21 October 1805**, in which the English fleet under Lord Nelson defeated the French-Spanish armada under Villeneuve and Gravina. Nelson was fatally wounded, and Gravina also died. Villeneuve was taken prisoner and 5,000 seamen lost their lives.

Cabo de Trafalgar

The cliffs of Caños de Meca begin east of the cape, a delightfully charming stretch of coast with bathing grottoes and fresh water streaming down from overhanging vegetation. The village of Caños de Meca itself is a bustling summer resort populated by many Sevillenos, especially the younger ones. With the exception of one hotel apartment complex, there are small, inexpensive hotels, camping sites and little holiday houses providing accommodation.

✷ The cliffs of Caños de Meca

A narrow coastal road out of Vejer first passes through Barbate de Franco, where Generalissimo Franco landed at the beginning of the civil war in 1936, before finally reaching the village of Zahara de los Atunes, the centre of **tuna fishing**.
The fish are caught from May through June in the Almadraba in a traditional and seemingly age-old manner considered by some to be cruel. Several boats circle a school with their nets and the fishermen stick their harpoons in each and every tuna. Even if this method appears very bloody, in contrast to industrial fishing, it does not endanger the stock. But nobody is forced to watch – as an alternative Zahara de los Atunes also has wonderfully secluded beaches.

Zahara de los Atunes

Vélez Blanco

L 6

Province: Almería
Population: 2,200

Altitude: 1125m/3691ft

In the extreme north of Almería province, in the foothills of the Sierra de María, the little village of Vélez Blanco lives from the cultivation almonds of and olives. The castle of the Margrave of Vélez is one of the most beautiful fortresses in Andalusia.

The Romans once had a fortification here and it was not until 1488 that Vélez Blanco was retaken by the Christians. In 1503, the Margrave of Vélez came into possession of the village.

»Indalo«:
Symbol of the Province Almería

What to See in and around Vélez Blanco

The castle, Castillo de los Fajardo, looms high over the little white houses of the village. It is, as is also the castle of La Calahorra (► Guadix, surrounding area), a Renaissance structure, begun in 1506 and completed in 1515; but in contrast to La Calahorra, it has a more complex and irregular ground-plan, the long rows of battlements and the ramp connecting the keep with the other parts of the castle. It was designed by Francesco Florentini. Unfortunately, practically nothing remains of its interior. Almost the entire furnishings, including a magnificent patio, were bought up by a French art dealer in 1904 and resold in 1913 to George Blumenthal, a New York millionaire and former president of the Metropolitan Museum of Art. He bequeathed the patio to the museum, where it has stood reconstructed since 1964.

✱
► **Castillo de Véle Blanco**

Stone Age rock paintings were found barely half a mile south of the village in **Cueva de los Letreros**. They depict humans and animals. Named Indalo, the human figure has become the symbol of Almería province.

Vélez Rubio, the former capital of the county of Vélez, possesses the impressive Baroque church, Santa María de la Encarnación.

Vélez Blanco and Vélez Rubio lie in the **Sierra de María National Park**. This craggy mountain range with a height of up to 1500m/4900 was declared a nature reserve in the 1990s. The starting point for hiking tours is the village of María 6km/ 3.5mi west of Vélez Blanco. Information about the flora and fauna and hiking can be had at the visitor centre 3km/2 mi outside María in the direction of Orce or the information centre in Almacen del Trigo in Vélez Blanco.

VÉLEZ BLANCO

INFORMATION (OFICINA DE TURISMO)

in Almacen del Trigo
Avenida Marqués de los Vélez, s/n
E-04830 Vélez Blanco
Tel. 950 41 56 51

WHERE TO EAT

► **Inexpensive**
El Molino
Curtidores
Tel. 950 41 50 70
Grilled meat is the mainstay in the old mill.

WHERE TO STAY

► **Budget**
Casa de los Arcos
San Francisco, 2
Tel. 950 61 48 05
Fax 950 61 49 47
www.casadelosarcos.net, 14 rooms
In a palace from the 18th and 19th centuries with an arcade offering attractive views. Pleasant rooms.

← *The ocean at the cliffs of Caños de Meca is joy coloured blue.*

GLOSSARY OF ART AND ARCHITECTURAL TERMS

Ajaraca Diamond pattern on Moorish buildings

Ajimez Twin (gemel) window with a central support

Alcázar (from Arabic al-kasr) Moorish castle or palace

Alcazaba Palace

Alfiz Rectangular frame with arched windows and doors

Aljibe Arabian cistern

Artesonado Richly decorated ceiling with geometric patterns

Ayuntamiento Town hall

Azulejos Painted and glazed tiles (originally blue: azul)

Camarín Altar niche behind the main altar

Capilla Mayor Main chapel with the high altar

Capital Upper part of a column, usually decorated

Cartuja Charterhouse

Casa House; residence of noble family

Castillo Castle

Churrigueresque style Baroque style with sumptuous decoration, named after the sculptor and architect José Benito Churriguera (1665–1725)

Cimborio Dome over the crossing of a church

Convento Convent, monastery

Coro Choir, area of church for the clergy

Crucero Transept

Custodia Housing for the monstrance, usually made of silver

Ermita Small country church, pilgrims' chapel

Estrella Rose window

Fuenta Fountain, well

Herrera style Ceremoniously austere Renaissance style, named after the architect Juan de Herrera (1530–1597)

Isabelline style Late Gothic style named after Isabella the Catholic (1451–1504), combining Gothic and Moorish elements and characterized by rich ornamentation and sculptural decoration

Mantilla Covering for head and shoulders made of lace and tulle

Manueline style »Portuguese decorative style of the first half of the 16th century, typically employing forms from the New World (shells, corals) and maritime motifs (ropes).

Medrese (Koran school

Mezquita Mosque

Midhâ Basin for ritual ablutions in the forecourt of a mosque

Mihrâb Prayer niche in a mosque directed towards Mecca

Mirador Terrace, solar, viewing point

Mozarab style Architectural style of Christians living under Moorish rule

Mudejar style Style of Moors living under Christian rule, a mixture of Gothic and Moorish elements

Muqarnas Cavities and plasterwork looking like stalactites

Parroquia Parish church

Paso Processional group with saints' figures

Patio Inner court in Moorish and Spanish houses

Plateresque style Intricately ornamented architectural style; the name is derived from its resemblance to the forms of silversmith work (platero: silver)

Predella The lower part of a retable

Puerta del Perdón Name of the main gate of many cathedrals, because those who entered here received remission of sins

Reja House of correction or education

Retablo Retable, screen or shelf behind an altar, decorated with paintings or sculpture

Sala capitular Chapter house

Seo Cathedral, (from seda, meaning bishop's throne)

Sillería Choir stalls

Taifa Independent emirate

Tracery Gothic geometrical architectural decoration

Trascoro Wall around the coro

Trassagrario Rear side of the high altar

Triforium Gallery below the upper windows of a church

Tympanum Area within an arch and above the door lintel

INDEX

PHOTO CREDITS

LIST OF MAPS AND ILLUSTRATIONS

PUBLISHER'S INFORMATION

Illustrations etc: 201 illustrations, 43 maps
and diagrams, one large map
Text: Rainer Eisenschmid, Reinhard Zakrzewski,
Martina Johnson
Editing: Baedeker editorial team
(John Sykes, Robert Taylor)
Translation: all-lingua, David Andersen, John
Sykes, Robert Taylor
Cartography: Franz Huber, München; Falk
Verlag, Ostfildern (map)
3D illustrations: jangled nerves, Stuttgart
Design: independent Medien-Design, Munich;
Kathrin Schemel

Editor-in-chief: Rainer Eisenschmid,
Baedeker Ostfildern

1st edition 2008
Based on Baedeker Allianz Reiseführer
»Andalusien«, 10. Aufl. 2007

Copyright: Karl Baedeker Verlag, Ostfildern
Publication rights: MAIRDUMONT GmbH & Co;
Ostfildern

DEAR READER,

We would like to thank you for choosing this Baedeker travel guide. It will be a reliable companion on your travels and will not disappoint you.
This book describes the major sights, of course, but it also recommends the best beaches, as well as hotels in the luxury and budget categories, and includes tips about tapas bars or shopping and much more, helping to make your trip an enjoyable experience. Our author Rainer Eisenschmid ensures the quality of this information by making regular journeys to Andalusia and putting all his know-how into this book.

Nevertheless, experience shows us that it is impossible to rule out errors and changes made after the book goes to press, for which Baedeker accepts no liability. Please send us your criticisms, corrections and suggestions for improvement: we appreciate your contribution. Contact us by post or e-mail, or phone us:

▶ **Verlag Karl Baedeker GmbH**
Editorial department
Postfach 3162
73751 Ostfildern
Germany
Tel. 49-711-4502-262, fax -343
www.baedeker.com, www.baedeker.co.uk
E-Mail: baedeker@mairdumont.com

Baedeker Travel Guides in English at a glance:

▶ Andalusia

▶ Dubai · Emirates

▶ Egypt

▶ Ireland

▶ London

▶ Mexico

▶ New York

▶ Portugal

▶ Rome

▶ Thailand

▶ Tuscany

▶ Venice